STUDIES IN THE NEW EXPERIMENTAL AESTHETICS:

STEPS TOWARD AN OBJECTIVE PSYCHOLOGY OF AESTHETIC APPRECIATION

STUDIES IN THE NEW EXPERIMENTAL AESTHETICS:
STEPS TOWARD AN OBJECTIVE PSYCHOLOGY OF AESTHETIC APPRECIATION

EDITED BY D. E. BERLYNE

UNIVERSITY OF TORONTO

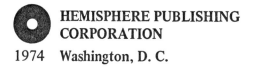 HEMISPHERE PUBLISHING CORPORATION

1974   Washington, D. C.

A HALSTED PRESS BOOK

JOHN WILEY & SONS
New York   London   Sydney   Toronto

Hemisphere Publishing Corporation
1025 Vermont Avenue, N. W., Washington, D.C. 20005

Distributed solely by Halsted Press, a Division of John Wiley & Sons, Inc., New York.

Library of Congress Cataloging in Publication Data:

Berlyne, D. E.
　Studies in the new experimental aesthetics.

　1. Aesthetics. 2. Art—Psychology. I. Title.
N71.B42　　　701′.17　　　74–13600
ISBN 0–470–07039–0

CONTENTS

Preface   vii

1   THE NEW EXPERIMENTAL AESTHETICS, *D. E. Berlyne* . . .   1

2   VERBAL AND EXPLORATORY RESPONSES TO SOUND
     SEQUENCES VARYING IN UNCERTAINTY LEVEL,
     J. B. Crozier   27

3   THE DEVELOPMENT WITH AGE OF VERBAL AND
     EXPLORATORY RESPONSES TO SOUND SEQUENCES
     VARYING IN UNCERTAINTY LEVEL, *B. W. E. Bragg and*
     J. B. Crozier   91

4   VERBAL RESPONSES TO VISUAL SEQUENCES VARYING
     IN UNCERTAINTY LEVEL, *L. F. Normore*   109

5   VERBAL AND EXPLORATORY RESPONSES TO VISUAL
     PATTERNS VARYING IN UNCERTAINTY AND IN
     REDUNDANCY, *D. E. Berlyne*   121

6   ARTISTIC TRAINING AND RESPONSES TO VISUAL AND
    AUDITORY PATTERNS VARYING IN UNCERTAINTY,
    F. G. Hare   159

7   VERBAL RESPONSES TO VISUAL PATTERNS VARYING
    IN DISTRIBUTIONAL REDUNDANCY AND IN VARIETY,
    F. G. Hare   169

8   NOVELTY, COMPLEXITY, AND INTERESTINGNESS,
    D. E. Berlyne   175

9   DIMENSIONS OF PERCEPTION OF PAINTINGS,
    D. E. Berlyne and J. C. Ogilvie   181

10 HEDONIC TONE AND REWARD VALUE OF EXPOSURE
    TO PAINTINGS, *D. E. Berlyne*   227

11 AN EXPERIMENTAL INVESTIGATION OF PERCEPTUAL
    AND STYLISTIC DIMENSIONS OF PAINTINGS
    SUGGESTED BY ART HISTORY, *G. C. Cupchik*   235

12 A CROSS-CULTURAL STUDY OF EXPLORATORY AND
    VERBAL RESPONSES TO VISUAL PATTERNS VARYING
    IN COMPLEXITY, *D. E. Berlyne, M. C. Robbins, and
    R. Thompson*   259

13 CORRELATES OF HUMOR: VERBAL AND NONVERBAL
    AESTHETIC REACTIONS AS FUNCTIONS OF SEMANTIC
    DISTANCE WITHIN ADJECTIVE-NOUN PAIRS,
    M. Godkewitsch   279

14 CONCLUDING OBSERVATIONS, *D. E. Berlyne*   305

Author Index   333
Subject Index   337

PREFACE

This book is devoted to an area of study for which "the new experimental aesthetics" seems an appropriate name. It reports some experiments that have been carried out since 1970. We hope that readers interested in psychology and readers interested in the arts will consider our findings worthy of their attention. But our main aim is to give some idea of the techniques that are now available to the experimental aesthetician and of the kinds of questions that can and cannot be answered with their help. Apart from one chapter (Chapter 12), for which the data were collected in Uganda by two anthropologists from the University of Missouri, the book is the work of persons affiliated with the Psychology Department of the University of Toronto.

Chapter 1 discusses the objectives of the experiments and attempts to place these objectives in perspective. Consequently, there is little left for this preface to do except record our thanks to those, other than the authors, who have contributed in indispensable ways to the completion of more than one of these projects. They include our senior research technician, Miss Mary Louise King, and two other research technicians, Mrs. Merle Nudelman and Mrs. Patricia Hunter; our research secretary, Mrs. J. E. Peters; Mrs. R. Niedra, who drew many of the illustrations; Mr. R. S. Young and his assistants in the Department of Psychology electronics workshop; and the National Research Council of Canada and the Canada Council, whose research grants (Nos. A-73,

S70-1570-X2, and S72-1405-XI, respectively) provided the financial wherewithal for the execution of the experiments and the preparation of this book.

We have had to provide detailed information on the statistical techniques that we used for analyzing our data and, occasionally, to make some comments on the underlying mathematics. This is for the benefit of readers who are psychologists or specialists in neighboring disciplines. They are accustomed to receiving such information and will expect it. It is hoped that other readers, who lack the necessary background, will not be put off by these technical passages but will feel free to skip them. We trust that they will be able to gather the essentials of what the statistical analyses tell us. There are a few points they will have to understand. For example, we have to apply tests to verify that differences are statistically significant, i.e., that they are unlikely to be the result of chance fluctuations. Only then are we entitled to conclude that the factors we are studying have had genuine effects. Also, they will realize that the various correlation indices that we mention are simply numbers representing the degree of relationship or association between two measures or sets of measures, i.e., the extent to which scores on one give some indication of how high scores on the other are likely to be.

Although experimental aesthetics is over a hundred years old, the new experimental aesthetics is still in its infancy. We are well aware that the faltering first steps of any infant, while they may elate family and friends, will not seem to a disinterested observer to be moving very far very fast. But they are indispensable preliminaries to the achievements of the polar explorer or the marathon runner. We trust that readers will judge psychological aesthetics to be a deserving field of study, at least as worthwhile as many that currently receive much more attention from researchers, and that others will undertake the investigations that will overcome the limitations of our own.

D. E. Berlyne

August 1974

1
THE NEW EXPERIMENTAL AESTHETICS

D. E. Berlyne

The field of aesthetics is notoriously difficult to define, although many writers have not hesitated to do so at the expense of imposing their own preconceptions. The term, derived from the classical Greek verb *aisthanomai,* meaning "to perceive," acquired its present connotations almost by accident. The eighteenth-century German philosopher, Baumgarten (1735, 1750), set out, under this rubric, to investigate the acquisition of knowledge through perception and imagination, as contrasted with reason and logic. He found himself discussing the peculiarities of poetry and other arts, which have remained inseparably associated with the word "aesthetics" to the present day.

But what has this word denoted since Baumgarten wrote? We can confidently place some matters within its province, but we cannot state nearly so confidently where the limits of that province lie. Aesthetics is certainly concerned with the arts, but it is not confined to the arts. There is an aesthetic aspect to many other activities, from mathematics to housework. In fact, one can argue that everything in life has its aesthetic side. And, in any case, what are the arts? The notion of a "work of art" has grown up in our western society over the last few centuries, and particular attitudes have become firmly attached to it. We are supposed to approach something labeled as art with a certain aesthetic stance, with a certain awe and spellbound seriousness that are withheld from most of the objects that we encounter. A conception of art quite like ours is not to be found in many other cultures or even in western society before the Renaissance. These other cultures have all produced objects, patterns, and activities that we class as art and treat as we treat our own works of art as soon as we gain access to them. But their significance for their originators will often have been quite different.

Questions regarding beauty belong indisputably to aesthetics. But they do not exhaust its scope. Beauty, however defined and explicated, is far from being the only quality attributed to works of art and to other objects of aesthetic value. Others, including sublimity, interestingness, and even ugliness have also been held to characterize them. Aesthetics has sometimes been identified with the "theory of pleasing and displeasing" (Fechner, 1876, I., p. 1) in general, especially among the early experimental psychologists.

The impossibility of drawing a sharp line to mark off the subject matter of aesthetics need not, however, disquiet the psychologist. One of his prime aims must be to find links between what is inside it and what is outside it, and psychological aesthetics, in particular, has suffered in the past from the excessive tendency to isolate it for study. Since it is not possible to investigate everything at once, areas of inquiry have to be mapped out, at least provisionally, but the demarcation lines recognized by tradition and by everyday language are all too often found to lack scientific usefulness. Definitions of areas, in contrast with definitions of concepts and of terms, can be fuzzy and shifting without harmful consequences.

DISCIPLINES CONCERNED WITH AESTHETICS

The objects and activities that fall within the purview of aesthetics are investigated, with different methods and different objectives, by several disciplines, falling into two groups.

Speculative Aesthetics

First of all, there are speculative disciplines. They can be pursued in a study or in a library. They depend heavily on deduction—from definitions of concepts, from self-evident principles, from generally accepted propositions, from an author's own beliefs, intuitions, and experience. To a large extent, their method is "hermeneutic," to use a term that is currently popular in continental Europe, i.e., they rely heavily on interpretative examination of particular texts, particular specimens of literary, musical, or visual art. Their ultimate criterion of validity is whether they leave the reader with a feeling of conviction.

Within speculative aesthetics, a distinction can be drawn between the kinds of investigation for which training is received in university departments of philosophy and the kinds for which training is received in departments of fine arts, literature, and music.

Philosophical aesthetics (which is what the word "aesthetics" most often denotes when it is used alone) aims to make general statements about the entities, concepts, terms, and values connected with art, beauty, etc. The best term to cover other forms of speculative aesthetics is *art theory*. This seems to be the best translation for expressions like *sciences de l'art, Kunstwissenschaft,* etc., which are widely used in non-English-speaking countries. A great deal of confusion has arisen from failure to realize that words like the French *science* and the German *Wissenschaft* (with their equivalents in other European languages) do not mean what the English word "science" means. A more accurate translation for them would be "scholarship."

Although terms like "art theory" can appropriately denote approaches to the study of the arts in general, they frequently imply specialization in the visual arts. "Musicology" and "theory of literature" (in German, *Literaturwissenschaft*) are used with reference to the other major media. Art theory differs from philosophical aesthetics in spending more time on discussion of individual works, artists, and styles. But, since this can hardly be done without seeking principles that are applicable to art in general, there is an inevitable interpenetration between its subject matter and that of philosophical aesthetics.

Within art theory, a not very sharp distinction is commonly recognized between art history and art criticism. Once again, these terms sometimes pertain to the visual arts in particular and sometimes to all the arts, in which case the words "music" and "literary" are substituted for the word "art" where appropriate. "Art history" is self-explanatory. There has been a great deal of controversy over the various tasks of criticism (see Venturi, 1964; Wimsatt & Brooks, 1957), but the primary aim of this discipline is, one may say, to help in the understanding, enjoyment, and evaluation of particular works. This can hardly be done without considering the historical succession of styles and the nature of art, so that overlaps with art history and philosophical aesthetics are unavoidable.

Empirical Aesthetics

The second group of disciplines concerned with aesthetics are the behavioral sciences. These must accept responsibility for studying the forms of behavior that center around works of art and other aesthetic phenomena. They study them, however, with the methods and objectives peculiar to empirical science. That is to say, they derive their conclusions from observation and, in particular, controlled observation, which means observation under circumstances that enable the effects of one factor to be distinguished from those of other factors that commonly accompany it. This entails due attention to sampling procedures, research design, and statistical analysis of data.

Among the behavioral sciences, the domain of empirical aesthetics is divided up (again, without clearcut lines of demarcation) among psychology, sociology, anthropology, and linguistics, with perhaps smaller shares accruing to economics and political science.

One prominent branch of empirical aesthetics is *psychobiological aesthetics*. As explained elsewhere (Berlyne, 1971), the term "psychobiology" is a useful one to distinguish what most contemporary psychological researchers do from what many laymen think of as "psychology" and from what was pursued under this heading before the advent of psychology as a scientific discipline. Psychobiology applies the methods of empirical science to the investigation of human and animal behavior and its relations to the observable conditions that can influence behavior. Moreover, it investigates behavior from a biological point of view. The term "psychological aesthetics" is useful but could not be limited to empirical approaches. All the branches of speculative aesthetics have much to say about the psychological processes involved in the creation and appreciation of works of art. But they do not use empirical methods to arrive at new knowledge about these processes. They either formulate answers to psychological questions deductively or make use of the answers contributed by behavioral scientists.

One part of psychobiological aesthetics is *experimental aesthetics*. This, as the term indicates, consists of the study of aesthetic problems through experiments, i.e., through situations in which an experimenter systematically manipulates causal factors so that their effects on some aspect of behavior can be ascertained. It excludes, however, two very important empirical approaches to psychological aesthetics. One is the *correlational study*, in which two or more factors vary naturally and statistical techniques are used to find out how strongly they are associated. For example, there are studies of the correlations between characteristics of societies and the kinds of art they produce. Secondly, there are investigations using *content analysis*, i.e., measurement of characteristics, especially statistical characteristics, of artistic and other artifacts typifying specific social groups or historical periods.

Experimental aesthetics has had a long but not particularly distinguished history (Berlyne, 1972b). It was founded by Fechner, who is generally recognized as the father of experimental psychology, in the 1860s and 1870s. For most of the ensuing century, it made some tangible progress (see Valentine, 1962), but, in comparison with other branches of experimental psychology, its products were relatively sparse and, on the whole, not profoundly enlightening. There has, however, been a marked reinvigoration of experimental aesthetics since about 1960. This latest phase is characterized by some new approaches, new techniques, new aims, and new ideas coming from a variety of sources. For these reasons, one can appropriately speak of the *new experimental aesthetics* (Berlyne, 1971, 1972b).

Research identifiable with the new experimental aesthetics possesses one or more of the following features, none of which characterized much experimental aesthetics until recently:

1. It concentrates on collative properties of stimulus patterns. Collative properties (of which more will be said later) are "structural" or "formal" properties, such as variations along familiar-novel, simple-complex, expected-surprising, ambiguous-clear, and stable-variable dimensions.

2. It concentrates on motivational questions (see Berlyne, 1960, 1970, 1971).

3. It studies nonverbal behavior as well as verbally expressed judgments.

4. It strives to establish links between aesthetic phenomena and other psychological phenomena. This means that it aims not only to throw light on aesthetic phenomena but, through the elucidation of aesthetic problems, to throw light on human psychology in general.

This book presents some examples of the new experimental aesthetics, all carried out since 1970 in our laboratory in the Department of Psychology, University of Toronto. This laboratory is known to its members by the not very serious and not very official title of "Laboratory of Aplopathematic and Thelematoscopic Pneumatology." These terms taken from Bentham (see Berlyne, 1973b) denote the aims of unraveling the determinants of hedonic processes and unraveling the role of hedonic processes in the determination of behavior.

THEORETICAL ORIENTATION

Those responsible for the experiments that are going to be reported are well aware of being pioneers who are exploring largely uncharted territory, where every step can be hazardous and conclusions must be offered with circumspection and hesitancy. They recognize that much more work must be done before answers can be more than provisional and before even provisional answers to many questions can be ventured.

The guiding theoretical notions—they can hardly be represented as a coherent "theory" or "model"—have been expounded in detail elsewhere (Berlyne, 1971). Tentative as they are, the hypotheses constructed from them receive support from several quarters inside and outside psychology, from recent findings in the psychology and neurophysiology of motivational processes, from other lines of research, both old and new, in psychology, and from the writings of speculative aestheticians, information theorists, and semioticians. There is no room here for a recapitulation of the theoretical scheme, but its principal ingredients can be indicated roughly as follows:

1. A work of art is analyzed in information-theoretic terms (see Berlyne, 1965, Chap. 2) as an assemblage of elements, each of which can transmit information from four distinct sources (depicted in Fig. 1). This is another way of saying that there is some degree of correlation between the characteristics of an element and characteristics of events or objects belonging to the four sources or, alternatively, that acquaintance with the four sources can help one to predict what an element will be like and vice versa. Information traceable to the four sources is labeled, respectively, semantic, expressive, cultural, and syntactic information. There are, however, complications because there is usually some transmission of information (correlation, causal influence) between every one of the four sources and every other. This means that there is some overlap (redundancy) between the four kinds of information reaching the work of art. But to some extent, the four sources emit independent information, which means that there will be competition between them for the limited capacity of the channel linking them with the work. More information transmission (i.e., influence) from one will therefore generally mean less from the others, and different styles of art characterized by relative predominance of information from different sources.

Extending and slightly modifying some usages introduced by information-theoretic aestheticians such as Moles (1958), Frank (1959), and Bense (1969), we may refer to expressive, cultural, and syntactic information collectively as "aesthetic information." The importance of these three kinds of information is one of the salient features that distinguish artistic (poetic) and nonartistic (prosaic) forms of communication, since, in the latter, accurate conveyance of semantic information is what matters (cf. the

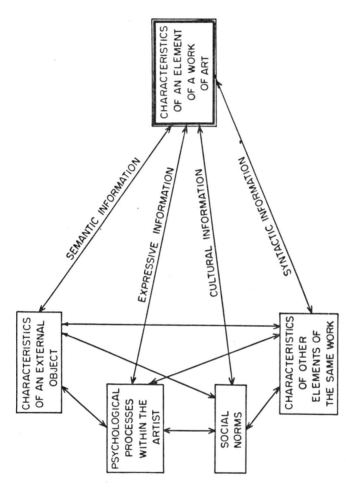

FIG. 1. Channels through which information can be transmitted to an element of a work of art.

contrasts between scientific and poetic language pointed out by Marcus, 1970). In nontechnical language, artistic communication is characterized by the relative importance of how something is communicated, as compared with what is communicated, and by the relative importance of formal properties in the selection of something to communicate.

2. A work of art is regarded as a collection of symbols in accordance with the conception of signs and symbols developed by the semiotic movement (Peirce, 1897; Morris, 1946; Osgood, 1952). According to Morris (1939), aesthetic symbols are distinguished by the presence of two characteristics: they are iconic (i.e., they have properties in common with the objects or events that they signify) and they serve to communicate "value properties." Modifying this suggestion, we may see the speciality of aesthetic symbols as the communication of intrinsic values, i.e., the artist's views on what objects, real or ideal, deserve attention.

3. A work of art is regarded as a stimulus pattern whose collative properties, and possibly other properties as well, give it a positive intrinsic hedonic value.

The term "hedonic value" embraces several distinct measurable variables (Berlyne, 1967, 1973b), which may or may not be aspects of the same underlying psychophysiological variable. They include degree of pleasure, preference, or utility, usually measured through verbal judgments, which have long been the principal source of data for experimental aesthetics. They also include such variables as reward value and incentive value, which must be measured through nonverbal behavior. When we say that something has a "positive intrinsic hedonic value," we mean that contact with it is pleasurable, rewarding, etc., in itself and not because it affords access to other events with beneficial or noxious qualities. This is close to what aestheticians have meant when they have spoken of art as an "end in itself" or of aesthetic appreciation as "disinterested."

There is abundant evidence (Berlyne, 1967) connecting hedonic value with fluctuations in arousal, and it is hypothesized that aesthetic patterns produce their hedonic effects by acting on arousal. This is, of course, a counterpart of the old belief that works of art generate pleasure through their emotional impact.

Indications are that positive hedonic values can come about in either of two ways, namely through a moderate increase in arousal (the "arousal-boost mechanism") or through a decrease in arousal when arousal has reached an uncomfortably high level (the "arousal-reduction mechanism").

Stimulus patterns that give rise to moderate arousal increments will be pleasurable and rewarding through the arousal-boost mechanism, whereas those that occasion sharper rises in arousal will be unpleasant, punishing, and aversive, in which case positive hedonic value can be produced by some subsequent event that lowers arousal. The magnitude of the arousal increment due to a stimulus pattern depends on a large assortment of factors, including intensity, association with, or resemblance to, biologically significant events, and collative properties. These properties are what we refer to collectively as "arousal potential."

The situation, as hypothesized, is represented by the curve in Figure 2, which is a reinterpretation of the well-known curve presented by Wundt (1874). This curve could be explained as the algebraic summation of the two curves in Figure 3, which represent the supposed degrees of activation of two antagonistic systems in the brain, a primary reward system and an aversion system. It must be pointed out that these curves concern only the conditions under which a stimulus pattern has either positive hedonic value through the arousal-boost mechanism or negative hedonic value. It does not cover stimulus patterns that have positive hedonic value through arousal-reduction (the arousal-jag mechanism), which is likely to involve a third system in the brain, a secondary reward system (Berlyne, 1967; Olds, 1973).

The upshot of these hypotheses is that the appeal of a work of art depends on the interplay of two sets of factors, one tending to drive arousal upwards and the other tending to reduce arousal or to keep it within bounds. The idea that aesthetic value requires a combination of two partly opposite and partly complementary factors has cropped up repeatedly over the centuries. They have been labeled "uniformity" and "variety" by Hutcheson (1725) and many later writers (see Eysenck, 1942), "order" and "complexity" by Birkhoff (1933), "subjective redundancy" and "statistical information" by information-theoretic aestheticians (Gunzenhäuser, 1962), "concinnity" and "empathy" by Coates (1972), "coherence" and "mystery" by Kaplan (1973). With one exception, these terms are all insufficiently comprehensive and capture some, but not all, of the numerous ingredients of each factor. The exception is Coates's "concinnity," a word that has existed in the English language since at least 1531 and is defined by the Oxford English Dictionary as "skillful putting together of parts; harmony." If "concinnity" will serve to cover the arousal-moderating properties of a pattern, we might adopt the word "tension" as a rubric for arousal-increasing properties. This word has so often been seconded from its original duties in mechanical engineering to perform widespread metaphorical service for both psychologists and writers

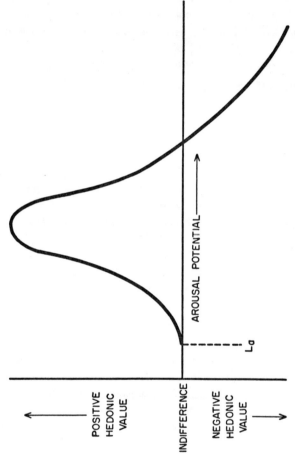

FIG. 2. The reinterpreted Wundt curve, representing relations between hedonic value and arousal potential.

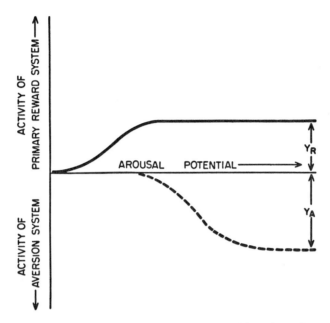

FIG. 3. Hypothetical curves representing activity of a primary reward system and an aversion system in the brain, whose resultant produces the Wundt curve.

on art. It has the appropriate connotations of a strain pulling something out of its normal shape or state. In elastic bodies, the resulting deformation or stress is accompanied by storage of potential energy, so that a force tending to correct the deformation arises as soon as the strain is removed. This makes the analogy with psychological "tension" imperfect, since the latter is characterized not merely by resilience but by negative or compensating feedback: counteracting processes normally come into play soon after an arousing influence has made itself felt and before it is withdrawn. There is neurophysiological evidence (Dell, 1963) that, when the brain structures controlling the indices of heightened arousal are activated, they are usually subjected to corrective inhibitory influences from other structures. These influences are, of course, frequently inadequate to bring arousal down again, so that more complex devices are brought into play, such as information-analyzing processes that make sense of disturbing experiences or actions that remove environmental threats.

Concinnity and tension are, it seems, sometimes at work simultaneously, so that they oppose and balance each other. This presumably serves to ensure that arousing effects are limited, so that pleasure and reward can be generated through the arousal-boost mechanism. At other times, arousal-raising and arousal-moderating factors come into play in turn, which presumably means that a phase of uncomfortably high arousal is succeeded by a phase of arousal reduction, so that the discomfort or disturbance is relieved. At yet other times, pleasure and reward may result from activation of both mechanisms in turn, as a moderate rise in arousal is succeeded by a drop (the "arousal boost-jag").

OBJECTIVES OF THE EXPERIMENTS TO BE REPORTED

The experiments to be reported in the ensuing chapters of this book were not designed primarily to provide crucial tests for the hypotheses that have just been outlined. What evidence there is to support these hypotheses has already been set forth (Berlyne, 1967, 1971). Before more conclusive evidence for or against them can be gathered and before more details can be filled in, it is evident that several advances will have to be made. Measuring procedures will have to be devised and refined, so that the concepts figuring in the hypotheses can be anchored more firmly in the world of empirical data. And some essential methodological, perceptual, and theoretical questions must be cleared up.

With regard to the experiments concerned, the theoretical scheme has two primary guiding roles. It points to some variables that should repay investigation. And it points to some problems that must be resolved before substantial advances can be made.

The experiments, as will be seen, are addressed to a fairly wide variety of topics. But some experimental techniques and some independent and dependent variables will come up repeatedly. While each experiment had its specific aims, they shared the following overall objectives:

1. to try out some techniques of data collection, measurement, and statistical analysis that seem to have great potential value for experimental aesthetics,

2. to examine the relations between certain independent variables and certain dependent variables, and

3. to examine the relations among certain dependent variables.

Dependent Variables

The dependent variables fall into three groups:

1. Verbal ratings. Most by far of the contributions that have been made to experimental aesthetics since its beginnings have concentrated on verbal evaluative judgments. Subjects have been asked to state how much they like particular stimulus objects or patterns, which they prefer to which and by how much, how pleasing or pleasant or beautiful they find each one, etc. Beginning with Day's (1965) doctoral thesis, rank-orderings and ratings of Pleasingness have been recorded in our laboratory. But judgments of another evaluative attribute, namely Interestingness, were also obtained. Interestingness and Pleasingness generally behave differently: they vary with some of the same independent variables, particularly complexity (objective or subjective) and novelty, but the curves relating them to these variables are generally dissimilar. Interestingness seems generally to rise monotonically with collative stimulus properties, whereas Pleasingness and equivalent attributes reach a peak, or sometimes several peaks, in the middle range. Other experiments were concerned with judgments of Complexity (beginning with Day, 1965) and novelty (Berlyne & Parham, 1968).

Since then, we have settled on the type of seven-point rating scale introduced by Osgood (1952), i.e., a row of seven compartments with opposite words or phrases labeling the two extremes. We have also come to use a progressively wider range of scales, as have researchers in other laboratories (see Berlyne, 1972a; Berlyne, Chap. 14, this volume).

Several of the experiments to be reported use batteries of scales belonging to the following three classes: (a) *descriptive scales*, referring to collative properties of stimulus patterns, which include subjective equivalents of the measures introduced by information theory (Berlyne, 1974), (b) *evaluative scales*, indicative of hedonic value and related attributes, and (c) *internal-state scales*, referring to attributes of the subject's reaction or mood while exposed to a pattern. Scales of a rather different nature, namely *stylistic scales*, referring to technical attributes of works of art, make an appearance in a few of the experiments (Chaps. 9 and 11, this volume).

2. Psychophysiological measures. Recordings of bodily processes, formerly discussed as manifestations or accompaniments of "emotion" but nowadays more frequently connected with fluctuations in arousal, were used quite early by students of experimental aesthetics (e.g., Diserens, 1926). Earlier investigations in our laboratory studied effects on GSR and EEG measures of conflict (Berlyne, 1961), uncertainty (Berlyne & Borsa, 1968), and various properties of sounds (Berlyne, McDonnell, Nicki, & Parham, 1967). There have also been plenty of investigations in other laboratories confirming the effects of collative stimulus properties on indices of arousal (see Berlyne, 1971, Chap. 13).

3. Behavioral measures. Several of the experiments recorded measures of exploratory or stimulus-seeking behavior.

Two such measures appear repeatedly. One is *Exploration Time* (Looking Time or Listening Time). The subject sees or hears each of a succession of patterns for as long as he wishes, and the duration of self-exposure to each pattern is recorded. The second is *Exploratory Choice*. Two visual or auditory patterns are first presented to the subject. He is then given a choice between two responses, either of which will cause one of the patterns to reappear, and his choice is recorded.

In recent years, we have resorted to wiring up the subject and giving him to understand that psychophysiological processes are being registered, as a means of disguising the true purpose of experiments on exploratory behavior. This is to obviate the possibility that his knowledge of the true purpose may bias the results in one direction or another. There is, however, no clear evidence that this contrivance produces different results from those that used to occur when instructions for the task were simply described without a rationale.

Exploration Time has been variously interpreted as a measure of the intensity of the orientation reaction, the intensity of attention (shown by how long competing targets for attention can be warded off), or perceptual curiosity (shown by how long it takes for curiosity to be reduced to a threshold value). Exploratory Choice seems to be governed by some of the same variables, particularly collative variables, as Exploration Time, but the stimulus patterns that are more likely to be chosen are not always those that attract longer Looking or Listening Time.

Exploratory Choice can be regarded as an index of *incentive value* or *utility* (Berlyne, 1973b). This attribute of a stimulus event is identifiable with the extent to which a response becomes more probable when it is expected to lead to that event. It is a central concept of decision theory and of cognitivist brands of behavior theory.

Another behavioral hedonic concept is *reward value*. This is identifiable with the power of an event to promote a learned, i.e., lasting, increase in the strength of association between some stimulus condition and a response that is frequently followed by the event in question (Berlyne, 1967). Since reinforcement is defined in terms of learning and learning implies a durable change in behavior, the only conclusive way to detect and measure the reward value of an event is to observe behavior some time (24 hours or more) after the last occurrence of the event. In particular, it is important not to confuse reward value with some transient effects that can temporarily raise the frequency of a particular response and can thus be easily mistaken for reward value. These include a cue effect (i.e., the occurrence of the event, after a particular response, evokes a prompt repetition of the same response), and a rise in drive or arousal (i.e., a rise in the subject's overall activity level). A technique for measuring the reward value of visual or auditory patterns in human beings (Berlyne, 1972d) was suggested by a pigeon experiment carried out by Catania (1963). It involves two instrumental responses producing reinforcement with concurrent but independent variable-interval schedules. The subject has access to two telegraph keys and can press either of them (but not both together) as often as he wants. Most of the time, the depression of a key has no effect. But now and then, it will produce a brief exposure of a pattern or picture on a screen. Once this has occurred, a variable, randomly determined time (20 seconds on the average in our experiments) must elapse before pressing the same key will have the same consequence. Although this technique does not involve a delayed test in the absence of the event whose reward value is to be measured, it can be argued that the relative rates of responding on the two keys reflect the relative reward values of the stimulus events they produce. The interval between successive appearances of a pattern is long enough to exclude the cue effect that was discussed earlier. And the fact that the frequencies of two concurrent responses are being compared rules out the possibility that changes in overall activity level are alone responsible for the findings. So, this technique seems promising as a way to probe the reward value of aesthetic patterns, and it was used in several of the projects with which this book is concerned (Chaps. 5, 10, and 13).

Relations among Dependent Variables

As our armory of measuring devices has grown, it has become imperative to study the intercorrelations of the measures they yield, to find out the degree to which some of them may be reflecting a common underlying variable. This means establishing R-R laws (Spence, 1944), which experimental psychologists have been somewhat inclined to disdain, because, unlike S-R laws, they permit prediction, but not control or explanation, of phenomena. Nevertheless, R-R laws can verify predictions from theories that include S-R principles and, in any case, they are needed if the significance of dependent measures is to be understood. Another way of putting it is to say that intercorrelations will help us to "isolate organically unitary and unique behavioral structures, i.e., 'significant variables'" (Cattell, 1959, p. 258) or "convenient 'dimensions'" (p. 259). This overall problem encompasses a number of more specific questions to which answers are worth having:

1. We need to know in what ways our verbal scales are interrelated. In particular, it is important to look for connections among the three main kinds of scales that we have used, namely the descriptive (collative) scales, the evaluative scales, and the internal-state scales. It has often been assumed that, when a subject expresses his evaluation of a stimulus, he is informing us about the affective reactions that the stimulus evokes in him. Correlations between evaluative and internal-state scales will show how justified this assumption may be. Correlations between these two kinds of scales, on the one hand, and ratings of collative properties on the other, can, despite all the cautions that correlations and R-R laws call for, test hypotheses regarding the influence of collative properties on evaluative and affective reactions.

Factor analysis suggests itself as soon as one is faced with data from a battery of verbal scales. Factor analyses are reported in several of the chapters that follow, and several have been carried out already in our own laboratory and in others (see Berlyne, 1972a; Berlyne, Chap. 14, this volume). The factor-analytic technique that has been used in these studies is a variant of P technique (Cattell, 1952). When this technique is used, each of the correlations that undergo analysis is a correlation between two measures of behavior over a set of occasions within the life of one individual. In our and other writers' studies in experimental aesthetics, the occasions are distinguished by presentation of different stimulus patterns and, instead of confining attention to one subject, data are collected from a number of subjects and their mean scores are used. Correlations between mean scores on different measures (usually rating scales, but occasionally other measures as well) over stimulus patterns are then factor-analyzed.

One preliminary experiment, with a miscellany of visual patterns, has already been published (Berlyne, 1973a). It produced three factors, of which the first and third were mutually oblique. They were provisionally labeled Complexity-Uncertainty, Hedonic Value, and Cortical Arousal. Some of the chapters of this book report similar factor analyses with more restricted kinds of visual or auditory stimulus material, designed to reveal effects of selected independent variables.

2. Information relating verbal to behavioral measures can help to fill a rather glaring gap that disfigured the history of experimental aesthetics before

the recent period. Investigators used to focus their attention more or less exclusively on verbal evaluative measures, either failing to consider what verbal judgments have to tell us about behavior or making assumptions on this question that had insufficient empirical backing. Correlations between measures of exploratory behavior and verbal ratings can test hypotheses regarding the influence of collative variables and of changes in arousal on exploration (Berlyne, 1960, 1963, 1966). Another vital question concerns the relations between verbal judgments indicative of hedonic value—which can be conveniently placed under the label of "hedonic tone"—and behavioral hedonic concepts, like incentive value and reward value. This is a question, in other words, of how much justification there is for using the term "hedonic value" to embrace both hedonic tone and behavioral hedonic concepts.

3. Bartenwerfer (1963, 1969), Thayer (1967, 1970), and Godkewitsch (1974) have presented data indicating high correlations between relevant internal-state ratings and psychophysiological measures of arousal. Their work raises the important theoretical and practical question of whether verbal ratings might, with comparable precision and with superior convenience, be able to measure what psychophysiological recordings measure. Experiments reported in later chapters have an indirect bearing on this question. They incorporate rating scales such as Bartenwerfer and Thayer found to be correlated with psychophysiological arousal indices and that sound as if they should reflect variations in arousal. And they show us how some independent variables that have previously been found to affect psychophysiological arousal indices affect ratings on these scales in the same way.

Independent Variables

Before discussing the main independent variables whose effects were selected for study, it may be helpful to take note of two directions that experimental aesthetics can take. One of these is what we may call the *synthetic* approach. It consists in singling out particular variables or factors that might play a part in aesthetic appreciation and designing stimulus patterns that will enable these variables or factors to be isolated and manipulated for study. The objects to which subjects are required to respond are thus artificial and relatively simple. Nobody would call them works of art, but they are such as might well be found among the elements of works of art. The synthetic approach has the advantage of permitting control over independent variables, so that an experimenter can be reasonably sure which ones are responsible for observed variations in subjects' reactions. But it might be objected that it misses some of the essential and decisive attributes of art. The impact of a work of art surely depends in large measure on how its elements are combined and arranged, and on how its attributes interact with one another.

The other alternative, which does not have this drawback but has others, is to study reactions to genuine works of art or to portions of works of art. This, which we may call the *analytic* approach, clearly brings one closer to what happens when people encounter art in real life, but any specimen of existing art will inevitably incorporate many elements, variables, attributes, and factors that could have some influence over the reactions that are recorded. It is, consequently, hard to tell which of them are affecting the subject most deeply. It is difficult, to say the least, for the experimenter to control the operative independent variables or even to measure them.

Both of these approaches were introduced by Fechner (see Berlyne, 1971, Chap. 2). He initiated the synthetic approach with his famous experiment on the golden-section rectangle, and his study on preferences between the two versions of a Holbein painting was apparently the first experiment illustrating the analytic approach. The synthetic approach has characterized the majority of contributions to both the old and the new experimental aesthetics. There were, however, some instances of the analytic approach in the early twentieth century, especially when individual differences in aesthetic preference were under investigation. Both approaches are certainly necessary to experimental aesthetics, and the experiments to be reported include examples of both.

The synthetic approach. Our experiments following the synthetic approach use stimulus patterns, auditory or visual, that were specially constructed with collative stimulus properties in view. The so-called collative variables are virtually identical with the constituents of aesthetic "form," "structure," or "composition." There are artistic genres, e.g., absolute music, concrete painting, in which form or, in other words, syntactic information is virtually all there is. But even when content is important, i.e., when semantic, cultural, and expressive information play major roles, formal factors account for a great deal. The motivational importance of form (i.e., syntactic information dependent on collative variables) as distinct from content seems, in fact, to be the common ingredient that binds together the highly variegated realm of art and the aesthetic.

Nevertheless, collative stimulus properties play an indispensable role even in connection with content or, in other words, with semantic, cultural, and expressive information. No work of art is indistinguishable from an object that it depicts. There are always cues to remind us that we are dealing with a replica in another medium, and there are frequently deliberate distortions, simplifications or ornamentations of the subject matter, as well as other departures from exact reproduction of appearance. So here also, degree of similarity or dissimilarity to something familiar, degree of expectedness or surprisingness, are what matter, which means that collative variables are crucial.

There are close relations between the collative stimulus properties and the principal statistical measures introduced by information theory. Novelty and surprisingness are associated with high information content, complexity, ambiguity, and variability with high uncertainty. And fundamental links have been established between information-theoretic concepts and some of the attributes of stimulus patterns that are essential to aesthetics. "Goodness," degree of "structure," "unity," and "order" have been analyzed in terms of redundancy; "tension" and "variety" in terms of uncertainty. European writers (Moles, 1958; Frank, 1959; Gunzenhäuser, 1962; Bense, 1969) have based psychologies of aesthetics on information theory.

The collative variables are actually subjective, in the sense that they depend on the relations between physical and statistical properties of stimulus objects and processes within the organism (Berlyne, in press). A pattern can be more novel, complex, or ambiguous for one person than for another or, for the same person, at one time than at another. Nevertheless, many experiments, using rating scales and other techniques, have confirmed that collative properties and subjective informational variables tend, as one would expect, to vary concomitantly with the corresponding objective measures of classical information theory.

Summing up then, there are ample grounds for believing that the variables to which information theory has drawn attention have a great deal to do with the motivational effects of aesthetic form. Informational factors are not the only ones that govern aesthetic appreciation, and they are unlikely to be the only constituents of aesthetic form. Nevertheless, they seem important for aesthetics, and, in contrast with many other variables of concern to aesthetics, they suggest quantitative manipulations. Consequently, in many of the experiments to be reported in this book, interest was concentrated on information-theoretic variables and on how they influence the dependent variables that have already been discussed. Above all, we were interested in the effects of uncertainty, which, it will be remembered, is a measure associated with a class of patterns and is equivalent to the expected information content of a pattern selected from the class.

When we talk about uncertainty or information, we may be thinking of uncertainty or information per total pattern, per element of a pattern, per unit time, or per unit area. The uncertainty of a class of patterns can be varied in at least four ways, which are all used by artists. First, it can be increased by increasing the number of elements per pattern. Secondly, it can be increased by increasing the number of alternative forms that each element can take. Thirdly and fourthly, it can be decreased by introducing varying amounts of redundancy (internal constraint) in either of two ways (Garner, 1962). Distributional redundancy can be created by making some kinds of element occur more frequently than others. Correlational redundancy can be created by making some combinations of elements appear more frequently than others or, in other words, by producing similarities or other interdependencies between elements in different locations, which is identifiable with what we have called syntactic information.

In our experiments, uncertainty is varied in all four ways. This is necessary to find out how far the effects we observe are due to variations in uncertainty as such and how far particular uncertainty-altering operations have special consequences. For example, the information-theoretic theories of aesthetics that were mentioned above attribute a special significance to redundancy. Redundancy can be equated with "order" or amount of "structure." The psychological significance of redundancy is clearly different from that of other determinants of uncertainty. Unlike variation in number of elements or in amount of variety among elements, redundancy can become apparent gradually as the portions of a pattern are interrelated, organized, and grouped through perceptual processing.

While manipulation of information-theoretic properties of patterns is one way, with many advantages, of investigating the motivational effects of at least some collative variables, verbal judgments, scaling collative variables, provide another means to the same end. The data derived from such rating scales can be construed as yielding R-R laws. Alternatively, they can point to S-R laws if the scales are regarded as devices for measuring independent variables (see Berlyne, 1972a). In our experiments, rating scales were used, even when the stimulus patterns were designed to represent different values of information-theoretic variables, in order to ascertain how closely the experimentally manipulated variables and the rated variables were related.

The analytic approach. Some of our experiments, on the other hand, make a start on the ultimately unavoidable task of studying reactions to works of art and other aesthetic objects taken from everyday life. As already mentioned, the complexity of any genuine work of art confronts us with intricate methodological problems. Verbal scaling can be used to classify, and supply measures for, paintings and other artistic products. They are used for this purpose in our experiments, together with factor analysis. But they raise the old question of how one can be sure that the attributes that influence behavior most decisively have been covered by any battery of scales that might be chosen.

Some help in overcoming this difficulty, and more generally considerable promise for future research in experimental aesthetics, is offered by the multidimensional (nonmetric) scaling techniques that have become available in recent years and depend on the use of computers. These techniques can analyze verbal judgments of the degree of similarity between two patterns or of the degree to which one pattern is preferred to another, leaving the subject to determine, and computerized statistical analysis to reveal, which attributes are reflected predominantly in his judgments.

Some of the chapters that follow in this volume describe some initial attempts to tap the great potentialities of these techniques for aesthetics. They are applied to sound sequences varying in uncertainty level (Chap. 2), to a fairly representative selection of western painting since the Renaissance (Chap. 9), and to some paintings chosen to test a theoretical view of stylistic variation in paintings (Chap. 11).

Godkewitsch's experiments on humor, which have used both the synthetic (Chap. 13) and the analytic approaches (1974), take us into a special field some distance away from the central topics of aesthetics. But the experimental study of humor is an integral part of experimental aesthetics, both because of the recurrent role of the comic in all the arts and because of the dependence of humor on some of the same motivational processes as reactions to art, though on a shorter time scale (Berlyne, 1969, 1972c).

While we are considering the use of works of art as stimulus material for experimental aesthetics, some experiments carried out by Mr. T. Avital might be mentioned. Mr. Avital is an Israeli painter with training in psychology. He has lately been producing a series of nonrepresentational paintings, each member of which grows out of the previous member according to a logico-mathematical scheme. Working in our laboratory in 1972–73, Mr. Avital used multidimensional analysis of similarity judgments, various rating scales, and Looking Time, applied to his own works. The results confirmed his expectations in large measure but, in some respects, they surprised him and caused him to revise his system. His findings are not reported in this book, because they will appear in a chapter of his own book (Avital, in press). He is likely to be the first artist in history who carried out controlled studies in experimental aesthetics on his own works and who took the results of such studies into account in planning future works!

Individual Differences

Many people, as soon as they think of aesthetics, call to mind maxims such as "Tastes differ," "Every man to his taste," "There is no accounting for tastes," and "One man's meat is another man's poison." They have come to believe that generalization about aesthetic reactions and aesthetic phenomena is impossible. The implication is that one can only discuss particular works, particular artists, the likes and dislikes of particular appreciators, or, at most, of particular societies or periods of history. This is, in fact, precisely what is done in a high proportion of the literature in speculative aesthetics, especially in art theory.

This belief is mistaken. The aesthetic reactions of differing individuals turn out to have an appreciable degree of consistency underlying their undeniable differences. We and other investigators have frequently found statistically significant group tendencies with a dozen or so subjects, who are admittedly usually drawn from one relatively homogeneous population. Individual and cultural variations in aesthetic taste can hardly be overlooked. But a search for general principles that apply to everybody is a necessary preliminary to examining, and accounting for, the range of variation. This search can bring to light the variables that influence aesthetic reactions, even if they influence them in different ways in different people. Dissimilar preferences can represent differences in degree, e.g., curves of the same shape relating dependent to independent variables but with peaks and troughs in different locations.

Most of the studies in the present book are concerned with reactions of groups of subjects. The results enable one to predict mainly descriptive statistics—means, trends, correlations—of other samples of the same subject population. It would be risky to generalize them to other populations or to use them to predict the reactions of an individual subject. It must, however, be borne in mind that information about the average reactions of groups of people is not only of interest theoretically and as a first stage towards understanding individual differences, it can also be of practical importance. Designers of custom-made objects—the architect or interior director concerned with a unique dwelling house, the tailor who takes an order for a made-to-measure suit—must be interested in the tastes of individual clients and be well aware of how widely they can differ. But for those responsible for the design of public buildings, urban environments, mass-produced objects, and works of art intended for mass audiences, predictions about group reactions—what will appeal to the greatest number of people, what will receive the highest average evaluation—are what matter.

Nevertheless, questions regarding individual differences are of compelling importance, and some of our experiments broach them. Some differences between subjects with and without specialized training in the arts are presented and discussed in Chapters 2 and 6. Changes with age are considered in Chapter 3.

Almost all the experimental aesthetics of the past, remote and recent, has concentrated on the reactions of western subjects with above-average education. This is true of most of the work done in our own laboratory, including most of the studies in this book. Such findings are of theoretical and practical interest, even if they are confined to persons with one kind of social background. But it is clearly essential to find out how far the findings that have been obtained reflect universal characteristics of the human nervous system and how far they are due to the kinds of learning that members of one culture or subculture undergo. The only way to settle this question is to extend research to subjects from a wide variety of cultures. Chapter 12 reports an initial foray in this direction and its results. The same stimulus material and the same procedures (apart from translation of terms) were used with subjects drawn from three Ugandan populations and with Canadian subjects representing the kind of population that has served the vast majority of studies in experimental aesthetics hitherto. Such cross-cultural research in experimental aesthetics calls for a great investment of effort in coming years.

REFERENCES

Avital, T. *Artonomy: Systematic art*, in press.

Bartenwerfer, H. Über Art und Bedeutung der Beziehung zwischen Pulsfrequenz und skalierter psychischer Anspannung. *Zeitschrift für experimentelle und angewandte Psychologie*, 1963, **10**, 455–470.

Bartenwerfer, H. Einige praktische Konsequenzen aus der Aktivierungstheorie. *Zeitschrift für experimentelle und angewandte Psychologie*, 1969, **16**, 195–222.

Baumgarten, A. G. *Meditationes philosophicae de nonnullis ad poema pertinentibus.* Halle: Grüner, 1735.

Baumgarten, A. G. *Aesthetica*. I. Teil. Frankfort-on-Oder: Kunze, 1750.

Bense, M. *Einführung in die informationstheoretische Ästhetik*. Reinbek: Rohwolt, 1969.

Berlyne, D. E. *Conflict, arousal and curiosity*. New York: McGraw-Hill, 1960.

Berlyne, D. E. Conflict and the orientation reaction. *Journal of Experimental Psychology*, 1961, **62**, 476–483.

Berlyne, D. E. Motivational problems raised by exploratory and epistemic behavior. In S. Koch (Ed.), *Psychology—A study of a science.* Vol. 5. New York: McGraw-Hill, 1963.

Berlyne, D. E. *Structure and direction in thinking.* New York: Wiley, 1965.

Berlyne, D. E. Curiosity and exploration. *Science*, 1966, **153**, 25–33.

Berlyne, D. E. Arousal and reinforcement. In D. Levine (Ed.), *Nebraska symposium on motivation*, 1967. Lincoln, Nebr.: University of Nebraska Press, 1967.

Berlyne, D. E. Laughter, humor and play. In G. Lindzey & E. Aronson (Eds.), *Handbook of social psychology.* (2nd ed.) Vol. III. Boston: Addison-Wesley, 1969.

Berlyne, D. E. Motivational problems. In J. Linhart (Ed.), *Proceedings of the International Conference on Psychology of Human Learning.* Vol. I. Prague: Institute of Psychology, Czechoslovak Academy of Sciences, 1970.

Berlyne, D. E. *Aesthetics and psychobiology.* New York: Appleton-Century-Crofts, 1971.

Berlyne, D. E. Ends and means of experimental aesthetics. *Canadian Journal of Psychology*, 1972, **26**, 303–325. (a)

Berlyne, D. E. Experimental aesthetics. In P. C. Dodwell (Ed.), *New horizons in psychology 2.* Hammondsworth: Penguin, 1972. (b)

Berlyne, D. E. Humor and its kin. In J. H. Goldstein & P. E. McGhee (Eds.), *The psychology of humor.* New York & London: Academic Press, 1972. (c)

Berlyne, D. E. Reinforcement values of visual patterns compared through concurrent performances. *Journal of the Experimental Analysis of Behavior*, 1972, **18**, 281–285. (d)

Berlyne, D. E. Interrelations of verbal and nonverbal measures used in experimental aesthetics. *Scandinavian Journal of Psychology*, 1973, **14**, 177–184. (a)

Berlyne, D. E. The vicissitudes of aplopathematic and thelematoscopic pneumatology (*or* The hydrography of hedonism). In D. E. Berlyne & K. B. Madsen (Eds.), *Pleasure, reward, preference.* New York: Academic Press, 1973. (b)

Berlyne, D. E. Information and motivation. In A. Silverstein (Ed.), *Human communication: Theoretical explorations.* Washington, D.C.: Erlbaum, 1974.

Berlyne, D. E., & Borsa, D. M. Uncertainty and the orientation reaction. *Perception & Psychophysics*, 1968, **3**, 77–79.

Berlyne, D. E., McDonnell, P., Nicki, R. M., & Parham, L. Effects of auditory pitch and complexity on EEG desynchronization and on verbally expressed judgments. *Canadian Journal of Psychology*, 1967, **21**, 346–367.

Berlyne, D. E. & Parham, L. C. C. Determinants of subjective novelty. *Perception & Psychophysics*, 1968, **3**, 415–423.

Birkhoff, G. D. *Aesthetic measure.* Cambridge, Mass.: Harvard University Press, 1933.

Catania, A. C. Concurrent performances: A baseline for the study of reinforcement magnitude. *Journal of the Experimental Analysis of Behavior*, 1963, **6**, 299–300.

Cattell, R. B. The three basic factor analytic research designs—Their interrelations and derivatives. *Psychological Bulletin*, 1952, **49**, 499–570.

Cattell, R. B. Personality theory growing from multivariate quantitative research. In S. Koch (Ed.), *Psychology—A study of a science.* Vol. 3. New York: McGraw-Hill, 1959.

Coates, F. D. In search of the sense of beauty. *Design Journal*, 1972, **5**, 8–13.

Day, H. I. Exploratory behaviour as a function of individual differences and level of arousal. Unpublished Ph.D. thesis, University of Toronto, 1965.

Dell, P. Reticular homeostasis and critical reactivity. In G. Moruzzi, A. Fessard, & H. H. Jasper (Eds.), *Brain mechanisms.* Amsterdam: Elsevier, 1963.

Diserens, C. M. *The influence of music on behavior.* Princeton, N.J.: Princeton University Press, 1926.

Eysenck, H. J. The experimental study of the "good Gestalt"–A new approach. *Psychological Review*, 1942, 49, 344–364.

Fechner, G. T. *Vorschule der Ästhetik.* Leipzig: Breitkopf & Härtel, 1876.

Frank, H. *Grundlagenprobleme der Informationsästhetik und erste Anwendung auf die mime pure.* Quickborn: Schnelle, 1959.

Garner, W. R. *Uncertainty and structure as psychological concepts.* New York: Wiley, 1962.

Godkewitsch, M. Verbal, exploratory and psychological responses to stimulus properties underlying humour. Unpublished Ph.D. thesis, University of Toronto, 1974.

Gunzenhäuser, R. *Aesthetisches Mass und ästhetische Information.* Quickborn: Schnelle, 1962.

Hutcheson, F. *An inquiry into the original of our ideas of beauty and virtue.* London: Darby, 1725.

Kaplan, R. Predictors of environmental preference: Designers and "clients." In W. F. E. Preiser (Ed.), *Environmental design research.* Stroudsberg, Pa.: Dowden, Hutchinson & Ross, 1973.

Marcus, S. Two poles of the human language. *Revue roumaine de linguistique*, 1970, 15, 187–198, 309–316, 495–500.

Moles, A. *Théorie de l'information et perception esthétique.* Paris: Flammarion, 1958. (*Information theory and esthetic perception.* Urbana, Ill.: University of Illinois Press, 1966.)

Morris, C. Esthetics and the theory of signs. *Journal of Unified Science (Erkenntnis)*, 1939, 8, 131–150.

Morris, C. *Signs, language and behavior.* New York: Prentice-Hall, 1946.

Olds, J. Brain mechanisms of reinforcement learning. In D. E. Berlyne & K. B. Madsen (Eds.), *Pleasure, reward, preference.* New York: Academic Press, 1973.

Osgood, C. E. The nature and measurement of meaning. *Psychological Bulletin*, 1952, 49, 197–237.

Peirce, C. S. Logic as semiotic: The theory of signs. In A. W. Burks (Ed.), *Collected papers of Charles Sanders Peirce*, Vol. II. Cambridge, Mass.: Harvard University Press, 1932. (Written, 1897.)

Spence, K. W. The nature of theory construction in contemporary psychology. *Psychological Review*, 1944, 51, 47–68.

Thayer, R. E. Measurement of activation through self-report. *Psychological Reports*, 1967, 20, 663–678 (Monograph Supplement 1–V20).

Thayer, R. E. Activation states as assessed by verbal report and four psychophysiological variables. *Psychphysiology*, 1970, 7, 86–94.

Valentine, C. W. *The experimental psychology of beauty.* London: Methuen, 1962.

Venturi, L. *Storia della critica d'arte.* (New rev. ed.). Turin: Einaudi, 1964. (*History of art criticism.* New York: Dutton, 1964.)

Wimsatt, W. K., & Brooks, C. *Literary criticism.* New York: Knopf, 1957.

Wundt, W. M. *Grundzüge der physiologischen Psychologie.* Leipzig: Engelmann, 1874.

2

VERBAL AND EXPLORATORY RESPONSES TO SOUND SEQUENCES VARYING IN UNCERTAINTY LEVEL[1]

J. B. Crozier

Only one aspect of music composition—melody—has been found to be common to the music of all times and all cultures (see Apel, 1964, p. 436; Lomax, 1968, p. 13). Recognizing this central role of melody, one would expect the investigation of melodic structure and perception to be well advanced. However, for a variety of reasons, this is not the case. And so the prospective investigator is faced with a dearth of previous research on which to build his efforts. The results of earlier investigations, which in many areas provide a reasonable blueprint for further action, are only suggestive in this particular context.

The first conclusion to be drawn from a survey of the literature is that experiments using real musical examples have been beset with interpretational problems (see Simon & Wohlwill, 1968; Werbik, 1969). These studies, while employing the methodology of an experimental aesthetic, lose much of the precision of the laboratory because of the elusive and only qualitative nature of the independent variable. As Simon & Wohlwill (1968) ultimately conclude, "Control over extraneous variables—always a challenge in psychological investigation—seems almost impossible to ensure in an experiment concerned with music [p. 238]."

[1] Based on a thesis submitted in accordance with the requirements for the Ph.D. degree of the University of Toronto. The author would like to thank Dr. C. D. Creelman for the use of his computer and Howard L. Kaplan for help with programming.

The alternative to this *analytic* approach is a *synthetic* one (see Chap. 1), and it is here that one finds the greatest degree of success in exploring listeners' judgments and reactions to melodic stimuli. Experiments by Overmier (1962), Mindus (1968), and Vitz (1966) can be taken as representative of the synthetic approach. The first point these experiments establish is the utility of an information-communication analysis in quantifying melodic sequences for laboratory investigation. Since the limitations of any method of melodic analysis will carry through all subsequent levels of any investigation, a more than cursory look at this issue is warranted.

The Stimulus Material

Our first and most obvious task under this heading is to define a melody, and according to the Harvard Dictionary of Music (1964), a melody is most simply "a succession of tones." A further step in our process of quantification is the formal statement that a melody can be considered a stochastic process—that is, a system of symbols (tones or notes) that is sampled according to probability laws in order to produce a succession of symbols (i.e., a melody).

Musical composers, while obviously aware of the probabilistic nature of their craft, tended up to 1940 to shun this particular conceptualization of melodic style. Early attempts by the composer Arnold Schönberg to base choice of pitch on the probabilistic principle of equal occurrence of the 12 pitches in the chromatic scale were considered revolutionary, and musical works based on this procedure, called 12-tone serial technique, were not particularly well received. After 1945, a new generation of composers extended serialization to the remaining three dimensions of a tone—duration, loudness, and timber (see Stockhausen, 1962; Babbitt, 1962). This "total-serialization" technique was important, for it signaled an overt recognition that melodic composition could consist of a simple permutation of the four parameters defining a single tone.

As composition and analysis of music and melodies in terms of stochastic principles became commonplace in the 1950s, (see Brooks, 1957; Pierce, 1956; Olson & Belar, 1961; Sowa, 1956), there was perhaps an historically inevitable attempt to quantify a given degree of serialization in information-theory terms. Many of the early applications of the theory were basically descriptive in nature and not essential to the analysis of a melody in serial terms (see Attneave, in Quastler, 1955b; Kraehenbuehl & Coons, 1959; Youngblood, 1960; Brawley, 1959; Pinkerton, 1956). However, some later applications (such as Vitz, 1966; Overmier, 1962) clearly employed the operational techniques of information theory to provide a metric expressing specific levels of serial construction.

Information theory, as formally outlined by Shannon and Weaver (1949), is an analysis of communication at the level of symbol transmission. Of the three broad levels of communication problems that they differentiate– "technical," "semantic," and behavioral "effectiveness"–their concern is with an adequate quantification of the transmission process, regardless of the semantic or motivational consequences of the message. While the most extensive applications of the theory have been outside the field of psychology, its applications to specific psychological problems have been reviewed by a number of writers (see Quastler, 1955a; Moles, 1958; Attneave, 1959; Garner, 1962). The extension of this method of "logical multivariate analysis," to use Garner's phrase, to melodic structure requires that for a given melody we must be able to (1) specify our "alphabet" (i.e., the total number of possible combinations of pitch, duration, loudness, and timber), and (2) specify the rules for sampling the "letters" of this "alphabet" (i.e., unconditional and conditional probability matrices for all possible tones). If these two sets of constraints can be specified, then the average information-content of a given melody can be expressed by the basic formula:

$$U = -[p_1 \log_2 p_1 + p_2 \log_2 p_2 + \cdots + p_n \log_2 p_n]$$

$$= -\sum_{i=1}^{n} p_i \log_2 p_i$$

$$= \sum_{i=1}^{n} p_i \log_2 \frac{1}{p_i} \tag{1}$$

where n is the total number of possible tones. In the simplest case, defined by an independent choice of successive tones and equiprobability of selection of all tones, formula (1) reduces to:

$$U = \log_2 n \tag{2}$$

This second formula is the one that will be employed in this chapter, and successions of tones metricized according to this formula will be referred to as *sound sequences*. Reflecting common usage within psychology, the measure U for a specific sound sequence will be calculated using logarithms to the base 2 (although logarithms to any base are equally appropriate), and the resultant single number will be referred to as the "uncertainty in bits per tone."

For this measure of uncertainty to be appropriate, assumptions regarding the stochasticity, ergodicity, stationarity, and transitional (Markov) properties of the sequences must be tenable. These assumptions make it obvious why melodies composed by famous composers will not be appropriate as stimuli through post hoc analysis using information-theory calculus. Any tone sequences employing information-theory principles must of necessity be so constructed as to meet the constraints of the sampling formula.

Of the studies reviewed in preparation for this project, the sound sequences employed by Vitz (1966) were clearly superior in their conceptualization. As Vitz was able to provide tape recordings of his sound sequence material, these ready-made stimuli were used in the initial experiments presented in this chapter. Table 1 presents the number of pitches, durations, and loudnesses defining each of the six levels of uncertainty of Vitz's sequences. Since Vitz employed the simplest case (independent choice and equiprobability of successive tones), uncertainty is expressed here by formula (2): $U = \log_2 n$.

It should be noted that the uncertainty measure cannot encompass compositional aspects of the sound sequence such as its tonal (i.e., "key-centeredness") or metric (rhythmic) qualities. Such conceptual aspects

TABLE 1

Summary of the Structural Characteristics
of the Vitz (1966) Sound Sequences

Stimulus uncertainty (rank order)	Number of pitches	Number of durations	Number of loudness levels	Number of equi-probable tones	U per tone (in bits)
1	2	1	1	2	1.00
2	4	2	2	16	4.00
3	6	4	3	72	6.17
4	8	6	3	144	7.17
5	12	6	4	288	8.17
6	18	8	4	576	9.17

of the stimulus must be resolved outside of the information theory metric. Vitz handled the question of key-centeredness by expanding the pitch range with uncertainty such that the specific frequencies chosen formed a whole-tone scale centering around A (447 Hz). Rhythmic implications, which may be viewed as an interaction of tone duration and loudness, were not incorporated in any systematic fashion beyond having the range of tone durations expand in both directions from an initial value of 500 msec. Vitz treated these conceptual variables as a form of intertone stimulus variation and expressed their increased magnitude by use of the descriptive statistic σ^2. (See Vitz, 1966 for a tabulated summary of these variables.)

Theoretical Considerations

Considering the theoretical background in which prior experiments were conducted, it can be noted that one hypothesis has prevailed. This hypothesis states that humans have a preferred or optimal level of stimulus variation in their environment. Regarding the organism as an information-processing system, this position attributes negative affect and avoidance behavior to small and large degrees of stimulus variation and positive affect and approach behavior to moderate degrees of variation. The attribute of the melodic stimulus implicated by this position is stimulus variation or complexity, and listeners' reactions to this stimulus property have been monitored using both verbal rating scales and listening time responses. However, neither the verbal nor the nonverbal data obtained in previous experiments have provided unequivocal support for the inverted U-shaped function predicted by this optimal-level-of-stimulation hypothesis.

An alternative and historically older hypothesis than the above is one that can be called the arousal-minimization position. The argument here is that approach behavior tends to occur as stimuli increase in complexity, due to the arousal and resultant need for resolution engendered in the subject. As in the optimization case, stimulus variation, complexity, etc., have been the primary stimulus attributes implicated by this position. However, note that the behavioral function predicted in this latter case is one of increasing exploration as stimulus complexity increases.

Some researchers have attempted to incorporate both information-optimization and arousal-minimization functions into their theorizing. Noteworthy in this respect is the work of Berlyne (1950, 1960, 1965, 1971; see also Chap. 1, this volume). An attempt by the present writer to capture the terminology and sequence of events incorporated in Berlyne's position is presented in the form of a flow diagram in Figure 1. (*Caveat lector*: this

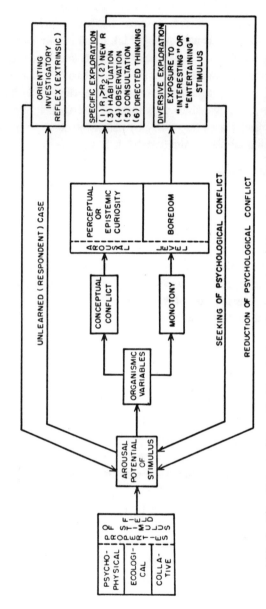

FIG. 1. Flow diagram of theoretical terminology. (Terms extracted from Berlyne, 1950, 1960, 1965, 1971.)

presentation should be taken for what it is and no more, namely, a summarization of some guiding theoretical notions to be used in this chapter.)

SUBJECTS' TRAINING IN MUSIC

The effect of *S*s' formal music background and training on sound sequence perception is also a variable considered in this chapter. There are many reasons for expecting those persons who have had extended exposure to music to exhibit different judgments and patterns of exploration (or, if you prefer, different "aesthetic tastes") than those who have had less. The effects of ear-training and explicit instruction in the principles governing auditory composition are only two of the more obvious aspects of environment, while the unknown contribution of endowment in terms of natural musical ability cannot be overlooked either.

In this investigation, the division of *S*s in terms of musical background was simply accomplished by reference to the *S*s' course of study. Those *S*s enrolled as students within the Faculty of Arts and Science of the University of Toronto were considered to form a sample from a "nonexpert" population and were called "nonmusic majors"; those enrolled within the Faculty of Music were considered a sample from an "expert" population and were called "music majors." Sampling from these two populations was such that comparisons of the effects of background on aesthetic judgment and choice were possible.

In order to assess differences between the two groups in terms of their formal music training and interest in music, a "music background" questionnaire and a "music interest" scale were administered to the *S*s. The music background questionnaire was a 10-item form consisting of elementary questions on the rudiments of music (such as, "What is the key signature of B minor?"). The music interest scale was simply an 11-point scale on which the *S*s indicated their interest in music, ranging from none to high absorbing interest.

It was expected that music majors would have a much greater knowledge of the rudiments of music than would nonmusic majors, and that this difference could be conveniently assessed by the music background questionnaire. The a priori expectations for the music interest scale were not so clearcut. A conjecture was that the music group would exhibit a significantly greater interest in music than the nonmusic group, but that this intergroup difference would not differentiate the two groups to the same degree as would the music background questionnaire.

Of primary interest was the extent to which the music and nonmusic groups showed significant differences in sound-sequence perception and exploration, for any effects found here reflect differences generalizable to much larger populations than in previous research. These earlier studies have typically limited their generalizability by taking only the extremes of music and nonmusic S distributions on some training criterion (e.g., Vitz, 1966) or by screening out Ss exhibiting hearing deficits (e.g., Overmier, 1962). In the present case, the selection of Ss on the basis of enrollment alone was seen as contributing to the generalizability of the concept of musical experience as a factor in aesthetic response.

THE DEPENDENT VARIABLES

The dependent measures have already been discussed in some detail in Chapter 1. In this chapter, verbal rating scales belonging to all four classes—descriptive, evaluative, internal-state, and stylistic—were utilized. These verbal judgments were gathered because they seemed to tap the intervening perceptual processes that constitute much of what we call criticizing, theorizing, and evaluating one's environment. They therefore presumably play some mediating role in determining nonverbal preference.

However, while man may talk endlessly about music, its most important impact on human behavior is shown by the amount of time spent in listening to the auditory stimuli we call music. Our laboratory analogues of natural, unrestrained listening and choice behavior were Listening Time and paired-comparison choice (or Exploratory Choice). Both "free" Listening Time and Rating Time were measured in different experiments. Free Listening Time involved presenting S with the full range of auditory stimuli available and letting him hear each sound sequence for as long as he saw fit. There was no experimental task for Ss in this setting other than to listen to the melodic material. The dependent variable was S's Listening Times (in seconds) as a function of sound-sequence uncertainty.

Rating Time involved a similar measure. However, when this was measured, the primary purpose of the experiment was to obtain Ss' verbal judgments of the sound sequences. In some of the experimental settings employed, the amount of time available to listen to a sound sequence in order to complete the rating judgments was under the control of the individual S. When this was the case, Rating Time was recorded as a variable of secondary interest. It was thought that this measure might result in a different pattern of exploration than that obtained with free Listening Time, as Rating Time would presumably reflect the degree of difficulty S had in filling out the verbal scales with reference to a particular sound sequence.

Exploratory Choice, our second class of sound sequence exploration, is a variant of what has been described as "the standard method of experimental aesthetics (Woodworth, 1938)." As employed in this investigation, it consisted of presenting listeners with two 10-second long sound sequences differing in uncertainty level, and permitting them to choose either the first or the second of the two sequences for 10 seconds of further listening.

STATEMENT OF THE RESEARCH PROBLEMS

Five experiments, involving manipulation of sound sequence uncertainty, stimulus incongruity/congruity, and Ss' musical background, are reported in this chapter. In the first three experiments, verbal judgments on 7-point rating scales are presented. The principal questions considered are:

1. What is the relation between the information-theory measure of uncertainty and subjective judgments of sound-sequence structure?

2. What is the relation between judgments of visual and auditory patterns on scales such as DISPLEASING-PLEASING and UNINTERESTING-INTERESTING?

3. What are the stimulus determinants of melodiousness?

4. What effect(s) do the sound sequences have upon listeners' internal-state judgments of discomfort and pleasure?

5. What is the dimensionality of the semantic space derivable from adjectival judgments of the sound sequences?

The final two experiments recorded Ss' listening times and exploratory choices to the sound sequences. The questions of primary interest here were:

6. What patterns of Listening Time and Exploratory Choice are found as a function of sound-sequence uncertainty and stimulus incongruity/congruity?

7. What relations do these measures of stimulus exploration bear to any derived semantic structure?

And finally,

8. In what manner, if any, do musical background and training qualify any answers gained to the above questions?

Some general implications and limitations of the investigation are presented following the reports of these experiments.

EXPERIMENT 1: COLLATIVE AND EVALUATIVE JUDGMENTS

The first concern of this experiment was to assess the relation between the information-theoretic measure of uncertainty and listeners' subjective judgments of the sound sequences. As a review of the experimental literature will show, the uncertainty measure has been the predominant method of quantifying differences in stimulus structure. However, most previous uses of uncertainty have employed this statistic without consideration of how uncertainty and subjective assessments of melodic Complexity may be related. Given the importance of structural variation to the study of aesthetic behavior, establishing this relationship suggested itself as the first step in any investigation.

A second concern of this experiment was to consider how verbal judgments of Interestingness and Pleasingness are affected by the uncertainty level associated with sound sequences. It has been noted in Chapter 1 that very particular and stable functions have been established between Pleasingness, Interestingness, and the objectively defined complexity of visual patterns. Will the rated Interestingness of sound sequences increase as a function of sound-sequence complexity also? Will Pleasingness increase and then decrease as a function of sequence complexity, as has been the case with visual patterns? The answers to these questions were seen as fundamental to the integration of this investigation with theoretical positions derived from research employing visual stimuli.

A final question considered in this experiment was the relationship between verbal judgments of Beauty and sound-sequence uncertainty. The question of the beautiful has been debated by philosophers since at least the fifth century B.C. In the present context of an experimental aesthetics, the question is reduced to one of group judgments of the stimuli. If inter-S agreement on ratings of Beauty are found, how will these judgments relate to judgments on the previous three rating scales? Will the most beautiful sound sequence be the most pleasing one or the most interesting one? At this point, the evidence drawn from visual research favors a positive correlation between Pleasingness and Beauty (cf. Chap. 5, this volume; Berlyne, 1973).

Subjects

Forty-eight undergraduates, 24 enrolled in the Faculty of Music and 24 in the Faculty of Arts and Science of the University of Toronto, participated in this study. Although all 48 *S*s were enrolled in an introductory course in psychology, all were experimentally naive.

Stimulus Material

The stimuli consisted of 12 of the sound sequences constructed by Vitz (1966) using traditional tape-splicing techniques. There were two sound sequences, designated A and B, respectively, at each of six levels of uncertainty. Each sound sequence was 20 seconds long (± .5 seconds), with a mean presentation rate of 2.06 tones per second.

Design

The 12 sound sequences and four rating scales were treated as within-*S* factors. The orders of presentation for the sound sequences and rating scales were based on 12 x 12 and 4 x 4 balanced Latin squares, respectively. The balanced square for ordering the 12 sequences was generated using an algorithm by Williams (1949) cited in Edwards (1968, p. 193). This square was further balanced such that, between periods (i.e., Latin-square columns), half of the *S*s had an increase and half a decrease in uncertainty.

Because of time-tabling constraints, the arts and science students were assigned to rows 1, 3, 5, 7, 9, and 11 of the sequence presentation square, and the music students to rows 2, 4, 6, 8, 10, and 12. Upon completion of a given rating scale, the Latin square for a subsequent scale was obtained by a one-step cyclic permutation of the square (see Winer, 1962, p. 518). A 4 x 4 balanced Latin square was used to order the rating scales for presentation to the four *S*s assigned to each row of the sequence presentation square.

Procedure

The experimental environment consisted of two identical 3.3m x 2.1m rooms. Each room contained a standard office table and two chairs. The tables were divided in the middle by three-foot high wooden partitions, thereby eliminating visual contact between *S*s. The four *S*s assigned to a row of the sound sequence presentation square were fitted with Sharpe high fidelity headphones (Model HA-10-A), given a copy of the instructions to read, and simultaneously heard a prerecorded reading of the instructions over their headphones. The instructions were adapted from Osgood, Suci, and Tannenbaum (1957, pp. 82–84).

The two sound sequences of lowest uncertainty value (1.00 bit/tone) were preset to a sound pressure level of 80 db (B2 scale-GRC SPL meter type 1565-A and GRC earphone coupler type 1560-P82), with the overall range for the six levels of uncertainty being 70–86 db. This intensity range was considered physically comfortable, and in none of the experiments did Ss express any discomfort as to the loudness levels of the sound sequences. Upon completion of the four rating scales, the Ss were administered the music background and music interest questionnaires described earlier.

Results

The arts and science and music groups reported a "moderate" and "high" interest in music, respectively, with the mean interest responses for the two groups being 6.75 and 7.79 ($t = 2.69$, 46 df, $p < .01$). On the music-background questionnaire, the mean scores (out of a maximum of 10) for arts and science and music Ss were 1.13 and 8.50, respectively ($t = 7.95$, 46 df, $p < .001$). From these results it was concluded that, as well as expressing significantly different interest in music, the two groups also differed greatly in terms of their knowledge of the rudiments of music.

Two a priori criteria were established for the inclusion of data. First, each S had to complete the experimental session, making a total of 48 responses on the four rating scales. Second, each S had to use at least two of the seven available categories of scale response during the experiment. All 48 Ss met these criteria, and their data were divided according to rating scale and analyses of variance carried out. A four-factor summary table, with two between-S and two within-S factors, was adopted for purposes of this analysis (Groups x Rating-scale-temporal-position x Uncertainty x Randomization).

SIMPLE–COMPLEX scale. The analysis of variance pointed to a highly significant Uncertainty main effect ($F = 213.41$, 5,200 df, $p < .001$), with mean Complexity rating a monotonically-increasing linear function of uncertainty level. Trend analysis indicated that the linear component accounted for 99.14% of the uncertainty sum of squares ($F = 1057.89$, 1,200 df, $p < .001$). However, there was also a significant quadratic trend component ($F = 7.86$, 1,200 df, $p < .01$). Plotting this effect, we see that this quadratic component did not reflect a downturn in perceived complexity as a function of uncertainty, a result that would have been indicative of a "ceiling" effect. Rather, the deviation in the trend has resulted in a slight positive acceleration in the curve [Fig. 2(a)].

The trend analysis also revealed a highly significant linear component in the Uncertainty x Groups interaction sum of squares indicating a significant difference between the slopes of the trends of music and nonmusic groups ($F = 10.06$, 1,200 df, $p < .01$). Inspecting Figure 2(b), it is apparent that mean ratings of the music group have resulted in a scale of greater range than

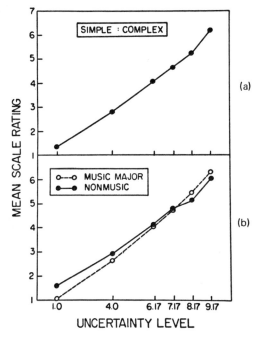

FIG. 2. (a) Uncertainty main effect: SIMPLE-COMPLEX scale; (b) Uncertainty x Groups interaction: SIMPLE-COMPLEX scale.

those of the nonmusic group (5.29 scale units versus 4.48 units, respectively). There are two possible explanations of this effect. First, this difference in scale lengths may be due to greater spacing of the sound sequences on the SIMPLE-COMPLEX dimension by the music as compared to the nonmusic group. Or second, this difference may reflect greater variability, and hence greater judgmental error, by the nonmusic as compared to the music group.

One way of deciding between these two interpretations was by analysis of rating-scale-range scores for Ss across treatments (uncertainty). If there were no group difference in consistency of judgments, then the mean range of stimulus ratings between groups should not show any significant difference. If the nonmusic group were more variable in repeated judgments of the same uncertainty level, then their mean range score should be significantly greater than that of the music group. Analysis of variance of the range scores revealed no significant Groups effect. Therefore, the first account of the Uncertainty x Groups interaction, namely of greater spacing of the sound sequences on the complexity dimension, was accepted.

There was also a marginally significant Uncertainty x Rating-scale-temporal-position interaction ($F = 1.85$, 15,200 *df*, $p < .05$). Like most task-order effects, this reflected a confounded mixture of learning, shifts in perceptual judgments, and fatigue. Inspection of the means did not implicate any particular one of these explanations. However, what was particularly noteworthy here was that SIMPLE-COMPLEX judgments by the 12 *S*s first assigned to this scale indicated that *S*s were able to differentiate the six levels of uncertainty without prior exposure to the full range of stimuli to be judged.

UNINTERESTING–INTERESTING scale.   Mean ratings of Interestingness corresponded closely to those reported for the previous scale, with Interestingness increasing as a function of stimulus uncertainty ($F = 78.58$, 5,200 *df*, $p < .001$) [Fig. 3(a)]. Trend analysis showed that the linear component once again accounted for 99.13% of the uncertainty sum of squares ($F = 389.47$, 1,200 *df*, $p < .001$).

A marginally significant Uncertainty x Groups interaction ($F = 2.53$, 5,200 *df*, $p < .05$), accompanied by a significant linear trend component

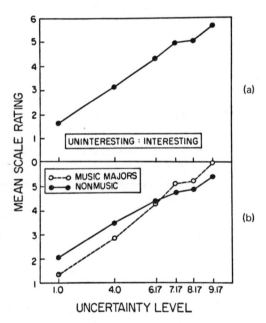

FIG. 3.   (a) Uncertainty main effect: UNINTER-
ESTING–INTERESTING scale; (b) Uncertainty x
Groups   interaction: UNINTERESTING–INTER-
ESTING scale.

($F = 11.81$, 1,200 df, $p < .001$), was once again indicative of a significant difference between groups in terms of mean scale range (music group range = 4.67 units; nonmusic = 3.36 units) [Fig. 3(b)]. As in the case of SIMPLE-COMPLEX ratings, this difference may be accounted for either in terms of greater spacing of the sequences by the music group, or greater variability in the judgments of the nonmusic group. These alternate explanations were tested by an analysis of variance on range scores for the two groups across uncertainty level. This analysis revealed no significant Groups effects, a result corresponding to that found with SIMPLE-COMPLEX scale ratings. On the basis of this range test, the explanation of the Uncertainty x Groups interaction in terms of greater stimulus spacing by the music group on the Interestingness dimension was accepted.

A marginally significant Uncertainty x Rating scale temporal position effect ($F = 2.05$, 15,200 df, $p < .05$) was attributed to the same factors suggested in considering the SIMPLE-COMPLEX scale, namely a confounded mixture of learning, judgment criterion shifts, and fatigue. As in the case of SIMPLE-COMPLEX ratings, the 12 Ss first assigned to rating the stimuli in terms of Interestingness were able to differentiate the six levels of uncertainty without prior exposure to the range of stimuli.

DISPLEASING-PLEASING scale. The analysis of variance once again implicated uncertainty as a major determinant of the Ss' patterns of response ($F = 18.98$, 5,200 df, $p < .001$). Visual inspection of the plotted means indicated that DISPLEASING-PLEASING ratings [Fig. 4(a)] appeared to be an inverted U-shaped function of uncertainty. This interpretation was supported in part by the trend analysis that showed highly significant linear ($F = 57.94$, 1,200 df, $p < .001$) and quadratic ($F = 33.96$, 1,200 df, $p < .001$) components. Further analysis of the treatment means using Duncan's New Multiple Range Test showed that all uncertainty levels greater than 4.00 bits/tone were more pleasing than 1.00 bit/tone ($\alpha = .001$). Therefore, while there was the suggestion of an inverted U-shaped function here, these data are better described as being an "r-shaped" function.

The Groups main effect was also significant ($F = 4.00$, 5,200 df, $p < .01$), with a highly significant linear ($F = 12.86$, 1,200 df, $p < .001$) and a marginally significant quadratic ($F = 4.07$, 1,200 df, $p < .05$) component of the Uncertainty x Groups interaction indicating a difference between the responses of the two groups. Inspection of Figure 4(b) shows that there was a "crossover" effect around uncertainty levels 3 and 4 (6.17 bits and 7.17 bits/tone), and a marked contrast between groups at the highest uncertainty level. Nonmusic Ss rated 9.17 bits/tone as the second-most displeasing uncertainty level, and music Ss rated it the most pleasing. Analysis of variance

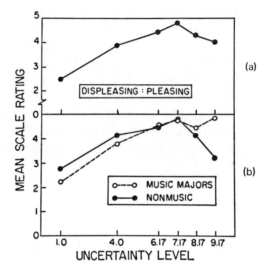

FIG. 4. (a) Uncertainty main effect: DISPLEAS-
ING–PLEASING scale. (b) Uncertainty x Groups
interaction: DISPLEASING-PLEASING scale.

on the range scores of Ss across the six uncertainty levels revealed no significant Groups effects. Therefore, differences in group variability in repeated
judgments of the same uncertainty level did not appear to be a contributing
factor to this interaction.

UGLY-BEAUTIFUL scale. The analysis of variance showed highly
significant Uncertainty $(F = 11.10, 5,200$ *df,* $p < .001)$ and Uncertainty x
Groups $(F = 5.54, 5,200$ *df,* $p < .001)$ effects, with the plotted mean ratings
suggesting an inverted U-shaped pattern of responding [Fig. 5(a)]. Significant
linear $(F = 10.06, 1,200$ *df,* $p < .01)$ and highly significant quadratic
$(F = 44.40, 1,200$ *df, $p < .001)$ trend components of the Uncertainty sum of
squares supported this interpretation. Further analysis using Duncan's New
Multiple Range Test indicated that intermediate uncertainty levels (4.00-8.17
bits/tone) were rated more beautiful than the two extremes of uncertainty
(1.00 and 9.17 bits/tone, $\alpha = .01$). No statistically significant difference was
found between these latter two uncertainty values $(\alpha = .05)$. Based on
the range test results, an inverted U-shaped interpretation of the function was
accepted.

The highly significant Uncertainty x Groups interaction was similar to that
found with ratings of Pleasingness, in that the trends of the groups' responses
differed both in slope (linear trend component, $F = 22.04, 1,200$ *df,*

$p < .001$) and in curvature (quadratic trend component, $F = 4.58$, 1,200 df, $p < .05$) [Fig. 5(b)]. The crossover point between the two groups once again occurred between uncertainty levels three and four (6.17 bits and 7.17 bits/tone). The ugliest sound sequence for the nonmusic majors was the most complex (9.17 bits/tone); the ugliest for the music majors was the least complex (1.00 bit/tone). Analysis of variance on the range scores of Ss across the six uncertainty levels revealed no significant Groups effects.

UGLY-BEAUTIFUL ratings produced the only statistically significant between-Ss effect in this experiment, this being a marginally significant Groups x Rating-scale-temporal-position interaction ($F = 3.26$, 3,400 df, $p < .05$). Inspection of the means showed that this effect reflected a clear change between groups in evaluative perception of the sound sequences as a function of repeated exposure. For the nonmusic group, the sequences tended to the negative pole of the scale as a function of repetition; for the music group, just the opposite occurred, with the sound sequences being perceived more positively over time.

While much could be made of this interaction in terms of the effects of "mere exposure" upon aesthetic perception, what will be noted here is that repeated exposure has *not*, as many theorists have postulated (see Zajonc,

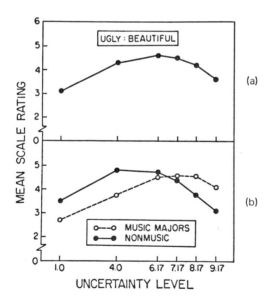

FIG. 5. (a) Uncertainty main effect: UGLY-BEAUTIFUL scale; (b) Uncertainty x Groups interaction: UGLY-BEAUTIFUL scale.

1968; Harrison & Zajonc, 1970; Matlin, 1970) been a sufficient condition for more positive evaluation of the stimuli by both groups of Ss. As the effects of repeated exposure have been of infrequent and only minimal statistical significance throughout this first experiment, the question of repeated exposure would not appear to be a crucial one in this experimental setting. Any shifts in aesthetic judgment that have occurred have been completely overshadowed by Ss' responses to stimulus uncertainty.

Intercorrelations of the rating scales. The mean ratings at each uncertainty level across all four rating scales were obtained. Using this data matrix, a 4 x 4 correlation matrix between rating scales across the six uncertainty levels (4 *df*) was calculated. This method of correlation focuses on the relationship between verbal judgments as a function of varying sound sequence uncertainty, and has been used extensively in research assessing the effects of stimulus variation on verbal ratings (see Berlyne, 1973).

Not unexpectedly, only two of the six possible correlation coefficients were statistically significant. Mean ratings of Complexity and Interestingness, both of which were monotonically-increasing linear functions of stimulus uncertainty, were almost perfectly correlated, the coefficient being .99 (4 *df*, $p < .001$). Mean ratings of Pleasingness and Beauty, which were, respectively, "r-shaped" and "n-shaped" functions of uncertainty, were significantly correlated, in this case the coefficient being .88 (4 *df*, $p < .02$).

Discussion

On all four rating scales, uncertainty has been the most important determinant of listeners' verbal judgments. Turning first to SIMPLE-COMPLEX ratings, the marked degree of linearity between Complexity judgments and uncertainty supports the assertion that "the collative stimulus properties can be usefully discussed in the language of information theory" (Berlyne, 1971, p. 69). Given this degree of correspondence between the measure of average information and judged complexity, to equate stimulus uncertainty with Complexity would not appear to misinterpret the data.

This correspondence between Complexity and uncertainty also tells us something about the manner in which people perceive variations in melodic structure. If one plots mean ratings of Complexity against the total number of possible tones at each uncertainty level, it is readily seen that increases in stimulus variation become less detectable as the number of tones becomes greater. This type of relationship, in which psychological judgments are a negatively accelerating function of the stimulus property under investigation, is a recurrent theme in investigations of perceptual processes (see Stevens, 1957).

Further evidence that the measure of uncertainty is not just a "pseudo-language cribbed from information theory" (Green & Courtis, 1966) is found in the similarity of ratings given to the 2 sound sequences (simply designated "A" and "B") at each level of uncertainty. This indicates that Ss have not discriminated 12 sequences, but six classes of sequence. This lack of discrimination of the 2 sequences also suggests that the assumptions for appropriate application of information theory have been reasonably realized within Vitz's 20-second sampling period.

Rated Interestingness has been a linearly increasing function of uncertainty nearly identical to that of Complexity ($r = .99$, 4 df, $p < .001$). This relationship corresponds to that found between Interestingness and visual patterns of varying complexity and provides a link with previous theoretical positions based on responses to visual stimuli of varying complexity. For, according to these accounts (see Berlyne, 1971), Interestingness reflects arousal-raising stimulus properties, making possible the achievement of positive hedonic value through the arousal reduction mechanism (see Chap. 1, this volume; Berlyne, 1967, 1971). The association of this verbal function with the minimization hypothesis of nonverbal exploration is congruent with the accepted meaning of "interestingness." Funk & Wagnalls (1968, p. 704) define "interest" as "(1) a feeling of curiosity or attentiveness, [and] (2) the power to arouse curiosity or attentiveness."

DISPLEASING-PLEASING ratings have also conformed to the previous relationship established using visual patterns of varying complexity. And as expected, ratings on the UGLY-BEAUTIFUL scale were similar to those for Pleasingness ($r = .88$, 4 df, $p < .02$). This finding that a moderate degree of uncertainty is the most pleasing and the most beautiful provides us with another link with the previous visually-based literature. For, pleasing and beautiful visual stimuli seem likely to reflect arousal-moderating motivational processes, favoring positive hedonic value through the arousal-boost or moderate-arousal-increment mechanism.

The division of Ss in terms of background in music has resulted in statistically significant Uncertainty x Groups effects on all four rating scales. In the two cases where verbal ratings were linearly-increasing functions of uncertainty, the music group has shown greater sensitivity to changes in uncertainty, in the sense that they have been able to space the sequences further apart than the nonmusic group. This difference may reflect the ear-training and explicit instruction in the principles governing auditory composition that music majors bring to the task and that are presumably lacking in the case of nonmusic majors. It should be noted that these group differences were not main effects, with perceived Complexity and Interestingness of all sound sequences being less for the music than for the nonmusic group. Music training has *not* caused a given level of uncertainty to be perceived as less complex and less interesting (i.e., less "curiosity-inducing"), as has been suggested by a number of authors (see Goldstein, 1961; Harrison, 1968; Harrison & Zajonc, 1970).

In the remaining two cases, where verbal ratings have increased and then decreased as a function of stimulus uncertainty, the music group's apex has occurred at a much higher level of complexity than has the nonmusic group's. In illustration, the most beautiful sound sequence for the music group was sampled from 144 alternative tones; for the nonmusic group it was selected from 16 alternative tones. This difference lends itself to explanation in terms of habitual group differences in tolerance for, and reward value of, sound sequences as a function of varying complexity.

Considering finally the correlations between the four rating scales across the six stimulus uncertainty levels, the two significant relationships were indicative of some degeneracy in verbally-assessed perception of melodic sequences. Even at this early stage of the investigation, it could be suggested that perception of the sound sequences was at least two-dimensional. The search for further dimensions continued in the next experiment.

EXPERIMENT 2: STYLISTIC AND INTERNAL-STATE JUDGMENTS

Purpose

The first concern of this study was to present *S*s with rating scales that might tap additional perceptual dimensions not considered in the previous experiment. One dimension of obvious interest concerned judgment of musical quality. Did the sound sequences have any "musical" quality, or were they, as some authors have suggested (see McLaughlin, 1962), devoid of any "musical meaning"? Did the quality of melodiousness depend principally upon environmental context, or was it to some degree inherent in particular arrangements of tones? These questions were considered by having listeners judge the sequences on an UNMELODIC-MELODIC scale.

It was also of interest to obtain *S*s' ratings of their internal reactions to the sound sequences. All the previous rating scales have clearly demanded ratings of the stimuli themselves. However, semantic techniques could also probe the effects of stimulus exposure upon internal transient states of the organism. The use of verbal reports in this manner has received some endorsement in the experimental literature (see Nowlis, 1965; Thayer, 1967). In line with this approach, the scales NO PLEASURE-EXTREME PLEASURE and NO DISCOMFORT-EXTREME DISCOMFORT were included in this study. Two patterns of interaction were seen as possible between these scales of positive and negative affect. First, the two scales might be negatively correlated. Or alternately, the two scales might be positively correlated, so that positive and negative affective reactions occur together.

The SIMPLE-COMPLEX scale was included in an attempt to confirm the linear relationship between rated Complexity and uncertainty found in the previous experiment. Given the use of uncertainty as a summary statistic of collative properties by previous and present Es, such confirmation was considered mandatory. This scale was also included to facilitate comparison of this experiment with the previous one.

Subjects

Twenty-four Ss were tested. Twelve were enrolled in a variety of summer music courses at the Faculty of Music; the remaining twelve consisted of transient adults taking part in a variety of credit and noncredit activities on the University of Toronto campus during the summer session.

Stimulus Material

Six of Vitz's (1966) sound sequences, one from each level of uncertainty, were taken as a representative sample of the sequences used in the previous experiment. Six additional sound sequences, one at each level of uncertainty, were constructed using a P.D.P. 8/S computer to monitor a Wavetek Waveform synthesizer. While specific values of pitch and duration were taken directly from Vitz, it was necessary to establish a loudness function due to the failure of traditional sources (Fletcher & Munson, 1933; Robinson & Dadson, 1956) to approximate the experimental setting (i.e., presentation of stimuli via Sharpe headphones). This loudness function was used to establish four different levels of subjective loudness, and these were incorporated into the computer sequences according to Vitz's procedure (see Vitz, 1966).

The auditory tapes generated by the computer were therefore comparable to Vitz's tapes on all dimensions except one, namely, rise-decay time. As Vitz's method of construction involved diagonal splicing of tape that traveled at 7.5 inches per second on the recorder, rise and decay times of approximately 15 msec. at the onset and termination of each tone were present. The P.D.P.-Wavetek combination did not permit this adjustment, with rise-decay time on the computer generated sound sequences being virtually instantaneous. This was unfortunate, since the onset of each tone generated by the computer was accompanied by a faint but audible burst of transient energy. However, it was felt that this difference between the spliced and computer sequences would not result in any systematic effects on verbal judgments of the sequences.

Design

The design was essentially the same as that used in Experiment 1, with 12 x 12 and 4 x 4 balanced Latin squares being employed to counterbalance presentation orders of the sound sequences and rating scales. Two Ss, one from the music and one from the nonmusic group, were assigned to each row of the stimulus presentation square. As in Experiment 1, these two Ss received the rating scales in the same order, there being four possible scale orders drawn from a 4 x 4 balanced square.

Procedure

The Ss were run individually, and the experimental environment was the same as in the previous study. Aside from one minor change in the instructions, the procedure was identical to that of the previous experiment.

Results

The music and nonmusic groups exhibited the previously-established split in interest and background scales. The mean interest scores for music and nonmusic Ss were 7.83 and 5.08 respectively ($t = 2.85$, 22 df, $p < .01$), and the background scores were 7.08 and 2.00 respectively ($t = 4.88$, 22 df, $p < .001$). This suggested that degree of formal training was again an objective factor on which the two groups differed. The a priori criteria for the inclusion of data previously described were applied, and analyses of variance on individual rating scales carried out. The design was viewed as a fractional replication of a 12 Treatments x 12 Stimulus temporal positions x 12 Latin square rows x 2 Groups factorial experiment, and the analysis-of-variance summary table adopted was based on plan 10 of Winer (1962, p. 563). The Treatments factor was further broken down into 6 Uncertainty levels x 2 Methods of construction (splicing versus computer generation).

SIMPLE-COMPLEX scale. Ss' ratings of the sound sequences on this scale paralleled those found in Experiment 1 (Fig. 6). The only statistically

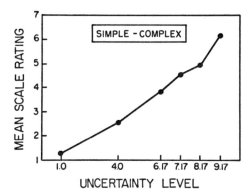

FIG. 6.   Uncertainty   main   effect: SIMPLE-
COMPLEX scale.

significant analysis of variance effect was an Uncertainty main effect
($F = 116.52$, 5,220 df, $p < .001$). Ninety-eight percent of the uncertainty
sum of squares was accounted for by the linear component of the trend
analysis ($F = 567.87$, 1,220 df, $p < .001$). Plotting this effect, we see that the
uncertainty response curve had a slight positive acceleration once again. While
there also were differences in the overall range of rating scale used by the two
groups (music range = 5.04 scale units versus nonmusic range = 4.58), this
difference failed to reach an acceptable level of statistical significance (linear
component of Uncertainty x Groups interaction, $F = 2.54$, 1,220 df,
$.05 < p < .10$).

Method of construction (splicing versus computer generated sound
sequence) was not a significant factor in subjective judgments of Complexity,
a result that one would expect given the structural correspondence between
the two sets of stimuli.

UNMELODIC-MELODIC scale.   The analysis of variance revealed a highly
significant Uncertainty main effect ($F = 7.09$, 5,220 df, $p < .001$). The
plotted mean ratings (see Fig. 7) suggested an inverted U-shaped pattern of
responding. The presence of a highly significant quadratic trend component
($F = 31.33$, 1,220 df, $p < .001$) and absence of a significant linear component
($F = 1.25$, 1,220 df, n.s.) indicated that ratings increased and then decreased
sharply, the apex of Melodiousness for both music and nonmusic groups
being at an uncertainty level of 4.00 bits/tone. Further analysis of treatment
means with Duncan's New Multiple Range Test confirmed this picture, there
being a significant difference between the two extremes of uncertainty and
the intermediate range of 4.00-7.17 bits/tone ($\alpha = .01$). However, there was no

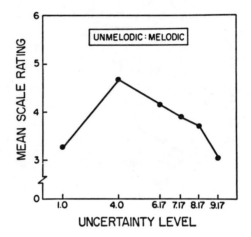

FIG. 7. Uncertainty main effect: UNMEL-
ODIC–MELODIC scale.

significant difference between the mean ratings of the sequences at the two
extremes of uncertainty ($\alpha = .05$). On the basis of these analyses, it was
concluded that mean rated Melodiousness was an inverted U-shaped function
of uncertainty.

A highly significant Method-of-construction main effect ($F = 25.04$, 1,220
df, $p < .001$) indicated that the computer generated sequences were judged to

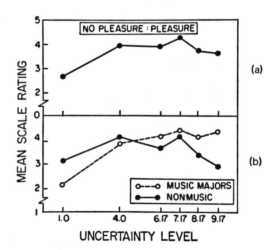

FIG. 8. (a) Uncertainty main effect: NO PLEA-
SURE–PLEASURE scale; (b) Uncertainty x Groups
interaction: NO PLEASURE-PLEASURE scale.

be less melodic than their spliced counterparts ($\bar{x}$ computer = 3.34; $\bar{x}$ spliced = 4.25). Unexpectedly, there was no evidence of any differences in judgments between music and nonmusic majors on this scale.

NO PLEASURE-EXTREME PLEASURE scale. The analysis of variance once again implicated uncertainty as a major determinant of the overall pattern and intergroup differences in response. Visual inspection of the plotted means suggested NO PLEASURE-PLEASURE ratings to be an "r-shaped" distribution, with Pleasure ratings reaching a peak by uncertainty level four [Fig. 8(a)]. Highly significant linear ($F = 15.16$, 1,220 *df*, $p < .001$) and quadratic ($F = 19.54$, 1,220 *df*, $p < .001$) trend components contributed to this interpretation. Further analysis of the treatment means with Duncan's New Multiple Range Test indicated that uncertainty levels from 4.00 to 9.17 bits/tone were comparable in contribution to pleasure ($\alpha = .05$) and were more pleasurable than uncertainty level 1 ($\alpha = .01$), thereby confirming the initial impression of an "r-shaped" function.

This Uncertainty main effect ($F = 7.49$, 5,200 *df*, $p < .001$) was qualified by a significant Uncertainty x Groups interaction ($F = 4.10$, 5,220 *df*, $p < .01$), with a highly significant linear component ($F = 19.04$, 1,220 *df*, $p < .001$) of the interaction pointing to a difference in slope between the trends of the two groups. Inspection of Figure 8(b) shows that this interaction reflected a crossover effect between uncertainty levels two and three (4.00 and 6.17 bits/tone). Ratings of Pleasure have generally increased for music majors and decreased for nonmusic majors beyond an uncertainty level of 4.00 bits/tone. A highly significant Method-of-construction main effect ($F = 17.46$, 1,220 *df*, $p < .001$) indicated that the computer generated sequences were considered less pleasurable than their spliced counterparts ($\bar{x}$ computer = 3.35; $\bar{x}$ spliced = 4.06).

NO DISCOMFORT-EXTREME DISCOMFORT scale. According to the analysis of variance, Uncertainty was only a marginally significant factor ($F = 2.53$, 5,220 *df*, $p < .05$), with trend analysis indicating the presence of a marginally significant quadratic trend component ($F = 6.59$, 1,220 *df*, $p < .05$). Plotting the means for this main effect [see Fig. 9(a)], we see that ratings of Discomfort have been highest at the extremes and lowest in the mid-range of uncertainty. Duncan's New Multiple Range Test revealed that uncertainty level two (4.00 bits/tone) was rated as less discomforting than level five ($\alpha = .01$), and that mean ratings of the extremes (1.0 and 9.17 bits/tone) did not differ significantly ($\alpha = .05$).

Group differences on this scale were found as a highly significant Groups main effect ($F = 28.57$, 1,16 *df*, $p < .001$) and a marginally significant Groups x Rating-scale-temporal-position ($F = 4.64$, 3,16 *df*, $p < .05$). The

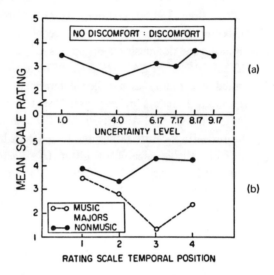

FIG. 9. (a) Uncertainty main effect: NO
DISCOMFORT-DISCOMFORT scale; (b) Groups x
Rating scale temporal position interaction: NO
DISCOMFORT-DISCOMFORT scale.

highly significant music:nonmusic effect clearly indicated that across all
uncertainty levels, the sound sequences elicited higher rated discomfort in the
nonmusic than in the music majors (nonmusic $\bar{x}$ = 3.94; music $\bar{x}$ = 2.47).

The Groups x Rating-scale-temporal-position interaction, plotted in Figure
9(b), suggested that, as a function of repetition, the sequences became less
discomforting for the music while becoming more discomforting for the
nonmusic Ss. However, like previous Rating-scale-temporal-position effects,
this one was of only marginal significance. The conclusion suggested by
Experiment 1, namely, that "mere exposure" is of secondary importance to
uncertainty and group membership in determining the pattern of verbal
ratings, does not seem challenged by this one significant effect.

Method of construction again appeared as a significant main effect
(F = 9.71, 1,220 df, $p < .01$), with the computer constructed sequences
leading to higher ratings of Discomfort than the spliced tapes, ($\bar{x}$
computer = 3.52; $\bar{x}$ spliced = 2.89). This result was clearly consistent with the
Method-of-construction effects found with UNMELODIC-MELODIC and NO
PLEASURE-PLEASURE rating scales.

Intercorrelations of the rating scales. A 3 x 3 correlation matrix between
rating scales (excluding SIMPLE-COMPLEX) across sound sequences

collapsed across Ss was calculated. Inspection of the three coefficients revealed that ratings of Pleasure and Melodic quality were positively correlated ($r = .64$, 10 df, $p < .05$) while both these scales were negatively correlated with ratings of Discomfort (Pleasure and Discomfort, $r = -.65$, $p < .05$; Melodiousness and Discomfort, $r = -.71$, $p < .02$).

Discussion

The highly significant differentiation by Ss of the computer-generated versus spliced sound sequences on the scales UNMELODIC-MELODIC, NO PLEASURE-PLEASURE and NO DISCOMFORT-DISCOMFORT was not expected, as the two sets of stimuli were structurally equivalent. The only apparent explanation for the relatively negative evaluation of the computer generated sequences would seem to be rise-decay time, with the transient energy accompanying the instantaneous onset of tones produced by the P.D.P.-Wavetek combination being responsible. Musical composers working in the genre of *musique concrète* have long considered this factor an important contributor to total affect, with tape splices at a 90° angle across the tape (resulting in an instantaneous rise time) being considered less pleasant than long diagonal splices producing graduated tone onset. Differences in acoustic rise time have also been shown to affect physiological indices of arousal and have been interpreted in terms of orientation and startle responses (see Hatton, Berg, and Graham, 1970). Noteworthy here is the absence of any Method-of-construction effect on the SIMPLE-COMPLEX scale. This suggests that, while Ss found the two sets of stimuli to be structurally equivalent, differences in affect were detectable within a given level of uncertainty, regardless of judgments of Complexity.

Comparing the mean ratings of Complexity obtained in these first two experiments [see Figs. 2(a) and 6], it is evident that the relation between the perception of stimulus structure and uncertainty found in Experiment 1 has reappeared with a subject sample of a somewhat different nature than the undergraduate population of the University of Toronto. That the two experiments have produced essentially the same function is evidenced in a linear correlation of .998 between the two response curves.

The UNMELODIC-MELODIC scale, included to encompass some clearly "musical" criterion within the range of the dependent variables, addresses itself to the question of what is a melody. Newman (1961) in considering this question, states that "satisfying proportions are as necessary to a melody as they are to the recipe for a cake" (pp. 74–75). This homespun prescription is born out in the case of our sound sequences, as the highest degree of

Melodiousness was attributed to sound sequences of intermediate uncertainty level. Relating this scale to Experiment 1, it is seen that the peak of Melodiousness occurs at a lower uncertainty level than that of Pleasingness or Beauty. However, the overall pattern of response is still that of an inverted U-shaped function of stimulus uncertainty.

The use of verbal report as a method of assessing transient internal hedonic processes associated with Ss' reactions to a controlled environment has not produced any unexpected results. The semantic similarity between the scales DISPLEASING-PLEASING and NO PLEASURE-PLEASURE would lead one to expect some similarity in verbal function. Comparison of the two response curves [Figs. 4(a) and 8(a)] strikingly suggests this to be the case. The linear correlation between mean ratings of uncertainty on these two scales was .96. Of the two alternative kinds of relation that were anticipated between the NO PLEASURE-PLEASURE and NO DISCOMFORT-DISCOMFORT scales, the one implying a negative correlation was supported. More Pleasure tended to coincide with less Discomfort and vice versa $(r = -.65;$ 10 $df, p < .02)$. In an experiment involving ratings of visual patterns and paintings, Berlyne (1973) found a similar relationship between these two rating scales $(r = -.56, 38 \ df, p < .001)$.

The relatively compressed scale ranges that Ss have employed while rating the sound sequences on these two scales raises the question of the efficacy and appropriateness of this semantic method in assessing internal reactions to the auditory patterns. This compression may, in part, reflect the labeling of one semantic pole as "extremely . . . ," since Ss may have avoided judging stimuli as "extremely" Discomforting or Pleasurable. Alternatively, this compression might reflect difficulty in making this type of internal-state judgment. Ss' comments to E at the conclusion of the experiment support this latter explanation. Given the similarity of Ss' ratings of Pleasure to DISPLEASING-PLEASING ratings, and given the relative lack of differentiation of sound-sequence uncertainty on the Discomfort scale, the value of rating scales for measuring such subjective reactions is debatable. For these reasons, these internal-state-rating scales were not used in subsequent experiments.

In summary, the three additional rating scales—UNMELODIC-MELODIC, NO PLEASURE-EXTREME PLEASURE and NO DISCOMFORT-EXTREME DISCOMFORT—have been interpretable in a manner similar to that of DISPLEASING-PLEASING and UGLY-BEAUTIFUL scales. No unique additional dimensions of judgment seem to have resulted from this extension of rating scales to encompass musical and internal reactions to the sound sequences. As in the previous experiment, it was concluded that perception of the sequences was at least two-dimensional. The question of semantic dimensionality was investigated in the following experiment.

EXPERIMENT 3: MISCELLANEOUS SCALES AND FACTOR ANALYSIS

Purpose

In the two preceding experiments, the relations between specific rating scales (such as UNINTERESTING-INTERESTING and DISPLEASING-PLEASING) and the sound sequences were investigated. Previous research employing visual patterns of varying complexity provided a priori hypotheses with respect to the relations between these scales and uncertainty level. Given the hundreds of adjectival modifiers that could conceivably be used to describe melodic sequences, the use of particular rating scales can be extended to address a more general question. This question concerns the number of ways or dimensions in which adjectival judgments of the stimuli may vary.

This use of rating-scale data to measure affective reactions is closely identified with Osgood, Suci, and Tannenbaum's (1957) development of the "semantic differential" technique. Based on the research reported by Osgood and his associates, three experimentally-derived dimensions of "connotative" or affective meaning have consistently emerged from a variety of research contexts. These dimensions have typically been labeled Evaluation, Potency, and Activity. Largely on the basis of one study by Tucker (1955) using representational paintings as stimuli, Osgood has conjectured that, in the case of aesthetic stimuli, the ubiquitous Evaluative factor and "a type of activity factor" will be the primary dimensions of aesthetic judgment (Osgood, et al., 1957, p. 74). This prediction of an Evaluation-Activity semantic space for aesthetic stimuli has remained relatively dormant since its initial exposition. Its relevance to the judgment of melodic sequences was assessed in this experiment by having Ss judge sound sequences on a battery of 20 rating scales.

Berlyne's writings (1971) also provided some support for a two-dimensional structure of sound sequence judgment. Verbal judgments of Interestingness and Pleasingness, the independence of which have been amply illustrated (see Berlyne, 1971, pp. 213-220), have been central to the theoretical notions summarized in Figure 1. According to this position, there are two motivational conditions of importance to exploratory, and hence aesthetic, behavior. In the case of the internal conditions resulting in specific exploration, the organism seeks out the complex, surprising, and hence *interesting*, stimuli in the environment. In the case of the conditions resulting in diversive exploration, the organism seeks out the beautiful, *pleasing* patterns. From these relationships it can be suggested that perception of the aesthetic environment is two-dimensional, and that subjects discriminate stimuli in terms of their interestingness and pleasingness.

The relation between this Pleasingness-Interestingness semantic space and Osgood's Evaluation-Activity formulation was an obvious, and at this point unresolved, question. It was therefore decided to select a battery of rating scales such that direct comparison and possibly integration of these two hypothesized structures could be carried out.

The grouping of *S*s according to faculty enrollment was continued in this experiment. In the context of semantic-space analysis, the reason for including this variable was not whether music and nonmusic majors varied significantly in their use of a specific rating scale, a question which was answered in the previous two experiments. The question here was whether any derived semantic space would be different for music and nonmusic groups. In case the dimensionality of the semantic space itself were not different between groups, with groups only varying in their relative placement of stimuli within the perceptual framework, the assumption of a common perceptual framework would be acceptable. However, in case the dimensionality of the semantic space differed between groups, the association of this intervening perceptual structure with nonverbal behaviors, such as Listening Time and Exploratory Choice, would be much more complicated.

Subjects

Twenty-four experimentally naive undergraduates, twelve enrolled in the Faculty of Music and twelve in the Faculty of Arts and Science, participated in the study.

Stimulus Material

The sound sequences constructed by Vitz (1966), having served their purpose as ready-made stimuli for the initial experiments, were replaced by computer-generated stimuli. These new sequences incorporated refinements such as: (1) a constant mean rate of tone presentation across all uncertainty levels, (2) two sound sequences of 30-minutes length at each uncertainty level, and (3) conceptual aspects (i.e., tonal and rhythmic implications) differing from those employed by Vitz.

This Incongruous/Congruous set of stimuli, as they will be called, were based on the same structural restrictions (i.e., same numbers of pitches, durations, and loudnesses) as Vitz (1966) employed. However, rather than construct the two sequences at each uncertainty level in a conceptually identical manner, the concept of "stimulus incongruity" was introduced to differentiate the sequences. This term has been used to characterize a stimulus property studied in connection with exploration of visual stimuli (see Berlyne, 1971, p. 196), and its extension to auditory sequences seemed straightforward. Sequences incorporating western aspects of music such as key-centeredness and metric pulse would accord with expectations due to prior experience, and hence be "congruous," while sequences violating expectations concerning key and meter would be culturally "incongruous."

With regard to pitch, an equal-tempered chromatic scale, representing a gradual expansion of the key of F major as uncertainty increased, was used for the pitch values of the congruous sequences. A simple mathematical algorithm was employed to derive an objective mistuning of this scale, and these "out-of-tune" frequencies were used for pitch values of the incongruous sequences. The congruous tone durations were integral multiples of each other, while the incongruous tone durations were not. The result of this manipulation was that the congruous sequences exhibited an underlying pulse or metrical rhythm, which was lacking in the incongruous sound sequences. A further point to be noted is that the specific millisecond values assigned to these ratios were chosen such that the mean duration of a tone for all 12 sound sequences was 500 msec.

The specific values of duration (in msec.) and pitch (in Hz) employed in the 12 sound sequences are summarized in Table 2. The rise and decay times for each tone were controlled by a Grason & Stadler Electronic Switch and Interval Timer (Models #829 and #471-1), which permitted rise-decay interval adjustments as fine as one millisecond. This equipment eliminated the audible burst of transient energy at tone onset that was implicated in listeners' relatively negative reactions to the computer-generated sequences in the previous experiment.

The Rating Scale Battery

The three scales, SIMPLE-COMPLEX, UNINTERESTING-INTERESTING and DISPLEASING-PLEASING, used in the previous two studies were included both for their theoretical importance and to permit direct

TABLE 2

Summary of the Information Characteristics: Incongruous/Congruous Sound Sequences

Uncertainty level	Congruous sequences			Incongruous sequences		
Bits/tone (U)	Pitch (Hz)	Duration (msec)	Loudness*	Pitch (Hz)	Duration (msec)	Loudness*
1.00	349(F) 392(G)	500	3	353(F+) 383(G–)	500	3
4.00	plus 440(A) 523(C)	333 667	2,3	plus 440(A) 526(C+)	378 622	2,3
6.17	plus 466(B♭) 587(D)	200 400 600 800	1,2,3	plus 458(B♮) 570(D–)	205 336 552 907	1,2,3
7.17	plus 294(D) 262(C)	90 182 364 546 728 1090	Same as above	295(D+) 257(C–)	103 170 279 458 753 1237	Same as above
8.17	plus 220(A) 175(F) 698(F) 784(G)	Same as above	1,2,3,4	plus 215(A–) 173(F–) 682(F–) 784(G)	Same as above	1,2,3,4
9.17	plus 147(D) 131(C) 87(F) 880(A) 1047(C) 1397(F)	40 81 162 323 485 646 970 1293	Same as above	plus 144(D–) 133(C+) 89(F+) 901(A+) 1017(C–) 1397(F)	49 81 133 219 360 591 971 1596	Same as above

*Level 1 = 70 db at 1000 Hz.
Level 2 = 75 db at 1000 Hz.
Level 3 = 80 db at 1000 Hz.
Level 4 = 85 db at 1000 Hz.

comparison of the results of the three rating-scale experiments. In order to relate any semantic space derived from this experiment to that previously established by Osgood, et al. (1957), reference or "marker" scales representative of their three primary dimensions were included. Three of them were chosen to represent each dimension. Their factor loadings are reported in Osgood, et al. (1957, pp. 37 & 69), and they are listed in the first nine columns of Table 3.

In view of the lack of a professional jargon among musicians to describe the melodic structure of western music (except for questions of syntax), the following four stylistic rating scales were included as representative of adjectival modifiers of music in general: UNMUSICAL-MUSICAL, NOT RHYTHMICAL-RHYTHMICAL, DISSONANT-CONSONANT, and SLOW-FAST.

Finally, in order to make the sample of scales more representative of the semantic sample space as a whole, four further scales were included. These scales were chosen because of their low loadings on all three of Osgood's dimensions in a visual-art study reported by Tucker (see Osgood, 1957, p. 69). They were viewed as unrelated to the semantic structure suggested by Osgood, et al. Their function, then, was simply to increase the range of scaled attributes. The scales adopted were REMOTE-INTIMATE, STALE-FRESH, EMPTY-FULL, and SUPERFICIAL-PROFOUND.

Design

The design was similar to the previous two rating scale experiments, with the 12 sound sequences and 20 rating scales treated as within-S factors. The order in which Ss were exposed to the sound sequences was determined by the 12×12 balanced Latin square used in the preceding studies, and as before, one music and one nonmusic S were assigned to each of the 12 rows of this square. To make the collection of 240 scale ratings from each S practicable, it was necessary to have the Ss judge each sound sequence against the complete set of rating scales before shifting to a new sequence. According to Osgood, et al., this procedure not only permits a response rate of 10 to 20 judgments per minute (versus the 2 judgments per minute obtained in Experiments 1 and 2 where the sound sequences were rotated against scales), but also makes "no differences in results" (Osgood, et al., 1957, p. 49).

Twelve random orderings of the 20 rating scales were made up, with the constraint that no scale could follow any other scale more than once. The 20 rating scales were then bound in booklets, one rating scale per page, according to one of the 12 orders. Each booklet order was assigned to one of the 12 columns of the sound sequence presentation square. This meant that

TABLE 3

Summary of Levels of Statistical Significance: Univariate Analyses of Variance

Sources of variance	Semantic differential scales																			
	STILL-VIBRANT	PASSIVE-ACTIVE	REPETITIVE-VARIED	AWFUL-NICE	BAD-GOOD	UGLY-BEAUTIFUL	WEAK-STRONG	HUMOROUS-SERIOUS	LIGHT-HEAVY	SIMPLE-COMPLEX	UNINTERESTING-INTERESTING	DISPLEASING-PLEASING	UNMUSICAL-MUSICAL	NOT RHYTHMICAL-RHYTHMICAL	DISSONANT-CONSONANT	SLOW-FAST	REMOTE-INTIMATE	STALE-FRESH	EMPTY-FULL	SUPERFICIAL-PROFOUND
Groups								mS												
Latin square rows																				
Uncertainty (Unct.)	HS	HS	HS	HS	HS	HS		HS	HS	HS	HS	HS	HS	HS	HS	S	HS	HS	HS	HS
Linear trend	HS	HS	HS	HS	HS	S		HS	mS	HS	HS	HS	HS	HS	HS	HS	HS	HS	HS	HS
Quadratic trend	S	mS		HS	HS	HS		mS	HS		HS	HS	HS	mS	HS		HS	HS	HS	
Incongruity/Congruity (I/C)	S			HS	HS	HS			mS				HS	HS			HS	mS	HS	mS
Unct. x I/C																				
Linear trend							mS													
Quadratic trend							mS													
Unct. x Groups																				
Linear trend													S							
Quadratic trend													HS							
I/C x Groups															S					
Unct. x I/C x Groups							S		mS									mS		
Stimulus Temporal Position (S.T.P.)								HS												
S.T.P. x Groups																		S		S

HS: p < .001.
S: p < .01.
mS: p < .05.

all 24 Ss had the same rating scale order within periods (Latin square columns).

Procedure

Each of the 24 Ss was run individually, and the experimental setting was the same as that described previously. Ss were given a copy of the instructions to read, and the rating of the sound sequences was carried out in the manner outlined in the instructions. It should be noted that Ss first heard 20-second excerpts of all 12 sound sequences before beginning the rating scale task, and that once they began rating a sequence on the 20 rating scales, a prerecorded computer realization of 30 minutes duration was available. The amount of time that Ss spent completing each rating-scale booklet was recorded without their knowledge. This measure of Rating Time has been discussed earlier. Due to limitations in time, the music-interest and music-background forms used in previous experiments were not administered.

Results

Univariate analyses of rating scales. As in the previous rating scale experiments, univariate analyses of variance were carried out on the Ss' responses across sound sequences to each semantic differential scale. The treatment of the design and the summary table adopted for these analyses were similar to that of Experiment 2. The levels of statistical significance of the sources of variance among the 20 scales are presented in summary form in Table 3. In this table, the rows correspond to sources of variance extracted by the univariate analyses, and the columns correspond to rating scales.

The uncertainty level of the sound sequences has clearly been the most powerful manipulation of the experimental environment, with only 1 of the 20 scales not exhibiting statistical significance on this factor. Incongruity/ Congruity of the stimuli has been the second most powerful effect, with a highly significant effect on one-half of the rating scale judgments, and at least a marginally significant effect on 6 of the remaining 10 scales. The prominence of this factor indicates that the attribute labeled "incongruity" is readily discriminated by the Ss. Interactions of these two factors with each other and with Groups were clearly of secondary importance in determining the pattern of responses. Only 5 of the 60 interactions showed any degree of statistical significance. Stimulus temporal position, a control factor, was also of very limited influence on the results, an indication of the appropriateness of the "doubly-balanced" sequence presentation square used in ordering the stimuli.

Turning to the three blocks of scales included as reference-points for Osgood's et al. three dimensions, the most straightforward method of factor estimation was employed at this point. By summing mean ratings on the three scales representing each of Osgood's factors, the three functions plotted in Figure 10 were obtained. The rating scales representative of the ubiquitous Evaluative factor were inverted U-shaped functions of uncertainty, with the most Beautiful, Good, and Nice sequence being in the range 4.00–7.17 bits/tone.

The three scales representative of the Activity factor were reasonably linear monotonically-increasing functions of stimulus uncertainty, with some evidence of a "ceiling" effect by uncertainty level 9.17 bits/tone. The Potency dimension was not well defined, with a relatively flat response trend across uncertainty levels.

The Incongruity/Congruity manipulation was strongest for the three evaluative rating scales, the incongruous version being rated more Ugly, Bad, and Awful than its congruous counterpart. The incongruous version was also perceived as significantly more Still and marginally more Passive, Heavy, and Serious.

Multivariate analyses of rating scales. A 20 x 20 correlation matrix between rating scales across mean ratings of the 12 sound sequences was

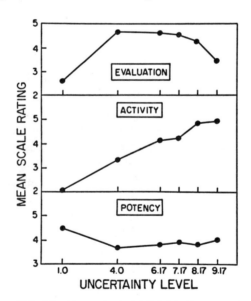

FIG. 10. Mean estimates of Osgood, Suci, and
Tannenbaum's three primary factors.

calculated. The degree of degeneracy in this matrix was examined by a principal-components analysis, a traditional and widely accepted method of extracting dimensions or factors accounting for progressively smaller proportions of variance. Ten factors, covering 99.96% of the total variance, were extracted using Veldman's (1957) FACTOR computer program.

While the question of when to stop extracting factors has not yet been answered definitively, a number of criteria have been put forward. The one which will be adopted here, as advanced by Kaiser (1960), consists of including only those factors whose eigenvalues (or latent roots) are greater than 1.0 (given that unities were used in the diagonal of the intercorrelation matrix). Using this criterion, a Varimax rotation was carried out on the first three dimensions derived in the principal components analysis. The results of this rotation are presented in Table 4.

The first three eigenvalues cover 91.45% of the total with rotated factors accounting for 48.34%, 36.06%, and 7.05% of the extracted variance, respectively. The final column of Table 4 presents the communalities of the factor solutions (which represent the proportion of the variance of each of the original variables preserved in the solution). We can see that the reduction of the 20 variables to three factors has preserved quite a large proportion of the information contained in the original data matrix.

Guidance towards psychological interpretation of these semantic dimensions can be obtained both from the relative size of the loadings of individual scales on the vectors and from mean estimated factor scores. The latter were calculated according to accepted procedures (Nunnally, 1967), using the factor weights included in the computer output. Analyses of variance on these three sets of estimates were then carried out.

Mean-estimated-factor-score analysis. The analysis of variance on the mean estimated scores for Factor I pointed to highly significant Uncertainty ($F = 31.66$, 5,220 df, $p < .001$) and Incongruity/Congruity ($F = 59.17$, 1,220 df, $p < .001$) main effects on this factor, and a marginally significant Uncertainty x Groups ($F = 2.63$, 5,220 df, $p < .05$) interaction. Plotting the mean estimated factor scores for the Uncertainty main effect [see Fig. 11(a)], we see that the factor of first magnitude was an inverted U-shaped function of stimulus uncertainty. Highly significant linear ($F = 11.90$, 1,220 df, $p < .001$) and quadratic ($F = 145.88$, 1,220 df, $p < .001$) trend components corroborated this interpretation. Inspection of the factor loadings of the 20 semantic differential scales (Table 4) indicates that Factor I had high and pure loadings on the scales AWFUL-NICE, BAD-GOOD, DISPLEASING-PLEASING, LIGHT-HEAVY, REMOTE-INTIMATE,

TABLE 4

Rotated Factor Loadings

Rating scale sample	Factors			h^2
	I	II	III	
AWFUL-NICE	.98	−.13	.08	.98
BAD-GOOD	.96	−.22	.10	.98
DISPLEASING-PLEASING	.97	−.14	.10	.97
DISSONANT-CONSONANT	.42	.87	.06	.94
EMPTY-FULL	.75	−.61	.15	.96
HUMOROUS-SERIOUS	−.38	.61	−.24	.57
LIGHT-HEAVY	−.95	.19	−.02	.94
NOT RHYTHMICAL-RHYTHMICAL	.51	.81	−.16	.94
PASSIVE-ACTIVE	.31	−.86	.17	.86
REMOTE-INTIMATE	.98	−.02	−.12	.98
REPETITIVE-VARIED	.32	−.92	.13	.97
SIMPLE-COMPLEX	.21	−.97	.06	.99
SLOW-FAST	.13	−.64	.36	.56
STALE-FRESH	.74	−.62	.02	.93
STILL-VIBRANT	.52	−.79	.20	.93
SUPERFICIAL-PROFOUND	.49	−.75	.31	.90
UGLY-BEAUTIFUL	.98	−.01	.05	.96
UNINTERESTING-INTERESTING	.75	−.62	.14	.97
UNMUSICAL-MUSICAL	.99	−.05	.07	.99
WEAK-STRONG	−.02	−.24	.96	.98
Percentage of total variance accounted for	48.34%	36.06%	7.05%	91.45%

UGLY-BEAUTIFUL, and UNMUSICAL-MUSICAL, with sound sequences in the range 4.00–6.17 bits/tone being evaluated most favorably.

This interpretation was qualified by the marginally significant Groups x Uncertainty interaction [see Fig. 11(b)]. The apex on this first factor occurred at an uncertainty level of 4.00 and 6.17 bits/tone for nonmusic and music majors, respectively. There was a "crossover" between the two groups at 7.17 bits/tone, the result being a resemblance between these group curves and those found with ratings of Pleasingness, Beauty, and Pleasure in Experiments 1 and 2. The Incongruity/Congruity main effect was straightforward, the incongruous versions being rated less positively than their congruous counterparts ($\bar{X}$ incongruous = −0.29, $\bar{X}$ congruous = 0.29).

The analysis of variance on the mean estimated scores for Factor II revealed only one statistically significant effect, this being a highly significant Uncertainty main effect ($F = 92.61$, 5,220 df, $p < .001$). Plotting the mean estimated factor scores for this effect (see Fig. 12), we see that this factor of second magnitude was a monotonically-increasing function of uncertainty. The presence of a highly significant linear ($F = 447.22$, 1,220 df, $p < .001$) and a significant quadratic ($F = 12.22$, 1,220 df, $p < .01$) trend component indicates that ratings on this factor were a monotonic, slightly positively accelerating function of stimulus uncertainty. Verbal ratings of Consonance, Rhythmicalness, Activity, Variation, and Complexity had high and pure loadings on this factor (see Table 4), and this factor would seem to behave like the Complexity and Interestingness ratings in the previous experiments.

Analysis of variance of the mean estimated scores on Factor III revealed only marginally significant Uncertainty and Stimulus temporal position main effects. This factor, accounting for only 7% of the total variance, had its only large factor loading on WEAK-STRONG, the only variable not to show a significant uncertainty effect in the univariate analysis. For lack of a more appropriate term, and since WEAK-STRONG was included as a reference variable for Osgood's Potency factor, this third factor was labeled Potency. Having said that, it should be noted that the other two scales included as reference items for this third dimension each had high and pure loadings on the first two factors. Because of the lack of definition and limited variability

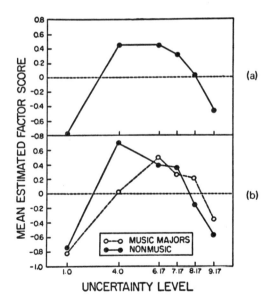

FIG. 11. (a) Uncertainty main effect: Factor I;
(b) Uncertainty x Groups interaction: Factor I.

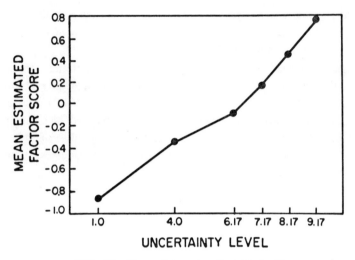

FIG. 12. Uncertainty main effect: Factor II.

associated with this third factor, it was felt that its exclusion from further consideration would not seriously compromise the semantic-space analysis.

Assistance in attaching formal labels to the first two factors was obtained by correlating mean ratings of the 12 sound sequences on these two factors with mean scores on the previously presented Osgood dimensions (Fig. 10) and on the univariate ratings of Pleasingness and Complexity obtained in this experiment. This correlation matrix, presented in Table 5, shows Factor I to be highly correlated both with Osgood's Evaluative dimension ($r = .99$) and

TABLE 5

Intercorrelations between the Estimates of Osgood's Factors,
Factors I and II, and Ratings of
Pleasingness and Complexity

	Complexity	Pleasingness	Evaluation	Activity	Factor I
Pleasingness	.37				
Evaluation	.34	.99***			
Activity	.97***	.52	.50		
Factor I	.22	.98***	.99***	.38	
Factor II	.97***	.20	.19	.93***	.05

***$p < .001$ (10 df).

with ratings of Pleasingness ($r = .98$). Factor II is highly correlated with Osgood's Activity dimension ($r = .93$) and ratings of subjective Complexity ($r = .97$).

Consequently, Factor I was identified with a general Evaluative dimension, reflecting an attitudinal variable that, because of its pervasiveness and prominence, may be a primary factor in aesthetic perception. Factor II was seen as a general Activity dimension, reflecting structural aspects of sound sequences captured by the information-theory measure of uncertainty.

Rating time. Rating time, which was the amount of time Ss listened to each sound sequence while completing the 12 rating scale booklets, was recorded and treated as a 21st dependent variable. An analysis of variance was carried out on these data (expressed in seconds) and indicated the presence of highly significant Uncertainty ($F = 11.90$, 5,220 df, $p < .001$) and Stimulus temporal position ($F = 11.96$, 11,220 df, $p < .001$) main effects, along with a marginally significant Versions effect ($F = 3.81$, 1,220 df, $p < .05$).

The Uncertainty main effect, plotted in Figure 13(a), points to relatively equal Rating Times across uncertainty levels two to six, with uncertainty level one listened to relatively less than the other five levels. The presence of highly significant linear ($F = 47.89$, 1,220 df, $p < .001$) and quadratic ($F = 11.03$, 1,220 df, $p < .001$) trend components supports this interpretation. Further analysis of the uncertainty means using Duncan's New Multiple Range Test showed that the mean Rating Time for uncertainty level one was significantly less than Rating Times for the other levels ($\alpha = .001$), and that Rating Times for stimuli above 1.00 bit/tone did not differ significantly from one another ($\alpha = .05$).

Looking at the means for the remaining two significant effects, we see that Ss listened slightly longer to the Incongruous than to the Congruous versions in making their judgments ($\bar{X}$ Incongruous = 192″, $\bar{X}$ Congruous = 183″). The Stimulus-temporal-position effect [see Fig. 13(b)], which points to a general decline in Rating Time across periods, reflects a learning trend over trials, with subjects familiarizing themselves with the experimental context and response format during their first 100 responses or so. Further consideration of the Rating-Time variable will be deferred to the following experiment, in which Listening Time was the principal dependent variable.

The partial correlation between Rating Time and Factor I (Evaluative) with Factor II held constant came to .56, 10 df, $p < .05$. The partial correlation between Rating Time and Factor II (Activity) with Factor I held constant came to .89, $p < .01$. The two factors account for 65% of the Rating-Time variance of which 16% is covered by Factor I and 49% by Factor

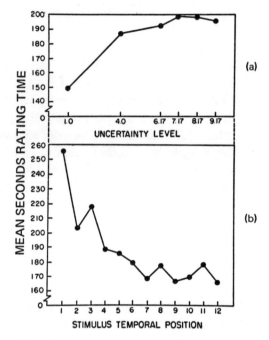

FIG. 13. (a) Uncertainty main effect: Rating time measure; (b) Stimulus temporal position main effect: Rating time measure.

II. The role of the Activity factor is easy to understand, since it would presumably take longer to assimilate the information in more complex sequences and thus to rate them. The role of the Evaluative factor, however, suggests that there was also some tendency to listen longer to more pleasing sequences.

Discussion

The 20 dimensions corresponding to the 20 rating scales have been seen to degenerate largely into two orthogonal factors, accounting for 84.40% of the total variance. Uncertainty level emerges as the most influential determinant of where sound sequences stand in relation to these two factors. Incongruity/Congruity, embracing conceptual aspects of construction not encompassed within the information-theory metric, has exercised an influence only on the Evaluative factor, the culturally inappropriate versions being evaluated less positively than the culturally appropriate ones. On the other hand, Incongruity/Congruity had no significant effect on the Activity factor.

The Groups factor, which the previous experimental literature has regarded as a major determinant of aesthetic perception, has been of little prominence outside of Experiment 1. The reduction of sample size from 48 to 24 Ss reduced this initial prominence considerably, and in the present experiment, the influence of Ss' formal music background has been of only marginal statistical significance. The decline of this factor may be, in large part, a result of the demands inherent in the procedure. Compared to the first two rating scale experiments, Ss in this study had to make five times as many responses in a comparable period of time, with no periods of silence in which to make their judgments. Rating scales were rotated against sound sequences, a method which, in spite of Osgood's assertions, is neither identical to, nor as sensitive as, the method of rotating stimuli against one specific scale. Regardless of the reasons for the lack of striking Group effects, the effects of this factor seem minor compared with those of Uncertainty level and of congruity.

The two perceptual dimensions that emerge from this experiment— Evaluation and Activity—bear a close resemblance to factor structures put forward by other experimenters. Unfortunately, none of the previous work involves judgments of sound sequences. However, the presence of a similar dimensionality across sense modalities is highly suggestive.

Other studies (reviewed by Berlyne, 1972; and Chap. 14, this volume) have produced factors bearing various labels but clearly resembling the Evaluative and Activity factors that Osgood has discussed and that emerged from the present experiment. Earlier experimenters working within very different frameworks, have also drawn attention to dimensions of perception or affective reaction that seem close to these two. Schlosberg's (1952) classification of emotional states in terms of PLEASANTNESS-UNPLEASANTNESS and ATTENTION-REJECTION, Wundt's (1893) classification of "feeling" in terms of PLEASANT-UNPLEASANT and EXCITEMENT-CALM, are noteworthy examples.

Philosophers, in their attempts to capture the essence of aesthetic response and beauty over the centuries, have asserted that aesthetic pleasure depends on the interaction of two antagonistic factors. Many different pairs of terms have been used to designate these factors, most of which are variations on the basic theme of "unity versus diversity." This philosophical tradition is reviewed in Berlyne (1971; see also Chap. 1, this volume). Musicians have tendered nonexperimental evidence supporting a two-dimensional structure that is perhaps more to the point, and a representative summary of the dimensions that composers and music educators have discovered through listening is given in Table 6.

Response to music in a natural setting, then, is viewed by these authors as an interaction of two perceptual processes. The first process is one of comprehension of the formal, structural, technical, compositional aspects of the flow of sound, and can be identified with our Activity factor. The second process, which occurs simultaneously with the first, is one of comprehension of the content, conceptual aspects, balance, and degree of affect, and can be identified with our Evaluative factor.

The three rating scale experiments just described have indicated that *S*s' verbal responses to sound sequences are not wholly idiosyncratic, individualistic, and unstable. The intervening perceptual structure revealed by both univariate and multivariate analyses points to a similar framework of judgment and comprehension amongst individuals and between groups. In fact, the 12 sound sequences can be represented as points in a

TABLE 6

Sample of the Dimensions of "Musical Experience"
Advanced by Musicians

Musician	Dimensions of music cited	
	Dimension #1	Dimension #2
A. Copland, (1939)	"The sheerly musical plane"	"The sensuous and expressive planes"
H. Tischler, (1956)	"Syntactical or internal relations"	"Nonsyntactical or external relations"
L. B. Meyer, (1956)	"Intellectual response"	"Affective response"
E. Levy, (1970)	"Formal and technical"	"The expressive"
D. Cooke, (1959)	"Technical knowledge"	"Emotional"
S. Zink, (1960)	"Perceiving," "understanding"	"Appreciating," "feeling"
D. N. Campbell, (1967)	"Formal," "technical"	"Expressive," "sensuous"

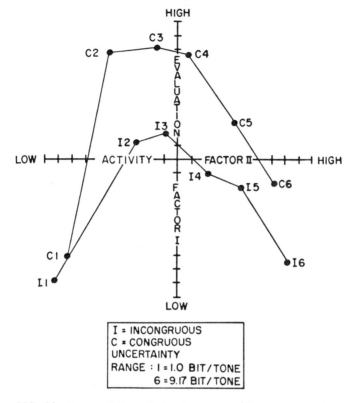

FIG. 14. Representation of the Incongruous/Congruous sound sequences in two dimensional "semantic" space.

two-dimensional perceptual space as in Figure 14. This two-dimensional classification will be used to analyze the results of the next two experiments, concerned with nonverbal, exploratory responses to sound sequences.

EXPERIMENT 4: LISTENING TIME

Two measures of exploration were reviewed in the introduction, namely Listening Time and Exploratory Choice. These behaviors were seen as experimental analogs of the listening and choice behaviors that form the core of musical response in a natural setting. There were two complementary reasons for including measures of exploratory behavior in this investigation. First, it was important to determine the effects of uncertainty level and of musical experience on Ss' patterns of listening and choice behavior in a controlled setting. Second, it was of interest to relate any exploratory behavior to the verbally derived perceptual structure presented in Figure 14.

A priori speculation regarding the strength and direction of exploration poses an interesting question. Will the Ss listen more to the most Pleasing, Beautiful, Musical sound sequence, thus responding to stimulus aspects associated with the Evaluative factor? Or will they listen more to the most Active, Varied, Complex sequences, thus responding to stimulus aspects associated with the Activity factor? In the former case, there will be, first, increasing and, then, decreasing self-exposure to patterns as uncertainty level increases. In the latter case self-exposure will increase monotonically with uncertainty level.

Which of these two hypotheses should be favored at this point in the investigation? Only two previous studies using sound-sequence stimuli have employed nonverbal measures. Overmier (1962) found Listening Time to be an inverted U-shaped function of stimulus uncertainty. Simon & Wohlwill (1968) found listening time to be greatest for their highest levels of "stimulus variation." Thus, both hypotheses had some experimental support. Since both these previous studies used Listening Time rather than Exploratory Choice as their dependent variable, this measure was also employed in this initial experiment on exploration.

Subjects

A total of 24 experimentally naive Ss were tested, 12 from the Faculty of Arts and Science, and 12 from the Faculty of Music.

Stimulus Material

As the computer-generated set of Incongruous/Congruous sound sequences were not yet available when this experiment was conducted, the 12 Vitz sequences used in Experiments 1 and 2 were used in this study. Since each of the Vitz sequences lasted 20 seconds (± .5 second), it was obvious that if Listening Time was to be the dependent variable, some extension of these sequences would be necessary. The most expedient solution to this problem was to make a tape-loop of each sequence, so that, after each 20 seconds of listening, the sequence would repeat itself. The effects of this repetition are hard to estimate. It was presumed that the effects of this structuring would be relatively constant over all levels of uncertainty and that it would not bias Ss' listening in any particular systematic fashion. Postexperimental questioning of Ss suggested that these assumptions were tenable.

Design

The 12 sound-sequence loops were presented to each *S* twice, with the first presentation being called "Run One" and the second "Run Two." The order of presentation within each run was determined by a 12 x 12 balanced Latin square. One arts and science and one music student were assigned to each of the rows of the square, and the Latin square for Run Two was obtained by a cyclic permutation of the initial square.

Procedure

On arriving for the experiment, each *S* was seated in a comfortable, lounge-type chair in the experimental room. The *S*s were told that they were "to listen to 24 sound sequences, each sequence consisting of a number of single, consecutive tones. . . . any one of the 24 sequences will continue for as long as you wish to listen to it. Whenever you want to go on to the next sequence, just press the button on the box in front of you, and this will cause the next sequence to begin . . . this is not a tonal memory test, and it will not be necessary for you to recall any specific sound sequence or to memorize details of the sound sequences . . ."

The *S* was then fitted with the headphones, and the sound sequence loops were presented. Every time *S* pressed the button, there was one second of silence before the next tape loop began; the rise and decay time at the start and end of each loop was 100/msec. As in the previous rating-scale experiments, sound sequences of uncertainty level one (1.00 bit/tone) were set at a sound pressure level (SPL) of 80 db, and the overall SPL range was 70-86 db (B2 scale—GRC SPL meter and earphone coupler). *S*s' Listening Times were automatically logged in 1/3 second intervals throughout the experiment.

Upon completion of the listening task, *S*s were given the music-interest scale and music-background questionnaire to fill out. Then they were asked the following question:

> While you were listening to the sound sequences, did you think that I might be timing how long you listened to each auditory sequence? If you did, do you think this feeling affected the amount of time you spent listening to any one pattern?

Results

As in Experiments 1 and 2 the nonmusic and music groups reported a "moderate" and "high" interest in music respectively, with the mean interest responses for the two groups being 6.08 and 7.83 ($t = 3.28$, 22 *df*, $p < .01$).

The two groups also differed greatly in terms of formal knowledge of music. The nonmusic Ss scored an average of 2.63 and the music Ss an average of 8.75 on the 10-item music background questionnaire ($t = 8.68$, 22 df, $p < .001$). Fifteen of the 24 Ss reported that they thought their Listening Times might have been recorded by E. Of these 15, only 1 stated that this feeling had influenced the amount of time spent listening, with his reaction being to "listen to the less complex patterns longer."

Twenty-two of the 24 Ss listened to the sound sequences for total time periods ranging from 5.31 to 27.85 minutes. However, two Ss in the nonmusic group listened for 35.82 and 58.91 minutes, confining most of their listening to Run One. These two "outliers" resulted in marked heterogeneity of variance between Groups and between Runs. This eliminated any meaningful consideration of differences in absolute listening time as a function of group membership and stimulus exposure (Runs). A logarithmic transformation of the raw scores failed to eliminate the heterogeneity between groups (Cochran's $C_{2,287} = .652, p < .01$). This being the case, it was decided to analyze the data in terms of proportional listening time. Ss' 24 listening time scores were collapsed within Runs into 12 scores corresponding to sequences, and these 12 scores were converted to proportions. An analysis of variance on these proportional listening times was carried out.

The analysis of variance revealed that only Uncertainty ($F = 16.94$, 5,440 df, $p < .001$) and Stimulus temporal position ($F = 2.08$, 11,440 df, $p < .05$) were influential in determining proportional Listening Time. Plotting the mean proportions for these two statistically significant effects [see Figs. 15(a) and 15(b)], we see that Listening Time has increased up to uncertainty level 4 (7.17 bits/tone), followed by a leveling off beyond this point. The presence of a highly significant linear component ($F = 80.21$, 1,440 df, $p < .001$), accounting for 94.81% of the uncertainty sum of squares, along with the absence of statistically significant higher-order components confirmed that Listening Time increased with uncertainty level. Further analysis on the mean proportional Listening Times with Duncan's New Multiple Range Test indicated that sequences at uncertainty levels 7.17 bits/tone and 9.17 bits/tone were listened to longer than sequences at 1.00 bit/tone and 4.00 bits/tone ($\alpha = .001$). Thus, there was evidence that proportional Listening Time increased up to 7.17 bits/tone, beyond which point there was no further increase.

The significant Stimulus-temporal-position effect was not unexpected. The Ss' response tendency, which may be termed a "novelty-fatigue" effect, was

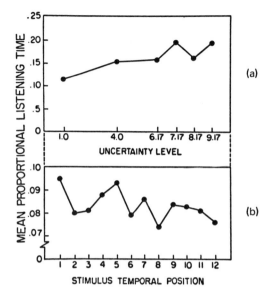

FIG. 15. (a) Uncertainty main effect: Proportional listening time analysis; (b) Stimulus temporal position main effect: Proportional listening time analysis.

marked by a decrease in the amount of time spent listening as trials followed one another. This was probably due to dissipation of novelty, together with fatigue or even boredom. The Groups and Sequences-within-uncertainty-level main effects and their interactions were not significant.

Discussion

The lack of variation in proportional Listening Time with group membership added support to the view that musical experience does not affect this kind of listening behavior materially. Evidence independent of this experiment corroborates this negative result. The previously reviewed study by Simon & Wohlwill (1968), in which Listening Times of musically trained and untrained Ss were compared, revealed no significant differences between groups. The Rating Time measure recorded in Experiment 3 was likewise devoid of significant group differences.

The results of the present experiment do not tally very well with the conclusion that Overmier (1962) drew from his own data, i.e., that "listening time was ... an inverted U-shaped function of complexity." In his experiment, a peak was reached at 3.00 bits/tone, whereas, in the experiment just reported, there was an increase in Listening Time up to 7.17 bits/tone and no significant decrease when that level was exceeded. It is interesting that sequences within the range of 7.17–9.17 bits/tone (i.e., 14.34–16.14 bits/second) were listened to longest. The German school of information-theoretic aestheticians (e.g., Frank, 1959) has contended that the limits of human information-processing capacity, and consequently maximum aesthetic appeal, are to be found around 16 bits/second.

Nor do the results provide strong support for the hypothesis, suggested by Simon and Wohlwill's experiment, that Listening Time will rise steadily as complexity goes up. In the present experiment, the rise ceased at 7.17 bits/tone, even though Ss could evidently detect further increases in uncertainty level.

Differences in stimulus material and in procedure could account for these failures to confirm what other experimenters have found. Our data, however, do not fit very closely either optimization-of-complexity or maximization-of-complexity positions. An alternative hypothesis, amounting to a synthesis of both these positions therefore recommends itself.

According to this hypothesis, which may be called the "additive" hypothesis, Ss tend to some extent to devote more Listening Time to stimuli that are higher on the Evaluative dimension (i.e., those that are judged more pleasing, beautiful, etc.) and to some extent to listen longer to stimuli that are higher on the Activity dimension (i.e., those that are judged more complex, interesting, etc.). Mean Listening Time would then depend jointly on these two factors. The Listening-Time curve of Figure 15(a) has, in fact, the kind of shape that one would expect if it represented a weighted sum of the ordinates of the curves in Figures 11(a) and 12, displaying mean estimated scores on the Evaluative and Activity factors, respectively (see Fig. 16).

A partial-correlation analysis (Garrett, 1926; Nunnally, 1967) was carried out, using mean Listening Times (L) for the six uncertainty levels as the criterion variables and the mean scores on Factor I (FI) and on Factor II (FII) from Experiment 3 as the predictor variables. It turned out that $r_{LFI.FII} = .63$ (4 df, not significant), while $r_{LFII.FI} = .93$ ($p < .001$). The two factor scores together for 88% of the variance of mean Listening Time, Factor I covering 10% and Factor II 78%. The failure of the first partial correlation to reach significance deprives us of any firm basis for concluding that the Evaluative factor contributes anything to predictive power as compared with the Activity factor alone. But this is hardly surprising in view of the small number of uncertainty levels and thus of

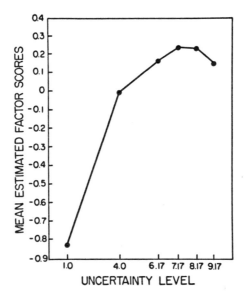

FIG. 16.   Equally weighted arithmetic summation of Factors I and II.

degrees of freedom. It would seem that the additive hypothesis is worth further consideration in future research.

EXPERIMENT 5: EXPLORATORY CHOICE

Purpose

Exploratory Choice, our second measure of sound-sequence exploration, offers a number of advantages over Listening Time. First, this method pairs each sound sequence with every other sequence an equal number of times, systematically exposing the Ss to the full range of stimuli. Second, it results in the same amount of absolute exposure to the stimuli by all Ss, thus eliminating the problem of "outliers." Third, it forces the Ss to make a clear-cut choice between alternative sequences. A final point, which should be made, is that in research using visual material, Exploratory Choice and Looking Time do not always favor the same stimuli (see Berlyne, 1963, 1971, 1972). These last two points were considered particularly relevant, in that this forced-choice situation was considered more likely than the Listening-Time situation to reveal systematic group and/or individual differences in exploratory behavior.

Subjects

Twenty-four Ss, twelve enrolled in the Faculty of Music and twelve in the Faculty of Arts and Science, participated in the study.

Stimulus Material

The six Incongruous and six Congruous sound sequences used in Experiment 3 replaced the stimuli used in the Listening-Time experiment.

Design

Each S received all possible pairings of the 12 treatments (six uncertainty levels x two versions), but not both orders (A-B and B-A) within each pair. Thus, there were $(12 \times 11)/2 = 66$ paired presentations of the 12 sound sequences ($132/12 = 11$ presentations per sequence). The Ss' task was to choose the first or second member of each paired presentation for 10 seconds further listening. The order of presentation of the 66 pairs of stimuli for each S was derived from an algorithm proposed by Ross (1934). Twelve orders, balanced according to Ross's criteria, were generated. One nonmusic and one music student were arbitrarily paired and assigned to each of these orders. The order of stimuli within each paired comparison (A-B versus B-A) was such that, for each order, the more and less complex stimulus and the Incongruous and Congruous versions were present equally often in the first and second stimulus positions.

Procedure

As no experimental precedent was found on which to base paired presentation of sound sequences, a pilot experiment was conducted to consider questions such as the discriminability of the paired sequences, the possible presence of stimulus-temporal-position bias, and the determination of an appropriate duration of presentation. This pilot experiment established that the Ss could discriminate between paired sequences without significant temporal position bias, and that a 10-second presentation of a sequence was sufficient for S to make his choice.

In the present experiment, each of the 66 paired presentations consisted of a 10-second sample of a sound sequence; 2 seconds of interstimulus silence; 10 seconds of a second sequence, followed by a further 10-second continuation of whichever of the two sequences S chose to hear. S was told, "your task is to choose the first or the second sequence of the two sequences in each pair for 10-seconds further listening." He was given no explicit criteria whatever on which to base his choice. He indicated his choice by pressing one of two buttons, which were clearly marked "First" and "Second."

As 30 minutes of each of the 12 types of sound sequence was available, it was not necessary (as in the previous experiment) to repeat any specific succession of tones in order to present Ss with 66 exploratory choices. Upon completion of the Exploratory-Choice task, the music-interest scale and music-background questionnaire were administered.

Results

Both groups expressed relatively high, but significantly different, degrees of interest in music as measured on the 9-point interest scale. The mean Interest rating for music students was 8.38, and, for nonmusic students, it was 7.29 ($t = 5.03, 22$ df, $p < .001$). On the music-background questionnaire, the mean scores for music and nonmusic subjects were 9.08 and 1.94, respectively ($t = 10.16, 22$ df, $p < .001$). Thus, as in previous experiments the Ss in the two groups were readily differentiated in terms of acknowledged interest and formal training in the field of music.

There was no significant difference in the number of first-position versus second-position stimuli chosen. The first-position stimulus was, on the average, chosen 34.0 times per S and the second-position stimulus 32.0 times. Thus, there was apparently no stimulus-position bias in the pattern of choice, sequences being chosen on some other basis than their presentation order.

The degree of consistency or transitivity of Ss' choices was determined by calculating coefficients of consistency for each subject (Kendall, 1962). Twenty-three of the twenty-four coefficients were found to be significantly greater than could have arisen by chance, given that the listener was making choices at random or was completely incompetent. This indicated that only one S deviated in any significant fashion from a consistent pattern or strategy of choice.

A Friedman two-way analysis of variance by ranks on stimulus choices across the 12 sound sequences pointed to a highly significant Treatments effect ($\chi^2_{RANKS} = 133.69, 11$ df, $p < .001$). This effect was further broken down into stimulus Uncertainty and Incongruity/Congruity effects. Friedman analyses on each S's choices involving paired sequences differing in uncertainty level (60 pairs per S) and differing in Incongruity/Congruity (36 pairs per S) indicated that both variables had significant effects on Exploratory Choice ($\chi^2_{RANKS} = 53.25, 5$ df, $p < .001$; $\chi^2_{RANKS} = 9.79, 1$ df, $p < .01$). Plotting the mean number of choices as a function of uncertainty (see Fig. 17), we see that the probability of stimulus choice once again

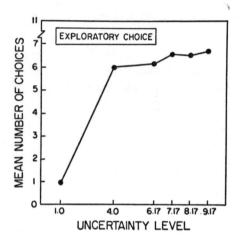

FIG. 17. Mean number of sound sequence
choices as a function of stimulus uncertainty.

increased as a function of uncertainty, leveling off beyond uncertainty level
four (7.17 bits/tone). Ferguson's (1965) nonparametric trend analysis
corroborated this interpretation. A highly significant monotonic trend
component pointed to an increase in choice across uncertainty ($z_M = 5.45$,
$p < .001$), and a highly significant bitonic component pointed to a bend or
"elbow" in this linear trend ($z_B = 5.75, p < .001$).

There was a tendency to choose a congruous sequence rather than an
incongruous one (mean number of choices per $S = 22.2$, 13.8, respectively).
When stimulus uncertainty was held constant and choices involving only
differences in version were examined, this tendency still appeared, with the
congruous version being chosen 67% of the time. Considering the interaction
of Version with Uncertainty, the congruous sequence was chosen a greater
number of times than the incongruous at all six levels of uncertainty,
suggesting that the effect of stimulus incongruity on sound sequence choice
was essentially a main effect, with congruous being favored over incongruous
sequences.

Assessment of the remaining experimental factor—group membership—
required a nonparametric procedure for examining the Groups x Sequences
interaction. The specific procedure adopted was Carroll and Chang's (1964)
"nonparametric multidimensional analysis" of paired-comparison data. This
analysis, available as a computer program called MDPREF (Chang & Carroll,
1968), performed a procedure resembling a linear factor analysis on the
choice data. It provided, first, an analysis of the perceptual dimensions

underlying stimulus choice derived from the preference data alone (the "stimulus space"), and second, an analysis of the differential importance of these dimensions in determining the strength (vector length) and direction (vector angle) of Ss' preference judgments in n-dimensional perceptual space (the "subject space"). Further details can be found in the chapter by Carroll (in Shepard, Romney, & Nerlove, 1972, pp. 123–129).

Turning to the data at hand, the MDPREF analysis of the perceptual dimensionality underlying exploratory choice indicated that a 12-dimensional solution was necessary to account for all the variance. However, the first two dimensions accounted for over 80% of the total variance, and no subsequent dimension accounted for more than 5.9% of the residual variance. A two-dimensional solution was therefore adopted.

The first MDPREF stimulus dimension, plotted in Figure 18(a), was an inverted U-shaped function of uncertainty level. Dimension I and Factor I were highly correlated ($r = .91$). The second MDPREF stimulus Dimension, plotted in Figure 18(b) was a monotonically increasing linear function of

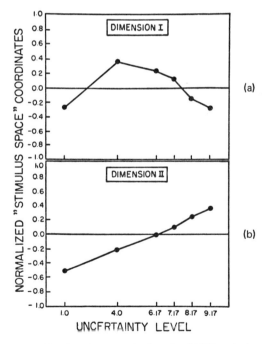

FIG. 18. (a) Dimension I of the MDPREF analysis;
(b) Dimension II of the MDPREF analysis.

uncertainty level. Dimension II and Factor II were essentially identical ($r = .99$).

Representing the 12 sound sequences as points in this two-dimensional space, the interstimulus topography presented in Figure 19 was obtained. The degree of correspondence between this stimulus space and that established by verbal-rating-scale analysis (see Fig. 14) was examined by correlating all 66 interstimulus distances in Figure 19 with the corresponding 66 distances in Figure 14. The resulting product-moment correlation was .92, indicating that 85% of the variance was common to these two representations of the sound sequences. This high degree of agreement between verbal and nonverbal representations of the stimuli was interpreted as strong support for a two-factor model of sound-sequence perception.

The reference axes plotted in Figure 19 were obtained by rotation of the subject space according to the Varimax criterion. Representing the 24 Ss as vectors in this two dimensional "stimulus space," with vector length indicating the magnitude and vector angle the directions of Ss' choices, the subject-space configuration presented in Figure 20 was obtained.

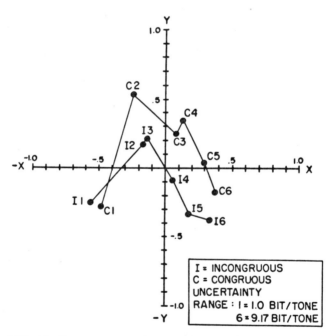

FIG. 19. Representation of the Incongruous/Congruous sound sequences in two dimensional MDPREF "stimulus space."

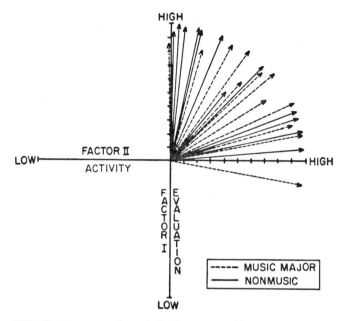

FIG. 20. Representation of the Incongruous/Congruous sound sequence in two dimensional MDPREF "subject space."

The Groups x Sequences interaction was examined following Tucker and Messick's (1963) "points of view" concept, in which the S structure is examined to find clusters of listeners corresponding to different "points of view." This rationale has also been advanced by Cliff (1968), who has suggested that factor analysis be regarded as a method of clustering in order to find "ideal" Ss. In the present case, it was expected that if group membership did systematically influence exploratory choice, there would be two "points of view" or "ideal subject" clusters. These two clusters of S vectors would largely consist of music and nonmusic Ss, respectively. It was also expected that, given these two differing "points of view," the music Ss would be more inclined than nonmusic Ss to choose sound sequences of relatively high uncertainty level.

Even if there were no clustering in terms of group membership, MDPREF can tell us whether there is any noticeable clustering of S vectors in the stimulus space. That is, was there one common "point of view" adequately represented by the function relating mean numbers of choices of uncertainty level? Or were there 24 individual "points of view," so that to look at means alone would be to miss important individual differences?

Inspection of Figure 20 in the light of the above rationale did not reveal any apparent clustering of Ss and certainly no separation of the two groups.

The individual patterns of choice depicted in Figure 20 support an additivity hypothesis resembling the one that was proposed with reference to the Listening-Time data of Experiment 4. It would appear that there was both a tendency to choose the sound sequence with the higher score on Factor I (Evaluation) and a tendency to choose the one with a higher score on Factor II (Activity). In some Ss, the former tendency predominated, so that they usually chose the more pleasing, beautiful sequence, while others were governed preponderantly by the latter tendency, choosing most often the more complex, interesting sequence. Yet other Ss' were apparently influenced by both tendencies, acting simultaneously and additively, so that their choices represented a compromise between what would happen if either tendency were operative alone. Our findings do not indicate that the choices depend on degree of musical experience or training. However, they indicate important differences between individuals in how preferences are determined. Future research might relate these differences in Exploratory Choice to differences in personality.

The additivity hypothesis also seems applicable to the mean numbers of times (C) that particular sound sequences were chosen over all Ss. This is shown by the partial correlation coefficients: $r_{CFI.FII} = .90$, 10 df, $p < .01$; $r_{CFII.FI} = .94$, $p < .01$. The multiple correlation coefficient comes to .95. The Evaluative and Activity factors together account for 96% of the variance of which 52% is covered by the former and 44% by the latter.

Further data bearing on the additivity hypothesis are reported in Chapter 3.

Discussion

It appears, then, that the probability that a particular sequence will be selected for further listening depends jointly on its location on the Evaluative dimension (i.e., how pleasing, beautiful, etc., it is judged to be) and on its location on the Activity dimension (i.e., how complex, interesting, etc., it is judged to be). These two factors or dimensions have about equal influence on the mean probability of choice over all Ss. But individual Ss differ widely in the degree to which their choices depend on the two factors.

These conclusions accord with what has been found when visual Exploratory Choice has been studied (see Chap. 14, this volume). Choice has sometimes tended to favor more complex, more interesting, patterns, and sometimes less complex, more pleasing patterns. The presumption is that Exploratory Choice is partly specific exploration, motivated by perceptual curiosity and aimed resolution of uncertainty through absorption of information, which means that more satisfaction would result from inspection of more complex stimuli (Berlyne, 1960). It is also partly diversive exploration, aimed at exposure to maximally pleasing stimuli, i.e., stimuli of moderate complexity and information content. These two forms of exploration may depend on the arousal-reduction and moderate-arousal increment mechanisms of hedonic value (Berlyne, 1967, 1971), respectively. The relative preponderance of the two evidently varies from one experimental condition to another and from one individual subject to another.

Ss tended to shun incongruous sound sequences, i.e., sequences that diverge from expectations derived from experience of western music. How close this kind of incongruity is to the incongruity whose effects have been studied in visual patterns is an open question. It has invariably been found that incongruous visual patterns attract longer Looking Time than congruous patterns, whereas visual Exploratory Choice seems to favor the incongruous in some conditions and the congruous in others (Berlyne, 1971, Chap. 13).

GENERAL DISCUSSION

We seem to have arrived at reasonably convincing answers to the questions that were raised at the beginning of this chapter. It appears that both verbal and nonverbal measures of aesthetic reaction depend quite sensitively on two dimensions along which sound sequences can be ordered. These dimensions are reflected in Pleasingness and Interestingness ratings, respectively, and are evidently close to Osgood's Evaluative and Activity dimensions, respectively. Both vary with information-theoretic properties, namely the uncertainty associated with the class from which a sequence is chosen or the information content of a particular sequence, but in different ways. One is curvilinearly, and the other linearly, related to uncertainty level. As shown in Chapter 14, equivalent dimensions have emerged in several recent investigations with a variety of visual material.

There turned out to be a remarkably high degree of interpredictability between mean verbal ratings and nonverbal measures of exploratory behavior taken from distinct samples of Ss belonging to the same population. High correlations between group means also emerge repeatedly from the experiments reported in other chapters of this book. The way in which all our dependent measures were sensitive to relatively slight differences in uncertainty level casts doubt on arguments (e.g., Arnheim, 1943; Albrecht, 1956; McLaughlin, 1962) dismissing information-theoretic analysis of music as "inappropriate" and "meaningless."

At the same time, it cannot be claimed that information-theoretic variables are the only ones of importance. We obtained evidence for substantial individual differences, some related to degree of musical training, and some (pertaining to Exploratory Choice) unrelated to this. There must also be effects of variations in subject's motivational and conditional mood. For example, a study by Konečni, Crozier, and Doob (1974) showed that induced anger can significantly influence Exploratory Choice of sound sequences.

On the other hand, some obvious limitations of the present investigation must be acknowledged. In our sequences, which consisted of some constructed by Vitz and modifications of these, degrees of uncertainty with respect to the three parameters, pitch, duration and loudness, were correlated. So, it is impossible to tell how much variation of each of these parameters contributed to the effects we observed. Musical tradition would lead one to suppose that variations in pitch loom largest in melodic perception, with duration coming second. Nevertheless, twentieth-century composers using serial techniques have given all three factors and timbre equal weight (see Meyer, 1967, pp. 246-247). Furthermore, Vitz, who was interested in "stimulus variation" rather than in uncertainty level alone, designed his sequences so that the range of values for each parameter would covary with the uncertainty. This may have played some part in his and our findings.

Avant-garde composers might derive some encouragement from one implication of the data, namely that listeners do not shun sequences judged to be BAD, AWFUL, DISPLEASING, UNMUSICAL, UNMELODIC, etc., provided these sequences possessed such redeeming qualities as judged Interestingness, Activity, Vibrancy, and Complexity. On the other hand, our Ss showed both verbally and nonverbally that they preferred sound sequences conforming to the melodic and rhythmic properties associated with traditional western tonal music.

Skeptically inclined musicians will no doubt point out that, although sound sequences must be classed as "melodies" according to the dictionary definition, they lack many of the ingredients found in real-life music. Members of our laboratory were actually quite surprised to find out how much the sequences of the higher uncertainty levels sound like contemporary serialized music (although they were constructed according to completely different principles) and how far the congruous sequences of intermediate uncertainty levels resemble folk tunes. But it must be noted that, unlike our sound sequences, melodies of virtually all major musical cultures possess distributional redundancies: there is usually one pitch (the tonic) that occurs more often than any other, and often another (the dominant) that is the second most frequent. There is virtually always correlational redundancy: certain motifs or sequences appear more often than others, e.g., in tonal western music, sequences embodying consecutive notes of the scale or the notes of common chords. Traditional western melodies begin and end on the tonic, they finish with a cadence, they more often than not reach their highest pitch somewhere in the middle and then decline. All of these features were absent from the stimulus material we used. But this investigation belongs to an initial stage. All the ingredients of familiar melodies that were missing can be added one by one, using the same experimental techniques, so that this line of research can bring us gradually nearer to the study of genuine music and the analysis of its components.

REFERENCES

Albrecht, G. Letter in *Scientific American*. 1956, 194(4), 18–19.

Apel, W. *Harvard Dictionary of Music*. Cambridge, Mass.: Harvard University Press, 1964.

Arnheim, R. Gestalt and art. *Journal of Aesthetics and Art Criticism*, 1943, 2, 71–75.

Attneave, F. *Application of information theory to psychology*. New York: Holt, 1959.

Babbitt, M. Twelve-tone rhythmic structure and the electronic medium. *Perspectives of New Music*, No. 1, Fall, 1962, 49–79.

Berlyne, D. E. Novelty and curiosity as determinants of exploratory behavior. *British Journal of Psychology*, 1950, 41, 68–80.

Berlyne, D. E. *Conflict, arousal and curiosity*. New York: McGraw-Hill, 1960.

Berlyne, D. E. Complexity and incongruity variables as determinants of exploratory choice and evaluative ratings. *Canadian Journal of Psychology*, 1963, 17, 274–290.

Berlyne, D. E. Measures of aesthetic preference. Paper read at the First International Colloquium on Experimental Aesthetics, Paris, 1965. In J. Hogg (Ed.), *Psychology and the visual arts*. London: Penguin, 1969.

Berlyne, D. E. Arousal and reinforcement. In D. Levine (Ed.), *Nebraska Symposium on Motivation*, 1967. Lincoln, Nebr.: University of Nebraska Press, 1967.

Berlyne, D. E. *Aesthetics and psychobiology*. New York: Appleton-Century-Crofts, 1971.

Berlyne, D. E. Ends and means of experimental aesthetics. *Canadian Journal of Psychology*, 1972, 26, 303–325.

Berlyne, D. E. Interrelations of verbal and nonverbal measures used in experimental aesthetics. *Scandinavian Journal of Psychology*, 1973, 14, 177–184.

Brawley, J. G., Jr. Application of information theory to musical rhythm. Unpublished M.A. thesis, Indiana University, 1959.

Brooks, F. P., Jr., Hopkins, A. L., Neumann, P. G., & Wright, W. V. An experiment in musical composition. *IRE Transactions on Electronic Computers*, 1957, EC-6, 175; correction, EC-7, 60.

Campbell, D. N. Education for the aesthetic experience. *Music Educators' Journal*, 1967, 53, 77–83.

Carroll, J. D., & Chang, J. J. Nonparametric multidimensional analysis of paired-comparisons data. Paper presented at the joint meeting of the Psychometric and Psychonomic Societies, Niagara Falls, Ontario, 1964.

Chang, J. J., & Carroll, J. D. How to use MDPREF, a computer program for multidimensional analysis of preference data. Unpublished report, Bell Telephone Laboratories, 1968.

Cliff, N. The "idealized" individual interpretation of individual differences in multidimensional scaling. *Psychometrika*, 1968, 33, 225–232.

Cooke, D. *The language of music.* London: Oxford University Press, 1959.

Copland, A. *What to listen for in music.* New York: McGraw-Hill, 1939.

Edwards, A. L. *Experimental design in psychological research.* New York: Holt, Rinehart and Winston, 1968.

Ferguson, G. A. *Nonparametric trend analysis.* Montreal: McGill University Press, 1965.

Fletcher, H., & Munson, W. A. The definition of loudness and its measurement. *Journal of the Acoustical Society of America*, 1933, 5, 82–108.

Frank, H. *Informationsästhetik.* Quickborn: Schnelle, 1959.

Funk & Wagnalls *Standard College Dictionary.* New York: Reader's Digest Association, 1968.

Garner, W. R. *Uncertainty and structure as psychological concepts.* New York: Wiley, 1962.

Garrett, H. E. *Statistics in psychology and education.* London: Longmans, Green, and Company, 1926.

Goldstein, A. G. Familiarity and apparent complexity of random shapes. *Journal of Experimental Psychology*, 1961, 62, 594–597.

Green, R. T., & Courtis, M. C. Information theory and figure perception: the metaphor that failed. *Acta Psychologica*, 1966, 25, 12–36.

Harrison, A. A. Response competition, frequency, exploratory behavior and liking. *Journal of Personality and Social Psychology*, 1968, 9, 363–368.

Harrison, A. A., & Zajonc, R. B. The effects of frequency and duration of exposure on response competition and affective ratings. *Journal of Psychology*, 1970, 75(2), 163–169.

Hatton, H. M., Berg, W. K., & Graham, F. K. Effects of acoustic rise time on heart rate response. *Psychonomic Science*, 1970, 19(2), 101–103.

Kaiser, H. F. Comments on communalities and the number of factors. Paper read at an informal conference, "The Communality Problem in Factor Analysis," St. Louis, Washington University, 1960.

Kendall, M. G. *Rank correlation methods.* New York: Hafner, 1962.

Konečni, V., Crozier, J. B., & Doob, A. N. Effects of anger and expression of aggression on exploratory choice. Unpublished manuscript, 1974.

Kraehenbuehl, D., & Coons, E. Information as a measure of the experience of music. *Journal of Aesthetics and Art Criticism*, 1959, 17, 510-522.

Levy, E. Compositional technique and musical expressivity. *Journal of Research in Music Education*, 1970, 18(1), 3-15.

Lomax, A. *Folk song style and culture*. Washington: McCall, 1968.

Matlin, M. W. Response competition as a mediating factor in the frequency-affect relationship. *Journal of Personality and Social Psychology*, 1970, 16, 536-552.

McLaughlin, T. P. Music and communication. *Music Review*, 1962, 23, 285-291.

Meyer, L. B. *Emotion and meaning in music*. Chicago: University of Chicago Press, 1956.

Meyer, L. B. *Music, the arts, and ideas*. Chicago: University of Chicago Press, 1967.

Mindus, L. The role of redundancy and complexity in the perception of tonal patterns. Unpublished M.A. thesis, Clark University, 1968.

Moles, A. *Théorie de l'information et perception esthétique*. Paris: Flammarion, 1958. (*Information theory and esthetic perception*. Urbana, Ill.: University of Illinois Press, 1966.)

Newman, W. S. *Understanding music*. New York: Harper, 1961.

Nowlis, V. Research with the mood adjective check list. In S. S. Tomkins, & C. E. Izard (Eds.), *Affect: measurement of awareness and performance*. New York: Springer, 1965.

Nunnally, J. C. *Psychometric theory*. New York: McGraw-Hill, 1967.

Olson, H. F., & Belar, H. Aid to music composition with a random probability system. *Science*, 1961, 133, 3461, 1368. (Abstract)

Osgood, C. E., Suci, G. J., & Tannenbaum, P. H. *The measurement of meaning*. Urbana, Ill.: University of Illinois Press, 1957.

Overmier, J. B. Auditory pattern preference as a function of informational content. Unpublished M.A. thesis, Bowling Green State University, 1962.

Pierce, J. R. *Electrons, waves and messages*. Garden City, New York: Hanover House, 1956.

Pinkerton, R. C. Information theory and melody. *Scientific American*, 1956, 194(2), 77-86.

Quastler, H. *Information theory in psychology*. Glencoe: Free Press, 1955. (a)

Quastler, H. Discussion following mathematical theory of word formation, by W. Fucks. In E. C. Cherry (Ed.), *Information theory—third London symposium*, New York: Academic Press, 1955, p. 168. (b)

Robinson, D. W., & Dadson, R. S. A re-determination of the equal loudness relations for pure tones. *British Journal of Applied Physics*, 1956, 7, 166-181.

Ross, R. T. Optimum orders for the presentation of pairs in the method of paired comparisons. *Journal of Educational Psychology*, 1934, 25, 375-382.

Schlosberg, H. A. A description of facial expressions in terms of two dimensions. *Journal of Experimental Psychology*, 1952, 44, 229-237.

Shannon, C. E., & Weaver, W. *The mathematical theory of communication*. Chicago: University of Illinois Press, 1949.

Shepard, R. N., Romney, A. K., & Nerlove, S. B. (Eds.) *Multidimensional scaling*. New York: Seminar Press, 1972.

Simon, C. R., & Wohlwill, J. F. An experimental study of the role of expectation and variation in music. *Journal of Research in Music Education*, 1968, 16(3), 227-238.

Sowa, J. *A machine to compose music*. New York: Oliver Garfield, 1956.

Stevens, S. S. On the psychophysical law. *Psychological Review*, 1957, 64, 153–181.

Stockhausen, K. The concept of unity in electronic music. *Perspectives of New Music*, 1962 (1, Fall), 39–48.

Thayer, R. E. Measurement of activation through self-report. *Psychological Reports*, 1967, 20, 663–678.

Tischler, H. The aesthetic experience. *Music Review*, 1956, 17, 189.

Tucker, L. R., & Messick, S. An individual difference model for multidimensional scaling. *Psychometrika*, 1963, 28 333–367.

Tucker, W. T. Experiments in aesthetic communication. Unpublished Ph.D. thesis, University of Illinois, 1955.

Veldman, J. *FORTRAN programming for the behavioral sciences*. New York: Holt, Rinehart and Winston, 1957.

Vitz, P. C. Affect as a function of stimulus variation. *Journal of Experimental Psychology*, 1966, 71, 74–79.

Werbik, H. L'indétermination et les qualités impressives des modèles stimulants mélodiques. *Sciences de l'Art*, 1969, 6(1-2), 25–36.

Williams, E. J. Experimental designs balanced for the estimation of residual effects of treatments. *Australian Journal of Scientific Research*, 1949, 2, 149–168.

Winer, B. J. *Statistical principles in experimental design*. New York: McGraw-Hill, 1962.

Woodworth, R. S. *Experimental psychology*. New York: Holt, 1938.

Wundt, W. M. *Grundzüge der physiologischen psychologie*. Leipzig: Engelmann, 1874. (*Principles of physiological psychology*. New York: Macmillan, 1904.)

Youngblood, J. E. Music and language: some related analytical techniques. Unpublished Ph.D. thesis, Indiana University, 1960.

Zajonc, R. B. Attitudinal effects of mere exposure. *Journal of Personality and Social Psychology*, 1968, 9 (Monograph Supplement 2, Pt. 2).

Zink, S. Is the music really sad? *Journal of Aesthetics*, 1960, 19(2), 197–207.

3

THE DEVELOPMENT WITH AGE OF VERBAL AND EXPLORATORY RESPONSES TO SOUND SEQUENCES VARYING IN UNCERTAINTY LEVEL[1]

B. W. E. Bragg and J. B. Crozier

Does preference for complex music increase with age? We know that young children listen to simple nursery rhymes in our culture. Is this because adults assume that children cannot appreciate complex musical passages and hence impose a children's culture on the young or are children, in fact, incapable of learning to detect structure in complex musical passages? The experimental evidence on this relationship is virtually nonexistent. Petzeld (1969) found no difference in the ability of 4-, 5-, and 6-year-old children to learn to read tonal configurations. In all cases, the ability was low. Taylor (1969) found increasing differentiation of preference as a function of age for 20-second extracts of classical composers from Monteverdi to Stravinsky. The age range was from six to adult. Duke and Gullickson (1970) found that 5-year-olds chose to listen to four 500 ms tones rather than to simpler alternatives.

Speculation on the relation between age and ability to learn complex musical passages is abundant. Music educators (e.g., Farnsworth, 1958; Lundin, 1967; Mursell, 1948) have suggested that young children prefer simple musical passages because they are unable to detect the subtlety in a

[1] The authors would like to express their appreciation for the cooperation they received from Dr. P. Anderson and his staff at the Ontario Science Centre in seeking subjects to participate in the experiments. They also acknowledge the help of Valerie March in collecting data for Experiment 1.

complicated musical passage. Presumably, these educators are assuming that young children are incapable of learning to detect the complicated structure of complex musical passages. Piaget's (1952) developmental theory would support this position. Piaget suggests that the developing child increases in his ability to organize the external environment—the process of assimilation and accommodation—with increased age. It would follow from this position that older individuals would have greater ability to detect complexity in musical passages.

The evidence on the relation between aesthetic evaluation and visual complexity is relevant to this issue. Munsinger, Kessen, and Kessen (1964) found the youngest age group (6-year-olds) liked the most complex visual stimuli best while older age groups liked intermediate levels of complexity best. They suggest the youngest age group were unable to detect the complexity in the most complex visual stimuli. Unfortunately they have no evidence for this interpretation because they have not assessed perceived complexity. The results of Thomas' (1966) research complicates the issue even more. Thomas (1966) found an increasing choice of the most complex stimulus from ages 6 to 16 with a decrease in choice of complex stimuli for older, teenage groups. The relationship between aesthetic preference and visual complexity, therefore, remains unresolved and does not clarify the relationship for auditory stimuli.

Observations of the evaluative responses of older individuals for more complicated musical passages are, of course, confounded by frequency of exposure and acquisition of cultural values. The present study, therefore, is designed to avoid these pitfalls and to answer two questions: (1) Are individuals of different age levels able to detect variations in complexity? and (2) How do different age groups differentially evaluate musical passages of varying degrees of complexity?

EXPERIMENT 1: METHOD

Subjects

Twelve male and female Ss at each of three age levels (8-9; 14-15; and 20+) were recruited from visitors to the Ontario Science Centre.

Stimuli

The use of known musical passages would confound complexity with familiarity, harmony, cultural values, etc. To avoid this problem randomly generated sound sequences patterned after those of Vitz (1966) were used (see Chap. 2, this volume). Sound sequences of six uncertainty levels constituted the stimuli. These ranged from 2 pitches presented randomly at equal loudness for equal durations (2 equiprobable events or 1 bit of information per note) to 18 pitches played at one of four loudness levels for one of eight durations (576 equiprobable events or 9.17 bits of information per note). Each of the elements on the three dimensions was randomly sampled with replacement.

There were six phases, during each of which all six sound sequences were presented. In each phase, new sequences were generated from the pool of available tones. A subject, therefore, never heard a particular sound sequence twice, but in each presentation of sound sequences he heard different tone randomizations at each of the six levels of complexity.

Rating Scales

Subjects were asked to rate the sound sequences on the following six rating scales: SIMPLE-COMPLEX, UNINTERESTING-INTERESTING, UGLY-BEAUTIFUL, DISPLEASING-PLEASING, CLEAR-HAZY, and WEAK-POWERFUL. These scales were chosen to reflect the three factors isolated by Crozier (1973; Chap. 2, this volume) in his factor analysis of ratings of the sound sequences. The first two scales reflect an Activity dimension, the second two an Evaluative dimension, and the last two a Potency dimension, as defined by Osgood, Suci, and Tannenbaum (1957).

Experimental Design

*S*s from three different age groups rated the six sound sequences on the six rating scales for a total of 36 judgments per person. Sound-sequence presentation order was determined by a 6 x 6 Latin Square. Every *S* heard the same orderings in turn of the sound sequences. The ordering of the rating scales was also determined by a 6 x 6 Latin Square. *S*s were assigned to rows of the Rating-Scale Latin Square so that columns corresponded to phases and cell entries determined the particular rating scale. The Rating Scale Latin Square was repeated for each age level.

Procedure

Subjects were tested individually. The rating procedure was explained, and then, after *S* put on the headphones to listen to the sound sequences, he was given the first rating scale (e.g., UGLY-BEAUTIFUL) as determined by the Rating-Scale Latin Square and he would rate all six sound sequences on that scale. He was then given the second rating scale (e.g., UNINTERESTING-INTERESTING) and would rate the six sound sequences on the second scale. He would continue this rating on the remaining four scales until a total of 36 judgments had been made.

EXPERIMENT 1: RESULTS

The first question to be answered in this study is whether Ss of different ages can discriminate sound sequences of different complexities. Analysis of variance of the Ss' ratings of the stimuli on the SIMPLE-COMPLEX scale revealed the only significant effect to be the linear component (see Fig. 1): $F = 101.28$, $df = 1$, 150, $p < .001$. The Age main effect ($F = .60$), the Age x Uncertainty interaction ($F = .99$), and all trend components were nonsignificant. We can conclude, therefore, that Ss from the ages of eight to adulthood have equal ability to differentiate sound sequences of different levels of complexity.

Having determined that all age levels perceive the variations in stimulus complexity with equal ability, we can now turn to the central question of the study. Are there differences in evaluation of sound sequences of differing uncertainty levels? Analysis of the ratings on the Ugly-Beautiful scale indicate a significant Uncertainty main effect ($F = 19.83$, $df = 5$ and 150, $p < .01$) and a significant Age x Uncertainty interaction ($F = 6.03$, $df = 10$ and 150, $p < .01$). Figure 2 shows the Age x Uncertainty interaction. As can

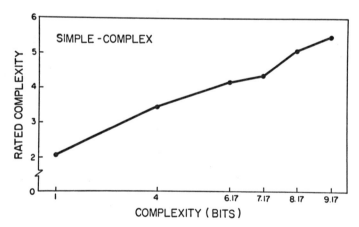

FIG. 1. Mean rated complexity for sound sequences of six levels of complexity.

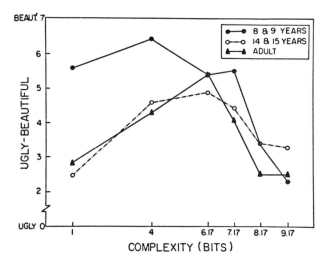

FIG. 2. Mean ratings of Beautifulness of three age groups for
sound sequences of six levels of complexity.

be seen, the 8-year-olds found the lowest Uncertainty levels most beautiful,
the 14-year-olds the third level (6.17 bits) most beautiful, and the adults the
fourth level (7.17 bits). This pattern of findings is also shown in the
PLEASINGNESS-DISPLEASINGNESS ratings. Analysis of variance shows an
Uncertainty main effect ($F = 9.17$, $df = 5$ and 150, $p < .01$) and an
Age x Uncertainty interaction ($F = 3.89$, $df = 10$ and 150, $p < .01$). Figure 3
shows this interaction. Again the 8-year-olds find the three lowest
Uncertainty levels most pleasing; 14-year-olds and adults rate the
intermediate (second, third, and fourth) levels more pleasing than the high
(fifth and sixth) or lower (first) levels.

We can conclude, therefore, that the uncertainty level that is found most
pleasing increases with age. These data, then, confirm our hypothesis.

Another scale included in the present study was UNINTERESTING-
INTERESTING. Crozier (1973; Chap. 2, this volume) had previously found
that mean ratings of subjective Complexity and Interestingness were highly
correlated ($r = .99$) for adults. The present data have revealed that there are
no differences as a function of age for judgments of subjective Complexity.
From Crozier (1973), then, it should follow that an Uncertainty main effect
would be the only term in the analysis of variance to be significant for the
UNINTERESTING-INTERESTING scale. The analysis reveals, however, an
Uncertainty main effect ($F = 3.36$, $df = 5$ and 150, $p < .01$), an Age main

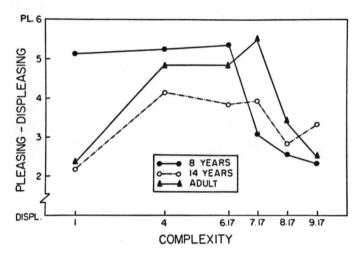

FIG. 3. Mean ratings of Pleasingness of three age groups for sound sequences of six levels of complexity.

effect ($F = 8.55$, $df = 2$ and 18, $p < .01$) and an Age × Complexity interaction ($F = 4.10$, $df = 10$ and 150, $p < .01$). Inspection of Figure 4 shows that 8-year-olds found the lowest uncertainty levels more interesting than the higher levels, while the 14-year-old and adult Ss found the higher levels more interesting.

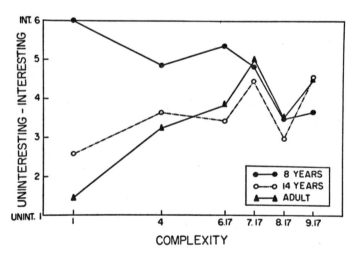

FIG. 4. Mean ratings of Interestingness of three age groups for sound sequences of six levels of complexity.

This age difference in Interestingness ratings raises a question about the use of language. How have these adjectives been used as a function of age? In order to answer this question, a factor analysis for each age group was performed on the mean ratings of the sound sequences for each scale. Crozier (1973) found that three factors were adequate to describe the way adults perceive sound sequences. If all age levels used the rating scales in the same manner, even though they may rate the sound sequences quite differently, then three factors should also emerge.

The results of the factor analysis for adults (see Table 1) indicate three factors accounting for 99% of the variance with Factor I, a structural factor, accounting for 45%, Factor II, an Evaluative factor, accounting for 40% of the variance, and Factor III, a Potency factor, accounting for 14% of the variance. The factors correspond to the Activity (i.e., Simple-Complex), Evaluative (i.e., Ugly-Beautiful), and Potency (i.e., Weak-Powerful), factors found previously by Crozier (1973; Chap. 2, this volume) with sound sequences, Tucker (1955) with representational paintings and Berlyne (1972) with visual patterns. The factor analyses of the 14-year-old Ss' ratings (see Table 1) indicate two factors accounting for 90% of the variance with Factor I (Simple-Complex) accounting for 44% of the variance and Factor II (Ugly-Beautiful) accounting for 46%.

For 8-year-old subjects the factor analysis (see Table 1) reveals a different semantic structure. Factor I accounts for 81% of the variance while Factor II accounts for only 11%. It can be seen from the data in Table 1 that the

TABLE 1

Factor Loadings for Ratings of Sound Sequences on Six Rating
Scales for Three Age Groups: P Technique

Rating scale/factor	Adults			14–15 Year olds		8–9 Year olds	
	I	II	III	I	II	I	II
CLEAR-HAZY	.73	–.67	–.01	.52	–.75	–.85	.48
DISPLEASING-PLEASING	.45	.86	.21	.56	.81	.95	–.25
SIMPLE-COMPLEX	.93	–.28	–.20	.96	–.24	–.87	–.40
UGLY-BEAUTIFUL	.37	.87	.29	.35	.89	.98	–.12
UNINTERESTING-INTERESTING	.97	.13	–.12	.90	.19	.90	.10
WEAK-POWERFUL	.12	–.38	.80	.41	–.79	.83	.40
Percent of Variance	43	40	13	43	45	82	11

judgments of the 8-year-olds are primarily unidimensional. If a sound sequence is simple it is judged to be pleasing, beautiful, interesting, clear, and powerful.

An analysis of variance on the factor scores for Factor I (see Harman 1960) indicates a significant Uncertainty main effect ($F = 10.02$, $df = 5$ and 90, $p < .001$) and a significant Age x Complexity interaction ($F = 17.28$, $df = 10$ and 90, $p < .001$). Figure 5 shows this Age x Complexity interaction. Inspection of the factor loadings in Table 1 indicate that this factor is primarily a structural factor for 14-year-olds and adults with the primary loadings on the SIMPLE-COMPLEX and the UNINTERESTING-INTERESTING scales. For 8-year-olds Factor I has both evaluative and structural components intermingled, with all of the scales loading highly on this factor. In general, this factor reflects a tendency for higher uncertainty levels to be evaluated more negatively by 8-year-olds.

Analysis of variance of the factor scores for Factor II reveals an Age x Complexity interaction ($F = 7.07$, $df = 5$ and 90, $p < .001$). Figure 6 shows a curvilinear relationship between uncertainty level and the factor score for 14-year-olds and adults. The major contributors to Factor II for 14-year-olds and adults are the DISPLEASING-PLEASING and

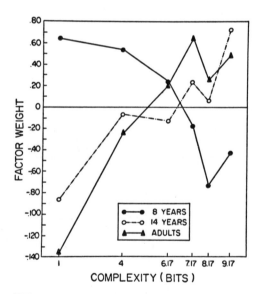

FIG. 5. Weighted factor scores on Factor I of three age groups for sound sequences of six levels of complexity.

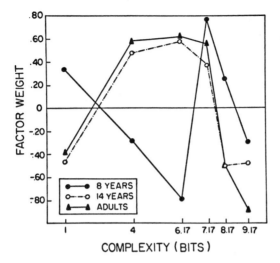

FIG. 6. Weighted factor scores on Factor II of three age groups for sound sequences of six levels of complexity.

UGLY-BEAUTIFUL scales. This factor is clearly an Evaluative factor for the older age groups. For the 8-year-olds, Factor II is not interpretable. However, it accounts for only 11% of the variance, whereas Factor II for 14-year-olds and adults accounts for approximately 45% of the variance.

EXPERIMENT 1: DISCUSSION

The results of this study show that sound sequences varying in uncertainty level can be differentiated by persons as young as 8 years of age. However, 8-year-olds evaluate more favorably simple sound sequences, whereas 14-year-olds and adults evaluate more favorably sound sequences of intermediate complexity. It appears further that 8-year-olds use verbal scales differently from older age groups. Eight-year-olds do not differentiate between structural and evaluative components of a stimulus. If, for example, a sound sequence is judged interesting, it will also be judged pleasing. Older age groups do differentiate between structural and evaluative components. They might find a particular sound sequence interesting but not pleasing.

The present data are verbal ratings of preference for sound sequences. The simplest logical extension of these data to choice would suggest that Ss would choose to listen to the more pleasing of two sound sequences.

Alternatively, the structural component may dominate and the more interesting of the two stimuli may be chosen. A more complicated prediction would suggest that both evaluative and structural (Interestingness) properties would contribute to a choice decision, possibly in an additive fashion or possibly in some weighted multiplicative fashion. The relation between verbal ratings and behavioral choice, then, is not a simple extension from the present data but requires empirical investigation.

Finally the results of the present study reflect upon current music education procedures. At present, emphasis in lower grade music education is placed on the training in "rudiments of music" or, in the terms of this study, detecting structural elements in musical passages. The present data suggest that 8-year-olds are quite capable of making structural differentiations but that emphasis should be placed on evaluative differentiation of auditory complexity and that music training may be essentially a development of the listeners' evaluation of auditory complexity.

We have shown that the verbal evaluation of sound sequences differs as a function of age. Are these cognitive differences reflected in behavioral differences? Crozier (Chap. 2, this volume) found that adult *S*s chose to listen to the simplest sound sequence significantly less frequently than all others. There were no differences in the frequency with which the more complex sound sequences (4 bits to 9.17 bits) were chosen. Crozier suggests that this asymptote in probability of choice may be determined by the interaction of the perceived complexity (Interestingness) of the stimulus and the listener's evaluation (Pleasingness) of the stimulus (an "additive" model). For Crozier's adult ratings, an additive model would predict the asymptote found in Crozier's exploratory choice data. If such a model is correct, a very different pattern should be reflected in the choices of 8-year-olds. Our rating-scale data indicate that 8-year-olds find the simplest sound sequence the most pleasing and the most interesting, with a general decrease in Pleasingness and Interestingness as uncertainty increases. An additive model for Exploratory Choice would predict that 8-year-olds would choose the simplest sound sequence most frequently and select more complex sound sequences less frequently.

The second study was, therefore, designed to investigate differences in Exploratory Choice in three age groups and to determine whether Crozier's additive model is tenable.

EXPERIMENT 2: METHOD

Subjects

Twelve male and female Ss at each of three age levels (8, 14, and 20+) were recruited from visitors to the Ontario Science Centre.

Stimuli

The stimuli consisted of the same six sound sequences used in the previous rating scale study.

Exploratory-Choice Measure

The subject was requested to listen to 10 seconds of one sound sequence, then 10 seconds of a second sound sequence, and then to choose which of the two sound sequences he would like to hear a second time. This choice constitutes the dependent measure. The exact instructions to the subject were as follows:

> In this study you will be presented with two sound sequences, each ten seconds long. After listening to these two sound sequences which we shall call "first" and "second," you are to press one of the two buttons on the box in front of you. If you press the button labeled "first" you will hear a 10-second continuation (not repetition) of the first sound sequence. . . .

Design

All possible pairs of sound sequences (15 pairs) were arranged into six presentation orders using an algorithm suggested by Ross (1934) in order to balance temporal positions of pairs within the presentation order and to balance the order of presentation of sound sequences within each pair.

This 6 x 15 matrix was replicated for each age and each sex resulting in a 3 x 2 x 6 x 15 factorial design.

EXPERIMENT 2: RESULTS

A 3 x 15 Friedman two way analysis of variance by ranks of the Exploratory-Choice data indicates a significant main effect of uncertainty level: $\chi^2 = 14.00$, $df = 5$, $p < .05$. A 3 x 6 chi square analysis of the choice data indicates no significant Age x Uncertainty interaction ($\chi^2 = 3.41$, $p = .98$).

Ferguson's (1965) nonparametric trend analysis indicates that the monotonic trend is not significant ($z = 0.96, p =$ ns) while the bitonic trend is highly significant ($z = 3.43, p < .001$). No differences as a function of sex were observed.

All age groups chose to listen to sound sequences of an intermediate uncertainty level rather than to higher or lower levels. This reflects a tendency to choose those sequences that adults judge to be most pleasing and beautiful.

Figure 7 shows that uncertainty levels 2, 3, and 4 were chosen significantly more frequently than complexity levels 1, 5, and 6.

A nonparametric multidimensional scaling (Carroll & Chang, 1964; Chang & Carroll, 1968) was performed on the choice data, using the MDPREF program. Inspection of the roots of the first score matrix reveals that two factors account for most of the variance (68%). The ordering of the stimuli on the first dimension show that this dimension reflects primarily uncertainty level. The only inconsistency is that uncertainty level five is judged less complex than level four. Inspection of the verbal-rating data (see Table 1) indicates that level four was rated higher on Factor I (Complexity) than level

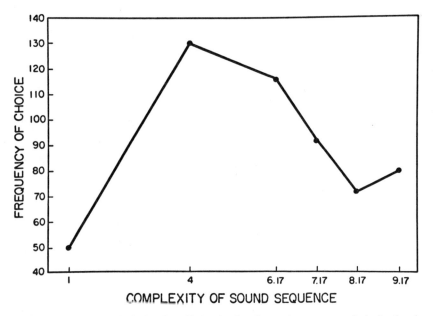

FIG. 7. Frequency of choice for all age levels of sound sequences of six levels of complexity.

five. Dimension I on the choice data thus reflects psychological complexity rather than the actual complexity of the stimuli. A comparison of the factor loadings of Factor I on the verbal-rating data and Dimension I on the choice data indicates a correlation of $r = .82$ ($df = 4$, $p < .05$), which further substantiates this interpretation.

Similarly, the ordering of the choice data on Dimension 2 reflects scores on verbal-rating Factor II for 14-year-olds and adults. This factor and Dimension 2 of the choice data have a correlation of .81 ($df = 4, p = .05$).

EXPERIMENT 2: DISCUSSION

The results of this study fail to support the prediction from Crozier's additive model that 8-year-old children would choose the simplest sound sequence most frequently and increasingly complex stimuli progressively less frequently. All age levels chose intermediate levels of complexity more frequently than higher or lower levels of complexity. This suggests that the discrepancy between age groups in verbal ratings was due to differential use of language rather than to differential nonverbal preference. When a procedure is employed that avoids the use of verbal responses, no age differences appear. This contention is investigated further in the next study, where a different behavioral dependent measure (Listening Time) is employed.

The adult Exploratory-Choice data from the present experiment also differ from those reported by Crozier (Chap. 2, this volume). Crozier's adult subjects chose uncertainty levels 5 and 6 as frequently as levels 2, 3, and 4. The present results indicate a tendency to choose intermediate levels of complexity.

The two experiments employed the same procedure and differed only in subject population. Crozier's study involved University of Toronto undergraduates, while the present study utilized visitors to the Ontario Science Centre. This population, while still selected, is probably more representative of the population in general in terms of age and (possibly) intellectual ability. This encourages to suggest that the results of this study may more accurately represent the preferred level of melodic uncertainty in the general North American population.

In the Exploratory-Choice study just reported, it was found that all age groups tended to choose sound sequences of intermediate uncertainty levels. It was suggested that a behavioral measure (as opposed to a verbal measure) bypasses the difficulties of language. Hence, it was suggested that the observed age differences in the verbal ratings reflect a difference in the use of language rather than an actual difference in preference. In order to substantiate this conclusion, more evidence is required. The next study, therefore, was designed to assess another nonverbal measure of exploratory behavior in order to determine if the present interpretation is justified. Listening Time was chosen as the measure, because of previous evidence (Crozier, 1973) that it is sensitive to differences in the complexity of sound sequences.

EXPERIMENT 3: METHOD

Subjects

Twelve adult (20 years and older), twelve 14- or 15-year-old, and twelve 8- or 9-year-old visitors to the Ontario Science Center participated in the present study. Half of each group were male.

Stimuli

The same sound sequences were used in the present study. Each sound sequence lasted 20 seconds. A tape loop was made so that each sequence could be repeated as long as S desired to listen. (N.B. No detection of repetition was made by subjects. The longest Listening Time averaged 39.2 seconds.)

Apparatus

Three Sony tape recorders (Model TC 252) were used to play the sound sequences. The tape recorders ran continuously with each sound sequence recorded on one of the six channels. The experimenter presented sound sequences according to a predetermined order. S indicated when he wished the sequence to terminate by pushing a control button. The interval between the onset of the sound sequence and the pressing of the button was recorded in hundreds of a minute on a Hunter timer.

There was a pause of approximately 30 seconds half way through the experiment while the second version of the sound sequences were placed on the tape recorders.

Design

The six sound sequences were presented to each S once as determined by a 6 x 6 balanced Latin Square, with each S being assigned to one row of the square.

S then listened to the second version of six sound sequences again as determined by a 6 x 6 balanced Latin Square. The Latin Square was repeated for each sex for all three age groups.

Procedure

When *S* arrived at the experimental room, he was given a metal box with a push button and was fitted with a set of head phones. He was informed that he was to listen to each sound sequence "for as long as you wish to listen to it" and then push the button to go on to the next sequence. After the listening task was completed, some information on *S*'s musical knowledge was obtained and the purpose of the experiment was explained to him.

EXPERIMENT 3: RESULTS

An analysis of variance was performed on the Listening-Time measures. The Groups main effect was not significant nor were the Age x Uncertainty Interactions significant. A highly significant linear component of the Uncertainty effect was observed ($F = 40.19$, $df = 1$ and 50, $p < .001$). There was also a significant sex difference in the linear component of the Uncertainty effect ($F = 11.41$, $df = 1$ and 50, $p < .001$). It can be seen from Figure 8 that females listened longer to the more complex sound sequences while males listened longer to the simplest sound sequence. In general, however, there is a tendency to listen to the more complex sound sequences longer. The linear component of the Uncertainty main effect accounts for four times as much variance as the linear component of the Uncertainty x Sex interaction. We conclude, therefore, that in general, *S*s, regardless of age, tend to listen longer to more complex sound sequences.

EXPERIMENT 3: DISCUSSION

The results of the present study confirm Crozier's (1973) finding that uncertainty level and Listening Time are linearly related. *S*s spend longer listening to more complex sound sequences. The results support Berlyne's (1965, p. 143) concept of "specific exploration," in that *S*s listened longest to stimuli containing more information to be absorbed.

The results of the present study also confirm the findings of our Exploratory-Choice study. The interaction between Age and Complexity was not significant. This further supports our contention that differences in verbal

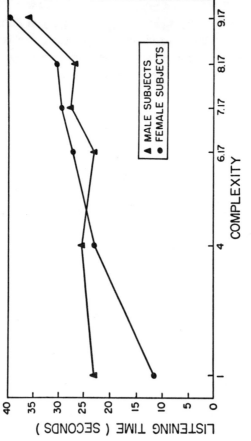

FIG. 8. Mean Listening Time in seconds of male and female subjects for the six levels of complexity.

ratings of sound sequences are due to differential use of language rather than to differences in preference as reflected by nonverbal measures.

The linear relation between uncertainty level and Listening Time suggests that *S*s listen longer to sound sequences that are judged more interesting rather than to those that are judged more pleasing. Conversely, *S*s in the previous experiment chose to listen to the more pleasing, rather than interesting, sound sequence. Why is there this discrepancy between the two behavioral measures? One possibility is that *S*s attempt to understand an interesting, but not necessarily pleasing, sound sequence when there is sufficient time to process the information but choose the more pleasing event when time is limited and insufficient for complete processing. In the Exploratory-Choice study, *S* heard each sound sequence for 10 seconds and then chose to listen to one of the two sequences for another 10 seconds (time being set by the experimenter). Listening Time ranged from 17.9 seconds for the simplest sound sequence to 39.2 for the most complex sound sequence. In all cases, the average Listening Time was two to four times as long as the listening time allowed by the experimenter in the choice study.

According to this interpretation, if *S* were given a choice between two sound sequences and could then listen to the one he chose as long as he wanted, the more complex sound sequence of the pair should be chosen, rather than the more pleasing one as found in Experiment 2.

REFERENCES

Berlyne, D. E. *Structure and Direction in Thinking.* New York: Wiley, 1965.

Berlyne, D. E. Ends and means of experimental aesthetics. *Canadian Journal of Psychology*, 1972, **26**, 303–325.

Carroll, J. D., & Chang, J. J. Non-parametric multidimensional analysis of paired-comparisons data. Paper presented at the joint meeting of the Psychometric and Psychonomic Societies, Niagara Falls, Ontario, 1964.

Chang, J. J., & Carroll, J. D. How to use MDPREF, a computer program for multidimensional analysis of preference data. Unpublished report, Bell Telephone Laboratories, 1968.

Crozier, J. B. Verbal and exploratory responses to sound sequences of varying complexity. Unpublished Ph.D. thesis, University of Toronto, 1973.

Duke, A. W. & Gullickson, G. R. Children's stimulus selection as a function of auditory stimulus complexity. *Psychonomic Science*, 1970, **19**, 119–120.

Farnsworth, P. R. *The Social Psychology of Music.* New York: Dryden Press, 1958.

Ferguson, G. A. *Non-parametric Trend Analysis.* Montreal: McGill University Press, 1965.

Harman, H. H. *Modern Factor Analysis.* Chicago: University of Chicago Press, 1960.

Lundin, R. W. *An Objective Psychology of Music.* New York: Ronald Press, 1967.

Munsinger, H. S., Kessen, W., & Kessen, M. L. Age and uncertainty: developmental variation in preference for variability. *Journal of Experimental Child Psychology*, 1964, 1–15.

Mursell, J. L. *Education for Musical Growth.* Boston: Ginn, 1948.

Osgood, C. E., Suci, G. J., & Tannenbaum, P. H. *The Measurement of Meaning.* Urbana, Ill.: University of Illinois Press, 1957.

Petzeld, P. G. Auditory perception by children. *Journal of Research in Music Education*, 1969, **17(1)**, 82–87.

Piaget, J. *The Origins of Intelligence in Children.* New York: International Universities Press, 1952.

Ross, R. T. Optimum orders for the presentation of pairs in the method of paired comparisons. *Journal of Education Psychology*, 1934, **25**, 375–382.

Taylor, S. Development of children aged 7 to 11. *Journal of Research in Music Education*, 1969, **17(1)**, 100–107.

Thomas, H. References for random shapes. Ages six through nineteen years. *Child Development*, 1966, **37**, 843–859.

Tucker, W. T. Experiments in aesthetic communication. Unpublished Ph.D. thesis, University of Illinois, 1955. Cited in C. E. Osgood, G. J. Suci, & P. H. Tannenbaum, *The Measurement of Meaning.* Urbana, Ill.: University of Illinois Press, 1957. Pp. 68–70.

Vitz, P. C. Affect as a function of stimulus variation. *Journal of Experimental Psychology*, 1966, **71**, 74–79.

4
VERBAL RESPONSES TO VISUAL SEQUENCES VARYING IN UNCERTAINTY LEVEL

L. F. Normore

Aesthetic judgments are apparently influenced by structural characteristics of works of art. One facet of structure is stimulus complexity, a construct bound up with the number of elements that a work of art embodies and the patterning of those elements. If the relation between structure and affect is to be understood, a coherent and comprehensive definition of complexity must be formulated.

Many early studies used experimenter-defined and/or subject-validated criteria to arrange a particular set of stimuli along a complexity dimension. While useful within a single experimental situation, such criteria fail to provide a wide-ranging metric for perceptual experience. The information-theoretic conceptualization of complexity as uncertainty has been thought to provide such a metric. A number of studies have examined the effects of stimuli varying in number of elements and in the interpredictability of their component parts. However, it soon became evident that other factors—organizational tendencies (cf. Snodgrass, 1971) and meaningfulness (cf. Munsinger & Kessen, 1954; Vitz, 1966b)—had to be considered if subjective and objective complexity measures were to be brought into accord.

Vitz (1966a) constructed a series of tone sequences representing different levels of variability or uncertainty. He found orderly relations between objective uncertainty and ratings of variability and of pleasantness. His tone sequences, and others like them, were used in two series of experiments reported in this book (Chaps. 2 and 3), and a greater variety of verbal ratings, as well as measures of exploratory behavior, were found to vary in simple ways with uncertainty level.

Many experiments have used visual displays varying in complexity (e.g., Chaps. 5 and 12, this volume). This chapter reports experiments using dynamic visual patterns, i.e., sequences of visual events. These were designed as visual equivalents of Vitz's tone sequences. The aim was to find out how the informational properties of visual sequences affect some of the dependent variables that have been shown to vary with the uncertainty level of tone sequences. It was of interest to see whether the effects that had already been observed depended on informational properties as such, regardless of the nature of the elements, and how far they would vary with the modality to which the elements belonged.

The first experiment looked at verbal responses to a series of film sequences constructed according to the parameters outlined by Vitz (1966a). The second experiment was a study of correlations among verbal judgments of the same film sequences. The third experiment used both visual and auditory sequences and revealed intermodality differences in the relations between verbal responses and uncertainty.

EXPERIMENT 1

Stimulus Material

Twelve sequences were constructed, two representing each of six uncertainty levels. The sequences were modeled after Vitz's tone sequences, substituting visual counterparts for the parameters he used (see Table 1). Vitz's sequences varied the frequency, loudness and duration of each tone. Here, location along a horizontal line was used as the visual dimension equivalent to auditory frequency—one could think of frequency as tonal location. Brightness was taken as the visual equivalent of loudness. Duration was a variable common to both modalities. The actual duration values were as close as possible to those selected for Vitz's tones, but they diverged from them slightly because of the limitations of working with 24 frames per second.

A sequence consisted of pictures of a dot, appearing in varying locations, at varying brightnesses, for varying lengths of time. There were 40 events per sequence. The range of alternatives over which each of the factors could vary depended upon the uncertainty level represented by that sequence. For example, as can be seen from Table 1, complexity level one consisted of a dot of brightness level three, moving between location 9 and location 10 (or

TABLE 1

Summary of the Information Characteristics of the
Film Sequences

Uncertainty level	Location		Duration		Brightness		Total U(bits)
	Values	U(bits)	Values (msec)	U(bits)	Values	U(bits)	
1	9,10	1.00	500	0.00	3	0.00	1.00
2	8,11 (plus the 2 above)	2.00	417,500	1.00	2,3	1.00	4.00
3	7,12 (plus the 4 above)	2.58	208,417, 500,583	2.00	1,2,3	1.58	6.17
4	6,13 (plus the 6 above)	3.00	83,208 417,500 583,1208	2.58	1,2,3	1.58	7.17
5	4,5 14,15 (plus the 8 above)	3.58	83,208 417,500, 583,1208	2.58	1,2,3,4	2.00	8.17
6	1,2,3 16,17,18 (plus the 12 above)	4.17	42,83, 208,417, 500,583, 1208,1500	3.00	1,2,3,4	2.00	9.17

reappearing at either one of these two locations) for 500 msec. at a time. The
value along each of the three dimensions was randomly and independently
determined for each event.

Stimuli were constructed using single frame photography with a Bolex
H16 reflex camera on to Kodak Plus-X reversal black and white film.

Subjects

There were 24 undergraduate Ss, of whom half were paid and half drawn
from an unpaid subject pool.

Method

Ss were first instructed in the use of a seven-point Osgood rating scale, the
mid-point of which was designated as neutral. They then began to rate the

film sequences, judging all 12 stimuli against a single scale before proceeding to the next scale. All of them completed four rating scales: SIMPLE-COMPLEX, UGLY-BEAUTIFUL, DISPLEASING-PLEASING, and UNINTERESTING-INTERESTING. Two Ss were assigned to each row of a 12 × 12 Latin square, which was used to balance stimulus order. Other experimental procedures corresponded closely to those outlined by Crozier (Chap. 2).

Results

Analyses of variance were performed on subject ratings for the four scales. Three of the scales, SIMPLE-COMPLEX, UNINTERESTING-INTERESTING, and DISPLEASING-PLEASING, showed significant effects of uncertainty level ($F = 132.51$, 47.05, 4.15, $df = 5,242$; $p < .001$, $< .001$, $< .01$). The linear component accounted for most of the variance ($p < .001$ in all cases). Ratings on the DISPLEASING-PLEASING scale showed a significant quadratic component as well ($F = 4.21$, $df = 1,424$, $p < .05$). The curves relating mean ratings to uncertainty level are shown in Figures 1–3, together with the corresponding curves from Crozier's (Chap. 2) data from 12 nonmusic specialists.

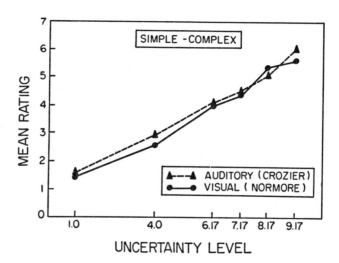

FIG. 1. Mean Complexity ratings for visual sequences in Experiment 1 and for auditory sequences, nonmusic subjects only, in Crozier's Experiment 1 (Chap. 2).

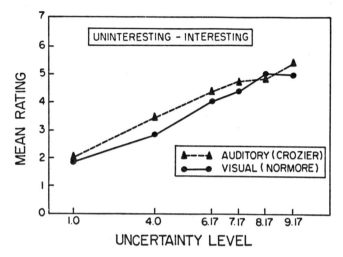

FIG. 2. Mean Interestingness ratings for visual sequences in Experiment 1 and for auditory sequences, nonmusic subjects only, in Crozier's Experiment 1 (Chap. 2).

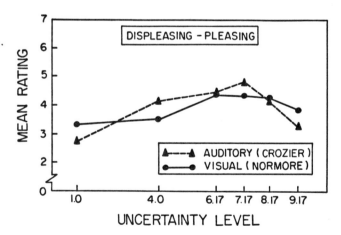

FIG. 3. Mean Pleasingness ratings for visual sequences in Experiment 1 and for auditory sequences, nonmusic subjects only, in Crozier's Experiment 1 (Chap. 2).

EXPERIMENT 2

Subjects

Twelve volunteer Ss were recruited from summer-school psychology classes.

Method

Having been instructed in the use of a seven-point Osgood scale, Ss were shown the 12 film sequences. The sequences were then presented again, Ss rating all scales for each stimulus before proceeding to the next stimulus. Twenty rating scales were used: SIMPLE-COMPLEX, UNINTERESTING-INTERESTING, DISPLEASING-PLEASING, STILL-VIBRANT, PASSIVE-ACTIVE, REPETITIVE-VARIED, AWFUL-NICE, BAD-GOOD, UGLY-BEAUTIFUL, WEAK-STRONG, HUMOROUS-SERIOUS, LIGHT-HEAVY, INARTISTIC-ARTISTIC, NOT RHYTHMICAL-RHYTHMICAL, CHAOTIC-ORDERED, SLOW-FAST, REMOTE-INTIMATE, STALE-FRESH, EMPTY-FULL, and SUPERFICIAL-PROFOUND. Other procedural details follow those of Experiment 1.

Results

Analyses of variance were conducted on each of the 20 scales. Eighteen of these showed significant effects of uncertainty level, the exceptions being LIGHT-HEAVY and REMOTE-INTIMATE. The linear component accounted for most of the variance. Fifteen scales showed increasing functions relating uncertainty to evaluative ratings, NOT RHYTHMICAL-RHYTHMICAL, CHAOTIC-ORDERED, and HUMOROUS-SERIOUS alone manifesting decreasing linear functions. Of the 18 scales showing significant effects of uncertainty, 16 manifested only linear trends. One, CHAOTIC-ORDERED, had a marginal quadratic component $(p < .05)$. HUMOROUS-SERIOUS exhibited a quadratic component that reached the same significance level as the linear $(p < .01)$.

A factor analysis using the FACTOR program was then performed on the uncertainty-level means for the 18 scales that were significantly affected by the independent variable. When instructed to extract all factors whose values exceeded 1.0, the program produced a single factor accounting for 93% of the variance. This should not be surprising, for the intercorrelation matrix (see Table 2) reveals very high correlations among all scales used in this study,

TABLE 2

Experiment 2: Correlations between Scales Included in the Factor Analysis

	AWFUL-NICE	BAD-GOOD	CHAOTIC-ORDERED	DISPLEASING-PLEASING	EMPTY-FULL	HUMOROUS-SERIOUS	INARTISTIC-ARTISTIC	NOT RHYTHMICAL-RHYTHMICAL	PASSIVE-ACTIVE	REPETITIVE-VARIED	SIMPLE-COMPLEX	SLOW-FAST	STALE-FRESH	STILL-VIBRANT	SUPERFICIAL-PROFOUND	UGLY-BEAUTIFUL	UNINTERESTING-INTERESTING	WEAK-STRONG
BAD-GOOD	.95																	
CHAOTIC-ORDERED	-.80	-.93																
DISPLEASING-PLEASING	.95	.97	-.87															
EMPTY-FULL	.91	.98	-.93	.93														
HUMOROUS-SERIOUS	-.85	-.73	.53	-.80	-.59													
INARTISTIC-ARTISTIC	.95	.99	-.94	.95	.98	-.72												
NOT RHYTHMICAL-RHYTHMICAL	-.81	-.91	.99	-.84	-.89	.56	-.93											
PASSIVE-ACTIVE	.91	.98	-.98	.95	.97	-.66	.99	-.96										
REPETITIVE-VARIED	.85	.96	-.99	.92	.95	-.59	.96	-.98	.99									
SIMPLE-COMPLEX	.86	.96	-.99	.92	.94	-.64	.97	-.98	.99	.99								
SLOW-FAST	.86	.95	-.99	.90	.94	-.61	.96	-.99	.99	.95	.99							
STALE-FRESH	.89	.97	-.98	.95	.95	-.67	.97	-.97	.99	.99	.99	.99						
STILL-VIBRANT	.94	.99	-.95	.97	.97	-.71	.99	-.94	.99	.98	.98	.97	.99					
SUPERFICIAL-PROFOUND	.91	.98	-.94	.90	.98	-.63	.99	-.94	.98	.96	.95	.96	.95	.97				
UGLY-BEAUTIFUL	.94	.99	-.89	.98	.95	-.79	.98	-.87	.90	.93	.94	.92	.95	.98	.94			
UNINTERESTING-INTERESTING	.90	.97	-.97	.95	.97	-.63	.97	-.95	.99	.99	.98	.98	.99	.99	.96	.94		
WEAK-STRONG	.82	.95	-.99	.90	.96	-.52	.95	-.96	.98	.99	.98	.98	.98	.97	.96	.91	.98	

$r > .81, p < .05.$
$r > .92, p < .01.$

115

despite the fact that the scales were found to produce three distinct factors when applied to sound sequences (Chap. 2).

EXPERIMENT 3

Subjects

Twelve paid college-educated Ss took part in the third experiment.

Method

All Ss were presented with 12 sequences, 6 of which were tone sequences used by Crozier (Chap. 2) and 6 film sequences, 1 from each uncertainty level in either modality. The aim was to ascertain effects of modality, by comparing responses to visual and auditory sequences of equal uncertainty level.

Three scales were used: SIMPLE-COMPLEX, DISPLEASING-PLEASING, and UNINTERESTING-INTERESTING. (See Figs. 4–6.) Ss were asked to rate each stimulus on all three scales before proceeding to the next stimulus. The method employed was essentially the same as in Experiment 2.

Results

Significant ($p < .001$) effects of uncertainty level were found for all three scales: $F = 53.33$, 5, 110 df, for SIMPLE-COMPLEX, $F = 17.30$ for

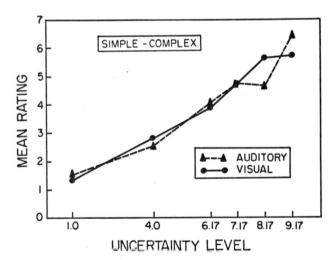

FIG. 4. Mean Complexity ratings for visual and auditory sequences in Experiment 3.

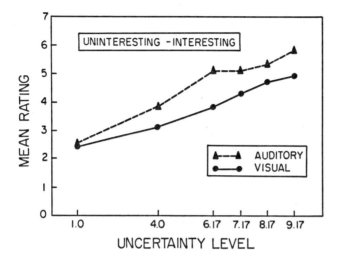

FIG. 5. Mean Interestingness ratings for visual and auditory sequences in Experiment 3.

UNINTERESTING-INTERESTING, $F = 8.86$ for DISPLEASING-PLEASING. Auditory sequences did not differ significantly from visual sequences in rated Complexity. But the auditory sequences were rated significantly more interesting $(F = 7.90, 1, 110 \, df, p < .01)$ and significantly more pleasing $(F = 7.95, p < .01)$. None of the Uncertainty x Auditory/Visual interactions approached significance.

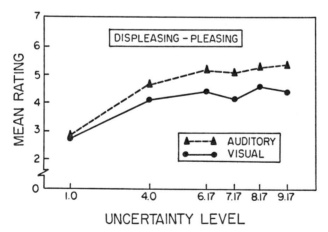

FIG. 6. Mean Pleasingness ratings for visual and auditory sequences in Experiment 3.

DISCUSSION

Experiments 1 and 3 show that subjective Complexity tends to increase monotonically with uncertainty level, the curves being essentially similar for both visual and auditory modalities. Ratings on the UNINTERESTING-INTERESTING scale, which have frequently been found to follow Complexity ratings quite closely, likewise increased monotonically with uncertainty level. In Experiment 3, auditory sequences were rated more interesting than film sequences of the same uncertainty level.

Ratings on the DISPLEASING-PLEASING scale differ, however. Crozier [Chap. 2, see Fig. 2(b)] found curvilinear relations between judged pleasingness and uncertainty, but the ratings of film sequences reveal a rising trend, whose linear component accounts for most of the variance with only a marginal quadratic component and no sign of a significant downturn. In other words, all the ratings of visual sequences that vary significantly with uncertainty level ascend monotonically. Similarly, the analyses from Experiment 2 reveal predominantly ascending linear effects across uncertainty levels for ratings on 17 out of 20 scales and, consequently, high positive correlations between almost all pairs of scales.

There are several possible explanations for these results. First, it may be that hedonic ratings of both tone sequences and film sequences rise and then fall as uncertainty increases. The peak, however, may correspond to a much higher uncertainty level in the visual than in the auditory modality. It may, in fact, occur beyond the range of uncertainty levels used in these experiments, which would explain why only the rising portion of the curve was represented. Since human beings generally receive much more information from visual than from auditory sources, they might well prefer higher levels of uncertainty or information content when the visual sense is stimulated.

Secondly, it may be that, even within a modality, the hedonic effects of variation depend on the dimensions along which variation is found. For example, the tone sequences included variations in pitch, loudness, and duration, which are important factors in music. The film sequences employed variations in position, brightness, and duration, which may be important factors in visual experience but are less important than, say, shape, color, or size. Different dimensions may be differently weighted as determinants of affect and thus give rise to curves of differing shapes when hedonic responses are related to amount of variation. The implication is that these dependent variables do not depend solely on level of stimulus uncertainty but on an interaction between uncertainty and other characteristics of a stimulus pattern.

Finally, inspection of the mean ratings of visual sequences on scales indicative of hedonic tone (e.g., DISPLEASING-PLEASING, UGLY-BEAUTIFUL, AWFUL-NICE, BAD-GOOD) reveals relatively narrow deviation of means around the neutral point (4.0) of each scale. Spontaneous comments of Ss suggested that the film sequences did not elicit strong affective responses. The question, "How can a dot be beautiful?" illustrates the difficulty that some Ss found in assimilating this kind of visual display with their everyday visual experience. The sound sequences, on the other hand, have some degree of resemblance to music, especially some kinds of contemporary avant-garde music. This suggests that evaluative responding may be strongly influenced by S's prior experience of similar stimulus events.

REFERENCES

Munsinger, H., & Kessen, W. Uncertainty, structure, and preference. *Psychological Monographs*, 1964, 78(Whole No. 586).

Snodgrass, J. G. Objective and subjective complexity measures for a new population of patterns. *Perception & Psychophysics*, 1971, 10, 217–224.

Vitz, P. C. Affect as a function of stimulus variation. *Journal of Experimental Psychology*, 1966, 71, 74–79. (a)

Vitz, P. C. Preference for different amounts of visual complexity. *Behavioral Science*, 1966, 11, 105–114. (b)

5

VERBAL AND EXPLORATORY RESPONSES TO VISUAL PATTERNS VARYING IN UNCERTAINTY AND IN REDUNDANCY[1]

D. E. Berlyne

The three last chapters report experiments with auditory and visual stimulus sequences. In these sequences, uncertainty per stimulus element was manipulated by varying the number of alternatives from which each element was selected. The number of elements per sequence was held constant at 40, so that the total uncertainty associated with a sequential pattern as a whole increased as the uncertainty per element increased.

The experiments with which the present chapter is concerned used static visual patterns, in which all the elements were present simultaneously rather than perceived one by one. Responses to two kinds of patterns were investigated. The first kind consisted of matrices, whose total uncertainty was varied in two ways, viz., by varying the number of alternative forms that each element could take and by varying the total number of elements. Consequently, the effects of total uncertainty per pattern and of uncertainty per element could be examined separately. The other kind of material consisted of modified checkerboards, i.e., patterns made up of equal numbers of black and white squares. Here again, two factors affecting total uncertainty per pattern were introduced in such a way that their effects could be separated; while all patterns were equal in area, three different "grains" (i.e., sizes of element

[1] The data for Experiments IA, IB and IC were ably collected and analyzed by Merle Nudelman, as were the data for Experiments IIA, IIB, and IIC by Patricia Hunter and the data for Experiment IID by Mary Louise King.

and therefore total numbers of elements) could be used, and, for each grain, there were six levels of redundancy.

Once again, verbal judgments were solicited as well as nonverbal measures of exploratory behavior. The aims were to see how the information-theoretic independent variables affect verbal judgments and exploratory responses, to see how the verbal judgments are related to one another, and see how the verbal judgments are related to exploratory responses.

I: MATRIX PATTERNS

Stimulus Material

Ten 9-element patterns (3 x 3 matrices) and twelve 36-element patterns (6 x 6 matrices) were constructed. Six levels of uncertainty or variability were contrived. They were made to correspond to the six levels represented by Vitz's (1966, see Chaps. 2, 3, and 4) sound sequences by substituting colors for pitches, shapes for durations, and sizes for loudnesses. Consequently, the number of alternative values of each of the three attributes for the six levels of variability are shown in Table 1, together with the corresponding uncertainty values per element and per total pattern. Sample patterns are represented in Figure 1. The elements were randomly selected with the restriction that all the values of a particular attribute appeared equally often (or as near equally often as possible) in each pattern.

For the 9-element patterns, this restriction made it possible to have only five levels, and, because of the small number of elements, the uncertainty

TABLE 1

Elements	Variability level	Colors	Shapes	Sizes	No. of possible elements	U per element	U per pattern
9	1	2	1	1	2	1.00	9.00
	2	4	2	2	16	4.00	36.00
	3	6	4	3	72	6.17	55.53
	4	8	4	3	96	6.58	59.22
	5	9	8	4	288	8.17	73.53
36	1	2	1	1	2	1.00	36.00
	2	4	2	2	16	4.00	144.00
	3	6	4	3	72	6.17	222.12
	4	8	6	3	144	7.17	258.12
	5	12	6	4	288	8.17	294.12
	6	18	8	4	576	9.17	330.12

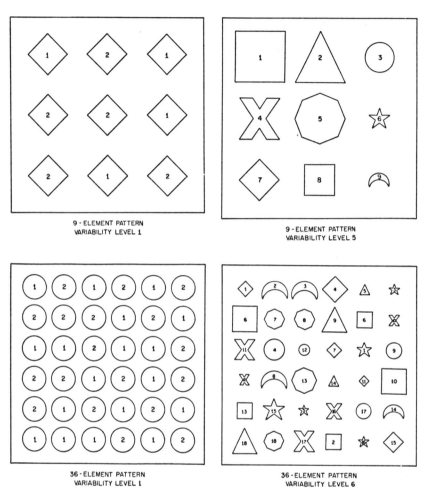

FIG. 1. Examples of matrix patterns used in Experiments IA, IB, and IC. In each pattern, elements bearing the same number were of the same color.

value associated with level four and the distribution of numbers of values among attributes in level five were changed, as compared with the Vitz sound sequences.[2]

[2] Because of the decision to have each of the values of all three attributes represented in at least one element of every pattern, the actual uncertainty value associated with the patterns (more properly, associated with the sample spaces from which the patterns are drawn) will be a little lower than the values given in Table 1. But the latter will serve as approximations. Examples of 9-element and 36-element patterns belonging to the highest and lowest variability levels are depicted in Figure 1.

There were two patterns corresponding to each combination of a number of elements and a variability level.

EXPERIMENT IA: VERBAL SCALING

Subjects

There were 11 male and 13 female Ss, all undergraduates taking psychology courses during the academic year.

Dependent Variables

Every S rated every one of the 22 patterns on 12 scales. The scales comprised the battery used in an earlier experiment (Berlyne, 1973) with a much wider variety of visual patterns, except for two replacements. The scales fall into three classes (see Table 3):

1. Scales descriptive of patterns (Nos. 1-3). These referred to collative properties, which are, as pointed out in Chapter 1, closely related to subjective equivalents of information-theoretic variables. Like all collative variables, the attributes measured through each of these scales must depend on an interaction between the physical properties of a pattern and the state of the S, but the task was presented to the S as one requiring characterization of the pattern. SIMPLE-COMPLEX has been used in many past investigations (see Berlyne, 1971, and earlier chapters of this book) and has been found to reflect information content reliably and sensitively. CLEAR-INDEFINITE was meant to tap something like subjective uncertainty or ease of perceptual organization, while DISORDERLY-ORDERLY was intended to explore the role of "order," which several theorists, notably Birkhoff (1933), have held to be an essential component of aesthetic value. Some writers, e.g., Frank (1959), have suggested that order can be identified with the information-theoretic variable of redundancy, but none of the patterns used in the present experiment possessed any redundancy, since the elements were chosen independently, apart from the restriction requiring all possible values of each attribute to appear in a pattern.

2. Evaluative ratings (Nos. 4-8). Each of these scales required some evaluative or preferential characterization of a pattern. UGLY-BEAUTIFUL, DISPLEASING-PLEASING and DISLIKE-LIKE are self-explanatory. UNINTERESTING-INTERESTING has been used frequently in previous investigations and has usually turned out to be nonmonotonically related to

DISPLEASING-PLEASING and similar scales. WEAK-POWERFUL was used in a previous study (Berlyne, 1973) as a representative of Osgood's (Osgood, Suci, & Tannenbaum, 1957) "potency" factor. There were indications that it may be closely related to cortical arousal.

3. *Scales descriptive of the subject's state* (Nos. 9–12). NO PLEASURE-EXTREME PLEASURE and NO DISCOMFORT-EXTREME DISCOMFORT sound as if they should represent a hedonic dimension viewed from different directions, but previous studies have shown that they are not exact opposites of each other. RELAXED-TENSE seems likely to reflect autonomic arousal, with DROWSY-ALERT reflecting cortical arousal. The positive but limited correlation between the two found in the previous experiment (Berlyne, 1973) corroborates this supposition, in view of the abundant evidence that cortical and autonomic indices of arousal vary together in many conditions but are to some extent independent (Berlyne, 1971).

Every *S* completed all 12 scales while watching one pattern and then pressed a button causing that pattern to be replaced by the next. The time he kept each pattern on the screen was recorded, and this duration, designated "Rating Time," was analyzed as a 13th dependent variable.

The stimulus patterns were projected by a Kodak Carousel Model 550 projector on to a screen standing 2.3 m in front of the subject. The image on the screen measured 42 cm x 65 cm.

S was given a booklet on which to mark his ratings. One page corresponded to each pattern and bore the 12 scales typed in the format introduced by Osgood for his semantic differential. The labels for the scales descriptive of the *S*'s state (Nos. 9–12) were typed in capitals. It was explained to *S* beforehand that capital letters would denote that he was to rate his own reaction and lower case letters that he was to rate the pattern.

After completing the 12 scales with reference to all 22 patterns, the subject was shown the patterns again for 5 seconds each, in the order in which they had appeared the first time, and was asked to indicate on a seven-point scale how much he would like to have a copy of each pattern framed and hanging on his wall at home. This was to follow up some suggestions in previous research (e.g., Berlyne, 1963; Ertel, 1973) that self-exposure to a stimulus pattern that has been present for a relatively long time is determined differently from self-exposure during the first few seconds of confrontation with a pattern (as in experiments on Looking Time or Listening Time), when subjective uncertainty and perceptual curiosity are major factors. It was hoped that this verbal rating would indicate the patterns that Ss would be more inclined to select for prolonged exposure, even though they had merely to imagine their continued presence and were not actually subjected to it. It constituted the 14th dependent variable.

Experimental Design and Procedure

A 22 x 22 Latin square, with columns randomly permuted, was constructed. Every S was allotted one row of this Latin square, which determined the order in which the 22 patterns were presented to him. The 12 scales were arranged in 22 different random orders. One order was assigned to each of the 22 temporal positions in which the patterns could appear.

Results

The 14 dependent variables were first subjected to independent analyses of variance. The F values for the 22 patterns and for the 11 classes of patterns (i.e., 11 pairs corresponding to the five variability levels of 9-element patterns and the six variability levels of the 36-element patterns) are presented in Table 3. Both of these F values are significant, implying significant intersubject agreement, for all variables with the exception of No. 10 (NO DISCOMFORT-EXTREME DISCOMFORT) and No. 12 (DROWSY-ALERT).

The mean score on each of the 12 scales and on Rating Time was calculated for each pattern, and the correlations among these 13 mean scores were computed. They appear in Table 2. These correlations, with the exception of those involving scales 10 and 12, which had not shown significant intersubject consistency, were then subjected to a principal-components factor analysis, with Varimax rotation, using Veldman's (1957) FACTOR Computer Program. The program revealed two factors, accounting together for 76.5 of the variance. The loadings are shown in Table 3. High loadings (defined as loadings with an absolute value of .50 or greater) are printed in bold type. It will be seen that every one of the 10 scales had a high loading on one or the other of the factors but not on both. Rating Time had a high loading on Factor I but not on Factor II.

Since the scales figuring prominently in Factor I consist of all the Evaluative scales and NO PLEASURE-EXTREME PLEASURE, this factor is provisionally labeled "Hedonic Tone." Elsewhere (Berlyne, 1967, 1971), the term "hedonic value" has been proposed to cover both verbal, postural, and facial indications of pleasure, on the one hand, and behavioral indications of reward value, incentive value, and positive feedback, on the other. The term "hedonic tone" is now proposed as a way of covering the variable manifested by verbal expressions of pleasure and the like. Factor II has high loadings for

TABLE 2

Experiment IA: Matrix Patterns
(Correlations)

Variable	1 (S-C)	2 (C-I)	3 (D-O)	4 (U-I)	5 (W-P)	6 (U-B)	7 (D-P)	8 (D-L)	9 (NP-EP)	10 (ND-ED)	11 (R-T)	12 (D-A)	13 (R.T.)
1													
2	.76**												
3	-.76**	-.73**											
4	.61**	.28	-.15										
5	.30	-.17	-.12	.56***									
6	.26	.04	.23	.72***	.44*								
7	.17	-.12	.34	.76***	.44*	.81**							
8	.19	-.10	.36	.77***	.49*	.79*	.92**						
9	.35	.10	.11	.85***	.50*	.85**	.79***	.77**					
10	.16	.27	-.43*	-.07	.04	-.21	-.29	-.31	-.12				
11	.73**	.65**	-.76**	.31	.16	-.04	-.05	-.03	.05	.35			
12	.49*	-.04	-.27	.56**	.83***	.41	.33	.46*	.43*	-.01	.36		
13	.33	.26	-.22	.44*	.24	.46*	.52*	.40	.48*	.26	.39	.27	

*$p < .05$.
**$p < .01$.
***$p < .001$.

TABLE 3
Experiment IA: Matrix Patterns

Variable	F(21,441) for patterns	F(10,441) for classes of patterns	Varimax factor loadings I (Hedonic Tone)	II (Uncertainty/ Arousal)	Correlation with "hanging on wall"	Correlation with Looking Time (Exp. IB)
1. SIMPLE-COMPLEX	13.58****	26.93****	.33	.88	.23	.79**
2. CLEAR-INDEFINITE	3.53****	6.03****	-.01	.86	-.04	.70**
3. DISORDERLY-ORDERLY	8.66****	17.65****	.19	-.93	.39	-.57***
4. UNINTERESTING-INTERESTING	2.59**	3.24**	.88	.33	.65**	.58**
5. WEAK-POWERFUL	3.34****	2.07*	.60	.10	.43	.27
6. UGLY-BEAUTIFUL	1.73*	2.40**	.90	-.05	.81**	.45*
7. DISPLEASING-PLEASING	2.30**	3.59****	.93	-.15	.72**	.36
8. DISLIKE-LIKE	1.96**	1.86*	.92	-.15	.81**	.31
9. NO PLEASURE-EXTREME PLEASURE	1.58*	2.33*	.92	-.07	.72**	.37
10. NO DISCOMFORT-EXTREME DISCOMFORT	1.11	1.56			-.41	.07
11. RELAXED-TENSE	2.21**	3.48****	.06	.88	-.11	.66**
12. DROWSY-ALERT	1.05	1.64			.39	.38
13. Rating Time	1.58*	2.34**	.55	.35	.15	.50*
14. "Hanging on wall"	2.49**	4.01**				.28
			% Variance			
FACTOR I (Hedonic Tone)	3.15****	3.84***	45.1	31.4	.76**	.44*
FACTOR II (Uncertainty/Arousal)	10.89****	22.08**			-.12	.74**

*p < .05.
**p < .01.
=**p < .001.

128

SIMPLE-COMPLEX, CLEAR-INDEFINITE, and DISORDERLY-ORDERLY, which presumably reflect subjective uncertainty, as well as for RELAXED-TENSE. So the factor is labeled "Uncertainty/Arousal." It may, however, reflect autonomic rather than cortical aspects of arousal: WEAK-POWERFUL, which seems to have a connection with cortical arousal (Berlyne, 1973), did not have a high loading on it.

UNINTERESTING-INTERESTING, which has in the past been found more often than not to be closely related to judgments of complexity but not to judgments of hedonic tone, was here highly loaded on the hedonic-tone factor alone. No explanation for this can be offered with any confidence. But it must be noted that, in view of the evidence that measures of pleasingness and, more generally, hedonic tone show nonmonotonic (inverted-U-shaped or multimodal) relations to complexity and that interestingness increases monotonically with complexity, the two kinds of measure can be expected to increase together when material is confined to the lower range of the complexity continuum. It is worth noting, however, that INTERESTING-NESS was quite highly correlated with SIMPLE-COMPLEX (see Table 2) but not with the other two descriptive scales (CLEAR-INDEFINITE and DISORDERLY-ORDERLY).

Rating Time had a fairly high loading on Factor I but not on Factor II. If this variable had depended mainly on the difficulty of taking cognizance of each pattern's properties in order to determine the appropriate ratings, one would have expected the loading on Factor II to have been greater. The finding suggests that how long the subject kept a pattern on the screen depended to some extent on how much he enjoyed seeing it.

An estimated factor score on each of the two factors was then worked out for each subject and each pattern, using the weights supplied by the computer output. The mean estimated factor score for each pattern on each factor was then calculated, and these means, shown in Figure 2, were subjected to analysis of variance. As can be seen from Table 3, the F values for patterns and for classes of patterns were significant beyond the .001 level for both factors, although they were distinctly higher for Factor II.

Planned orthogonal contrasts were then carried out as follows. The five variability levels for 9-element patterns were compared with one another, as were the six variability levels for the 36-element patterns. Linear and quadratic components of the trend were also examined for the 9-element and the 36-element patterns separately. Finally, the effect of number of elements was examined by contrasting the mean estimated factor scores for 36-element patterns and 9-element patterns at the four variability levels that were

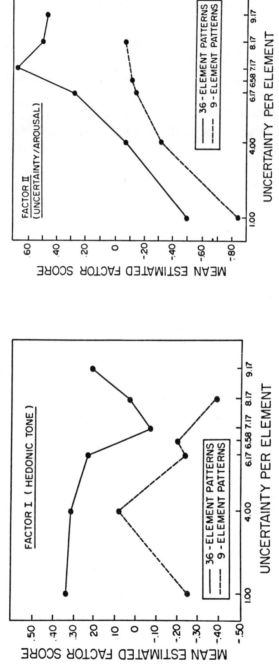

FIG. 2. Curves relating mean estimated factor scores, scores on hanging-on-wall scale, and Looking Time for matrix patterns (Experiments IA and IB) to number of elements and uncertainty per element.

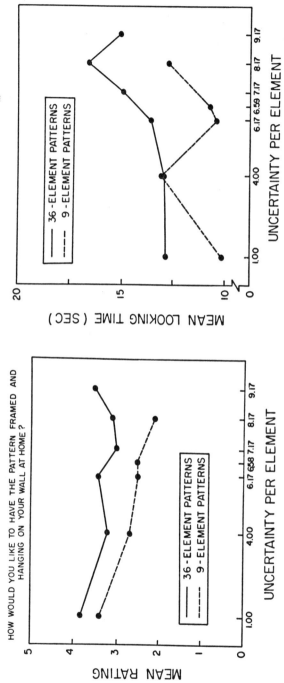

FIG. 2. (*Continued*) Curves relating mean estimated factor scores, scores on hanging-on-wall scale, and Looking Time for matrix patterns (Experiments IA and IB) to number of elements and uncertainty per element.

common to both, namely levels one, two, three, and five. The pertinent F values are shown in Table 4, and, where trend components are significant, the same table shows the percentage of the variance across variability levels that was accounted for by each component.

It will be seen that, as far as Factor I is concerned, the mean scores for 9-element patterns rise to a peak at variability level two and then decline, revealing a trend with a significant quadratic but not linear component. Scores are higher for 36-element patterns than for 9-element patterns having the same uncertainty (U) per element, but there are no significant differences or significant trend among 36-element patterns. Mean scores on Factor II rise, as one would expect, with U per element and with number of elements; there is a significant linear component with both 9-element and 36-element patterns, and 36-element patterns have higher scores than corresponding 9-element patterns. A significant quadratic component with 36-element patterns evidently stems from the flattening out at the highest variability levels. According to Duncan's New Multiple-Range Test, the difference between the mean for level four and level five is not significant, so that we are entitled to conclude only that there is a flattening out rather than a decline from a peak.

It seemed that it might be enlightening to look at the mean estimated factor scores in relation to total U per pattern (estimated simply by multiplying U per element by the number of elements) over the whole range of 11 classes of patterns. The corresponding curves are shown in Figure 3 and, while the relevant overall F values appear in the third column of Table 3, the F values for the linear and quadratic components of the trend, as well as for the deviation from quadratic trend, are shown on the right hand side of Table 4. There are only 10 points on each of the curves in Figure 2, because variability at level two of the 9-element patterns and level one of the 36-element patterns had the same total U. The trend analysis, however, was carried out over the 11 pairs of patterns.

Scores on both factors show a significant increasing linear component, and there is also a significant quadratic component for Factor II. Deviations from the quadratic trend are significant in both cases but account for 82% of the variance across levels for Factor I but only 12% of the variance for Factor II. The results are compatible with the view that the trend for hedonic tone is predominantly multimodal, which tallies with the results of several previous investigations relating judgments of pleasingness and the like to complexity (e.g., Munsinger & Kessen, 1964; Day, 1965, 1968). The results of Factor II agree, on the other hand, with those of numerous experiments showing

TABLE 4
Experiments IA and IB

Experiment	Variable	U per element										9 vs. 36 Elements (Levels 1,2,3,5)	U per pattern				
		9-Element patterns					36-Element patterns						All patterns				
		Linear	%	Quadratic	%	Overall	Linear	%	Quadratic	%	Overall	L	Linear	%	Quadratic	%	Deviation
		F(1,441)	%	F(1,441)	%	F(4,441)	F(1,441)	%	F(1,441)	%	F(4,441)	F(1,441)	F(1,441)	%	F(1,441)	%	F(8,441)
IA	Factor I (Hedonic Tone)	1.38		4.5*	76.0	1.48	3.01		0.18		1.51	22.01***	6.44*	16.8	0.49		3.93***
	Factor II (Uncertainty/Arousal)	48.27***	95.9	1.05		12.56***	87.76***	87.5	3.98*	9.4	20.00***	27.45***	176.58***	80.0	13.78***		3.80***
	Hanging on wall	12.85***	93.9	0.04		3.42*	2.58		2.07		1.36	14.95***	3.18		3.15		3.36***
IB	Looking Time	0.30		0.20		1.20	5.90*	66.8	0.36		1.77	9.93***	24.84***	71.9	0.04		4.22**

*p < .05.
**p < .01.
***p < .001.

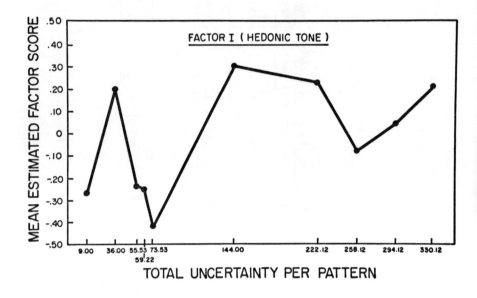

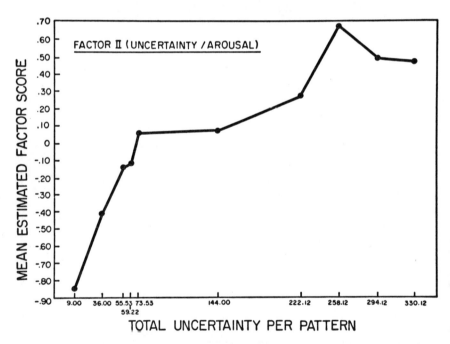

FIG. 3. Curves relating mean estimated factor scores, scores on hanging-on-wall scale, and Looking Time for matrix patterns (Experiments IA and IB) to total uncertainty per pattern.

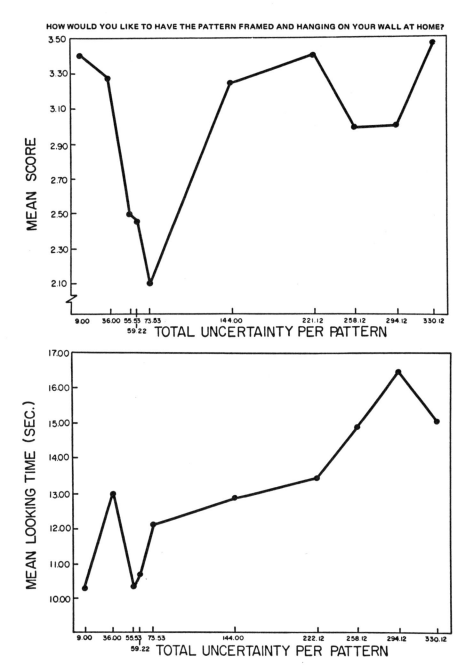

FIG. 3.(*Continued*) Curves relating mean estimated factor scores, scores on hanging-on-wall scale, and Looking Time for matrix patterns (Experiments IA and IB) to total uncertainty per pattern.

measures of subjective complexity and of arousal to increase with objective complexity and with information content.

The data generated by the second part of the experiment, in which subjects were asked how much they would like to have each pattern framed and hanging on the wall, received the same statistical treatments (see Figs. 2 and 3, Tables 3 and 4). Mean scores differed significantly over all 22 patterns and over the 11 classes of patterns. The 36-element patterns received higher mean ratings than corresponding 9-element patterns, and there was a decreasing linear trend over the variability levels of the 9-element patterns but no significant differences among the 36-element patterns. A significant linear, but not quadratic, component, with a significant deviation from quadratic trend, was apparent when the means were plotted against total U per pattern (Fig. 3 and Table 4).

As Table 3 shows, there was a fairly high and significant correlation between ratings on this question and mean estimated scores on Factor I, but the correlation for Factor II was negligible. The hanging-on-the-wall ratings were, in fact, significantly correlated with all the scales that had high loadings on Factor I, apart from WEAK-POWERFUL and Rating Time. If, as was hoped, ratings in response to this question show how strongly subjects are inclined to seek prolonged exposure to patterns, once the curiosity produced by their initial impact has been largely eliminated, there is some confirmation for the hypothesis that hedonic tone governs attraction to stimuli when uncertainty and curiosity are no longer dominant factors.

EXPERIMENT IB: LOOKING TIME

A second experiment, carried out with other subjects taken from the same population, used the same stimulus material to study Looking Time.

Subjects

There were 6 males and 16 females.

Procedure

Every S saw the 22 patterns in a different order, viz., one of the orders used in Experiment IA. A pretense of psychophysiological recording was used to disguise the purpose of the experiment. A GSR electrode was attached to the S's left hand, and he was told that physiological processes would be registered while he was looking at some patterns.

The remote-control button that came with the projector was placed in his right hand. He was instructed to look at each pattern for as long as he liked and then press the button to replace it with the next pattern. The time each pattern was left on the screen was recorded with a Rustrak recorder in the adjoining room.

Results

The mean Looking Times are displayed in Figures 2 and 3. Analysis of variance shows that the mean differs significantly over the 22 patterns—$F(21,441) = 1.66$, $p < .05$—and over the 11 classes of patterns—$F(10,441) = 3.32$, $p < .001$. As Table 4 shows, 36 elements were inspected significantly longer than their 9-element equivalents, and with the 36-element patterns, there was a significant rising linear component. Plotted against total U per pattern, the linear component and the deviation from quadratic trend are significant.

The correlations between mean Looking Time and the variables studied in Experiment IA are shown in Table 3. There is a substantial correlation with mean estimated factor scores on Factor II, agreeing with much previous research showing Looking Time and Listening Time to rise monotonically as complexity, information content, and factors conducive to arousal increase. There is, however, also a significant but lower correlation with scores on Factor I, suggesting that Looking Time is influenced by hedonic tone when the effects of complexity and cognate variables are held constant. It must be remembered, however, that the UNINTERESTING-INTERESTING scale, which has invariably turned out to be closely related to Looking Time, had a high loading in this experiment on Factor I but not on Factor II. Looking Time was, in fact, significantly correlated with this scale and with UGLY-BEAUTIFUL but not with the other scales that were highly loaded on Factor I. The partial correlation between Looking Time and Factor I, with the correlation of either with UNINTERESTING-INTERESTING scores removed, comes to .18, which is not significant.

The nonsignificant correlation between Looking Time and hanging-on-the-wall scores, coupled with the significant correlation of this latter variable with Factor I but not Factor II, adds still more weight to the hypothesis that Looking Time, when a pattern is first encountered, depends on different factors from self-exposure after curiosity has been largely allayed. There is, however, a moderate but significant correlation between Looking Time and Rating Time while completing the scales. One would not expect the time a pattern is kept on the screen under the two conditions to be very similar. But, as mentioned above, the significant correlation of Rating Time with Factor I scores suggests that the difficulty of recording judgments on the scales was not the sole determinant of Rating Time, and it turns out (see Table 2) that Rating Time, like Looking Time, was significantly correlated with UNINTERESTING-INTERESTING and with UGLY-BEAUTIFUL.

EXPERIMENT IC: EXPLORATORY CHOICE

The final experiment using the matrix patterns studied effects of number of elements and of U per element on Exploratory Choice. On each trial, the subject was shown two patterns and then required to choose one of the two to be presented to him again. In previous experiments (see Berlyne, 1971, Chap. 13) with visual material, Exploratory Choice has shown itself to be influenced by collative or information-theoretic variables but in a different way from Exploration Time. In Crozier's (Chap. 2) experiments with sound sequences, the curves relating mean Listening Time and Exploratory Choice to U were rather similar. However, experiments reported in Chapter 3 indicate a monotonic rising curve for the former and a nonmonotonic curve for the latter.

Subjects

There were 20 male and 20 female Ss, all taking undergraduate psychology courses during the summer session.

Experimental Design

Each S went through 30 trials as follows: (a) 15 trials pairing every one of the six variability levels of the 36-element patterns with every other, (b) 10 trials pairing every one of the five variability levels of the 9-element patterns with every other, and (c) 5 trials pairing a 36-element pattern with a 9-element pattern at each of the variability levels from one to five.

It will be recalled that, in Experiments IA and IB, there were two patterns representing each variability level with each number of elements. One member of each pair was allotted to half of the Ss in the present experiment. Half of the Ss in each of these two groups had the less complex pattern on the left on odd-numbered trials and on the right on even-numbered trials, while the remaining Ss had the opposite arrangement. There were equal numbers of males and females in each of the four subgroups formed in this way.

The 30 trials were arranged in 20 randomized orders, each assigned to one S. The inversions of these orders were used for the remaining Ss.

Procedure

On each trial, two cards bearing the appropriate patterns were placed face downwards on a table in front of S for 5 seconds. The E then turned the cards over and S had to point to the one chosen for further viewing. This card was then turned face upward for 5 seconds, after which the two cards were removed and the next trial was started.

After the 30 trials had been completed, all except the first eight Ss saw the patterns again twice. A different randomized order was used for each S, but the same order was used twice in succession. Sixteen of the Ss rated the patterns on a seven-point DISPLEASING-PLEASING scale the first time round and then on an UNINTERESTING-INTERESTING scale. The remaining 16 Ss filled in the scales in the opposite order.

Results

Since all patterns participated in an equal number of choices and thus had an equal number of opportunities to be chosen, the numbers of choices of the different U levels for 9-element patterns when paired with one another, for the different U levels for 36-element patterns when paired with one another, and for the 9-element and 36-element patterns of corresponding variability levels when paired with each other, were analyzed. The first two distributions were subjected to Friedman's nonparametric analysis of variance and to Ferguson's (1965) nonparametric trend analysis. The tests revealed no significant differences among U levels or monotonic or bitonic trends. On the other hand, a 36-element pattern was significantly more likely to be chosen when paired with a 9-element pattern of the same variability level; on the average, Ss chose 36-element patterns 3.0 times out of five trials, $t = 2.28$, $df = 39$, $p < .05$.

For each S, the number of times he had chosen the pattern of a pair that he later rated more interesting was calculated, as was the number of times that he had chosen the less interesting pattern. Trials with patterns that later received identical ratings for interestingness were disregarded. Choices of more interesting patterns exceed choices of less interesting patterns by 3.3 on the average: $t = 3.26$, $df = 39$, $p < .001$. The corresponding analysis was used to ascertain whether subjects tended to choose more often the patterns that they later rated more pleasing. The mean difference score this time was 4.0: $t = 3.88$, $df = 39$, $p < .001$.

It will be remembered that, in Experiment IA, the correlation over patterns between pleasingness and interestingness ratings came to +.76. In

Experiment IC, the corresponding correlation is equal to +.47 ($p < .05$). One more analysis was performed to determine whether subjects tended to choose the more or less complex member of a pair, the more complex pattern being either the one with more elements or the one with more U per element. The mean difference came to 1.3 in favor of the less complex patterns, which was far from significant, confirming the lack of a consistent effect of complexity over all subjects.

II. SMETS PATTERNS

The patterns used in the experiments to be reported next incorporated independent variations in number of elements and in redundancy (R). The special role that R, among all the factors that can affect U, is likely to play in aesthetic appreciation was discussed in Chapter 1. It was pointed out there that redundancy can be identified with degree of "structure," "order," or "organization," which can be discovered or generated gradually through perceptual and intellectual effort.

Stimulus Material

A collection of 216 patterns was kindly supplied by Dr. G. Smets of the University of Leuven, Belgium, who had constructed them and used them in some experiments of her own (Smets, 1973). Every pattern consisted of a square array of equally numerous, or as nearly as possibly equally numerous, black and white squares. They were, in other words, checkerboard patterns with rearranged elements. Such patterns have also been used by other experimenters concerned with motivational effects (Berlyne, 1958; Dorfman & McKenna, 1966; Karmel, 1969; Nicki, 1972).

Thirty-six patterns had each of three numbers of elements or grains: 64 (8 x 8), 225 (15 x 15) and 900 (30 x 30) (Fig. 4). If every element had been black or white with equal probability, regardless of the colors of other elements, i.e., if there had been sampling with replacement, the maximum-uncertainty (U_{max}) values associated with the three grains would have been 64, 225, and 900 bits, respectively. However, the requirement that black and white elements should be equally numerous reduced the U_{max} values to 60.63, 220.63, and 894.25 bits, respectively.

At each grain six patterns represented each of six R levels, designated as percentages of U_{max}. Patterns in which the black elements were distributed randomly among all possible positions were associated with 0% R. Patterns representing the other R levels were tested by Dr. Smets as follows.

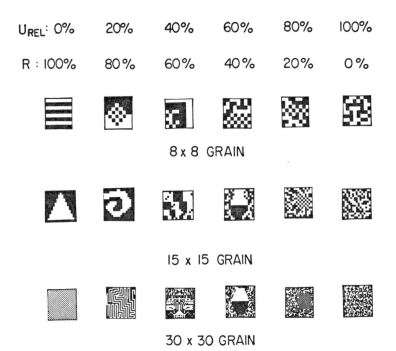

U_{REL}: 0%   20%   40%   60%   80%   100%

R : 100%   80%   60%   40%   20%   0%

8 x 8 GRAIN

15 x 15 GRAIN

30 x 30 GRAIN

FIG. 4. Examples of Smets patterns used in Experiments IIA, IIB, IIC, and IID. (*From Smets, 1973 by kind permission of the author.*)

The pattern was presented to each of seven Ss for 2 seconds. After it was withdrawn, S was required to reproduce the pattern, column by column and square by square (starting from the top left-hand corner), by inserting black and white blocks into compartments on a rack. Whenever he located a black or white element correctly, it was left in place. If he located one incorrectly, his error was corrected but noted. In this way, sets of six patterns were identified that produced, on the average, 0%–2%, 8%–12%, 18%–22%, 28%–32%, and 38%–42% errors, respectively. It was assumed that the number of blocks placed correctly by guesswork equaled the number placed incorrectly. Consequently, the sets of six patterns per grain, were identified, respectively, with R levels of 100%, 80%, 60%, 40%, and 20%. Alternatively, since relative uncertainty (U_{rel}), expressed as a percentage of U_{max}, is equal to 100-R, the six sets of patterns per grain were associated with 0%, 20%, 40%, 60%, 80%, and 100% U_{rel}, the last-named being the completely randomized set.

The six patterns associated with a particular grain and a particular R level were designated A, B, C, D, E, and F. Sample patterns are shown in Figure 4.

EXPERIMENT IIA: VERBAL SCALES

Subjects

There were 5 male and 13 female undergraduates enrolled in an introductory psychology course.

Procedure

Every S saw 36 patterns, representing every combination of a grain and an R level, projected on the screen and rated each on the same 12 scales as were used in Experiment IA. Apart from the stimulus material, the procedure and other conditions were the same as in that experiment. Rating Time was recorded, and S was shown the patterns he had seen again at the end of the session, with instructions to rate on a seven-point scale how much he would like to have each framed and hanging on the wall at home.

Experimental Design

A 12 x 12 counterbalanced Latin Square determined the orders of the scales for the first 12 patterns seen. The 12 orders were randomly redistributed among the next 12 patterns and then again among the last 12 patterns.

An 18 x 18 counterbalanced Latin Square was constructed in order to determine which patterns each S saw and in what sequence. Each of the six sets of patterns, A–F, was associated with three rows of the Latin Square. Every S went through a sequence of 36 patterns corresponding to two rows of the Latin Square, such that every pattern was seen by one of three Ss in the first half of the sequence and by three other Ss in the second half of the sequence. Consequently, when mean scores for grains and R levels are discussed below, they are based on all six sets of patterns appearing equally often over the 18 Ss.

Results

Analysis of variance (see Table 6) revealed significant differences among the means for the 18 classes of patterns (six R levels at each of three grains) of all variables except UGLY-BEAUTIFUL, NO DISCOMFORT-EXTREME DISCOMFORT and Rating Time. A principal-components factor analysis

TABLE 5
Experiment IIA: Smets Patterns
(Correlations)

Variable	1 (S-C)	2 (C-I)	3 (D-O)	4 (U-I)	5 (W-P)	6 (U-B)	7 (D-P)	8 (D-L)	9 (NP-EP)	10 (ND-ED)	11 (R-T)	12 (D-A)	13 (R.T.)
1													
2	.89**												
3	-.80***	-.93**											
4	.84***	.64**	-.54*										
5	.28	-.03	.16	.64**									
6	.75***	.47*	-.31	.89**	.65**								
7	.61**	.29	-.54*	.81**	.72**	.87**							
8	.76***	.49*	-.36	.92**	.68**	.86**	.90**						
9	.64**	.34	-.18	.84**	.75**	.90**	.94**	.91**					
10	.58*	.66**	-.62**	.40	-.08	.24	.08	.27	.06				
11	.64*	.61**	-.58*	.78**	.50*	.53*	.56*	.68**	.60**	.38			
12	.54*	.36	-.24	.81**	.70**	.65**	.74**	.76**	.74**	.03	.81**		
13	.68**	.71**	-.73**	.53*	-.12	.41	.27	.42	.24	.47*	.46	.36	

$*p < .05.$
$**p < .01.$
$***p < .001.$

with Varimax rotation was then carried out on the correlations among the 10 variables that remained after these three had been eliminated. The intercorrelations among all 13 variables are shown in Table 5 and the factor loadings in Table 6. The factor structure is very similar to that derived from Experiment IA with matrix patterns (see Table 1). All the scales that figured in both analyses had high loadings on the same factors in both cases, although, in Experiment IIA, UNINTERESTING-INTERESTING had a high loading on Factor II as well as on Factor I and RELAXED-TENSE on Factor I as well as on Factor II. The resulting factors can therefore be identified safely enough with those of Experiment IA and assigned the same provisional labels.

The mean estimated factor scores were then calculated and subjected to analysis of variance, including trend analysis (see Table 7 and Fig. 5). It will be seen that scores on both factors tend to rise with number of elements per pattern. But the predominant effects of R on the two factors are opposite. Scores on Factor II (Uncertainty/Arousal) increase, not surprisingly, as U_{rel} increases. But there is a tendency for scores on Factor I (Hedonic Tone) to vary inversely with U_{rel} or, in other words, to increase with R. The three curves in Figure 5 all reach a peak when $U_{rel} = 20\%$ and $R = 80\%$. This suggests that the trend may actually be nonmonotonic. According to Duncan's New Multiple-Range Test, however, the rise from 0% to 20% U_{rel} is not significant for any of the three curves separately or for the means taken over the three grains. So, the results justify only the conclusion that the mean factor score tends to decrease as U_{rel} increases but not the conclusion that there is an initial increase before the decrease, although there is a possibility that this may be the case.

The scores on the hanging-on-the-wall scale were subjected to similar analyses (see Table 7 and Fig. 5). Once again, the mean score is higher the greater the number of elements, and, with regard to the effects of redundancy, the quadratic, but not the linear, component of the trend is significant, suggesting a nonmonotonic relation. Correlations between mean ratings on this scale and the other 13 variables, as well as the mean factor scores, are presented in Table 6. All the correlations with individual scales that were significant in Experiment IA turned out to be significant in Experiment IIA also, but, this time, some additional correlations reached significance also. Whereas in Experiment IA, the correlation with Factor I was significant but not the correlation with Factor II, there were significant correlations with both factors in this experiment. This presumably reflected mainly the fact that both scores on the hanging-on-the-wall scale and scores on Factor II increased with the number of elements.

TABLE 6

Experiment IIA: Smets Patterns

Variable	F(17,289) for classes of patterns	Varimax factor loadings		Correlation with "hanging on wall"	Correlation with Looking Time (Exp. IIB)
		I (Hedonic Tone)	II (Uncertainty/Arousal)		
1. SIMPLE-COMPLEX	30.43***	.48	.84	.68**	.79**
2. CLEAR-INDEFINITE	10.37***	.15	.97	.55*	.73**
3. DISORDERLY-ORDERLY	14.45***	.01	-.98	-.44	-.63**
4. UNINTERESTING-INTERESTING	4.42***	.80	.55	.79**	.79**
5. WEAK-POWERFUL	2.21*	.90	-.18	.51*	.40
6. UGLY-BEAUTIFUL	1.53			.75*	.68**
7. DISPLEASING-PLEASING	1.87*	.92	.15	.77**	.56*
8. DISLIKE-LIKE	2.21*	.88	.38	.80**	.66**
9. NO PLEASURE-EXTREME PLEASURE	2.72**	.93	.19	.82**	.64**
10. NO DISCOMFORT-EXTREME DISCOMFORT	0.43			.17	.27
11. RELAXED-TENSE	1.92*	.62	.58	.62**	.63**
12. DROWSY-ALERT	2.38**	.84	-.26	.68**	.59*
13. Rating Time	.05			.42	.32
14. "Hanging on wall"	3.06***				.78**
		% Variance			
FACTOR I (Hedonic Tone)		35.4		.62*	.41
FACTOR II (Uncertainty/Arousal)		52.8		.52*	.70**

*p < .05.
**p < .01.
***p < .001.

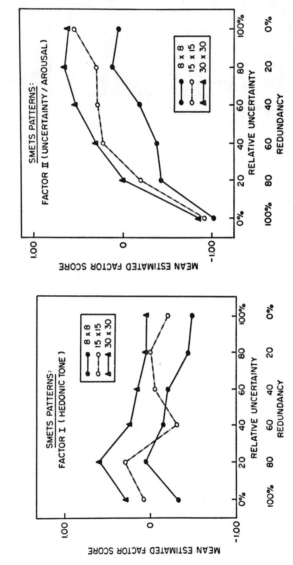

FIG. 5. Curves relating mean estimated factor scores, scores on hanging-on-wall scale, and Looking Time for Smets patterns (Experiments IIA and IIB) to Redundancy (R) or Relative Uncertainty (U_{rel}) for different grains.

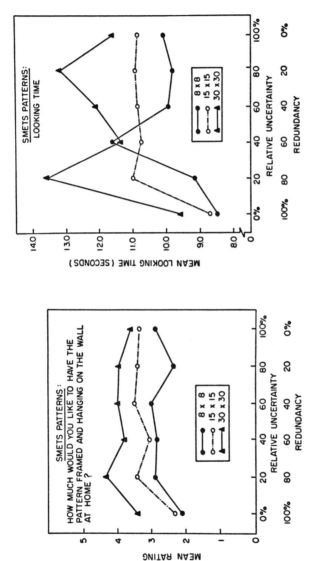

FIG. 5. (*Continued*) Curves relating mean estimated factor scores, scores on hanging-on-wall scale, and Looking Time for Smets patterns (Experiments IIA and IIB) to Redundancy (*R*) or Relative Uncertainty (U_{rel}) for different grains.

TABLE 7
Experiments IIA and IIB

Experiment	Variable	Grain (U_{max}) $F_{(2,34)}$	Redundancy (U_{rel})						Grain × Redundancy					
			L		Q		Overall		L		Q		Overall	
			$F_{(1,85)}$	%	$F_{(1,85)}$	%	$F_{(5,85)}$		$F_{(1,170)}$	%	$F_{(1,170)}$	%	$F_{(10,170)}$	
IIA	Factor I (Hedonic Tone)	5.98**	7.63**	60.0	0.37		2.54*		1.11		0.34		1.28	
	Factor II (Uncertainty/ Arousal)	28.62***	198.14***	81.7	39.38***	16.2	48.48***		3.62		9.15**	43.8	2.09*	
	Hanging on wall	6.26**	1.93		4.08*	26.6	3.07*		4.06*	45.6	0.34		0.89	
IIB	Looking Time	8.87***	7.99**	20.3	15.13***	38.4	7.88***		0.03		0.41		2.33*	

L = Linear Component.
Q = Quadratic Component.
*$p < .05$.
**$p < .01$.
***$p < .001$.

In her experiments, Smets (1973) used duration of EEG desyn-chronization as a measure of the extent to which arousal was raised by the 15×15 and 30×30 patterns. The resulting curves generally rose as U_{rel} increased and, in this respect, resembled our curves for the Uncertainty/ Arousal factor, although they reached maxima at 80% U_{rel}. She also used a Q-sort technique to obtain judgments of "pleasantness." This technique produced peaks of judged pleasantness in the middle range of U_{rel} for the 15×15 and 30×30 grains, but the curve for the 8×8 grain was low at 0% U_{rel} and level from 20% to 100% U_{rel}. These findings do not accord very well with our own findings regarding the Hedonic Tone factor. Whether the discrepancies are due to differences between experimental procedures or between subject populations is impossible to tell.

EXPERIMENT IIB: LOOKING TIME

Subjects

There were 3 male and 15 female undergraduates.

Procedure and Experimental Design

The procedure was the same as in Experiment IB.

Every S saw 54 patterns, 3 belonging to each combination of a grain and an R level, in a different order. He went through three rows of an 18×18 counterbalanced Latin Square in succession, associated with three different sets (A, B, and C or D, E, and F) of patterns. Consequently, every pattern was seen by equal numbers of Ss in the first, second, and third thirds of the sequence and in every temporal position within each third of the sequence.

Results

The means and results of analysis of variance are shown in Figure 5 and Table 7. Since the grain $\times R$ interaction was not significant, the means for the six R levels over all three grains are shown in Figure 6. Duncan's New Multiple-Range Test applied to the means of this last curve shows a significant difference between the 0% U_{rel} mean and the 20% U_{rel} mean and no other significant differences. The principal outcome of the experiment would therefore appear to be that Ss look longer at patterns possessing some relative uncertainty than patterns approximating 0% U_{rel} (100% R).

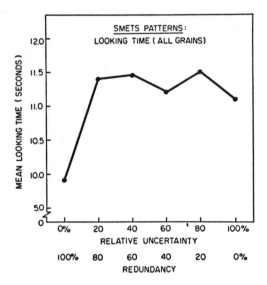

FIG. 6. Curve relating Looking Time for Smets patterns (Experiment IIB) to R (or U_{rel}) over all grains.

Correlations between Looking Time in Experiment IIB and the variables of Experiment IIA are shown in Table 6. A comparison with Table 3 shows that six variables were significantly correlated with Looking Time in both experiments and two variables in neither. There are, however, a few variables that have significant correlations in one experiment but not in the other. In contrast with Experiment IA, there is a fairly high and significant correlation between the hanging-on-the-wall scores and Looking Time, which may once again reflect principally the common effect of grain on both variables. Looking Time possesses a substantial correlation with scores on Factor II in both experiments. The correlation with scores on Factor I falls a little short of significance in Experiment IIB, but a little above the threshold of significance in Experiment IB.

EXPERIMENT IIC: EXPLORATORY CHOICE

Subjects

There were 6 male and 12 female undergraduates taking an introductory psychology course.

Procedure and Experimental Design

The procedure was the same as in Experiment IIC, except that each S went through 63 pairs of patterns. All the patterns belonged to one of the six sets, A-F, which were used for three Ss each. Of the 63 pairs, 45 consisted of the 15 possible pairs of R levels within each of the three grains. The remaining 18 pairs consisted of all possible pairs of grains within each R level.

Eighteen random permutations of the 63 pairs ensured that every S went through the pairs in a different order. Half the Ss had the more complex pattern (i.e., the one with the larger number of elements or the higher U_{rel}) on the left on odd-numbered trials and on the right on even-numbered trials, while this arrangement was reversed for the remaining Ss.

Results

Data for trials on which Ss chose between patterns of differing R levels at the same grain are shown in Figure 7. Friedman nonparametric analyses of variance show that the probabilities of being chosen differ significantly from R level to R level at the 8 x 8 grain ($\chi_r 2 = 14.24, p < .05$) and at the 15 x 15

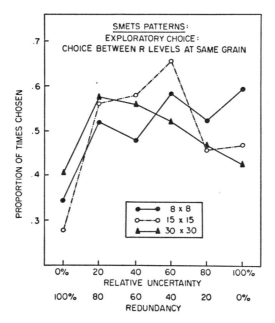

FIG. 7. Curves relating Exploratory Choice to R (or U_{rel}) at same grain.

grain ($\chi_r 2 = 29.95$, $p < .01$), but not at the 30 x 30 grain or over all three grains. Ferguson's (1965) nonparametric trend analysis shows a significant rising monotonic trend ($z = 2.63$, $p < .01$) at the 8 x 8 grain and a significant bitonic trend ($z = 3.35$, $p < .01$) at the 15 x 15 grain. Neither the monotonic nor the bitonic component of the trend was significant at the 30 x 30 grain, but the bitonic component was significant over all grains ($z = 2.20$, $p < .05$).

It will be seen that the R level corresponding to the highest point of the curve increases with grain. The reliability of this difference was tested by identifying for each S his most frequently chosen R level at each grain (taking the mean when there were two chosen equally often) and performing a Friedman test. The difference did not, however, reach significance.

Figure 8 shows the frequency with which each grain was chosen when it was paired with another grain at the same R level. According to the Friedman test, the means differed significantly from grain to grain when U_{rel} was 0% ($\chi_r 2 = 19.31$, $p < .01$), 20% ($\chi_r 2 = 7.50$, $p < .05$), 40% ($\chi_r 2 = 8.90$, $p < .01$), and 60% ($\chi_r 2 = 7.10$, $p < .05$), but not when it was 80% or 100%. $\chi_r 2$ was also significant over all levels: $\chi_r 2 = 10.33$, $p < .01$, the overall probabilities of choice being .32, .50, and .68 for the 8 x 8, 15 x 15, and 30 x 30 grains,

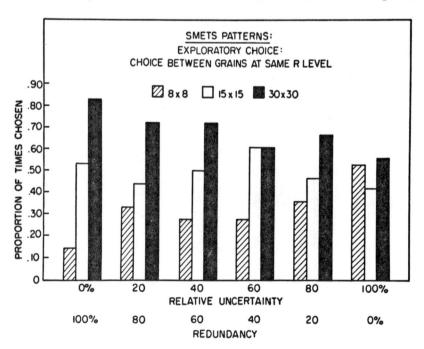

FIG. 8. Bar graphs relating Exploratory Choice to grain at same R level.

respectively. It will be seen from the bar graphs in Figure 8 that the probability of choosing the 8 x 8 grain tends to increase as U_{rel} increases, while the probability of choosing the 30 x 30 grain decreases. The reliability of these trends was confirmed by Ferguson's test: $z = 3.17$, $p < .01$ for the 8 x 8 grain and $z = 2.60$, $p < .01$ for the 30 x 30 grain. No significant trend appears at the 15 x 15 grain.

All in all, therefore, it would seem that Ss tend to choose patterns with many elements when there is a great deal of redundancy and patterns with relatively fewer elements when there is little redundancy. Similarly the results for choices between R levels suggest that the middle range of R levels attracts most choices. There is some suggestion, therefore, of a predilection for intermediate levels of U per pattern.

EXPERIMENT IID: REWARD VALUE

The final experiment sought to relate reward value to verbal judgments using the technique introduced by Berlyne (1972) and derived from a pigeon experiment by Catania (1963), measuring rates of responding on two keys producing different consequences according to concurrent variable-interval schedules. As argued in the cited article and in Chapter 1, rates of responding can be taken to reflect the relative reward value of the consequences, uncontaminated with the transient motivational and cue effects that can be confused with reward value when other commonly applied techniques are used.

Subjects

There were 18 male and 16 female undergraduates enrolled in an introductory psychology course.

Stimulus Material and Experimental Design

Three pairs of patterns were used for each S, one pair belonging to each of the three grains. One member of each pair represented the 0% R (100% U_{rel}) level and the other the 80% R (20% U_{rel}) level. It will be remembered (see Fig. 5) that these R levels were associated with, respectively, the highest and the lowest mean scores on Factor I (Hedonic Tone) but with a low mean score and the highest mean score on Factor II (Uncertainty/Arousal).

The three grains were assigned to the three phrases of the key-pressing part of the experiment, in the six possible orders for equal numbers of Ss. Half of the Ss in each of the six subgroups formed in this way had one set of six patterns, whereas a different set of six was used for the other half, so that 12 patterns from the collection were used altogether.

Two of the *S*s in each subgroup, one assigned to each of the two sets of patterns, had the pattern with the greater U_{rel} on the left, the right, and the left in successive phases, and the order was reversed for the remaining two *S*s.

Procedure

The procedure for the first and main part of the experiment was modeled on that used previously (Berlyne, 1972).

S sat in front of a 61 x 91 cm black plywood board, placed on a table top and bearing two telegraph keys mounted 25 cm apart. A screen was placed in front of the table, 120 cm from *S*. An adjoining room contained the scheduling and recording equipment and a three-channel Polymetric Tachisto-Projector, Model V-1459-3, which projected on to the screen through a window. The size of an image on the screen was 56 x 38 cm. A Gerbrands Model 2A tape puller maintained the VI schedules. *S* went through three consecutive phases, lasting 10 minutes each, for which different pairs of patterns were used.

To disguise the purpose of the experiment, a GSR electrode was attached to *S*'s left hand, and he was told that "physiological responses to some visual stimuli" were going to be measured. He was then given the following instructions:

> There are two telegraph keys in front of you. If you press the left key, some but not all of your key presses will produce a slide; this will always be the same slide. The same is true of the right key; if you press it, some but not all of your key presses will produce a slide, which will always be the same one. There are two slides involved, one of which is only on the left key, and the other only on the right. Your task is to press the keys whenever you wish, in any order you wish, and as often as you wish, as long as you do not press both keys at once. As soon as a slide appears, please stop pressing the keys, and look at the slide. When the slide disappears you may start pressing the keys again.
>
> There will be three sections to the experiment. During section one, the same two slides will be appearing, one on the left key and one on the right. The slides will be changed before section two and again before section three. The signal for you to start pressing the keys will be a single buzzer. At the end of a section I'll press the buzzer twice as a signal for you to stop, then once more when it is time to start again.

There was a 1-minute pause between phases to enable the slide magazine to be changed and the apparatus to be reset. A buzzer sound signified the start of a phase, and two buzzer sounds the end.

Each key was independently scheduled to produce reinforcements (5-second exposures to the corresponding slide) according to a VI 20-second schedule. The minimum interval elapsing between one reinforcement and the time when depression of the same key could produce the next reinforcement ranged from 5 seconds to 35 seconds in multiples of 5 seconds, with a mean of 20 seconds. In addition, to discourage alternation, neither key could produce reinforcement for 5 seconds following the end of a slide exposure, and a key could not produce reinforcement for 3 seconds after a response on the other key.

After this part of the experiment was completed, the GSR electrode was removed. Half of the *S*s had then to rate each of the six slides on an UNINTERESTING-INTERESTING scale and then on a DISPLEASING-PLEASING scale, while the remaining *S*s completed the scales in the opposite order. Each slide appeared for 5 seconds followed by a 5-second interval during which a judgment was recorded. The sequences in which the six slides were presented were counterbalanced among *S*s, and they were presented once for the first scale and then again for the second scale.

Results

Over all three grains, the mean numbers of responses per phase were 279.8 for the less redundant pattern and 263.8 for the more redundant pattern. In an analysis of variance, this difference was found to be nonsignificant.

It was therefore decided to examine relations between the relative key-pressing rates of individuals and their ratings of the patterns on evaluative scales. Sign tests were performed, with *S*s having ties on either measure eliminated. Over all grains, 16 out of 19 *S*s ($p < .01$) pressed more often whichever key delivered the pattern they judged more pleasing. The response delivering the pattern judged more pleasing was performed more often by 11 out of 21 *S*s (not significant) at the 8 x 8 grain, by 17 out of 21 ($p < .01$) at the 15 x 15 grain, and by 17 out of 22 ($p < .05$) at the 30 x 30 grain. The corresponding sign tests revealed no significant associations between rates of responding and judgments of interestingness.

DISCUSSION

It is difficult to sum up all the data yielded by the seven experiments. They have, however, provided further confirmation for some of the conclusions favored by the experiments with sound sequences reported in Chapters 2 and 3 and by much previous research with visual patterns

(Berlyne, 1971, Chap. 13). We have evidence once again that information-theoretic and collative stimulus properties have a broad influence on a variety of verbal judgments and measures of nonverbal behavior. Once again, however, we find that there are two sets of dependent variables, both depending on these properties but in different ways. There are, in other words, two dimensions of aesthetic reaction. Dependent variables of one group tend to rise as complexity and uncertainty rise. Variables belonging to the other group reach a peak, or several peaks, in the middle range of complexity and uncertainty. The two dimensions correspond to what we have in this chapter called the Hedonic Tone and Uncertainty/Arousal factors, respectively, and to what Crozier in Chapter 2, calls, following Osgood, the Evaluative and Activity factors (see Chap. 14).

The experiments to which this chapter is devoted, in contrast with most earlier experiments using both visual and auditory material, showed judgments of interestingness to be more closely related to the Hedonic Tone factor, and to scales loaded on it, than to the Uncertainty/Arousal factor. In the experiments with the Smets patterns, this could have been due to redundancy, which tended to affect interestingness in a similar manner to pleasingness and the like. The presence of redundancy permits uncertainty to be resolved progressively as relations resulting from mutual dependences among elements are discovered and perceptual activities make use of them to organize a pattern. This fits in with the suggestion that highly interesting patterns are ones that cannot be assimilated immediately but offer promise of yielding reasonably quickly to perceptual and intellectual efforts.

In Experiment IA, using the matrix patterns, Pleasingness and Interestingness ratings were higher when the number of elements per pattern was greater, resulting in a positive correlation between the two. This suggests that the patterns were confined to the lower register of the complexity-uncertainty continuum, where curves for Interestingness and curves for the scales most representative of Hedonic Tone are both rising; they could be expected to diverge as the upper reaches of this continuum are entered.

Previous experiments have shown close connections between verbal judgments representative of complexity and uncertainty and a number of nonverbal measures, notably Exploration Time and psychophysiological measures of arousal. In these experiments, RELAXED-TENSE had significant correlations with SIMPLE-COMPLEX, CLEAR-INDEFINITE, and DISORDERLY-ORDERLY and shared high loadings with these scales on what we labeled the Uncertainty/Arousal factor. These findings lend further credence to the assumption that RELAXED-TENSE reflects some aspect of arousal. On the other hand, DROWSY-ALERT and WEAK-POWERFUL, which were thought (Berlyne, 1973) to measure something like cortical arousal, were not significantly correlated with those three scales (except for a correlation between DROWSY-ALERT and SIMPLE-COMPLEX in Experiment IIA) and were loaded not on the Uncertainty/Arousal factor but on the Hedonic Tone factor. RELAXED-TENSE also had a high loading on this factor in Experiment IIA. We also have confirmation for earlier findings in the high correlations between Looking Time and the Uncertainty/Arousal factor.

Nonverbal correlates of hedonic tone have been mysteriously lacking hitherto. In these experiments, they are beginning to come to light. In Experiment IB, there was some correlation between Looking Time and the Hedonic Tone factor with the Uncertainty/Arousal factor partialed out. Scores on the hanging-on-the-wall scale were predominantly correlated with Hedonic Tone, which provides another link with nonverbal behavior, assuming that ratings on this scale reveal the probability with which subjects would actually have taken the patterns to decorate their homes if given the opportunity. And in Experiment IID, there was evidence of a link between reward value and judged pleasingness.

REFERENCES

Berlyne, D. E. The influence of albedo and complexity of stimuli on visual fixation in the human infant. *British Journal of Psychology*, 1958, 49, 315–318.

Berlyne, D. E. Complexity and incongruity variables as determinants of exploratory choice and evaluative ratings. *Canadian Journal of Psychology*, 1963, 17, 274–290.

Berlyne, D. E. Arousal and reinforcement. In D. Levine (Ed.), *Nebraska Symposium on Motivation*, 1967. Lincoln, Nebr.: University of Nebraska Press, 1967.

Berlyne, D. E. *Aesthetics and psychobiology*. New York: Appleton-Century-Crofts, 1971.

Berlyne, D. E. Reinforcement values of visual patterns compared through concurrent performances. *Journal of the Experimental Analysis of Behavior*, 1972, 18, 281–285.

Berlyne, D. E. Interrelations of verbal and nonverbal measures used in experimental aesthetics. *Scandinavian Journal of Psychology*, 1973, 14, 177–184.

Birkhoff, G. D. *Aesthetic measure*. Cambridge, Mass.: Harvard University Press, 1933.

Catania, A. C. Concurrent performances: A baseline for the study of reinforcement magnitude. *Journal of the Experimental Analysis of Behavior*, 1963, 6, 299–300.

Day, H. I. Exploratory behaviour as a function of individual differences and level of arousal. Unpublished Ph.D. thesis, University of Toronto, 1965.

Day, H. I. The importance of symmetry and complexity in the evaluation of complexity, interest and pleasingness. *Psychonomic Science*, 1968, 10, 339–340.

Dorfman, D., & McKenna, H. Pattern preference as a function of pattern uncertainty. *Canadian Journal of Psychology*, 1966, **20**, 143-153.

Ertel, S. Exploratory choice and verbal judgments. In D. E. Berlyne & K. B. Madsen (Eds.), *Pleasure, reward, preference*. New York: Academic Press, 1973.

Ferguson, G. A. *Nonparametric trend analysis*. Montreal: McGill University Press, 1965.

Frank, H. *Grundlagenprobleme der Informationsästhetik und erste Anwendung auf die mime pure*. Quickborn: Schnelle, 1959.

Karmel, B. Z. The effect of age, complexity, and amount of contour on pattern preferences in human infants. *Journal of Experimental Child Psychology*, 1969, **7**, 339-354.

Munsinger, H. L., & Kessen, W. Uncertainty, structure and preference. *Psychological Monographs*, 1964, **78**, No. 9(whole no. 586).

Nicki, R. M. Arousal increment and degree of complexity as incentive. *British Journal of Psychology*, 1972, **63**, 165-171.

Osgood, C. E., Suci, G. J., & Tannenbaum, P. H. *The measurement of meaning*. Urbana, Ill.: University of Illinois Press, 1957.

Smets, G. *Aesthetic judgment and arousal*. Leuven: Leuven University Press, 1973.

Veldman, J. *FORTRAN programming for the behavioral sciences*. New York: Holt, 1957.

Vitz, P. C. Affect as a function of stimulus variation. *Journal of Experimental Psychology*, 1966, **71**, 74-79.

6
ARTISTIC TRAINING AND RESPONSES TO VISUAL AND AUDITORY PATTERNS VARYING IN UNCERTAINTY

F. G. Hare

INTRODUCTION

Berlyne (1971, pp. 262-263) has noted several reasons for believing that training and exposure can influence aesthetic preferences. Through exposure one learns the redundancies and transitional probabilities of a given mode of expression and acquires certain expectations. Familiarity also reduces novelty and thus the effect of recurrent element combinations. Finally, experience with a range of aesthetic stimuli may improve the capacity to process more complex stimuli which may, in turn, raise the amount of variability necessary for optimal hedonic value. Studies involving experimentally induced experience and experiments with specifically and generally trained Ss have tended to support these assumptions. These three approaches will be considered in turn.

A. Induced Experience

Washburn, Child, and Abel (1927) observed that repetition of musical excerpts produces different effects, depending upon the type of music used. For example, "with very popular selections the tendency is to attain maximum pleasantness at an early performance, whereas in the case of ... classical music the tendency is to reach maximum enjoyment at a late performance" (p. 205). The conclusion drawn is that factors lowering pleasantness or enjoyment over repetitions predominate in popular music, while factors having the opposite effect predominate in classical music. Similar results were reported by Razran (see Gernet, 1940, pp. 68-69). If one were to assume that the differences between "popular" and "classical" include, at least to a certain extent, differences in complexity, a link may be established between this music-preference research and two other types of investigation. In one, Dember, Earl & Paradise (1957) predicted that "any change in preference (of rats) will be from the less to the more complex path" (p. 514). In the other, Jones, Wilkinson & Braden (1961) found that *S*s who were allowed to choose among various sequential patterns of lights over a 12-hour period tended, the longer they were in the experiment, to choose the more complicated patterns. Thus, there seems to be at least some conceptual consistency among three different types of preference studies.

B. Modality-Specific Training

This type of study frequently uses existing "artistic" groups and compares them to "nonartistic" controls, on the assumption that the artistic group's preferences will reflect their history of exposure to the type of stimulus material being used. For example, one finds intergroup differentiation in studies by Washburn, et al. (1927), Barron & Welsh (1952), Rosen (1955), Raychaudhuri (1963), Eisenman & Coffee (1964), Munsinger & Kessen (1964), Vitz (1966), and Crozier (Chap. 2, this volume). The general results indicate that *S*s with training and interest in a particular modality of artistic expression tend to prefer greater stimulus variability in that modality. It must be noted, however, that demonstrations of group differentiation do not imply that training has a causal influence, since one could expect that *S*s preferring higher levels of variability are more likely to enroll in art and music schools.

C. Generalized Training and/or Predisposition

In experiments on induced experience, *S*s are retested one or more times on material *identical* to that of the original testing. The hypothesis under examination is that evaluation changes over successive exposures to a specific set of stimuli. In experiments relevant to generalized training, an element of transfer of training is introduced. Testing is done with stimuli *similar to* those used in training, so that evaluative changes over successive exposures to a class of stimulus material can be detected. This third kind of experiment compares groups who are, respectively trained and untrained in the course of the experiment or alternatively groups already trained in different modalities of artistic expression. Relevant studies include those of Williams, Winter & Woods (1938), Welsh (1959), Raychaudhuri (1966), Egger & Iminski (1969) and Hare & Gaier (1971). The results generally indicate a general ability or "artistic sensibility" factor, which interacts with the specific type of training received.

It is, however, virtually impossible to control for the possibility that artists who are expressive in one medium may be interested in, and consequently experienced in, another artistic medium, which would result in something akin to specific training. Furthermore, personality traits underlying several types of aesthetic behavior and common to artists working in different media (Bieri, 1961; Dellas & Gaier, 1970; Roubertoux, 1970), may play some part in Ss' responses.

The question to which this chapter is addressed is whether artistic training in one medium will affect responses to patterns in a different medium. With regard to the particular material used in this chapter, Crozier's (Chap. 2) work has established a differentiation between music and nonmusic (psychology) students in responses to sound sequences of varying uncertainty, and Munsinger & Kessen (1964) have shown differences between art and nonart students in responses to polygons of varying uncertainty. The question is thus whether responses to sound sequences of people trained in the visual arts will resemble those of people trained in music, and whether the responses to visual patterns of people trained in music will resemble those of people trained in the visual arts.

EXPERIMENT 1

The purpose of this experiment was to compare responses of fine arts and psychology students to auditory patterns. Forty-eight Ss were drawn from an undergraduate student population, 24 from the Fine Arts Department and 24 from the Psychology Department. Fine arts students were recruited from classes offered by their department and psychology students were selected from a subject pool. The latter had, on the average, participated in one psychology experiment.

Stimulus Material

The 12 sound sequences, representing six levels of uncertainty, that Crozier used, following Vitz (1966), served as stimulus material (see Chap. 2). Each of the levels was represented by two randomizations. The six levels consisted of 2, 16, 72, 144, 288, 576 equiprobable events, with an event defined as a tone of a particular frequency, a particular loudness and a particular duration. These values corresponded, respectively, to 1.00,

4.00, 6.17, 7.17, 8.17, and 9.17 bits of uncertainty. *S*s rated each of the 12 sequences on three 7-point scales, the poles of which were SIMPLE-COMPLEX, DISPLEASING-PLEASING and UNINTERESTING-INTERESTING.

Design and Procedure

Two *S*s from each group were assigned to each of the 12 rows of a 12 × 12 balanced Latin square, which determined the order of stimulus presentation. Each of six permutations of the three rating scales was randomly assigned to two rows of the Latin square. Each rating scale occurred equally often in each of the three rating-scale temporal positions (RSTP), i.e., first, second, or third. Within each group, there were thus three rating-scale temporal positions, each used for eight *S*s.

*S*s were run individually or two at a time. They entered the experimental room (approx. 3.4 × 2.1 m.), which contained an office table with one chair at either end. On arrival, they were fitted with Sharpe high-fidelity headphones (Model HA-10-A) and were instructed in the use of the rating scales. Instructions indicated that the seven points on the scale were to be treated as representing equal intervals. The 12 sound sequences were rotated against the scales, so that a *S* would rate all 12 sequences on the first scale before moving on to the second scale and then, in turn, the third scale. Responses to the two randomizations at each of the six uncertainty levels were averaged before analysis, giving one score per *S* for each level of uncertainty on each scale.

Results

Complexity. Analysis of variance revealed a strong Uncertainty effect ($F = 99.7$, $df = 5,210$, $p < .001$) with a significant linear component ($F = 308.4$, $df = 1,42$, $p < .001$). Rated Complexity of sound sequences increases linearly with uncertainty level. Complexity means for the six levels of uncertainty are graphically presented in Figure 1. The interaction between Groups and Uncertainty levels is not significant. Nor is the Groups main effect.

Interestingness. Analysis of variance indicates two significant effects. There was a significant effect of rating-scale temporal position ($F = 4.1$, $df = 2,42$, $p < .05$). *S*s rated the sound sequences less interesting the later they came in the experimental session. The other significant effect was that of uncertainty level ($F = 26.1$, $df = 5,210$, $p < .001$), with trend analysis indicating a significant linear component ($F = 50.5$, $df = 1,42$, $p < .001$). Interestingness means are plotted in Figure 2.

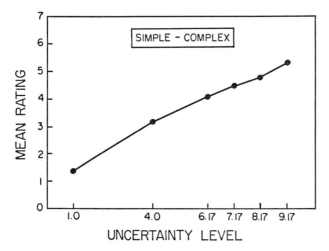

FIG. 1. Mean Complexity ratings of sound sequences by fine arts and psychology students in Experiment 1 (no significant interaction).

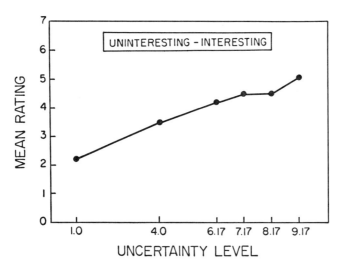

FIG. 2. Mean Interestingness ratings of sound sequences for fine arts and psychology students in Experiment 1 (no significant interaction).

Pleasingness. Analysis of variance again reveals a significant Uncertainty effect ($F = 12.02$, $df = 5,210$, $p < .001$), while trend analysis indicates significant linear and quadratic components ($F_{lin} = 13.5$, $df = 1,42$, $p < .001$; $F_{quad} = 18.24$, $df = 1,42$, $p < .001$). Rated Pleasingness appears to be a curvilinear function of stimulus uncertainty with a peak in the range of 7.17 bits. The Uncertainty x Groups interaction was significant ($F = 2.6$, $df = 5,210$, $p < .05$), with a significant difference in linear trend ($F_{lin} = 4.51$, $df = 1,42$, $p < .05$). The means for Pleasingness ratings are plotted in Figure 3.

Discussion

Results obtained in this study resemble those of previous experiments in that Complexity and Interestingness ratings are monotonic rising functions of uncertainty level and Pleasingness ratings are an inverted U-shaped function of uncertainty level. As far as the main purpose of the experiment is concerned, it appears that the Pleasingness ratings of fine arts students differ from those of psychology students but resemble those that Crozier obtained from music students. No difference between fine arts and psychology students appeared when Complexity or Interestingness were rated, just as none appeared between music and psychology students in Crozier's experiment.

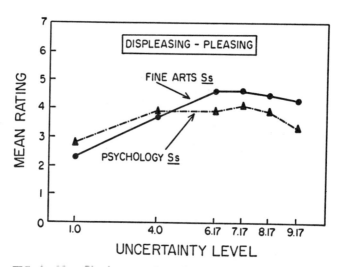

FIG. 3. Mean Pleasingness ratings of sound sequences for fine arts and psychology students in Experiment 1 (significant interaction).

EXPERIMENT 2

In this experiment, the responses of music students and psychology students to visual patterns were compared.

Subjects

Thirty subjects were drawn from an undergraduate student population, fifteen from the Faculty of Music and fifteen from the Psychology Department. Music students were recruited through the Faculty of Music Student Directory. The acceptance rate was approximately 75%. Psychology subjects were contacted through a subject pool and had, on the average, participated in one experiment.

Stimulus Material

Thirty random polygons, generated according to Attneave & Arnoult's (1956) Method 1, and ranging in number of sides from 3 to 146, served as the stimulus material. The polygons were photographed on slides (in black on white) and were selected from a population of polygons used by Day (e.g., 1968). Attneave & Arnoult's Method 1 involves plotting points with randomly and independently chosen coordinates on graph paper, so that, for example, a 10-sided figure is obtained by connecting 10 points. The thirty polygons used had, respectively, 3, 4, 5, 6, 8, 9, 10, 11, 12, 13, 14, 16, 18, 19, 20, 21, 24, 31, 34, 40, 46, 54, 62, 70, 80, 90, 100, 122, 140, 146 sides. Ss responded to the polygons with reference to the same Complexity, Pleasingness, and Interestingness rating scales as were used in Experiment 1.

Design and Procedure

A 30 x 30 balanced Latin square was generated to determine stimulus-presentation order. Fifteen rows of the square were selected at random. One S from each group was assigned to each of the fifteen rows. The six permutations of the rating scales were randomly assigned to rows, subject to the restriction that any given scale order must be assigned to no fewer than two and no more than three rows. Ss were run in the same experimental room as in Experiment 1, facing a screen approximately 2.1 m. away. Once again, Ss rated all polygons in turn on one scale and then all polygons on the next scale, and so on.

Results

Complexity. Analysis of variance revealed a significant Uncertainty effect ($F = 126.7$, $df = 29$, 812, $p < .001$) with a significant linear component ($F = 1130.3$, $df = 1,28$, $p < .001$). Complexity means are plotted in Figure 4. There was no significant Groups × Uncertainty interaction.

Pleasingness. Analysis of variance reveals a significant Uncertainty effect ($F = 3.14$, $df = 29$, 812, $p < .01$) although the function, plotted in Figure 4, appears to be highly irregular. Neither the linear nor the quadratic component is significant. Nor is the Groups × Uncertainty interaction.

Interestingness. Analysis of variance reveals a significant Uncertainty effect ($F = 24.4$, $df = 29,812$, $p < .001$), with a significant linear component ($F = 68.4$, $df = 1,28$, $p < .001$). Interestingness means are plotted in Figure 4. There was no significant Groups × Uncertainty interaction.

Discussion

The monotonic rising functions for rated Complexity and Interestingness, plotted against uncertainty level, are similar to results obtained in previous studies. The highly irregular Pleasingness function suggests that peculiarities of individual polygons may have masked uncertainty effects, since there was only one pattern at each level. Significant Groups × Uncertainty interactions

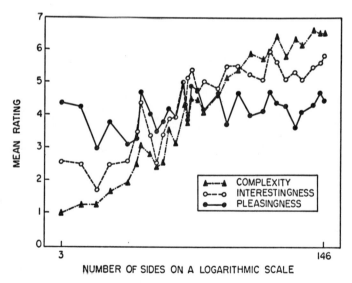

FIG. 4. Mean ratings of polygons by fine arts and psychology students in Experiment 2 (no significant interactions).

were not found on any of the three scales. So, there was no evidence that music and psychology students differ in responses to these visual stimuli.

GENERAL DISCUSSION

The results indicate some cross-modality transfer in so far as fine arts students find more complex sound sequences more pleasing than psychology students do. But no such transfer was found when music and psychology students rated visual stimuli.

Once again, there are alternative explanations of the difference that emerged. Fine arts students may be self-selected, in the sense that they may possess, before embarking on their specialized training, a high capacity for processing complex stimulation or a tendency to prefer it. Alternatively, their training or their frequent contact with complex stimulus patterns may have increased their ability to cope with such patterns and hence their liking for them. In any case, it is interesting to find some indication that whatever factor is at work may affect their responses to auditory stimulation as well as to stimulation in the visual modality with which they have a specialized concern.

REFERENCES

Attneave, F., & Arnoult, M. D. The quantitative study of shape and pattern perception. *Psychological Bulletin*, 1956, 53, 452–471.

Barron, F., & Welsh, G. S. Artistic perception as a possible factor in personality style. *Journal of Psychology*, 1952, 33, 199–203.

Berlyne, D. E. *Aesthetics and psychobiology*. New York: Appleton-Century-Crofts, 1971.

Bieri, J. Complexity-simplicity as a personality variable in cognitive and preferential behavior. In D. W. Fiske & S. R. Maddi (Eds.), *Functions of varied experience*. Homewood, Ill.: Dorsey Press, 1961.

Day, H. The importance of symmetry and complexity in the evaluation of complexity, interest and pleasingness. *Psychonomic Science*, 1968, 10, 339–340.

Dellas, M., & Gaier, E. L. Identification of creativity: The individual. *Psychological Bulletin*, 1970, 73, 55–73.

Dember, W. N., Earl, R. W., & Paradise, N. Responses by rats to differential stimulus complexity. *Journal of Comparative and Physiological Psychology*, 1957, 50, 514–518.

Egger, G. J., & Iminski, S. A. An investigation into the development of melodic interval discrimination. *Australian Journal of Psychology*, 1969, 21, 187-191.

Eisenman, R., & Coffee, S. Aesthetic preferences of art students and mathematics students. *Journal of Psychology*, 1964, 58, 375-378.

Gernet, S. K. *Musical discrimination at various age and grade levels.* College Place, Wash.: The College Press, 1940.

Hare, F. G., & Gaier, E. L. Perceptual characteristics of the creative process in musicians, artists and poets. *Sciences de l'Art*, 1971, 8, 39–45.

Jones, A., Wilkinson, H. J., & Braden, I. Information deprivation as a motivational variable. *Journal of Experimental Psychology*, 1961, 62, 126–137.

Munsinger, H., & Kessen, W. Uncertainty, structure and preference. *Psychological Monographs*, 1964, 78(Whole No. 586).

Raychaudhuri, M. Some perceptual characteristics of incipient artists. *Indian Journal of Psychology*, 1963, 38, 13–17.

Raychaudhuri, M. Perceptual preference patterns and creativity. *Indian Journal of Applied Psychology*, 1966, 3, 67–70.

Rosen, J. C. The Barron-Welsh Art Scale as a predictor of originality and level of ability among artists. *Journal of Applied Psychology*, 1955, 39, 366–367.

Roubertoux, P. Personality variables and interest in art. *Journal of Personality and Social Psychology*, 1970, 16, 665–668.

Vitz, P. C. Affect as a function of stimulus variation. *Journal of Experimental Psychology*, 1966, 71, 74–79.

Washburn, M. F., Child, M. S., & Abel, T. M. The effect of immediate repetition on the pleasantness of music. In M. S. Schoen (Ed.), *The effects of music.* New York: Harcourt Brace, 1927.

Welsh, G. S. *The Welsh Figure Preference Test.* Palo Alto, Calif.: Consulting Psychologists Press, 1959.

Williams, E., Winter, L., & Woods, J. M. Tests of literary appreciation. *British Journal of Educational Psychology*, 1938, 8, 256–284.

7

VERBAL RESPONSES TO VISUAL PATTERNS VARYING IN DISTRIBUTIONAL REDUNDANCY AND IN VARIETY

F. G. Hare

INTRODUCTION

The growing literature on the role of complexity and uncertainty in aesthetic behavior may be extended by the inclusion of new types of stimulus material that can be scaled in terms of Complexity. In this chapter, circles with colored sectors, based on material developed by Driscoll & Sturgeon (1969), are used in an experiment studying verbal ratings.

This uncertainty associated with a class of patterns can be varied in at least four ways (cf. Chap. 1). Uncertainty can be increased by increasing the number of elements per pattern and by increasing the number of alternative forms that each element can take. Uncertainty can be decreased by making some kinds of elements occur more frequently than others (distributional redundancy) as well as by making some combinations of elements more frequent than others (correlational redundancy). The material used in this experiment varies uncertainty through variation in number of elements and also through variation in amount of distributional redundancy. This latter method seems not to have been used in experimental aesthetics.

METHOD

Subjects

Eight paid Ss were recruited from a summer university student population and run individually.

Stimulus Material

Sixteen circles were prepared on gray cards. On the cards, each circle was 120 mm. in diameter and contained a concentric gray circle 42 mm. in diameter. The circles on the slides made from these cards, when projected on a screen approximately 2.1 m. away, measured 240 mm. in diameter.

There were two series of stimuli, each consisting of two patterns at each of four uncertainty levels. In series A, the uncertainty levels differed in amount of distributional redundancy, i.e., proportions of the total area allotted to two colors. In series B, the uncertainty levels differed in the number of colors among which the total area was equally divided. Specifications for the eight types of pattern are given in Table 1. The patterns were constructed by dividing the area between the two concentric circles into 48 sectors of 7.5 degrees. Randomly selected sectors were then assigned to each color in the specified proportions. The two patterns belonging to level A1 had equal areas of blue and yellow. At levels A2-A4, one pattern had a preponderance of yellow, with blue assigned to the smaller number of sectors, and the ratios of yellow and blue were reversed in the other pattern. In patterns of series B, succeeding levels included all the colors used for lower levels as well as some additional ones.

Procedure

One S was assigned to every second row of a balanced 16 x 16 Latin square that had been generated to determine stimulus presentation order, with stimuli randomly assigned to the columns of the square.

Upon entering the experimental room, S was seated at a table facing a screen (2.1 m. away). He was instructed in the use of the seven-point rating

TABLE 1

Stimulus Characteristics

Level	Number of colors	Proportions	Uncertainty value
A1	2	.96, .04	0.25
A2	2	.90, .10	0.47
A3	2	.77, .23	0.78
A4	2	.50, .50	1.00
B1	2	.50, .50	1.00
B2	4	each .25	2.00
B3	8	each .125	3.00
B4	16	each .0625	4.00

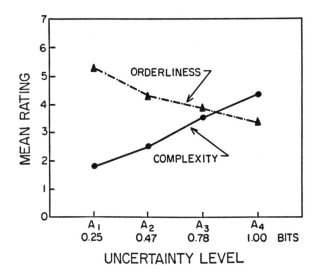

FIG. 1. Mean Complexity and Orderliness ratings for visual patterns varying in distributional redundancy (proportions occupied by two colors).

scales and told that, when *E* left the room, he was to judge each of the 16 slides on 12 rating scales. Random permutations of scale presentation orders for each *S* were rotated against stimuli, so that the *S* would complete all scales for one stimulus before moving on to the next one. The poles of the scales used were SIMPLE-COMPLEX, DISPLEASING-PLEASING, UNINTERESTING-INTERESTING, WEAK-STRONG, CLEAR-INDEFINITE, UGLY-BEAUTIFUL, DISORDERLY-ORDERLY, NO PLEASURE-EXTREME PLEASURE, NO DISCOMFORT-EXTREME DISCOMFORT, RELAXED-TENSE, DROWSY-ALERT, DISLIKE-LIKE. Rating time per stimulus was recorded. Responses to the two patterns at each uncertainty level were averaged before analysis.

Results

Analysis of variance on the distributional-redundancy manipulation (uncertainty levels A1 to A4) indicated significant effects of uncertainty level on the SIMPLE-COMPLEX scale ($F = 18.22$, $df = 3,21$, $p < .001$) and on the DISORDERLY-ORDERLY scale ($F = 4.04$, $df = 3,21$, $p < .05$). Mean ratings, plotted in Figure 1, show a monotonic increase in judged Complexity and a monotonic decrease in judged Orderliness with increasing uncertainty (i.e., decreasing redundancy).

Analysis of variance on the amount-of-variety manipulation (uncertainty levels B1 to B4) revealed significant effects of uncertainty level on the UNINTERESTING-INTERESTING scale ($F = 4.22$, $df = 3,21$, $p < .05$) and on the NO PLEASURE-EXTREME PLEASURE scale ($F = 3.89$, $df = 3,21$, $p < .05$). Means are plotted in Figure 2 and indicate monotonic rising functions for Interestingness and Pleasure with increasing uncertainty (i.e., increasing number of colors per pattern).

Discussion

The distributional-redundancy manipulation was found to affect judgments of order and complexity, which have played a large role in speculative aesthetics (cf. Berlyne, 1971, pp. 126–129). Other scales did not produce significant effects, which may be due to the small number of stimulus patterns and of Ss. It is interesting to have some evidence that this way of varying uncertainty, which does not seem to have been used by experimenters before, has effects on rating scales resembling those that have appeared when uncertainty has been varied in other ways. This adds a little further confirmation of the importance of the uncertainty variable for aesthetic behavior and for motivational and hedonic processes generally.

With regard to the amount-of-variety manipulation, the significant effect of uncertainty on Interestingness is consistent with previous research, although the usual effect of uncertainty level on judged Complexity did not emerge.

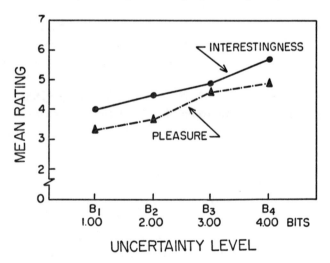

FIG. 2. Mean Interestingness and Pleasure ratings for visual patterns varying in amount of variety (number of colors).

The monotonic, as opposed to inverted U-shaped, function for Pleasure may have been due to the relatively restricted uncertainty range. If still higher uncertainty levels had been used, a downturn may well have appeared, producing the familiar inverted-U curve.

REFERENCES

Berlyne, D. E. *Aesthetics and psychobiology*. New York: Appleton-Century-Crofts, 1971.

Berlyne, D. E. Ends and means of experimental aesthetics. *Canadian Journal of Psychology*, 1972, 26, 303–325.

Driscoll, J. M., & Sturgeon, L. B. Uncertainty (H) estimation. *Journal of Experimental Psychology*, 1969, 79, 565–567.

8
NOVELTY, COMPLEXITY, AND INTERESTINGNESS

D. E. Berlyne

An earlier series of experiments (Berlyne, 1970) examined ways in which the novelty and the complexity of visual patterns interact to determine judged pleasingness. The experimental literature had shown that, as a stimulus pattern is repeatedly presented and thus becomes increasingly familiar, ratings indicative of hedonic tone might steadily rise (e.g., Zajonc, 1968), steadily fall (e.g., Cantor, 1968), or rise to a peak and then fall (e.g., Skaife, 1966).

It was hypothesized, in an attempt to resolve these apparent disparities, that the shape of the curve relating pleasingness to novelty might depend on how complex a pattern is. And, as expected, the rated pleasingness of relatively complex patterns was found to increase and then decline, while that of relatively simple patterns declined from the start, subsequently flattening out. Congruent findings were reported by Saegert & Jellison (1970) in the same year. It was not suggested that complexity is the only variable that affects the function connecting mean hedonic tone with novelty. For example, the same series of experiments (Berlyne, 1970) provided some evidence that the unvarying repetition of one pattern, as compared with repeated presentation of the pattern interspersed with other patterns, favors an inverse relation between hedonic tone and familiarity. But the observed novelty-complexity interaction was compatible with a theoretical model (Berlyne, 1967, 1971) embodying two assumptions, viz., (1) that both novelty and complexity contribute to arousal potential and (2) that the curve relating hedonic tone to arousal potential has the shape of the Wundt curve (see Chap. 1, Fig. 2, this volume). Repeated exposure to a pattern, implying decreasing novelty and therefore decreasing arousal potential, would correspond to a leftward movement along the horizontal axis of the curve. However, a relatively complex pattern would start this process at a point to the right of the peak. Consequently, progression to the left would mean rising and then falling ordinates. A simpler pattern would begin to the left of the peak, so that further movement to the left could only mean a steady drop in the ordinate.

Judged Pleasingness and Interestingness have both turned out regularly to vary with complexity (see Berlyne, 1971, Chap. 13; see also several chaps. this volume). But the curves relating them to complexity are generally found to differ, except when stimulus material is confined to a relatively simple range. Pleasingness and equivalent attributes usually vary nonmonotonically with complexity, producing an inverted U-shaped curve or else a curve with several peaks, while Interestingness tends to rise monotonically as complexity rises, at least until very high levels are reached.

If we are right in assuming that evaluative judgments depend on the intervening variable that we have called "arousal potential" and to which several factors, including novelty and complexity, contribute, we should expect novelty, as well as complexity, to affect both Pleasingness and Interestingness but to affect them in different ways. Close correlations have invariably appeared between Interestingness and Looking or Listening Time, and Looking Time (e.g., Berlyne, 1958) increases with novelty as well as with complexity. But there do not seem to have been any studies of judged Interestingness as a function of novelty.

Consequently, it was decided to repeat the experiment (Experiment V) from the previous series (1970) that revealed most clearly the interaction between novelty and complexity in determining Pleasingness, except that this time judgments of Interestingness would be solicited instead.

METHOD

Subjects

These were 20 undergraduates from elementary psychology courses.

Stimulus Material

The same four patterns were used as in Experiment V of the previous series (Berlyne, 1970). They consisted of one simple-nonrepresentational

(S-NR) pattern, one complex nonrepresentational (C-NR) pattern, one simple representational (S-R) pattern, and one complex representational (C-R) pattern. The nonrepresentational patterns were taken from a collection of line drawings used in many previous experiments (e.g., Berlyne, 1963). They consisted of the less complex member of the fourth pair in category A, and the more complex member of the second pair in category XA. The representational patterns were black-and-white reproductions of paintings, the simple one being Raeburn's *Portrait of a Man* and the complex one Rubens's *Massacre of the Innocents.*

Procedure

The design and procedure were modeled on those used for the NAI group of the Pleasingness experiment, apart from one modification. The four patterns were arranged in a sequence of sixty-four 4-second presentations at 4-second intervals, with each pattern appearing 16 times. First, the four patterns appeared in a random order, and S was required to rate each on a seven-point Osgood type scale labeled UNINTERESTING-INTERESTING. He was then told that he would see the patterns again a number of times. He then went through eight additional presentations comprising two of each pattern in a randomized order, without any judgments being required. There was a second test phase, in which each pattern appeared once and had to be rated. The sequence continued until six test phases had been completed, each separated from the last by eight presentations requiring no judgments.

The sole change in design was the use of two orders of presentation for half of the Ss each. The second order was derived from the first by interchanging S and C, as well as R and NR, patterns.

Results

The curves showing mean judged Interestingness with successive tests for the four patterns are displayed in Figure 1. The curves for C and S patterns in the corresponding Pleasingness experiment (Berlyne, 1970) appear below for comparison (Fig. 2). In that experiment, there was a significant Test x Complexity interaction, but no significant Tests x Representational/ Nonrepresentational interaction. Consequently, only two curves were drawn.

Interestingness declined significantly ($F = 2.84$, 5,90 df, $p < .05$), showing a trend with a significant linear ($F = 10.41$, 1,90 df, $p < .005$) component but no significant quadratic component.

No significant interactions emerged between the Tests effect, or the linear and quadratic components of the trend, and the S/C or R/NR variables.

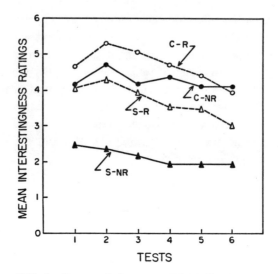

FIG. 1. Curves relating mean UNINTERESTING-INTERESTING ratings with increasing familiarization.

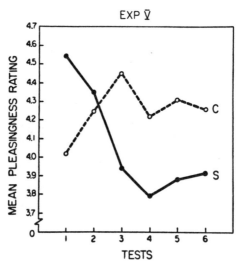

FIG. 2. Curves relating mean DISPLEASING-PLEASING ratings with increasing familiarization (*From Berlyne, 1970*).

Nevertheless, the mean rating was significantly higher for C than for S patterns ($F = 43.92$, 1,19 *df, $p < .001$*). It was also higher for R than for NR patterns ($F = 10.33$, $p < .005$). Finally, there was a significant interaction between these two variables ($F = 6.2, p < .025$).

CONCLUSIONS

The fact that more complex patterns were rated more interesting than less complex ones tallies with much previous research. It would be hazardous to generalize widely from our finding that representational patterns were deemed more interesting than nonrepresentational ones. But this finding fits in with the suggestion, made in several previous writings, that patterns are judged interesting to the extent that they contain information that cannot be absorbed immediately but seems likely to be absorbed relatively speedily through perceptual and intellectual efforts. Representational patterns contain semantic information in addition to the syntactic information that they, like nonrepresentational patterns, possess. Apart from that, it seems quite likely that our representational patterns were both more complex than our two nonrepresentational patterns.

The most important result, however, is the monotonic decline in judged Interestingness that all four patterns showed as they lost their novelty. So, there is evidence that novelty, like complexity, affects Interestingness monotonically but Pleasingness nonmonotonically. It appears, in fact, that Interestingness tends to increase with arousal potential, whether arousal potential stems from novelty or from complexity, while the effects of variations in arousal potential on hedonic tone conform, in most circumstances, to the Wundt curve. There is, in sum, further support for the view that the arousal potential of a stimulus pattern, of which its novelty and its complexity are two of many determinants, is a decisive variable.

REFERENCES

Berlyne, D. E. The influence of complexity and change in visual figures on orienting responses. *Journal of Experimental Psychology*, 1958, 55, 289–296.

Berlyne, D. E. Complexity and incongruity variables as determinants of exploratory choice and evaluative ratings. *Canadian Journal of Psychology*, 1963, 17, 274–290.

Berlyne, D. E. Arousal and reinforcement. In D. Levine (Ed.), *Nebraska Symposium on Motivation*, 1967. Lincoln, Nebr.: University of Nebraska Press, 1967.

Berlyne, D. E. Novelty, complexity and hedonic value. *Perception & Psychophysics*, 1970, 8, 279–286.

Berlyne, D. E. *Aesthetics and psychobiology*. New York: Appleton-Century-Crofts, 1971.

Cantor, G. N. Children's "like-dislike" ratings of familiarized and unfamiliarized visual stimuli. *Journal of Experimental Child Psychology*, 1968, 6, 651–657.

Saegert, S. C., & Jellison, J. M. Effects of initial level of response competition and frequency of exposure on liking and exploratory behavior. *Journal of Personality and Social Psychology*, 1970, 16, 553–558.

Skaife, A. M. The role of complexity and deviation in changing musical taste. Unpublished Ph.D. thesis, University of Oregon, 1966.

Zajonc, R. B. Attitudinal effects of mere exposure. *Journal of Personality and Social Psychology*, 1968, 9(Monograph Supplement 2).

9

DIMENSIONS OF PERCEPTION OF PAINTINGS[1]

D. E. Berlyne and J. C. Ogilvie

The experiments reported in earlier chapters have followed one of the two approaches described in Chapter 1, namely, what was termed the "synthetic" approach. It focuses on a particular factor that can be found in works of art and is likely to contribute to the effects they have on appreciators. It uses specially designed, relatively simple stimulus patterns, in which the factor of interest is present in differing degrees, so that its influence on subjects' reactions can be isolated. Such an approach is indispensable, particularly when an area of research is in its infancy. It is adopted, with good reason, by other branches of experimental psychology and indeed of experimental science in general.

Nevertheless, it has obvious limitations. The variables whose effects it covers can be presumed to figure among the constituents of at least some works of art. But it may be difficult to determine how large a part they play in the existing corpus of art and how they affect the appreciator in the combinations that artists contrive. Consequently, the "synthetic" approach must sooner or later be supplemented with "analytic" studies, in which reactions to genuine works of art are investigated with a view to unraveling their determinants.

[1] The data for experiments reported in Chapters 9 and 10 were collected by Mary Louise King, and the computer operations were handled by her and Bonnie Henderson. The authors wish to express thanks for their extremely able and conscientious work.

This, however, involves difficulties. Any two paintings, for example, must differ in at least a thousand respects. If we find a reliable difference between reactions to the two paintings, any one of these factors, or any combination of them, could be responsible for the difference.

The nonmetric multidimensional-scaling methods (Shepard, Romney, & Nerlove, 1972) that have grown out of recent advances in the theory of psychological measurement and in computer technology offer some possible ways of overcoming this difficulty. They would seem to have immense potentialities for psychological aesthetics, as for other fields.

Multidimensional-scaling procedures begin by obtaining data that can be interpreted as reflecting distances among stimuli in a psychological space. Many kinds of data can serve this purpose, and three were used in the project with which this chapter is concerned.

A particularly useful procedure, especially in the initial stages of a line of research, is to present subjects with pairs of stimulus patterns and ask for ratings of degree of similarity, leaving the subjects to set their own criteria. It is often assumed, especially by partisans of the various cognitivist currents that are popular in psychology at the moment, that such similarity judgments indicate how subjects "perceive" stimulus objects, how their brains or minds categorize, or organize, or conceptualize them. It is assumed that the degree of similarity attributed to a pair of objects represents the degree of similarity between the "cognitions" through which the objects are internally represented. These cognitions will reflect some of the characteristics of the objects faithfully and distort other characteristics. Processes that are often labeled "attention", but are more appropriately called "abstraction" (see Berlyne, 1969, 1970), prevent some characteristics from being reflected at all and cause some of the characteristics that are reflected to figure less prominently than others. It is further assumed that the nonverbal behavior elicited by a stimulus object depends primarily on the nature of the cognition that represents it.

. All these assumptions call for circumspection and more empirical testing than they have received. Nevertheless, multidimensional scaling, especially when coupled with the use of rating scales and nonverbal measures of behavior with reference to the same stimulus objects, can reveal which attributes govern judgments of similarity. These may be the attributes that predominantly govern behavior in general when such objects are encountered.

This chapter reports six experiments, in which a reasonably representative sample of western painting since the Renaissance provides the stimulus material for multidimensional scaling of similarity judgments and preference judgments, for various kinds of rating scales, and for recording of Looking Time. The chief aim was to examine the interrelations of all these dependent measures in the hope of finding out which attributes of paintings dominate subjects' reactions to them and what dimensions can be regarded as salient in the perception of paintings. The next chapter reports a couple of further experiments concerned with the relations between dimensions derived from this project and the reward value of exposure to paintings.

The multivariate and multidimensional methods of data analysis used in this project can best be characterized as "hypothesis-generating" rather than "hypothesis-testing." They summarize the information contained in a large body of data descriptive of various kinds of responses made to the same stimulus patterns. In default of objective external criteria, interpretation is difficult and must to some extent be subjective. It is especially dangerous to place heavy weight on conclusions from a single set of data. If, however, similar conclusions are supported by analyses of different sets of data using a variety of methods, it seems reasonable to take the conclusions seriously.

The hope is that, eventually, investigations of this sort might lead to an objective classification of works of art, based on the responses of ordinary appreciators. Such classifications are not only of intrinsic importance for psychological aesthetics; they are also a necessary preliminary for studies relating differences in style and differences in taste to personality and to culture. Measurement of interindividual and intercultural differences still confronts us with many problems, but a great deal of effort has been devoted to these problems over the years and a great deal of progress has been made. The measurement of differences between works of art is much further behind, which constitutes the principal obstacle at present to reliable knowledge concerning the determinants and the effects of artistic style.

Art historians have, of course, their own taxonomies, which have grown out of centuries of scholarship. There is a fair measure of agreement on them, although there is always room for dispute over the proper characterization of particular works or artists. The criteria and aims of traditional art-historical categories are, however, quite different from those that must be adopted by the psychological aesthetician. For one thing, they depend on the sensitivities of specially trained experts. So, while no experimental aesthetician is in a position to belittle their value, they cannot be accepted as adequate for empirical aesthetics, at least not without experimental investigation of their objective validity. The classificatory schemes that emerge from experimental work with nonexpert subjects and those that have emerged from the lucubrations of scholars may or may not turn out to resemble each other.

How far they do is one of the many interesting questions on which techniques like multidimensional scaling can throw light.

A few experimenters have already used multidimensional scaling with works of art. Two studies analyzed similarity judgments of paintings, but, while their findings were interesting, their scope was limited. Künnapas and Norman (1971) used nine paintings by Cézanne and found three dimensions relevant specifically to the composition of Cézanne's paintings. Goude (1972a, 1972b) used four crucifixions and four landscapes by the same four artists, selected to represent wide variations in style. The investigation that comes nearest to our present one in objectives and in scope is one carried out by Wedin (1972) with musical excerpts. A multidimensional-scaling analysis was also used in an earlier experiment by the present authors (Berlyne, Ogilvie, & Parham, 1968), but it differed in two respects from the project to be reported. The stimulus material consisted of nonrepresentational line drawings, and Ss judged how similar drawings were in degree of complexity, pleasingness, and interestingness, rather than how similar they were in general.

STIMULUS MATERIAL

Fifty-two slides, bearing colored reproductions of pictures, were selected from a collection offered for sale by the Art Gallery of Ontario, Toronto. All of the pictures are located in Toronto, the great majority belonging to the Art Gallery of Ontario. Artists, years of birth, and titles are specified in Table 1. Apart from one mixed media work and one silkscreen print, most are paintings of oil in tempera with one watercolor and one epoxy. Although the pictures do not represent a random or systematically constructed sample, they cover western painting from the fourteenth century to the mid-twentieth century and include most of the principal styles that have appeared during that period.

Since the multidimensional scaling technique necessitates presenting to a subject all possible pairs of the objects he is to judge, the 52 pictures were divided into two sets of 30, with 8 common to both sets. The 8 were chosen as follows. The 52 paintings were arranged in order of the artist's year of birth and divided into 8 subsets of 7 or 8 consecutive items. One picture was then randomly chosen from each subset. The remaining 44 pictures were then randomly assigned to set A or Set B.

TABLE 1

Pictures Used in Experiments 1, 2, 3, and 4

Number	Artist	Year of birth	Title	Experiment 3			Experiment 4			
				I Hedonic Tone	II Arousal	III Uncertainty	I Subjectivism	II Realism	III Classicism	IV Impressionism
			SET A							
1*	Andrea del Sarto	1486	The Madonna and Child with Infant St. John and Children	.52	-.24	-.26	-.46	.57	.80	-.53
2*	Orley, Bernard van	1491	Rest on the Flight into Egypt	.53	.17	-.41	-.23	.79	.58	.29
3*	Tintoretto, Jacopo	1518	Christ Washing His Disciples' Feet	.16	.02	-.11	.37	.78	.83	-.02
4	Hals, Frans	1580	Isaak Abrahamsz Massa	.31	-.07	-.70	-.64	.65	.35	.82
5	Arentsz, Arent	1585	Skaters on the Amstel	.54	.08	.22	-.75	.59	-.43	-.41
6*	Preti, Mattia	1613	St. Paul the Hermit	-.10	.89	.05	.70	1.01	.24	-.17
7*	Gainsborough, Thomas	1727	The Harvest Wagon	.16	-.64	.65	.39	-.12	.34	1.12
8*	Northcote, James	1746	Mrs Wells as Hebe	.07	.31	-.31	.19	.85	-.07	-.20
9	Degas, Edgar	1834	Woman in Bath	.42	-.33	.40	.36	-.24	.59	1.03
10*	Tissot, James	1836	La Demoiselle de Magasin	.80	.14	.32	-.18	-.02	.68	.19
11	Fantin-Latour, Henri	1836	Roses, Peaches and Plums	.15	-.75	-.11	-1.26	-.15	.20	1.14
12*	Redon, Odilon	1840	Vase de Fleurs	.11	-.84	-.36	-1.02	-.40	-.88	.34
13	Vlaminck, Maurice	1876	River Landscape with Stormy Sky	-.21	-.37	.86	.55	-.46	-.42	.23
14*	Dufy, Raoul	1877	Port du Havre	.63	-.18	.34	.41	-.72	.11	.51
15	John, Augustus	1878	The Marchesa Casati	-.49	.13	-.11	1.31	-.12	-.35	.88
16	Derain, André	1880	Fleurs dans un Panier	-.09	-.90	-.55	-.26	-.43	-.47	.87
17*	Picasso, Pablo	1881	Crouching Woman	-.17	.26	-.35	1.36	.38	-1.03	-.10
18*	Louis, Morris	1912	Lambda	-.68	-.30	-.09	-.36	-1.35	.24	-.95
19*	Kelly, Ellsworth	1923	Blue White	-.20	-.43	-.07	.21	-.95	.80	-1.51
20*	Noland, Kenneth	1924	"C"	-.31	.29	-.83	-.55	-1.55	.89	-.75
21*	Indiana, Robert	1928	The Demuth American Dream	-.36	.89	-.66	.05	.49	-.20	-1.29
22*	Dine, Jim	1935	Black Bathroom No. 2	-.97	-.45	-.07	-.63	.97	-2.39	-.39

TABLE 1 (Continued)

Pictures Used in Experiments 1, 2, 3, and 4

Number	Artist	Year of birth	Title	Mean factor scores						
				Experiment 3			Experiment 4			
				I Hedonic Tone	II Arousal	III Uncertainty	I Subjectivism	II Realism	III Classicism	IV Impressionism
			SET B							
23	Giovanni del Biondo	XIV c.	Vision of St. Benedict	-.53	.14	-.06	.47	.22	.42	-.23
24	Bartolommeo di Giovanni	1480	Lamentation with Saints and a Donor	-.58	.23	-.39	-.03	.31	.12	-.91
25*	Brueghel, Peter the Younger	1564	The Peasants' Wedding	.41	.34	.03	.96	-.31	-.01	-1.34
26	Rubens, Peter Paul	1577	The Elevation of the Cross	.07	1.04	.40	1.13	.47	.71	.65
27	Poussin, Nicolas	1594	Venus, Mother of Aeneas, Presenting Him with Arms Forged by Vulcan.	.28	.30	.26	.52	1.61	-.25	-.37
28	Claude, Lorrain	1600	Carlo and Ubaldo Embarking in Pursuit of Rinaldo	.74	-.20	.14	-.46	.36	-.93	-.02
29*	Rijn, Rembrandt van	1606	Portrait of a Lady with a Handkerchief	.53	.01	-.64	-.39	.42	-.86	.19
30	Rootius, Jan Albertsz	1615	Portrait of a Young Girl with a Carnation	.45	.17	-.48	-1.24	.82	-.56	.06
31*	Unknown (Netherlands)	XVII c.	Still Life with Roemer, Fruit and Roses	.56	.22	-.46	-1.35	.31	.72	.26
32*	Canaletto, Antonio	1697	Piazzetta, Venice	.62	.09	-.50	-1.46	.08	.17	-.29
33*	Chardin, Jean Baptiste	1699	Un Bocal d'Abricots, dit un Dessert	.42	-.27	-.30	-.26	.07	1.24	1.00
34	Delacroix, Eugene	1798	The Fanatics of Tangiers	-.08	.70	.38	.31	-.20	.32	.74
35	Pissarro, Camille	1830	Le Pont Boïeldieu à Rouen	.40	-.57	.33	-.32	-.23	-.40	.68
36*	Sisley, Alfred	1839	Paysage Près de Moret	.51	-.54	.03	.10	-.21	-.68	.40
37*	Renoir, Pierre Auguste	1841	Le Concert	.10	-.78	.67	-.11	-.21	.17	.81
38*	Bonnard, Pierre	1867	La Table Garnie	.16	-.48	.06	-.87	-.66	.40	.25
39	Vuillard, Edouard	1868	The Widow's Visit	-.51	-.80	.42	.27	-.31	.31	.73
40*	Utrillo, Maurice	1883	La Maison de Berlioz et Pavillon de Chasse Henri IV	-.21	.21	.70	-.03	.58	1.20	.48
41*	Albers, Josef	1888	Homage to the Square: Oasis	-.96	-.85	-1.19	-.83	-1.54	.33	-1.27
42*	Moore, Henry	1898	Group of Shelterers during an Air Raid	-.23	-.04	.38	1.11	.04	1.05	-.08
43	Warhol, Andy	1930	Elvis I and II	-.90	.10	-.77	.88	.51	-.74	-.77
44	Stella, Frank	1936	Ossippee II	-.83	.30	-.58	-.20	-1.22	.33	-.96

TABLE 1 (*Continued*)

Pictures Used in Experiments 1, 2, 3, and 4

Number	Artist	Year of birth	Title	Mean factor scores						
				Experiment 3			Experiment 4			
				I Hedonic Tone	II Arousal	III Uncertainty	I Subjectivism	II Realism	III Classicism	IV Impressionism
			COMMON TO SETS A AND B							
45*	Giovanni del Biondo	XIV c.	St. Benedict Restores Life to a Young Benedictine Monk	-.43, -.39	-.45, -.48	-.10, -.39	.47, .09	.72, 1.03	.02, .23	-.80, -.94
46	Dyck, Anthony van	1599	Michael de Blon	.31, .31	-.01, .25	-.57, -.72	-.67, -.60	.91, 1.04	-.06, -1.28	.79, -.12
47	Dyck, Anthony van	1599	Daedalus and Icarus	.02, .46	.35, .54	-.13, -.39	-.65, .44	.75, .93	.20, .24	-.31, .34
48*	Fuseli, Henri	1741	Lear Banishing Cordelia	-.09, -.05	.86, 1.06	-.18, -.33	-.35, .50	.76, .40	.33, -.13	-.60, -.44
49*	Monet, Claude	1840	Vetheuil en Été	-.10, .40	-.37, -.57	.82, .33	.70, -.35	-.52, -1.00	-.06, -1.16	1.22, .45
50	Gleizes, Albert	1881	Le Port	-.00, -.28	.70, .15	.89, 1.16	.68, .63	-.29, -1.01	.43, .63	-.51, -.90
51	Appel, Karel	1921	Nobody Knows It	-.48, -.31	.69, -.06	1.04, 1.12	.57, .86	-1.31, -1.07	-.73, -1.41	-.62, .83
52*	Ronald, William	1926	Herronton Woods	-.05, -.23	.56, -.27	.35, .48	-.28, .24	-1.60, -1.21	-.55, -.17	-.30, .77

*Used also in Experiments 5 and 6.

EXPERIMENT 1: PAIRWISE SIMILARITY JUDGMENTS

The first experiment should be regarded as a preliminary study of largely methodological interest. Prime aims were to find out how well subjects could rate differences between paintings without specification of criteria and whether there would be consistency both within and between subjects. The experiment afforded an opportunity to find out what kinds of results would be obtained when nonmetric scaling is applied to paintings. Comparisons of these results with the ratings and Looking Times recorded in the following experiments would also be suggestive.

Subjects

Ten paid volunteer Ss (three males and seven females) were obtained from the departmental subject pool of undergraduates. All had some postsecondary education, and none had formal training in art appreciation or a special interest in art as a hobby. They split randomly into two equal groups, who saw respectively stimulus set A and stimulus set B.

Procedure

The stimuli were projected by two Kodak Carousel (Model 860) projectors on to a 47 in. square Da-lite screen.

Each S was shown all 435 pairs from the appropriate stimulus set in a different sequence. The sequences were printed by the computer and generated from pseudo-random numbers.

S was seated in the experimental room, and instructions were read to him, explaining that his task was to judge on a 7-point scale how similar or different the two pictures of each pair were. The final six pairs in his permutation were presented in reverse order for practice trials. When S understood the task, he was given a computer-printed sheet of scales with four columns of scales to the page, and the experiment began.

E loaded projectors manually. Each pair appeared for approximately 4 seconds with an interval between pairs of about 7 seconds. Because of the length of the experiment, two sessions were required. After the first 200 pairs, the first session terminated. S was asked not to discuss the experiment and to avoid thinking about it as far as possible. The next day he returned to complete the experiment.

Results

First, an analysis of variance was performed for each stimulus set. The F value, with 434 and 1,736 degrees of freedom, for pairs of pictures came to 3.63 in group A and 3.08 in group B. These values are significant far beyond the .001 level and correspond to reliability coefficients of .72 and .67 (Winer, 1971, pp. 283ff.), respectively. There is therefore quite reasonable intersubject consistency.

Next, the 30 x 30 matrix of mean dissimilarity scores for each group was subjected to nonmetric scaling. This procedure is now so well known and well described (Kruskal, 1964; Shepard, Romney & Merlove, 1972) that it will be only briefly summarized here. In nonmetric scaling, a configuration of points is generated in a fixed number of dimensions, and the configuration is then modified iteratively to produce a set of points whose distances are as nearly as possible in the same rank order as the dissimilarities in the data matrix. Nonmetric scaling can be regarded as a kind of nonmetric factor analysis.

The program used here was NMSCAL ("numbskull"), which is a local variant of TORSCA-9. Scaling was done in one to five dimensions. The stress values for group A were .28, .18, .12, .09, .07, and for group B, .33, .20, .15, .11, .08. The interpretation of stress is not straightforward, but it seems clear that it would be unreasonable to assume more than three dimensions, because the further improvement in fit is negligible.

The configurations for the eight stimuli that the two sets had in common were compared for the two groups of Ss. The comparison was done visually with the two-dimensional scaling results, and the agreement was excellent. This is further evidence of intersubject consistency.

Secondly, individual-differences scaling (INDSCAL) was done on both sets of data. In this procedure, developed by Carroll & Chang (1970), it is assumed that the stimuli can be represented by a fixed configuration of points in Euclidean space and that this configuration is common to all Ss. There is, however, a weight vector associated with each S where the weights express the emphasis placed by the S on each dimension.

The results for the two groups are very similar; so, only those for group A will be described. They are shown in Table 2. The correlations improve as more dimensions are added, but again it seems unreasonable to go past three dimensions. For only one S is there much improvement as one goes from two to three dimensions. The same is true of group B. The variances associated with each dimension in the three-dimensional scaling show one dominant dimension and two of much less importance.

TABLE 2

INDSCAL Results for Group A in
Experiment 1
Correlations of Fitted Weighted
Coordinates with Input Ratings

Subject	Number of fitted dimensions		
	1	2	3
1	.71 ·	.73	.79
2	.22	.31	.53
3	.45	.57	.63
4	.68	.80	.83
5	.39	.53	.54
Overall	.525	.613	.676
Variance	1.38	1.04	1.17
for each		.74	.62
dimension			.40

The outputs of the NMSCAL and INDSCAL programs represent stimuli (in our case, paintings) as points in an n-dimensional space. As explained, the most reasonable number of dimensions to use with our data seems to be three. INDSCAL will also plot subjects as points in the same space, in which case each coordinate represents the relative weight of the corresponding dimension in determining the subject's judgments. Inspection of the painting plots suggested that the first and most important dimension contrasts old masters with modern art. Degree of realistic representation is the most obvious attribute in which older and newer paintings differ, but there are, of course, others. The second and third dimensions were difficult to identify even tentatively, although there was a hint that the relative importance of line and surface quality might have something to do with one of them. It was, however, doubtful that the second dimensions of the different analyses were the same.

A third analysis was of a rather different kind, outputting a hierarchical grouping of the pictures. Of the various hierarchical-grouping methods, "furthest-neighbor" analysis (Johnson, 1967; Lance & Williams, 1967; Cunningham & Ogilvie, 1972) seems to be one of the better ones. It was applied to the data from both of our groups. The tree obtained from group A is shown in Figure 1 as an illustration. The three clusters that first separate from one another seem to approximate the modern abstract and

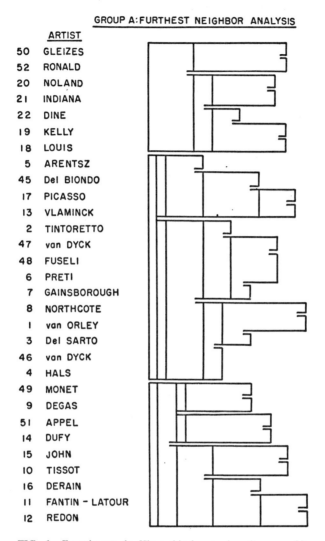

FIG. 1. Experiment 1: Hierarchical grouping (tree graph) derived from furtherest-neighbor analysis of dissimilarity judgments of group A.

nonrepresentational works, old masters, and impressionistic works, respectively.

EXPERIMENT 2: AFFECTIVE AND COLLATIVE SCALING

In Experiment 2, two new groups of Ss were asked to scale the two sets of paintings on each of 12 scales. The scales were those used in Experiments IA and IIA of Chapter 5 except that UNBALANCED-BALANCED replaced DISLIKE-LIKE, and they were those used in another study (Berlyne, 1973) except that DISORDERLY-ORDERLY replaced PASSIVE-ACTIVE.

Tables 3 and 4 list the scales. They fall into three classes. There are evaluative scales (e.g., DISPLEASING-PLEASING, UNINTERESTING-INTERESTING) and internal-state scales (e.g., NO PLEASURE-EXTREME PLEASURE, RELAXED-TENSE). Scales belonging to these two classes may appropriately be designated "affective" scales. Lastly, there are descriptive scales referring to collative or informational properties of patterns (e.g., SIMPLE-COMPLEX, CLEAR-INDEFINITE).

The purpose of Experiment 2 was twofold. First, it was of interest to see what kinds of intercorrelations and factor structures would emerge when scales of these kinds are applied to paintings. They could be compared with the intercorrelations and factor structures produced by previous experiments, which used, respectively, simple nonrepresentational patterns varying in information-theoretic properties (Chap. 5, this volume), and a miscellany of visual patterns including a few paintings (Berlyne, 1973). Secondly, it was hoped that the scaling data would throw some light on the dimensions generated by the similarity judgments of Experiment 1 and thus on the attributes that preponderated in our Ss' perceptions of paintings.

Subjects

Sixteen Ss rated each of the two sets of 30 paintings. There were 6 males and 10 females in Group A and 5 males and 11 females in Group B. In each group, 10 were unpaid and 6 were paid, but all were undergraduates taking psychology courses.

Procedure and Design

The 30 pictures were projected on to a screen in the same conditions as in Experiments IA and IIA of Chapter 5.

TABLE 3
Experiment 2: Affective and Collative Scaling
(Correlations)

	1	2	3	4	5	6	7	8	9	10	11	12	13
							Group A						
1. SIMPLE-COMPLEX	–	.57**	-.66**	-.31	.42*	.21	.81**	.50**	.68**	.24	.36	.49**	.50**
2. CLEAR-INDEFINITE	.46**	–	-.78**	-.46	.02	-.14	.33	.02	.30	.38*	.26	.12	.41*
3. DISORDERLY-ORDERLY	-.76**	-.73**	–	.78**	-.03	.21	-.44*	-.10	-.41*	-.33	-.24	-.26	-.35
4. UNBALANCED-BALANCED	.12	-.28	.21	–	-.11	-.15	-.10	.05	-.33	.01	-.04	-.10	-.16
5. DISPLEASING-PLEASING	-.14	-.31	.24	.22	–	.82**	.37*	.15	.84**	-.53**	.30	.12	.15
6. UGLY-BEAUTIFUL	-.13	-.40*	.33	.29	.91**	–	.08	-.04	.63**	-.57**	-.45*	-.26	-.04
7. UNINTERESTING-INTERESTING	.55**	-.12	-.21	.17	.35	.44*	–	.76**	.63**	.36	.54**	.76**	.50**
8. WEAK-POWERFUL	.51**	-.26	-.10	.19	.07	.20	.79**	–	.26	.30	.72**	.78**	.31
9. NO PLEASURE-EXTREME PLEASURE	.05	-.21	.16	.20	.87**	.85**	.57**	.19	–	-.31	-.16	.28	.37*
10. NO DISCOMFORT-EXTREME DISCOMFORT	.56**	.43*	-.55**	-.20	-.78**	-.70**	.13	.27	-.56**	–	.66**	.29	.19
11. RELAXED-TENSE	.62**	.31	-.57**	-.17	-.67**	-.62**	.28	.46*	-.52**	.88**	–	.70**	.13
12. DROWSY-ALERT	.45*	-.24	-.28	-.08	-.11	-.11	.58**	.68**	-.03	.37*	.60**	–	.28
13. Rating Time	.72**	.39*	-.68**	-.11	-.36	-.28	.36	.38*	-.20	.59**	.63**	.38	–
							Group B						

*

*p < .05.

**p < .01.

Within each group, every S saw the pictures in a different order, corresponding to a randomly selected row of a 30×30 Latin Square. A different randomly selected permutation of the 12 scales was associated with each temporal position.

After the instructions, one of the paintings not presented to S's group was used for practice. S then went through the 12 scales while each of the 30 paintings assigned to his group was projected in turn. The 12 scales to be used with a particular picture were printed in the format introduced by Osgood (a row of seven compartments with words representing the opposite poles of the scale printed at the two ends) on one sheet of a booklet. S pressed a button to advance the projector when he was ready to start on a new picture, and E recorded Rating Time with a stopwatch.

Results

Correlations and factor analysis. Analysis of variance showed the main effect of paintings to be significant at at least the .005 level for every scale in either group. The effect of Pictures on Rating Time was significant at the .05 level in Group B but not significant in Group A.

Table 3 shows the correlations over pictures between mean scores on the 13 variables, those for Group A appearing above the principal diagonal and those for Group B appearing below the principal diagonal.

A principal-components factor analysis, with Varimax rotation, was then carried out on the variables that showed significant intersubject agreement (i.e., all 13 variables in Group B but only the 12 scales and not Rating Time in Group A). The factor loadings are shown in Table 4, with those having an absolute value greater than .5 printed in bold face.

The first thing to notice is the striking similarity between the factor structures for the two groups. Apart from the fact that UNBALANCED-BALANCED has a high loading on Factor III in group A but no high loading on any factor in group B, the scales having high loadings (greater than .50) on particular factors are the same in both groups. When we compare the results with those of the factor analyses derived from ratings of simple nonrepresentational visual patterns in Chapter 5, we find that the scales that distributed themselves between two factors in those experiments are here distributed among three factors, which account for 84.0% of the variance in group A and 81.3% in group B. Whereas, in the experiments of Chapter 5, the UNINTERESTING-INTERESTING, WEAK-POWERFUL, DROWSY-ALERT, and, in one case, RELAXED-TENSE scales were loaded on the Hedonic Tone factor, they here produce a factor of their own. Consequently, the three

TABLE 4

Experiment 2: Affective and Collative Scaling
(Factor Analyses)

	Group A			Group B		
	I (Hedonic Tone)	II (Arousal)	III (Uncertainty)	I (Hedonic Tone)	II (Arousal)	III (Uncertainty)
1. SIMPLE-COMPLEX	.34	.62	.59	-.01	.54	.76
2. CLEAR-INDEFINITE	-.09	.14	.84	-.19	.34	.86
3. DISORDERLY-ORDERLY	.06	-.19	-.96	.17	-.14	-.91
4. UNBALANCED-BALANCED	-.03	.09	-.81	.29	.20	-.22
5. DISPLEASING-PLEASING	.95	.15	.08	.95	-.02	-.14
6. UGLY-BEAUTIFUL	.90	-.09	-.14	.93	.10	-.20
7. UNINTERESTING-INTERESTING	.24	.88	.29	.44	.80	.23
8. WEAK-POWERFUL	.04	.93	-.09	.11	.93	.02
9. NO PLEASURE-EXTREME PLEASURE	.82	.31	.42	.94	.13	.01
10. NO DISCOMFORT-EXTREME DISCOMFORT	-.68	.45	.24	-.71	.37	.47
11. RELAXED-TENSE	-.48	.79	.09	-.65	.57	.41
12. DROWSY-ALERT	-.05	.88	.08	-.16	.85	.04
13. Rating Time	–	–	–	-.24	.43	.68

factors descriptive of paintings are provisionally labeled Hedonic Tone, Arousal, and Uncertainty, respectively.

Comparisons with Results of Experiment 1

Each of the 30 pictures comprising set A and each of the 30 pictures comprising set B has a location along each of the three dimensions resulting from the INDSCAL analysis, which means that it has a location in the three-dimensional conceptual space derived from pair-wise dissimilarity judgments. Each picture also has a mean score on each of the 12 scales used in Experiment 2 and a mean estimated factor score on each of the three factors derived from the intercorrelations of these scales. This means that it has a location in a 12-dimensional scale space and a location in a 3-dimensional factor space.

There are two fundamental problems in interpreting the results of a multidimensional scaling analysis. The first is how many dimensions are appropriate. The second is how the axes should be oriented. In neither case are there statistical tests or adequate objective methods. In the absence of external information, one must make more arbitrary and subjective choices. But additional information can be used to make the choices a little more objective. Carroll & Chang (1970) have claimed that a configuration of points obtained through INDSCAL requires no rotation and is usually directly interpretable. If this holds true, one can treat the coordinates of the pictures as a fixed set of dependent variables and use techniques of multivariate regression to predict them from mean ratings.

Comparisons, and in particular correlations, relating the measures produced by Experiments 1 and 2 may therefore provide some clues to the principal attributes of paintings that underlie similarity-dissimilarity judgments and perhaps even to the identity of the INDSCAL dimensions.

Such correlations must, however, be treated with great caution. They are correlations between scores obtained from different groups of Ss (though drawn from the same population) carrying out different tasks. The groups of Ss are small, and the rapid judgments required must be subject to a great deal of test-retest unreliability. On the other hand, all these conditions make likely some attenuation of correlation coefficients, and all the measures to be discussed in this connection showed significant intersubject consistency. This makes high correlations all the more impressive when they emerge. It must be noted, however, that, whenever there is a significant correlation between a measure derived from a rating scale and a dimension derived from multidimensional scaling, it would be fallacious to conclude that the rated attribute plays a part in determining similarity judgments. It is possible that the rated attribute is correlated with some other attribute that looms large when S estimates similarity.

With all these limitations in mind, we can proceed to ask a number of questions. The first is whether there is a significant degree of relation between the INDSCAL space and the scale space (or its associated factor space), in the sense that knowledge of the location of a picture in the latter could reduce uncertainty regarding its location in the former. The appropriate index of association is the canonical correlation coefficient (R_C). Computation of this index amounts to finding linear combinations of each of two sets of measures such that the product-moment correlation between the two linear combinations will be maximal. R_C between the 12-dimensional scale space and 3-dimensional INDSCAL space comes to .90 in set A and .96 in set B[2]. If the 12-dimensional scale space is replaced by the 3-dimensional factor space, R_C drops to .73 for set A and .80 for set B. The significance of canonical correlations can be gauged by means of a χ^2 test (Bartlett, 1941). According to this test, all of the four canonical correlations just mentioned are significant at the .001 level. Finally, one can compute the redundancy (Stewart & Love, 1968)[3] from the rating data of Experiment 2 to the INDSCAL data of Experiment 1, i.e., the amount of variance shared by the two sets of data expressed as a proportion of INDSCAL variance. This provides a measure of the extent to which INDSCAL locations could be predicted from the rating data. The redundancies from the scale space to the INDSCAL space come to .58 for group A and .81 for group B. The redundancies from the factor space to the INDSCAL space are .27 for group A and .46 for group B.

These redundancy indices bear on one perennial difficulty that haunts all users of factor analysis and other multivariate techniques. When these techniques are used, everything depends on the choice of variables, which is sometimes rather arbitrary and, in any case, rarely represents a systematic sample of all the variables that could be used in approaching a particular problem area, let alone exhausting them. The choice of scales for Experiment 2 of the present project was dictated by a great deal of previous theoretical

[2] Whenever there is a reference to *the* canonical correlation coefficient (R_c) in this chapter and in Chapter 11, the maximum canonical correlation coefficient is meant. When an m-dimensional space and an n-dimensional space are compared, there are actually m different canonical correlation coefficients, where $m \leqslant n$. These correspond to m mutually orthogonal coefficient vectors or rotated axes.

[3] A few days before the typescript of this book was due to be sent to the publisher, Stewart and Love's redundancy index, which figures in this chapter and in Chapter 11, came under attack. W. A. Nicewander and D. A. Wood ("Comments on 'A general canonical index'," *Psychological Bulletin*, 1974, 81, 92–94) claimed that this index is invalid and does not represent what it purports to represent. Flaws in their arguments have been pointed out in rejoinders written by J. K. Miller, by S. D. Farr, and by R. B. Dunham and D. J. Kravetz. In an earlier article (J. K. Miller and S. D. Farr: "Bivariate redundancy: A comprehensive measure of interbattery relationship," *Multivariate Behavioral Research*, 1971, 6, 313–324), measures of redundancy were computed for the same data both from a canonical-correlation analysis (using Stewart and Love's method) and from multiple regression of principal components: the two procedures produced identical values. Dr. Miller (personal communication) has also confirmed the validity of the index by checking it against variance ratios calculated directly from product-moment correlations. He has, furthermore, worked out an algebraic demonstration of its validity.

discussion and experimental work, but, as in other lines of research, they may very well have excluded some attributes of prime importance. The redundancy values just mentioned imply at least a substantial overlap between the information obtained from the scales and the information obtained from the dissimilarity judgments. A fair proportion of the attributes determining how the pictures are perceived and coded is evidently reflected in the battery of scales. The remaining INDSCAL variance might be covered by other scales, which might have been included in the battery but were not, but much of it is no doubt identifiable with errors of measurement and random fluctuation.

We can go on to ask which scales (or factors) are most closely related to the INDSCAL space. The appropriate index for this question is the multiple correlation coefficient (R), measuring the degree of association between mean scores on that scale and the INDSCAL dimensions collectively. Two of the scales had significant multiple correlations with the three dimensional INDSCAL spaces for both sets of pictures. These were UGLY-BEAUTIFUL, WEAK-POWERFUL, and RELAXED-TENSE. The only one of the three factors to show a significant R with the INDSCAL spaces for both sets of pictures was Factor I (Hedonic Tone).

The upshot of these analyses is, therefore, that the location of a picture in the scale space, and to a lesser extent in the factor space, has a fair degree of affinity with its location in the INDSCAL space. But the rating-scale data do not permit us to identify the INDSCAL dimensions with any assurance, and there is strong reason to believe that the dimensions defining the INDSCAL space of set A are distinct from those defining the INDSCAL space of set B.

EXPERIMENT 3: LOOKING TIME

Looking Time was measured with yet another group of Ss from the same population. This was partly to find out whether there would be significant intersubject consistency. Many previous experiments have shown such consistency with regard to Looking Time, but most of them have used simple, nonrepresentational patterns rather than paintings. Apart from that, relations between mean Looking Time, a behavioral measure, and the measures derived from verbal responses, whether in the form of similarity-dissimilarity judgments or of ratings, seemed worth examining.

Since it was possible to go through all 52 paintings in one session, there was only one group of Ss.

Subjects

There were 8 male and 11 female Ss from a paid subject pool. All but one (who had completed high school) had had some postsecondary education. Ss with a special interest or training in art were not accepted.

Procedure

The procedure was essentially the same as that used in Experiments IB and IIB of Chapter 5. GSR and EKG electrodes with leads were attached to disguise the purpose of the experiment, S being given to understand that the intention was to record psychophysiological changes. Every S saw the 52 paintings in a different randomly selected order, pressing a button to replace one slide with the next whenever he chose to do so. There was a 5-minute break, during which S was given magazines to read, between the first 26 pictures and the last 26.

Results

Analysis of variance. The main effect for pictures produced an F value, with 51 and 918 degrees of freedom, of 2.50; $p < .01$. This corresponds to a reliability of 0.60. There is therefore enough consistency to justify using the mean Looking Times for paintings in comparisons with other data.

Comparisons with the results of Experiments 1 and 2. There were no significant correlations between Looking Time and any of the INDSCAL dimensions, apart from a correlation of $-.38$ ($p < .05$) with the third INDSCAL dimension in group B. The multiple correlation between Looking Time and the three INDSCAL dimensions comes to .41 (not significant) in group A, and to .56 ($p < .05$) in group B. There is therefore evidence for some relation, but a relatively tenuous one, between Looking Time and the attributes that determine similarity judgments.

We can now turn to the relations between Looking Time and the mean ratings and factor scores from Experiment 2. Information about the relation between Looking Time and each of these variables comes from two correlation coefficients from the two sets of pictures. Since, in some cases, the correlation is significant with one set and not with the other, it was decided to examine the combined significance levels, using the Stouffer method (Mosteller & Bush, 1954, p. 329). This method entails converting each product-moment coefficient to a z value and dividing the sum of the two z values by the square root of 2 (the square root of the number of observations). The resulting combined z values, where significant, are

TABLE 5

Experiments 2 and 3: Correlations

Variable (Experiment 2)	Looking Time (Experiment 3)	Artist's Year of birth
	Combined z	Combined z
1. SIMPLE-COMPLEX	5.87***	–
2. CLEAR-INDEFINITE	–	4.65***
3. DISORDERLY-ORDERLY	–3.12**	–
4. UNBALANCED-BALANCED	–	–
5. DISPLEASING-PLEASING	2.70**	–2.54*
6. UGLY-BEAUTIFUL	2.09*	–3.09***
7. UNINTERESTING-INTERESTING	5.29***	–
8. WEAK-POWERFUL	2.81**	–
9. NO PLEASURE-EXTREME PLEASURE	3.74***	–
10. NO DISCOMFORT-EXTREME DISCOMFORT	–	–
11. RELAXED-TENSE	–	–
12. DROWSY-ALERT	3.11**	–
I Hedonic Tone	2.79**	–2.65**
II Arousal	3.56***	–
III Uncertainty	2.99**	2.24*

$*p < .05.$
$**p < .01.$
$***p < .001.$

displayed in Table 5. A minus sign indicates that the correlation is negative. The z-test indicates that Looking Time is correlated with all three factors and with 8 out of 12 scales. In accord with a sizable body of previous research, the most substantial correlations are with SIMPLE-COMPLEX and UNINTERESTING-INTERESTING judgments.

EXPERIMENT 4: STYLISTIC SCALING

In the next experiment, two groups of Ss were required to rate the two groups of paintings on attributes of a different nature from those that figured in Experiment 2. This time, it was a matter of rating stylistic or technical attributes. For judgments of this kind, it seemed safe to enlist Ss with some training in the fine arts rather than Ss from the usual subject pool of psychology students that had been used in the previous experiments. The aims were, once again, multiple. It was hoped to find out how consistently subjects could produce rapid ratings of the attributes in question, how these rated attributes are related to one another, and what further clues they might provide with regard to the determinants of similarity-dissimilarity judgments.

Subjects

Three male and five female subjects were selected by faculty members of the Fine Arts Department of the University of Toronto from undergraduates taking studio courses. Although they were not students specializing in history or theory of art, they had all taken theoretical courses and had therefore been exposed to the terms and concepts current among art critics. They were divided randomly into two groups, who rated pictures of sets A and B, respectively.

Scales

The 12 scales used in this experiment are shown in Table 6. It was made clear to S that he was to judge the importance in each picture of each of

TABLE 6

Experiment 4: Stylistic Ratings

Scales

Importance of:

1. Reproduction of the appearance of objects or people (REPRODUCTION)
2. Composition or arrangement of elements (COMPOSITION)
3. The artist's feelings or emotions (EMOTION)
4. The artist's individual way of perceiving objects or the world as a whole (PERCEPTION)
5. The artist's beliefs or thoughts (BELIEFS)
6. The artist's imagination or fantasies (IMAGINATION)
7. Aesthetic norms or stylistic conventions characterizing the society or age in which the artist lived (AESTHETIC NORMS)
8. Beliefs or values characterizing the society or age in which the artist lived (NONAESTHETIC NORMS)
9. Surface qualities or textures (SURFACE)
10. Lines
11. Colors
12. Shapes

Note: Words in parentheses are abbreviations by which scales are designated in text.

the 12 factors. On each page of the answer booklet, the phrase describing each factor was printed above an Osgood-type scale, which had the words NOT AT ALL on the left and the word EXTREMELY on the right. The descriptive phrases appear in Table 6, together with the word that will, for convenience, be used hereafter to denote each scale.

The first eight scales were suggested by an information-theoretic analysis of artistic style outlined elsewhere (Berlyne, 1971; see Chap. 1, this volume). The basic assumption is that each element of a work of art can transmit information from four different sources, which will compete for the limited capacity of the channel. The four kinds of information are designated *semantic* information (originating in the perceptible properties of external objects or events), *syntactic* information (originating in other elements of the same work, i.e., constraints requiring similarities, contrasts, or other specifiable relations between one portion of a work and other portions, adjacent or remote), *expressive* information (originating in the artist's internal psychological processes), and *cultural* information (originating in the beliefs, values, or customs of the social group with which the artist identifies himself).

Scales 1 and 2 were intended to tap semantic and syntactic information, respectively. Scales 3 to 6 were aimed at expressive information, since it had been suggested (Berlyne, 1971) that, among the artist's psychological processes, the influence of affective, perceptual, intellectual, and imaginative processes might be distinguished. Scales 7 and 8 were concerned with cultural information, distinguishing the influence of aesthetic norms from those of norms relating to nonaesthetic matters. The last four scales pertain to technical features of paintings. The distinction between paintings emphasizing line and paintings emphasizing surface quality or texture is an old one, found, for example, in Wölfflin's (1915) influential "linear-painterly" dimension. Similarly the polarity between dependence on shape or form and dependence on color has appeared not only in many discussions of painting but also in many psychological studies of individual differences in perception (e.g., Oeser, 1932). The use of bipolar LINE-SURFACE and SHAPE-COLOR scales was considered, but it would have prejudiced the question of whether the factors that would then be paired are actually opposites. Consequently, it was decided to include four separate scales corresponding to tho four factors, so that the degree of negative correlation, if any, between those that are commonly contrasted with each other could be revealed.

Procedure and Design

Apart from the scales, the procedure and design were modeled after those used in Experiment 2. As in that experiment, every S saw the pictures in a different sequence, corresponding to a randomly selected row of 30 x 30 counterbalanced Latin Square, and a different randomly selected permutation of the scales was associated with each of the 30 temporal positions in which a picture could appear. Once again, a practice slide, taken from the set that was not used for S's group, was shown at the start to provide an opportunity for practice and for the explanation of anything that was not clear. After completing the scales for one picture, S pressed a button bringing on the next picture, and Rating Time was recorded.

Results

Analysis of variance. The Pictures main effect was significant for all scales in both groups, with the exception of SHAPES in group A and PERCEPTIONS, AESTHETIC NORMS, and NONAESTHETIC NORMS in group B.

Correlations and Factor Analyses

Correlations over pictures between mean scores and the 12 scales are presented in Table 7. Once again, the correlations for group A appear above the principal diagonal and those for group B below.

The correlations involving the 11 scales that were significantly consistent from subject to subject in group A and the 9 scales that were significantly consistent in group B were subjected to separate factor analyses, whose outcomes are shown in Table 8. As in Table 4, loadings with absolute values greater than .50 are printed in bold face. Both analyses produced four factors accounting for 82.9% of the variance in group A and 81.5% in group B.

There are enough similarities between the two factor structures to establish correspondences between factors derived from the two groups. However, some variables have a high loading on a factor in one group but not in the other, and some scales were included in one factor analysis but not in the other.

The task of selecting provisional labels for the four factors is perhaps a little more hazardous than most factor analyses, but nevertheless instructive. On Factor I, we find high loadings for all scales representing the artist's psychological processes but for no others. This factor was therefore labeled Subjectivism. The predominant variables in Factor II are REPRODUCTION

TABLE 7
Experiment 4: Stylistic Ratings
(Correlations)

	1	2	3	4	5	6	7	8	9	10	11	12
							Group A					
1. REPRODUCTION	—	-.11	-.40*	.00	-.40*	-.65**	.19	.49**	.18	-.18	-.58**	-.52**
2. COMPOSITION	.01	—	-.09	.08	-.26	-.07	.55**	.09	-.13	.64**	.26	.09
3. EMOTIONS	-.21	-.10	—	.60**	.69**	.72**	-.14	-.08	-.07	.09	.33	.17
4. PERCEPTIONS	.04	-.08	.28	—	.42*	.34	-.17	.06	.00	.13	.13	.07
5. BELIEFS	-.20	-.24	.49**	.24	—	.62**	-.03	.38*	-.37*	.05	-.17	-.01
6. IMAGINATION	-.36	.01	.70**	.05	.52**	—	-.21	-.15	-.27	.23	.27	.26
7. AESTHETIC NORMS	-.10	-.39*	-.02	-.09	.26	-.03	—	.58**	-.18	.33	-.23	-.07
8. NONAESTHETIC NORMS	-.03	-.11	.29	-.16	.63**	.41*	.48**	—	-.43*	.29	-.65**	-.24
9. SURFACE	.23	-.23	.09	.06	-.47**	-.11	-.02	-.42*	—	-.48**	.26	-.17
10. LINES	-.11	.50**	-.32	-.08	-.07	.00	-.16	.10	-.69**	—	.01	.44*
11. COLORS	-.40*	.04	.24	.32	.16	-.04	-.21	-.20	-.04	-.12	—	.44*
12. SHAPES	-.37*	.47**	.05	.30	.08	.01	-.38*	-.26	-.27	.39	.28	—
							Group B					

*$p < .05$.
**$p < .01$.

TABLE 8

Experiment 4: Stylistic Ratings

(Factor Analyses)

	Group A				Group B			
	I (Subjectivism)	II (Realism)	III (Classicism)	IV (Impressionism)	I (Subjectivism)	II (Realism)	III (Classicism)	IV (Impressionism)
1. REPRODUCTION	-.14	.79	-.05	.47	-.25	.72	-.10	.16
2. COMPOSITION	-.06	-.16	.94	.08	-.02	.06	.91	-.12
3. EMOTIONS	.88	-.26	-.05	-.17	.88	-.21	-.06	.21
4. PERCEPTIONS	.86	.03	.12	.23	–	–	–	–
5. BELIEFS	.74	.25	-.19	-.48	.61	-.19	-.36	-.54
6. IMAGINATION	.62	-.41	-.07	-.55	.93	.00	.06	-.09
7. AESTHETIC NORMS	-.11	.41	.69	-.06	–	–	–	–
8. NONAESTHETIC NORMS	.12	.86	.30	-.26	–	–	–	–
9. SURFACE	-.03	-.21	-.23	.82	-.04	.12	-.10	.94
10. LINES	.09	-.03	.77	-.39	-.16	.06	.50	-.76
11. COLORS	.16	-.86	.15	.21	-.03	-.88	-.08	.09
12. SHAPES	–	–	–	–	.02	.52	.65	-.19

and COLORS (with a negative loading), together with SHAPES in group B. Realism seems a not inappropriate label for this factor; the nineteenth-century Realist schools of painting in France (e.g., Courbet) and Russia (e.g., Repin) were characterized by faithful depiction of objects, coupled with relatively drab coloring. Prominent in Factor III are COMPOSITION, LINES, and, in the single analysis in which each participates, AESTHETIC NORMS and SHAPES. This factor is designated Classicism, since the styles that have borne this label (e.g., in Greek and Roman antiquity, in the seventeenth and eighteenth centuries) have given priority to harmony and clarity of structure, to form, to sharpness and gracefulness of line, and to conformity with accepted canons of beauty. Finally, SURFACE has the highest loadings on Factor IV, while there are negative loadings, in at least one analysis, for BELIEFS, IMAGINATION, and LINES. The designation that naturally comes to mind for this factor is Impressionism. The Impressionist school of the late nineteenth century placed a great deal of weight on reproduction of surface qualities and textures, while blurring outlines. Furthermore, although many people misinterpret Impressionism, and misuse the term, identifying it with the presentation of a subjective view of some external subject matter, the Impressionists intended to simulate with strict objectivity the qualities of light that are transmitted from objects to the eye and the reactions of the human optical apparatus. This fits in with the negative loadings shown by the scales most strongly associated with the Subjectivism factor, except for PERCEPTIONS, which has a moderate, positive loading in the one analysis including it.

Three of our factors, namely Subjectivism, Realism, and Classicism recall the three dimensions, named Expressionism, Geometricism, and Realism, that Knapp (1964, 1969) discusses. He states that Ss can be trained to a remarkably high degree of reliability in locating paintings along these dimensions, with the help of samples representing their opposite poles. They also correspond, of course, to concepts that have received a great deal of attention in the writings of art historians.

Our information-theoretic scheme is partially vindicated by the factor structures. The Subjectivism, Realism, and Classicism factors can be held to represent the relative prominence of expressive, semantic, and syntactic information, respectively. On the other hand, the two scales that were intended to probe cultural information do not generate a factor of their own but are divided between two of the other factors. The fourth factor, Impressionism, was not predicted. It is conceivable that what we have called the Realism and Impressionism factors correspond to two separable, and to some extent competing, kinds of semantic information, namely one originating in outlines of objects and the other in their surfaces.

The suggestion that styles emphasizing four different kinds of expressive information—corresponding to different psychological processes—can be reliably distinguished, receives no corroboration. Scales 3 to 6 are correlated with one another and predominate in the same factor. There are moderately high and significant correlations between the two scales associated with cultural information, AESTHETIC NORMS and NONAESTHETIC NORMS, but they, as already mentioned, show their strongest affinities with different factors. SURFACE and LINES, which were suspected of representing opposite poles of one continuum, show moderately high and significant negative correlations, but there is no evidence for a single dimension opposing COLORS to SHAPES; these two scales have moderate, positive correlations with each other.

Comparisons with the Results of
Experiments 1, 2, and 3

The 11 scales that showed significant intersubject consistency in group A of Experiment 4 define an 11-dimensional space in which the pictures of set A can be located. Similarly, there is a 9-dimensional space for group B. Locations of pictures within these scale spaces were compared with their location with the 3-dimensional INDSCAL spaces of Experiment 1. For set A, the canonical correlation between the stylistic scale space and the INDSCAL space comes to .95, and the redundancy from scale space to INDSCAL space is .73. In set B, the canonical correlation between the scale space and the INDSCAL space comes to .91, and the redundancy to .58. As for the relations between the 4-dimensional factor spaces and the 3-dimensional INDSCAL spaces, the canonical correlative coefficients are .90 for set A and .86 for set B, with redundancies of .55 and .47, respectively. The χ^2 test shows all four canonical correlations to be significant at the .001 level.

The multiple correlations between each of the scales and the two three-dimensional INDSCAL spaces of Experiment 1 were examined. Four of these coefficients were significant for both sets of pictures, namely those for the REPRODUCTION, IMAGINATION, NONAESTHETIC NORMS, and COLORS scales. The only one of the four factors to achieve a significant R with both INDSCAL spaces was Factor II (Realism).

The spaces defined by the collative and affective scales of Experiment 2 were also compared with the stylistic scale spaces of Experiment 4. In set A, the canonical correlation came to .99 and in set B to .94, which are significant at the .01 and .05 levels, respectively. The redundancies from the affective and collative scales to the stylistic scales are .50 and .56, and the redundancies in the opposite direction are .56 and .52. The canonical correlations for the factor spaces of the two experiments come to .78 for both set A and set B, $p < .001$. The redundancies are .28 and .31 from the factors of Experiment 2 to those of Experiment 4, and .38 and .40 in the opposite direction.

The mean Looking Time scores from Experiment 3 are not significantly correlated with any of the scales or factors in Experiment 4.

Table 9 presents information about correlations between the mean estimated factor scores for the individual factors from Experiments 2 and 4. Once again, the correlations from set A and set B were combined to produce the z values that appear in the table. It will be seen that the Classicism factor yields no significant correlations with the collative and affective factors. But there are indications that the other three stylistic factors have different combinations of direct and inverse associations with Hedonic Tone, Arousal, and Uncertainty.

The tastes of our Ss, as revealed by scores on the Hedonic Tone factor, apparently lean towards Realism and Impressionism and away from Subjectivism. Verbally indicated Arousal seems to increase with Subjectivism and Realism but to be negatively associated with Impressionism, whereas (subjective) Uncertainty is intensified by Subjectivism and Impressionism (which presumably impede prompt recognition of subject matter) but allayed by Realism.

TABLE 9

Experiments 2 and 4: Correlations between Mean Estimated Factor Scores (Combined z Values)

		Experiment 2		
		I (Hedonic Tone)	II (Arousal)	III (Uncertainty)
Experiment 4	I (Subjectivism)	−2.25*	2.16*	3.48***
	II (Realism)	1.96*	2.08*	−2.22*
	III (Classicism)	−	−	−
	IV (Impressionism)	2.94**	−2.31*	2.44*

*$p < .05$.
**$p < .01$.
***$p < .001$.

TABLE 10

Experiments 1 and 4: Correlations with
Artists' Year of Birth
Combined z Scores

Variable	Combined z
1. REPRODUCTION	−3.72***
2. COMPOSITION	−
3. EMOTIONS	−
4. PERCEPTIONS	1.96*
5. BELIEFS	−
6. IMAGINATION	2.08*
7. AESTHETIC NORMS	−2.89**
8. NONAESTHETIC NORMS	−4.29***
9. SURFACE	−
10. LINES	−2.08*
11. COLORS	4.87***
12. SHAPES	1.97*
I. Subjectivism	−
II. Realism	−5.83***
III. Classicism	−
IV. Impressionism	−

$*p < .05.$
$**p < .01.$
$***p < .001.$

Artist's Year of Birth

The data from the four experiments reported so far were compared with
one additional variable, namely the artist's year of birth. In a few cases, the
year of birth was not known exactly, and there was even one picture whose
painter was unknown. In these cases, however, the century was known and
the mid-year of the century was treated as the year of birth. Significant
combined z values derived from correlations between the year of birth and
the variables of Experiments 2 and 4 are presented in Tables 5 and 10. The
correlations with factor scores corroborate the widespread belief that, in the
course of the centuries, paintings have become less realistic and more difficult
to interpret. The negative correlation with Hedonic Tone indicates that our
subjects had rather conservative tastes.

Year of birth had significant ($p < .001$) multiple correlations of .88 and
.83 with the three-dimensional INDSCAL spaces obtained with both sets of
pictures in Experiment 1.

EXPERIMENT 5: SIMILARITY JUDGMENTS
AND DESCRIPTIVE RATINGS

In the next experiment, similarity judgments and ratings were obtained successively from the same Ss. It was hoped that this would make correlations between the two sets of measures more meaningful and more enlightening.

One set of 30 pictures, drawn from the two sets used in Experiments 1–4, was used for all subjects. The pictures were chosen to represent all octants of the three-dimensional INDSCAL space that emerged from Experiment 1, avoiding locations near the point of origin. Table 1 shows which of the 52 paintings were included in this set (the ones marked with an asterisk).

Every S went through three sessions of approximately one hour each. The first two sessions were taken up with similarity-dissimilarity judgments applied to all possible pairs, and the third session was devoted to the rating scales. These were taken partly from the descriptive (collative) scales of Experiment 2 and partly from the stylistic scales of Experiment 4 with the addition of two new scales corresponding to dimensions along which paintings can be distinguished, namely CURVED-ANGULAR and SOMBER-BRIGHT. The complete battery of 12 scales is shown in Table 12.

A further aim of the experiment was to compare the dissimilarity judgments of Ss who are relatively knowledgeable and relatively ignorant with respect to the visual arts. They could be governed either by different factors or by the same factors to different extents. The INDSCAL program, it will be recalled, provides a measure of the degree to which each S's judgments depend on each dimension.

Apart from the differences just mentioned, the procedures and experimental designs were the same as those used in Experiments 1, 2, and 4.

Subjects

Two groups of paid Ss were recruited through posters displayed in the corridors of a building housing several departments of the Faculty of Arts and Science of the University of Toronto. One poster called for the participation of people "highly interested in art" for a "research study in perception." The other poster, which was designed to appear unconnected with the first one, simply asked for volunteers to take part in an "experiment on perception" without mentioning any qualifications.

Three male and two female Ss responded to each poster. They were subjected to an informal questionnaire to make sure that they could be classified as relatively sophisticated or relatively unsophisticated about the visual arts, justifying the assignment of five Ss each to the A+ or A− group. Members of the A+ group had had several courses on the theory of fine art or art appreciation and visited art galleries frequently or regularly read books about art. Members of the A− group had had no more than one art course and visited galleries no more than a few times a year. Two of the A+ Ss and three of the A− Ss had taken some psychology courses.

Results

Similarity-dissimilarity judgments. In an analysis of variance performed on the ratings of pairs of pictures, the F value for pairs came to 5.51 ($p < .001$), corresponding to a reliability of .82.

One of the purposes of the experiment, it will be recalled, was to find out whether Ss differing in level of sophistication would differ in the degree to which their similarity judgments depended on particular dimensions. Figure 2

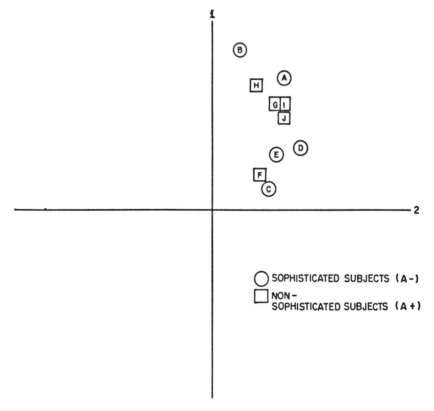

FIG. 2. Experiment 5: Subject plot for first two dimensions of three-dimensional INDSCAL analysis based on similarity-dissimilarity judgments.

presents a subject plot for the first two dimensions. It will be seen that there is a great deal of variation within groups in the relative influence in the two dimensions. But there is no sign of a differentiation between groups.

It must, of course, be recognized that our A+ group did not consist of real experts or specialists in art and that there are many people more ignorant about art than our A- group. If groups representing much greater differences in levels of sophistication could be found, the results might well be different if they were studied. In view of the absence of grounds for separating them, the results for the two groups of Ss were analyzed together. Both nonmetric scaling (NMSCAL and INDSCAL) were used. The stress values for nonmetric analyses in two to five dimensions were .16, .11, .08, and .07, which are very similar to those obtained in Experiment 1. The INDSCAL results for fits from one to three dimensions are shown in Table 11. Once again the results resemble those of Experiment 1.

Rating scales. Analysis of variance showed the Pictures effect to be significant with all scales except COLORS. The correlation between the mean judgments of the A+ group and the mean judgments of the A- group was significant beyond the .01 level for all scales except COLORS.

TABLE 11

INDSCAL Results for Experiment 5
Correlations of Fitted Weighted Coordinates
with Input Ratings

Subject	Number of fitted dimensions		
	1	2	3
1	.69	.78	.82
2	.84	.86	.87
3	.09	.29	.36
4	.35	.56	.62
5	.28	.42	.53
6	.19	.31	.38
7	.56	.63	.66
8	.66	.71	.74
9	.55	.65	.70
10	.50	.62	.68
Overall	.523	.609	.655
Variance	2.73	2.72	2.65
for each		.98	.86
dimension			.70

Because of these findings and because of the failure of the A+ and A– groups to cluster separately in the INDSCAL analysis, the rating-scale data for all 10 Ss were analyzed together.

The correlations between mean ratings of the 30 pictures are shown in Table 12. All these correlations except those involving the COLORS scale were then subjected to factor analysis with Varimax rotation, whose outcome appears in Table 13. The four factors displayed there account between them for 79.17% of the variance.

The factors are naturally different from those that emerge from Experiment 2 and Experiment 4, because the scales included some taken from the batteries using those two experiments and some that were used in neither. The labeling of the factors is even more hazardous than in the case of those two experiments.

The first factor has high loadings for two of the scales defining the Classicism dimension in Experiment 4 and negative loadings on two scaled attributes defining the Uncertainty factor in Experiment 2. Consequently, it may be called Classicism/Order. The second factor has a high positive loading for SIMPLE-COMPLEX and a high negative loading for CURVED-ANGULAR (which was not included in the two previous batteries). Complexity/Curvilinearity suggested itself as a label. It is noteworthy that SIMPLE-COMPLEX was loaded on this factor, whereas CLEAR-INDEFINITE and DISORDERLY-ORDERLY were loaded on Factor I. The correlations between the first of these scales and the other two were also exiguous (see Table 12). Factor III, with positive loadings for REPRODUCTION and for SURFACE, with a negative loading for IMAGINATION, is tentatively designated Realism vs. Subjectivism. The last factor has a high loading for EMOTIONS and a high negative loading for SOMBER-BRIGHT. The best provisional name for this factor, although it must be put forward with a great deal of hesitation, is Expressionism.

Relations between similarity-dissimilarity judgments and rating scales. Since the three-dimensional INDSCAL analysis produced one dimension whose index of importance is signally higher than those of the other two dimensions, it was decided to compare the rating-scale data with both the one-dimensional and three-dimensional INDSCAL solutions. The 11-dimensional scale space (omitting the COLORS scale) had a multiple correlation of .96 with the one-dimensional INDSCAL coordinates and a canonical correlation of .94 with the three-dimensional space. For both of the coefficients, $p < .001$.

TABLE 12
Experiment 5: Descriptive Scales
(Correlations)

	1	2	3	4	5	6	7	8	9	10	11	12
1. SIMPLE-COMPLEX	—											
2. CLEAR-INDEFINITE	.11	—										
3. DISORDERLY-ORDERLY	-.37*	-.58**	—									
4. CURVED-ANGULAR	-.29	-.13	.34	—								
5. SOMBER-BRIGHT	-.14	-.25	-.07	-.01	—							
6. REPRODUCTION	.42*	-.28	.29	-.11	-.30	—						
7. COMPOSITION	-.10	-.59**	.71**	.08	.00	.32	—					
8. EMOTIONS	.46*	.25	-.22	-.43*	-.48**	.06	-.04	—				
9. IMAGINATION	-.07	.06	-.15	-.17	-.01	-.51**	.07	.45*	—			
10. SURFACE	.32	.50**	-.35	-.36	-.19	.32	-.31	.23	-.29	—		
11. LINES	-.13	-.70**	.53**	.41*	-.13	.27	.58**	-.08	-.03	.62**	—	
12. COLORS	-.07	-.11	.00	-.16	.06	-.04	-.02	.30	-.11	.26	.04	—

*$p < .05$.
**$p < .01$.
***$p < .001$.

TABLE 13

Experiment 5: Descriptive Scales

(Factor Analysis)

	I (Classicism/ Order)	II (Complexity/ Curvilinearity)	III (Realism vs. Subjectivism)	IV (Expressionism)
1. SIMPLE-COMPLEX	-.09	.71	.23	.19
2. CLEAR-INDEFINITE	-.86	.00	-.05	.31
3. DISORDERLY-ORDERLY	.76	-.32	.17	.08
4. CURVED-ANGULAR	.17	-.82	.11	.14
5. SOMBER-BRIGHT	.01	-.01	-.10	-.94
6. REPRODUCTION	.38	.37	.75	.25
7. COMPOSITION	.85	.07	.01	.01
8. EMOTIONS	-.07	.62	.35	.61
9. IMAGINATION	.03	.18	-.91	.12
10. SURFACE	-.56	.41	.50	.15
11. LINES	.83	-.24	-.02	.19

The corresponding multiple and canonical correlations for the four-dimensional factor space came to .96 and .93, respectively. Once again, $p < .01$ in both cases. The redundancies were .82 from the scale space to the three-dimensional INDSCAL space and .67 from the factor space. The product-moment correlations and multiple correlations relating individual scales and factors to the dimensions of the one-dimensional and three-dimensional INDSCAL solutions appear in Table 14.

It will be seen that the scales showing the highest correlations with the one-dimensional solution are REPRODUCTION, SIMPLE-COMPLEX, and SURFACE. These are also the scales having the highest correlations with the first dimension (the dominant dimension) of the three-dimensional solution. EMOTIONS is the only scale having a significant correlation with the second dimension but with neither of the other two, and four scales have significant correlations with the third dimension only. All scales except SOMBER-BRIGHT and all factors except Factor IV have significant multiple correlations with the three-dimensional solution. The second and third factors both have significant product-moment correlations with the one-dimensional solution and with the first dimension of the three-dimensional solution. But Factor II is the only factor significantly correlated with the second dimension, while Factor I is significantly correlated with the third dimension only.

TABLE 14

Experiment 5: Similarity Judgments and Descriptive Scales
Product-moment and Multiple Correlations

Variable	One-dimensional	Three-dimensional			
	r	1	2	3	R
1. SIMPLE-COMPLEX	−.63**	−.60**	−.38*	−	.80**
2. CLEAR-INDEFINITE	−	−	−	.65**	.67**
3. DISORDERLY-ORDERLY	−	−	−	−.51**	.61**
4. CURVED-ANGULAR	.40*	.33*	−	−	.60**
5. SOMBER-BRIGHT	.44*	.42*	−	−	−
6. REPRODUCTION	−.82**	−.83**	−	−	.70**
7. COMPOSITION	−	−	−	−.42*	.55*
8. EMOTIONS	−	−	−.62**	−	.74**
9. IMAGINATION	.41*	.48**	−.51**	−	.69**
10. SURFACE	−.57**	−.61**	−	−	.72**
11. LINES	−	−	−	−.48**	.56*
12. COLORS	−	−	−	−	−
I Classicism/Order	−	−	−	−.63**	.69**
II Complexity/Curvilinearity	−.60**	−.56**	−.45*	−	.76**
III Realism vs. Subjectivism	.69**	.75**	−	−	.75**
IV Expressionism	−	−	−	−	−

Above the sub-header: **INDSCAL Solutions**

*p < .05.
**p < .01.
***p < .001.

It would therefore appear that similarity judgments are predominantly determined by attributes reflected in the REPRODUCTION, SIMPLE-COMPLEX, and SURFACE scales. There seems to be another dimension, of lesser importance (the third dimension of the three-dimensional INDSCAL solution), identifiable with Classicism/Order. A remaining dimension (the second dimension of the three-dimensional solution) is harder to characterize but seems to have something to do with what, in Experiment 4, was labeled Subjectivism.

EXPERIMENT 6: MULTIDIMENSIONAL PREFERENCE SCALING

The multidimensional analyses of Experiments 1 and 5 were derived from similarity-dissimilarity judgments. Ss' estimates of the degree of similarity between two pictures were treated as distances, so that the stimuli (and, when the INDSCAL program was used, the Ss themselves) could be located in a conceptual or "cognitive" space. In Experiment 6, multidimensional scaling techniques were applied to data of a different nature, namely judgments indicative of degree of preference for one picture over another. The analyses of these judgments enabled pictures and Ss to be located in an affective or preferential space. Two different analyses were applied to two different kinds of data obtained from the same Ss confronted with the same pairs of pictures.

The aims of the experiment were, first, to see whether Ss would show a significant measure of agreement with regard to the preferential judgments that were required of them. In Experiments 1 and 5, dissimilarity judgments had shown appreciable intersubject consistency. We are often reminded, however, that aesthetic tastes vary from individual to individual. This could mean either of two things. Preferences of different individuals might depend on different variables or attributes of stimulus objects. Alternatively, it is possible that different individuals have their preferences determined predominantly by the same variables but that they have predilections for different values of these variables. In the former case, we would not expect much intersubject consistency with regard to the location of stimulus objects in a preferential space. In the latter case, there would be such consistency; Ss would agree substantially on where stimulus objects should be placed with regard to the attributes that determine preferences, but different regions of the common preference space would be optimal for different individuals.

In addition, it was of interest to ascertain how far the arrangements of pictures within the two preferential spaces generated by Experiment 6 and the conceptual space generated by Experiment 5 would resemble one another. We also examined relations between the mean scores on the rating scales of Experiment 5 and the distributions of pictures within the preferential spaces of Experiment 6, although the fact that these comparisons require correlations between scores produced by different Ss calls once again for caution.

The same 30 pictures were used as in Experiment 5.

Subjects

The services of three male and seven female Ss were obtained with the help of the same poster, requesting volunteers for research on "perception," that was used to recruit the A– group in Experiment 5.

Procedure

Every S went through all possible pairings of the 30 pictures in a different randomly chosen order. This took two sessions of approximately one hour.

On seeing a pair of pictures, S had first to indicate which picture he liked better. Then, he had to estimate on a 7-point scale how much he preferred one to the other. As in previous experiments, he first went through six practice trials, using the last six pairs he was to receive in reverse order. During the practice trials, he was told that the seven compartments of the scale represented degrees of preference going from "a little" to "very much."

The two data gathered for every S and every pair of pictures, namely which member of each pair was preferred and to what degree it was preferred, were subjected to separate multidimensional analyses. Degrees of preference were treated as estimates of distance and put through the INDSCAL program, just like the similarity judgments of Experiments 1 and 5.

The information on which picture of each pair S preferred was subjected to "nonparametric multidimensional analysis of paired-comparison data" (Carroll & Chang, 1964), using the MDPREF computer program (Chang & Carroll, 1968). This technique was used for one of the experiments reported in Chapter 2 and is described there.

Results

Multidimensional analyses. Analyses of variance showed modest but statistically significant consistency among Ss with regard to the degree-of-preference judgments ($F = 1.23$ for the Pictures main effect, with 435 and 3,906 degrees of freedom, $p < .05$). This corresponds to a reliability of .19, which, while significant, falls far short of the reliabilities obtained in Experiments 1 and 5 with similarity-dissimilarity judgments. It is hardly surprising that preference judgments vary among Ss more than descriptive judgments.

A subsequent three-dimensional INDSCAL analysis produced dimensions whose indices of importance (mean squared subject weightings) came to .079, .058, and .065, respectively. The indices of importance (percentages of variance accounted for) for the three-dimensional MDPREF solution are 28.2, 21.1, and 11.9, respectively.

Two differences between the INDSCAL and the MDPREF analyses are worth pointing out. The one-dimensional MDPREF solution is identifiable with the first dimension of the two-dimensional solution, and so on. This is not necessarily true for INDSCAL. The first MDPREF dimension is thus identifiable with the one-dimensional MDPREF solution. A one-dimensional INDSCAL solution was computed. Its index of importance is equal to .27.

Secondly, the subject plots produced by the INDSCAL program display the relative weights of the various dimensions in determining Ss' judgments. Since such weights must be nonnegative, subject points will be confined to the positive orthant of the space. The MDPREF subject plot, on the other hand, represents each S's preferred point along each dimension, which means that subject points can be distributed all over the space.

Figures 3 and 4 show subject plots for the first two MDPREF dimensions and the first two dimensions of the three-dimensional INDSCAL space.

Comparisons among multidimensional-scaling spaces. The findings of Experiments 5 and 6 assigned to each of 30 pictures a location in each of three spaces. It must be remembered, once again, that these spaces are constructed out of three completely separate sets of data. The INDSCAL space of Experiment 5 comes from judgments of how similar or dissimilar two pictures are. The INDSCAL space of Experiment 6 uses solely information on the extent to which one picture of a pair is preferred to another but takes no account whatever of which of the two pictures S prefers. In other words, it reflects degree of preference but disregards the direction of preference. Finally, the MDPREF space of Experiment 6 reflects the number of Ss preferring each picture of each pair but not the ratings of degree of preference. Both the three-dimensional solutions produced by these analyses and the one-dimensional solutions will be discussed. The latter constitute the best that can be done to locate the pictures along a single linear scale corresponding to each kind of data.

Table 15 shows, below the principal diagonal, the canonical correlations among the three-dimensional spaces, while the product-moment correlations among one-dimensional solutions appear above the principal diagonal. The redundancies in Table 16 show how far knowledge of where a picture is located in one space helps prediction regarding its location in either of the other spaces.

It is evident that there is considerable interdependence and resemblance between every pair of spaces. The relation between the INDSCAL and MDPREF spaces of Experiment 6 show consistency between Ss' weightings of degree of preference and their statements regarding direction of preference; the more one picture is said to be preferred to another the greater the probability of choosing that picture as the one S likes more. The significant relations between these two spaces and the INDSCAL spaces of Experiment 5 support the hypothesis that Ss agree on where pictures stand with respect to

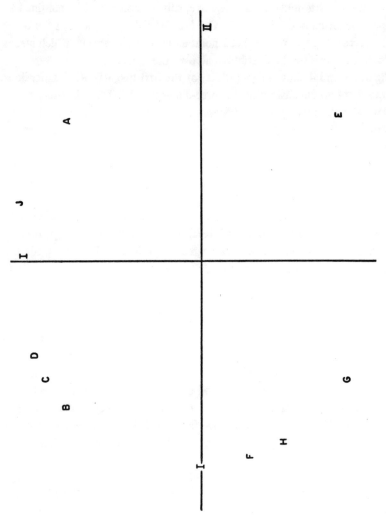

FIG. 3. Experiment 6: Subject plot for first two dimensions of MDPREF analysis based on paired-comparison preference choices.

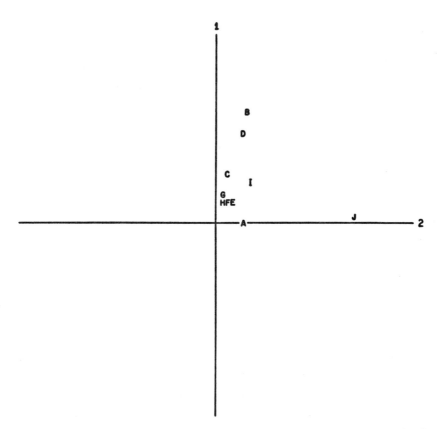

FIG. 4. Experiment 6: Subject plot for first two dimensions of three-dimensional INDSCAL analysis based on degree-of-preference judgments.

the attributes that govern preference, even when their individual preferences vary. Furthermore, the correlations between where pictures are located in the preferential space and where they are located in the conceptual space suggest that the attributes that dominate expressions of preference are, to a substantial extent, the attributes that dominate judgments of similarity-dissimilarity and therefore perceptions of pictures.

Comparisons of preferential spaces with rating scales of Experiment 5. The multiple correlations, canonical correlations, and redundancies linking the scale space and factor space of Experiment 5 to the one-dimensional and three-dimensional preferential spaces of Experiment 6 will be found in Table 17. There is evidence for quite close relations between the ratings made by the *S*s in Experiment 5 and the spaces emerging from the

TABLE 15

Experiments 5 and 6: Correlations between Spaces

		Experiment 5 Similarity INDSCAL	Experiment 6 Preference INDSCAL	Experiment 6 MDPREF
		Product-moment correlations between one-dimensional solutions		
Experiment 5	Similarity INDSCAL	–	.53**	.86**
Experiment 6	Preference INDSCAL	.85***	–	.70**
	MDPREF	.90***	.96***	–
		Canonical correlations between three-dimensional solutions		

*p < .05.
**p < .01.
***p < .001.

preference judgments of the Ss of Experiment 6, even though the two groups of Ss and their tasks were distinct. The coefficients involving the 4-dimensional factor space are a little lower than those involving the 11-dimensional scale space, but they are still significant.

Table 18 shows the correlation coefficients, where significant, connecting specific scales and factors from Experiment 5 with the 1-dimensional and 3-dimensional spaces produced by Experiment 6. It will be remembered that the first MDPREF dimension is the same as the 1-dimensional MDPREF solution. Looking at Table 18 together with

TABLE 16

Experiments 5 and 6: Redundancies from Row Space to Column Space
(Three-dimensional Solutions)

		Experiment 5 Similarity INDSCAL	Experiment 6 Preference INDSCAL	Experiment 6 MDPREF
Experiment 5	Similarity INDSCAL	–	.39	.46
Experiment 6	Preference INDSCAL	.39	–	.62
	MDPREF	.49	.64	–

TABLE 17

Experiments 5 and 6: Multiple and Canonical Correlations

Experiment 5 space	Experiment 6 space					
	INDSCAL			MDPREF		
	One-dimensional	Three-dimensional		One-dimensional	Three-dimensional	
	Multiple R	Canonical R_c	Redundancy	Multiple R	Canonical R_c	Redundancy
11 scales	.78*	.91***	.61	.88***	.97***	.71
4 factors	.60*	.82***	.36	.97***	.89***	.45

*$p < .05$.
**$p < .01$.
***$p < .001$.

Table 14, some instructive consistencies can be found. Among the scales, SIMPLE-COMPLEX and REPRODUCTION have the highest multiple correlations with the two 3-dimensional preferential spaces and the highest product-moment correlations with the two 1-dimensional preferential spaces. These two scales also have the highest and the fourth highest multiple correlations with the 3-dimensional conceptual INDSCAL space of Experiment 5 (see Table 14). Looking at individual dimensions, one finds again the SIMPLE-COMPLEX and REPRODUCTION scales having two of the three highest correlations with the first dimension of the 3-dimensional conceptual INDSCAL space (Experiment 5) and high correlations with the first and third dimensions of the three-dimensional preferential INDSCAL space (Experiment 6).

Turning to the factors, we note that Factor II (Complexity/Curvilinearity) and Factor III (Realism vs. Subjectivism) have more significant correlations than the others with all three multidimensional spaces.

There seems therefore to be a strong indication that how complex a picture is and how realistic it is play a large part in determining how the picture will be classified conceptually and how much it will be liked by Ss such as ours.

CONCLUDING COMMENT

Although the six experiments reported in this chapter have produced a fair number of worthwhile detailed findings, it must be recalled that they are

TABLE 18

Scales from Experiment 5 and Multidimensional Preference Analyses from Experiment 6 Product-moment and Multiple Correlations Analysis (Experiment 6)

Variable (Experiment 5)	One-dimensional INDSCAL	Three-dimensional INDSCAL				MDPREF			
		1	2	3	R	1	2	3	R
1. SIMPLE-COMPLEX	-.56**	-.51**	–	-.62**	.75**	-.78**	–	–	.80***
2. CLEAR-INDEFINITE	–	–	–	–	–	–	.40*	-.52**	.66**
3. DISORDERLY-ORDERLY	–	–	–	–	–	–	–	.37*	–
4. CURVED-ANGULAR	–	–	–	–	–	–	–	–	–
5. SOMBER-BRIGHT	.37*	–	–	–	–	–	–	–	–
6. REPRODUCTION	.47**	-.43*	–	-.59**	.69**	-.73**	–	–	.80***
7. COMPOSITION	–	–	–	–	–	–	–	–	–
8. EMOTIONS	–	–	–	–	–	–	–	–	–
9. IMAGINATION	–	.53**	–	–	.54*	–	-.43*	–	.63**
10. SURFACE	–	-.54**	–	–	.59**	-.59**	–	–	.68**
11. LINES	–	–	–	–	–	–	–	.48**	.54*
I Classicism/Order	-.40*	–	–	–	–	–	-.37*	.45*	.58*
II Complexity/Curvilinearity	–	–	–	-.50**	.56*	-.56**	–	–	.58*
III Realism vs. Subjectivism	–	.60**	–	.42*	.68**	.65**	–	–	.76***
IV Expressionism	–	–	–	–	–	–	–	–	–

*p < .05.
**p < .01.
***p < .001.

224

essentially exploratory in nature and that their principal objectives are methodological.

It has been verified that Ss, from the populations sampled, can apply to paintings pair-wise similarity-dissimilarity judgments, pair-wise preference judgments, as well as ratings on collative, evaluative, and stylistic scales, with sufficient consistency to warrant analysis of mean scores. The pair-wise judgments can be fairly well represented, after nonmetric multidimensional analysis, by spaces of no more than three dimensions. The mean ratings, after factor analysis, yield factors that resemble dimensions that have arisen out of previous research and that make some degree of theoretical sense. The canonical correlations and redundancy coefficients indicate that similarity judgments and preference judgments are in large measure governed by the same attributes of paintings. Other canonical correlations and redundancy coefficients indicate that the attributes reflected by the scale batteries overlap substantially with those that determine the pair-wise judgments and thus presumably dominate Ss' perceptions of paintings. Finally, the Looking-Time data from these experiments and the data on reward value that will be reported in the next chapter point to important relations between some of the verbal judgments under discussion and nonverbal forms of behavior.

All in all, the great potentialities of these techniques for experimental aesthetics have received confirmation.

REFERENCES

Bartlett, M. S. The statistical significance of canonical correlations. *Biometrika*, 1941, **32**, 29–38.

Berlyne, D. E. The development of the concept of attention in psychology. In C. R. Evans & T. Mulholland (Eds.), *Attention in neurophysiology*. London: Butterworths, 1969.

Berlyne, D. E. Attention as a problem in behavior theory. In D. Mostofsky (Ed.), *Attention: Contemporary theory and analysis*. New York: Appleton-Century-Crofts, 1970.

Berlyne, D. E. *Aesthetics and psychobiology*. New York: Appleton-Century-Crofts, 1971.

Berlyne, D. E. Interrelations of verbal and nonverbal measures used in experimental aesthetics. *Scandinavian Journal of Psychology*, 1973, **14**, 177–184.

Berlyne, D. E., Ogilvie, J. C., & Parham, L. C. C. The dimensionality of visual complexity, interestingness and pleasingness. *Canadian Journal of Psychology*, 1968, **22**, 376–387.

Carroll, J. D., & Chang, J. J. Non-parametric multidimensional analysis of paired-comparisons data. Paper presented at the joint meeting of the Psychometric and Psychonomic Societies, Niagara Falls, October, 1964.

Carroll, J. D., & Chang, J. J. Analysis of individual differences in multidimensional scaling via an N-way generalization of "Eckart-Young" decomposition. *Psychometrika*, 1970, 35, 283–319.

Chang, J. J., & Carroll, J. D. How to use MDPREF, a computer program for multidimensional analysis of preference data. Unpublished report, Bell Telephone Laboratories, 1968.

Cunningham, K. M., & Ogilvie, J. C. Evaluation of hierarchical grouping techniques: A preliminary study. *The Computer Journal*, 1972, 15, 209–213.

Goude, G. A multidimensional scaling approach to the perception of art. I. *Scandinavian Journal of Psychology*, 1972, 13, 258–271. (a)

Goude, G. A multidimensional scaling approach to the perception of art. II. *Scandinavian Journal of Psychology*, 1972, 13, 272–284. (b)

Johnson, S. C. Hierarchical clustering schemes. *Psychometrika*, 1967, 32, 241–254.

Knapp, R. H. An experimental study of a triadic hypothesis concerning the sources of aesthetic imagery. *Journal of Projective Techniques & Personality Assessment*, 1964, 28, 49–54.

Knapp, R. H. Une comparaison stylistique de Picasso et Cézanne. *Sciences de l'Art*, 1969, 6, 6–11.

Kruskal, J. B. Nonmetric multidimensional scaling. *Psychometrika*, 1964, 29, 1–27.

Künnapas, T., & Norman, M. Interindividual differences in similarity estimates of paintings. *Scandinavian Journal of Psychology*, 1971, 12, 161–167.

Lance, G. T., & Williams, W. T. A general theory of hierarchic and nonhierarchic classifications. *The Computer Journal*, 1967, 9, 373–380.

Mosteller, F., & Bush, R. P. Selected quantitative techniques. In G. Lindzey (Ed.), *Handbook of social psychology*. Vol. I. Cambridge, Mass.: Addison-Wesley, 1954.

Oeser, O. A. Some experiments on the abstraction of form and colour. I. Tachistoscopic experiments. *British Journal of Psychology*, 1932, 22, 200–215.

Shepard, R. N., Romney, K., & Nerlove, S. B. *Multidimensional scaling*. Vol. I. New York & London: Seminar Press, 1972.

Stewart, D., & Love, W. A general canonical correlation index. *Psychological Bulletin*, 1968, 70, 160–163.

Wedin, L. A multidimensional study of perceptual-emotional qualities in music. *Scandinavian Journal of Psychology*, 1972, 13, 241–257.

Winer, B. J. *Statistical principles in experimental design*. (2nd ed.) New York: McGraw-Hill, 1971.

Wölfflin, H. *Kunstgeschichtliche Grundbegriffe*. Munich: Bruckmann, 1915. (*Principles of art history*. London: Bell, 1922.)

10

HEDONIC TONE AND REWARD VALUE OF EXPOSURE TO PAINTINGS

D. E. Berlyne

In Experiment 2 of the project reported in the last chapter, factor analyses revealed a dimension of aesthetic reaction that was provisionally labeled Hedonic Tone. The DISPLEASING-PLEASING, UGLY-BEAUTIFUL, and NO PLEASURE-EXTREME PLEASURE scales had high positive loadings on it, while NO DISCOMFORT-EXTREME DISCOMFORT had a high negative loading. A similar factor has appeared invariably when verbal (and occasionally other) responses to diverse kinds of stimulus material have been factor-analyzed (see Berlyne, 1972a, 1973a; Chaps. 2, 5, and 14, this volume). The factor is clearly close to the Evaluative factor that Osgood and his associates (Osgood, Suci, & Tannenbaum, 1957) have derived from a comparably wide variety of stimulus material, mainly verbal.

The two experiments to be discussed in this chapter extend the search for behavioral correlates of verbal judgments and of the dimensions underlying them. One nonverbal measure of behavior, namely Exploration Time, figured in the project that Chapter 9 reported. This measure had a significant positive correlation with mean estimated factor scores on the Hedonic Tone factor, but, in accord with many previous findings (e.g., Berlyne, 1973a; Chaps. 2, 3, and 5, this volume), it was more highly correlated with other factors, in which SIMPLE-COMPLEX judgments were prominently represented.

The present experiments examined relations between the three factors emerging from Experiment 2, Chapter 9, and another behavioral measure, namely reward value. The reward values of exposure to different paintings were compared by means of the technique used in Experiment IID of Chapter 5, as well as in an earlier experiment (Berlyne, 1972b). It required two concurrent key-pressing responses, producing 5-second visual displays in accordance with independent variable-interval reinforcement schedules.

The general aim was to pursue further the associations between verbal and nonverbal measures with relevance to experimental aesthetics. But the experiments were directed, in particular, at one question of considerable theoretical significance, namely how far verbal evaluative judgments (which we have been grouping together under the term "Hedonic Tone") and reward value (power to reinforce an instrumental response) reflect a common underlying variable. It has often been assumed that they do, and we have been using the term "hedonic value" to refer to both verbal and behavioral hedonic variables, on the provisional assumption that they do (see Berlyne, 1967, 1973b). A few experimenters (Munsinger & Kessen, 1964; Finley & Staats, 1967; Witryol, 1971) have reported findings that support this assumption but with techniques that do not show unequivocally that reward value is involved rather than a temporary cue or arousal effect. Our technique, as argued in Chapter 1, seems to fulfill this requirement.

Although one would expect patterns of higher hedonic tone to be more rewarding, our first experiment using visual patterns (Berlyne, 1972b) indicated a closer relation between judged Interestingness and reward value than between judged Pleasingness and reward value. A later experiment (Chapter 5), with material that pitted Interestingness against Pleasingness, showed reward value to concur with the former attribute rather than the latter. And in Chapter 13, Godkewitsch reports an experiment with verbal material in which an inverse relation appeared between Hedonic Tone and reward value.

In Experiment 2 of Chapter 9, the UNINTERESTING-INTERESTING scale was loaded on the Arousal factor rather than on the Hedonic Tone factor. Other experiments (e.g., Berlyne & Crozier, 1971; Berlyne, 1971b), though not designed to test reward value directly, indicate a preference for responses that cause more complex material to be exhibited. In view of this and other findings, one might expect a relation between reward value and the third factor that appeared in Experiment 2, Chapter 9, the one labeled Uncertainty.

So, there are grounds for suspecting that any or all of the three factors, Hedonic Tone, Arousal, and Uncertainty, may turn out to be correlated with reward value. The scaled stimulus material of Chapter 9 provides us with an opportunity to test all these possibilities separately.

EXPERIMENT 1

Subjects

Twelve male and 12 female undergraduates taking introductory psychology courses participated without pay.

Stimulus Material

Pairs of pictures were selected from those used in Experiments 1-4, Chapter 9. Each pair comprised pictures whose mean estimated factor scores were as far apart as possible on one factor but as close together as possible on the remaining two factors. They were as follows, numbered as in Table 1, Chapter 9, with the picture representing the low extreme of each dimension mentioned first:

Factor I (Hedonic Tone)—22 (Dine), 10 (Tissot),
Factor II (Arousal)—11 (Fantin-Latour), 6 (Preti),
Factor III (Uncertainty)—46 (van Dyck), 51 (Appel).

Procedure

The apparatus and procedure were exactly the same as in Experiment IID of Chapter 5. Every S went through three consecutive 10-minute phases, for each of which a different pair of pictures was used. The three pairs were distributed among the three phases in the six possible orders for four Ss each. The picture representing a high value of the pertinent dimension was produced by the right key, the left key, and the right key in successive phases for half of the Ss in each subgroup. This arrangement was reversed for the remaining Ss.

Results

The mean numbers of responses per 10-minute phase are shown in Table 1 with the corresponding F values. The corresponding cumulative curves appear in the top half of Figure 1. The numbers of responses were subjected to a logarithmic transformation before analysis of variance, because mean rates of responding varied widely from S to S and one would expect a difference in reward value to produce a proportionate, rather than an absolute, difference in response rate.

It will be seen that the high-Hedonic Tone picture produced significantly more responses than the low-Hedonic Tone picture, implying that reward

TABLE 1

Mean Number of Manual Responses

Experiment	Dimension	Hedonic Tone	Arousal	Uncertainty
1	Low	91.4	299.5	272.1
	High	383.4	242.5	331.2
	$F(1,21)$	16.29	0.20	0.17
	p	<.001	n.s.	n.s.
2	Low	195.6	283.2	213.4
	High	325.5	290.0	257.4
	$F(1, 9)$	13.13	0.00	1.25
	p	<.01	n.s.	n.s.

value increased with score on the Hedonic Tone factor. Neither of the other two pairs produced a significant difference, so that the hypotheses linking Arousal and Uncertainty with reward value received no support.

EXPERIMENT 2

The results of Experiment 1 were reasonably clear-cut. But their generalizability is in doubt, since only one pair of pictures represented each dimension. Other attributes of these particular pictures might have been responsible for the findings, which might, therefore, not have occurred if other pictures had been chosen to represent those dimensions. Furthermore, although the two pictures of each pair had maximum separation on the dimension they were intended to represent, they were sometimes unavoidably some distance, but less far, apart on other dimensions also (see Table 1, Chap. 9, this volume).

Consequently, it was decided to carry out a second experiment with three other pairs of pictures, each designed, like those of Experiment 1, to represent points with coordinates far apart on one dimension but as close together as possible on the other two dimensions. Otherwise, the experimental design and procedure were exactly the same as in Experiment 1, except that 12 paid Ss participated.

Subjects

There were three male and nine female Ss, who were enrolled in summer-session day courses (not necessarily in psychology) and were paid $2.00 for their participation.

Stimulus Material

The three pairs of pictures were as follows, with a picture representing a low value of each dimension mentioned first:

Factor I (*Hedonic Tone*)—43 (Warhol), 32 (Canaletto),
Factor II (*Arousal*)—37 (Renoir), 26 (Rubens),
Factor III (*Uncertainty*)—41 (Albers), 50 (Gleizes).

Apparatus

There was a change in the equipment used to project the pictures. Instead of a Polymetric Tachisto-Projector, two Gerbrands (Model G 1166) shutters

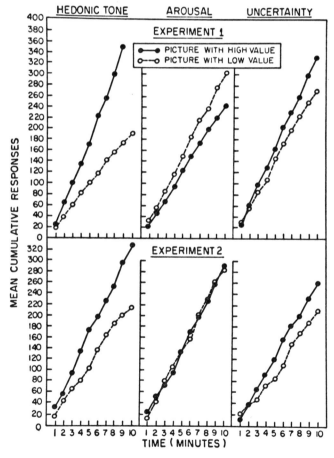

FIG. 1. Mean cumulative number of responses for pictures with high and low scores on the three factors.

were used in conjunction with two Kodak Carousel (Model 360) slide projectors.

Results

The results appear in the lower halves of Table 1 and Figure 1. Once again a logarithmic transformation was used. It will be seen that they are similar to those of Experiment 1. The number of responses on the key producing the high-Hedonic Tone picture significantly exceeded the number of responses on the key producing the low-Hedonic Tone picture. With regard to the other two dimensions, the differences were much lower and did not approach significance.

CONCLUSIONS

We therefore have evidence from two experiments, with different stimulus material, in support of the conclusion that the reward value of a picture increases with its score on the Hedonic Tone factor. There is no evidence that it depends on the other factors that were investigated. Although a much wider and more representative sample of pairs of pictures would be required to produce anything like a definitive demonstration of the conclusion, the similarity of the findings from the two experiments provides substantial corroboration for it. We have, therefore, a little more justification than we had before for using the term "hedonic value" to embrace both reward value and verbal judgments indicative of Hedonic Tone and for looking for their common determinants. On the other hand, we cannot evade the evidence that, in other circumstances, stimulus patterns with less Hedonic Tone may have more reward value.

At this stage, one can only venture the following conjecture, with a great deal of diffidence. It may be that reward value is closely related to Hedonic Tone, as revealed by verbal scaling, when it depends on the arousal-boost mechanism of hedonic value (Berlyne, 1967, 1971a; see Chap. 1, this volume), but it will have a closer association with scaled attributes indicative of arousal value (often including Interestingness) when the arousal-reduction mechanism is at work. It seems likely (Berlyne, 1967) that both mechanisms participate in the enjoyment of art and that the relatively greater importance of the arousal-reduction mechanism (activated by efforts to resolve uncertainties through perceptual and intellectual processing) is what distinguishes a profound appreciation of art from the shallower pleasures of entertainment. If so, our conjecture suggests that our Ss reacted to the pictures superficially. Different results (e.g., closer kinship between reward value and the Arousal and Uncertainty factors) might appear if the experiments were repeated with *S*s from more aesthetically sophisticated populations.

REFERENCES

Berlyne, D. E. Arousal and reinforcement. In D. Levine (Ed.), *Nebraska symposium on motivation*, 1967. Lincoln, Nebr.: University of Nebraska Press, 1967.

Berlyne, D. E. *Aesthetics and psychobiology*. New York: Appleton-Century-Crofts, 1971. (a)

Berlyne, D. E. Effects of auditory prechoice stimulation on visual exploratory choice. *Psychonomic Science*, 1971, 25, 193–194. (b)

Berlyne, D. E. Ends and means of experimental aesthetics. *Canadian Journal of Psychology*, 1972, 26, 303–325. (a)

Berlyne, D. E. Reinforcement values of visual patterns compared through concurrent performances. *Journal of the Experimental Analysis of Behavior*, 1972, 18, 281–285. (b)

Berlyne, D. E. Interrelations of verbal and nonverbal measures used in experimental aesthetics. *Scandinavian Journal of Psychology*, 1973, 14, 177–184. (a)

Berlyne, D. E. The vicissitudes of aplopathematic and thelematoscopic pneumatology (*or* The hydrography of hedonism). In D. E. Berlyne & K. B. Madsen (Eds.), *Pleasure, reward, preference*. New York: Academic Press, 1973. (b)

Berlyne, D. E., & Crozier, J. B. Effects of complexity and prechoice stimulation on exploratory choice. *Perception & Psychophysics*, 1971, 10, 242–246.

Finley, J. R., & Staats, A. W. Evaluative meaning words as reinforcing stimuli. *Journal of Verbal Learning and Verbal Behavior*, 1967, 6, 193–197.

Munsinger, H. L., & Kessen, W. Uncertainty, structure and preference. *Psychological Monographs*, 1964, 78(9, Whole No. 586).

Osgood, C. E., Suci, G. J., & Tannenbaum, P. H. *The measurement of meaning*. Urbana, Ill.: University of Illinois Press, 1957.

Witryol, S. Incentives and learning in children. *Advances in Child Development and Behavior*, 1971, 6, 1–61.

11

AN EXPERIMENTAL INVESTIGATION OF PERCEPTUAL AND STYLISTIC DIMENSIONS OF PAINTINGS SUGGESTED BY ART HISTORY[1]

G. C. Cupchik

Art historians have been repeatedly challenged by the problems of describing and classifying artistic styles. One solution to the classification problem has been the adoption of categories or labels, such as "Rococo," "Cubism," and "Pop Art," to identify the dominant styles of particular historical periods. An apparent shortcoming of this method is the tendency to overemphasize the uniqueness of period styles. A second solution has been the delineation of stylistic dimensions, such as linear versus painterly (Wölfflin, 1915), which can be applied to all works in a particular medium. The main virtue of the dimensional approach is that scholars can disregard period labels and explore the stylistic similarities as well as the differences between particular works. The success of the dimensional approach will depend on the development of an exhaustive list of independent dimensions

[1] The author wishes to thank Dr. J. Isaacson of the Department of Art History of the University of Michigan for his encouragement at the outset of this project and Dr. R. Beetem of the Department of Art History of the University of Wisconsin for aiding in the preparation of Experiment 1. Thanks are also due to Mary Louise King and Dr. J. Graef for their help with the data analysis, and to Dr. C. X. Poulos and Edith S. Klein for their careful reading of the manuscript. Experiment 1 was supported by NSF Grant GS-31450X (D. H. Leventhal of the University of Wisconsin, Principal Investigator). Experiment 2 and all data analyses were supported by Canada Council Grant No. S70-1570-X2 and National Research Council Grant No. A-73 (D. E. Berlyne, Principal Investigator). The author greatly appreciates Dr. Berlyne's helpful advice and support.

that can be applied to works of different cultures, historical periods, and media. In this study, an attempt is made to determine if a set of four dimensions, which appear to be important from an art-historical point of view, actually underlie the perception of paintings by modern viewers.

The Linear-versus-Painterly Dimension

Although the "linear"-versus-"painterly" dimension was described by Wölfflin in 1915, it was anticipated in the works of Zimmermann (1858), Riegl (1893), and Worringer (1908). The earlier conceptions of this dimension distinguished a tactile style (Riegl) or an "art of complete presentation" (Zimmermann) from a visual style or "art of incomplete presentation." The tactile style reflected a conception of the objects and events that were depicted in paintings as tangible, discrete, impermeable, and absolute (Shapiro, 1961). In contrast, the visual style represented a more subjective viewpoint of the field of perception as a directly given, yet more distant continuum, involving merging parts and spatial voids (Shapiro, 1961).

Worringer (1908) differentiated between an abstract style (derived from an "urge to abstraction") and a naturalistic style (derived from an "empathic urge"). These two styles seem to correspond respectively to the tactile and visual styles distinguished by earlier writers. He asserted that the goal of the artist who possesses an urge to abstraction is "to deliver the object from its relativity and eternalise it by approximation to abstract crystalline forms [p. 37]," and by emphasizing "the simple line and its development in purely geometrical regularity ... [p. 20]." These comments provide an insight into the technical processes that enable the artist to render an object both tangible and absolute. However, Worringer said little about the style associated with an empathetic urge except that it involves a "feeling for the beauty of organic form that is true to life [p. 27]," and that it is related to "naturalism in the higher sense [p. 14]."

The significance of Wölfflin's (1915) contribution lies in his detailed description of the stylistic factors associated with both the tactile and visual properties of Renaissance and Baroque art. These stylistic factors are represented by five pairs of visual qualities including: linear versus painterly, plane versus recession, closed versus open form, multiplicity versus unity, and absolute versus relative clarity. Wölfflin maintains that an objective or tactile "mode of perception" is reflected in a style that attains maximum clarity by treating all forms as independent and of equal value, separating them by outline, grouping them in ordered planes, and by using horizontals and verticals to fix the work structurally. In contrast, the subjective or visual "mode of perception" is realized by deemphasizing outlines and balanced composition, thereby forcing the viewer to see in masses, while affirming space and depth, and using color and light to give unity to the scene, independent of the subject matter. While Renaissance and Baroque art are contrasted using five dimensions, the linear-versus-painterly dimension, which distinguishes the use and deemphasis of outline, will be exclusively focused upon in this paper.

The linear-versus-painterly dimension provides a valuable distinction between two artistic styles that appear to reflect objective and subjective perceptions in art. However, the art-historical treatment of the problem is descriptive and lacks the theoretical and rigorous discrimination between the two styles that would be preferred by an experimental aesthetician. This interest in a theoretical distinction is motivated not so much by a concern for elegance, but rather by the fact that it is essential for further research. For example, an understanding of the defining properties of the linear style could facilitate the comparison of classical art in West European art with its equivalent in "exotic" cultures. Further, the formal specification of the unique qualities of the two styles would aid in the construction of stimuli embodying those properties and the investigation of their effects on both verbal and behavioral aesthetic responses.

As a first step toward formalizing the distinction, it is helpful to consider Wölfflin's suggestion that the linear and painterly styles are "still infinitely different from reality [p. 29]." Neither style depicts external reality with complete fidelity. Worringer argued similarly that abstraction (his definition of a linear style) and naturalism (i.e., painterly style) are not associated with the "impulse to imitation" which he relates to skills such as manual dexterity. Therefore, it may be deduced that the two styles reflect different operations or transformations of the content of the work undertaken by the artist. This leads to speculations concerning the type of transformation appropriate to each style.

The linear style has been associated with rendering objects absolute by idealizing them. Implicit in this discussion is the notion that the artist, and probably his society, have expectations concerning the appropriate characteristics of an object or event. Norms or expectations such as these led the academicians of the late nineteenth century in France to reject the new phenomenological perspective of the Impressionist painters. Expectations, therefore, function as templates to which the objects in the painting must be approximated through the use of outline. Consequently, outline can be interpreted as an interface between the properties of the object and the physical parameters of the form to which it is approximated. The process of approximating the given object to an ideal form can be termed *systematic normalization*. In sum, the unique features of the linear style in general, and classical styles in particular, would appear to be the salience and idealization of form as it is realized through a process of normalization.

The painterly style, on the other hand, was associated with seizing the "appearance of reality," which does not mean exact replication, but rather a presentation of essentials. The various techniques described by Wölfflin, such as deemphasizing outline, force the viewer to withdraw his attention from the edges of forms and instead to apprehend the interrelations of "patches of color or light and dark." The critical factor associated with the subjective viewpoint of the painterly style would seem to be indeterminacy of form. It may be conjectured that it is this indeterminacy or ambiguity that encourages the active participation of the viewer in the interpretation of the work of art. Worringer, without focusing on the motivating factor, acknowledged that an active or empathic response must be undertaken by a viewer to appreciate a naturalistic or "organic" work of art. He used Lipps' words to describe this active participation: "The form of an object is always its being-formed by me, by my inner activity [1908, p. 6]." A recent study of Berlyne and Borsa (1968) provides data that fit the predicted relationship between indeterminacy of form and active efforts at interpretation by the viewer. Specifically, they found that blurred colored pictures of common objects evoked longer EEG desynchronization than clear pictures when the blurred pictures are associated with greater subjective uncertainty. They interpreted this increase in cortical arousal as indicating that subjective uncertainty demands stimulus "structuring" or "organization" by the viewer.

A recent study dealing with indeterminacy of form (Posner and Keele, 1968) can provide an insight into the process of transformation which underlies the painterly style. The experimenters developed a series of variations based on prototype nonsense dot patterns and found that the subjects were able to learn a prototype pattern by abstracting the central tendency of the variations. In a similar fashion, the person who views a particular interpretation of a scene in a Baroque painting must look beyond the general perspective of this particular variation to infer the specific scene that underlies it. It is, therefore, suggested that an analogy can be drawn between the creation of a Baroque painting and a variation on a nonsense dot pattern. Consequently, the indeterminacy that characterizes the painterly style can be attributed to a similar transformation of the content of the scene. In accordance with the terminology used by Posner and Keele, the transformation performed by the painterly artist can be termed *systematic distortion.*

In sum, the normalization transformation associated with the linear style approximates the objects depicted in a painting by degrees and *in the direction* of a standard form. The more extreme examples of such transformations include nonrepresentational works by Mondrian and Malevich or representational works by the American artist Hopper. The distortion transformation associated with the painterly style involves successive approximation of the objects *away from* a standard form. This is most clearly evident in the development of Monet's painting from his early works such as *Women in the Garden* (1866) to the later series of waterlily paintings.

Another aspect of the distinction between the two art styles concerns their relation to the artist's expression of his beliefs and feelings. A formal treatment of this issue is facilitated by considering Moles's (1966) statement that "Within the same material message, there is a superposition of several distinct sequences of symbols. These symbols are made of the same elements grouped in different ways [p. 129]." The two basic symbol systems are the semantic and aesthetic (or syntactic).[2] The semantic system is logical, or structured, and corresponds to the content of the work while the aesthetic system is untranslatable and "determines internal states [p. 131]."

It may be hypothesized that the concern of the linear artist for idealized themes is expressed in an emphasis on the semantic aspect of the artistic message. Therefore, the linear style provides a vehicle for expressing the artist's ideas and beliefs to the exclusion of his emotions. This conclusion is dictated by limited and mutually exclusive capacities of the semantic and aesthetic channels. This point is made clear by considering the linear style within the framework of Garner's (1962) discussion of internal and external constraint. Predominance of external constraint is manifested in the artist's attempt to approximate a system of internal variables such as color and line to an external standard or referent system, such as physical objects or regular geometric forms. When the amount of external constraint is high, the amount of internal constraint is low, provided that the total amount of constraint remains constant. In other words, the use of colors and tones for the purpose of

---

[2] Moles proposes this twofold distinction, whereas Berlyne (1971, Chap. 5; Chap. 1, this volume) suggests that four kinds of information transmitted to an element of a work need to be distinguished.

elucidating forms that convey ideas limits their contribution to the aesthetic symbol system.

It may be further hypothesized that the indeterminacy of the painterly style makes the aesthetic structure a channel for the expression of the artist's feelings. Again using the framework elaborated by Garner, as the correlation between the internal system of variables and some external referent system decreases, the correlation within the system of variables increases, provided that the total amount of constraint remains constant. Therefore, the act of systematic distortion decreases the external constraint, thereby freeing the basic elements of the work (i.e., colors and tones) for expression of the artist's emotions. The potential affect-evoking properties of these basic elements are considered in the discussion of the third and fourth dimensions.

The Abstract-versus-Representational Dimension

A second dimension, which has become particularly salient in twentieth-century art, is "abstract" versus "representational." This dimension concerns the amount of detail in an external object or event (both real or imaginary) that is referred to or denoted in a work of art, including the pattern of detail. Toward the representational end of the dimension, a work of art will be characterized by successively greater amounts of detail while preserving its structure. Toward the abstract end of the dimension, a work of art will reflect the deliberate selection of certain details and properties of an object to the exclusion of others and, in addition, may involve changes in the pattern or structure of the detail. At the more extreme levels of abstraction, a particular sign may be used to denote an event or object which it may or may not resemble. Ultimately, events in the work of art cease to denote any external events. This general formulation leads to the conclusion that abstraction, as a process of selective denotation or reference, is not unique to twentieth-century art. From an information-theoretic point of view, abstract art differs from representational art in transmitting less semantic information.

Sorokin (1962) has developed a model of cultural and artistic development that incorporates the abstract styles of earlier historical periods. He describes an Ideational style that emphasizes the use of symbols to represent supernatural and nonmaterial concepts or events such as God, the Virgin, and Soul. He also describes a Visual style that aims at an accurate rendering of worldly events. This Visual style includes two subtypes, the naturalistic and the impressionistic. While the Visual-naturalistic stresses photographic accuracy the Visual-impressionistic reflects the artist's subjective perception of an event. Finally, he describes an Idealistic style of art that is similar to the Ideational style in its emphasis on idealized themes but resembles the Visual style in its depiction of forms drawn from empirical reality. Sorokin has indirectly described the poles of the two dimensions that have been discussed. The Ideational versus Visual-naturalistic apparently corresponds to the abstract versus representational, while the Idealistic versus Visual-impressionistic corresponds to the linear versus painterly. In addition, he has demonstrated that art resembling abstract painting has occurred repeatedly during the past 31 centuries.

The Multiplicity-versus-Unity Dimension

A third dimension is suggested by the findings of other art historians and scholars. Abell (1957) has argued that periods of continued insecurity are reflected in deformation in art style. Kavolis (1968) has also hypothesized a relationship between short-term severe upheavals or radical economic changes, emotional stress and expressionism in visual art. Hauser (1965) adopted a similar perspective, arguing that the "deformation or distortion of classical forms [p. 9]" which occurred during the Mannerist period was influenced by the alienation of a "conflict-torn generation." This deformation of forms can be contrasted with the "orientation of harmony with nature" that Kavolis finds present in the art of the Chinese landscapists. He describes the mechanism that underlies this harmony of self and forms as "'irregular' outlines—that is, neither geometrically regularized nor smoothed over, but capturing impressions of unordered fragments of nature [p. 145]."

These descriptions appear to contrast two styles of painting, including one that evokes feelings of tension and another that elicits feelings of harmony or calm. The feeling of tension is associated with the deformation of events or details, while the feeling of calm is related to an ordering of events. It is difficult, however, to specify the structural properties of the works that evoke these feelings. One solution to the problem is suggested by Berlyne's (1971) statement that: "There is always one factor, whether it be called 'multiplicity,' 'variety,' or 'complexity,' that can be expected to raise arousal ... " and further that "there is the other factor, 'unity,' 'order,' or 'lawfulness,' that can be expected to lower arousal ... [p. 129]." Accordingly, it can be hypothesized that the tension associated with Mannerism and other expressionist styles and the calm associated with the Chinese landscapes are determined by an interaction of two factors, complexity and orderliness. In the absence of data that show which of the two factors is crucial, the critical underlying dimension is tentatively labeled "multiplicity versus unity." In information-theoretic terms, it may represent variations in the total amount of information transmitted by a painting.

The Somber-Tonality versus Bright-Color Dimension

Hauser (1965) has distinguished between two postclassical styles. On the one hand, Mannerism reflects "the expression of the conflict between the spiritual and sensual impulses of the age," while Baroque art represents "the resolution of that conflict on the basis of spontaneous emotion [p. 20]." Thus, while the third dimension was related to the artist's harmony or discord with the outside world, a fourth dimension involves the degree of direct expression of private feelings. Kavolis (1968) has provided a general framework within which to conceptualize this development. He relates the emergence of intimacy structures characterized by social-emotional orientations with an emphasis on private experience and the appearance in art of emotional rather than socially accepted themes.

Both points are consistent with Ariès' (1962) discussion of the appearance in the mid-seventeenth century of the first modern family, characterized by domesticity, warmth in the parent-child relationship, and an emphasis on social interaction skills. Ariès relates the new concern for a private family life to the appearance of Baroque family portraits in which the actors are linked by gestures expressing reciprocal feelings rather than through objective compositional devices. However, it may be conjectured that, as well as expressive gestures (a semantic factor), certain aesthetic (or syntactic) attributes may also provide a vehicle for the expression of spontaneous emotion.

Some speculations suggest that color may be the crucial aesthetic factor. Kavolis (1968), for example, relates the urban middle class emphasis on individual personality, subjectivism, and romanticism to a "passion for color." He also describes the tension reducing effect that intense color may have during periods of social change. The emotional effects of colors are discussed by Arnheim (1971), who cites experimental evidence to demonstrate that intense brightness, high saturation, and hues that correspond to long wavelengths produce feelings of excitement. However, the mechanisms which mediate this effect are, as he emphasized, unknown.

Color, therefore, appears to be a factor that may underlie the spontaneous expression of emotion in art. However, it is difficult at this time to specify how the three parameters that contribute to color—hue, saturation, and value—can be related to the expression or elicitation of affect. Consequently, the nature of the color dimension will be hypothesized on the basis of art-historical data from West European art. On two occasions in West European art since the Renaissance, a somber-tonal use of color was followed by a brighter and more decorative use of color: the evolutions from Baroque to Rococo art and from French Realism and the Barbizon School to Impressionism. Therefore, as a first step, the fourth dimension will be tentatively labeled "somber tonality versus bright color." Paintings that are higher on the tonality-color dimension should evoke greater feelings of warmth or arousal. The dimension may reflect the relative importance of expressive information in Berlyne's (1971; Chap. 1, this volume) sense.

The Problem of Stylistic Development and Change

Four dimensions that may underlie artistic style have been derived from art-historical analysis. The first two dimensions, linear-versus-painterly and abstract-versus-representational, pertain, respectively, to the transformation and selection of detail in paintings. The third and fourth dimensions, multiplicity-versus-unity and somber tonality-versus-bright color, are related to the expression of tension or calmness and to a cold-warm distinction, respectively. The goal of this investigation is to determine whether these dimensions underlie the perception of paintings that were selected to represent these properties.

Before introducing the procedure and the findings of the investigation, it may prove valuable to consider briefly the problem of stylistic change as it relates to this dimensional analysis. In his discussion of stylistic change, Wölfflin (1915) stated that the evolution from the linear to the painterly style "follows a natural logic, and could not be reversed [p. 17]." Sorokin (1962) hypothesized that a cyclical pattern begins with the Visual style, which is followed by the Ideational style. When the Ideational phase declines and the Visual style is due to reappear, a brief Idealistic phase occurs, followed by the new Visual phase. Sorokin's model is similar to Wölfflin's in its description of a Classical (Idealistic) phase preceding a Visual phase. It differs from Wölfflin's model, however, in its more differentiated analysis of the styles that immediately follow Visual art into a purely conceptual (Ideational) as well as an Idealistic phase. In part, the Ideational phase is similar to the preclassical or archaic phase that Wölfflin mentions in passing as the primitive embodiment of the linear style. Shapiro (1961) has also concluded from a review of several theories of stylistic development that a sequence of stages, corresponding to Archaic, Classical, Baroque, and Impressionist in West European art occurs whenever an art form becomes increasingly naturalistic. The development proceeds from a schematized or conceptual form of representation to a more structured representation involving illusionist techniques.

One major shortcoming of these three models is the conspicuous absence of an anticlassical phase corresponding to Mannerism or Expressionism. A four-stage model of aesthetic development will be briefly presented, partly because it incorporates an anticlassical phase but also because each stage can be associated with an extreme development on one of the four stylistic dimensions and neutrality on the others. The model is adapted from a general theory of the development of beliefs or cognitive systems as a function of both structural (cognitive) and environmental factors (Harvey, Hunt, & Schroeder, 1961). In adapting this model, it is assumed that the "modes of perception" that art historians such as Wölfflin have related to stylistic development, can be related to cognitive and emotional systems and their development. It is also assumed that environmental factors such as political absolutism, social stability, and the emergence of intimacy structures, which have been discussed by art historians, correspond to the basic external factors of the model: democracy-autocracy and consistency-inconsistency of communication and reinforcement.

The first stage is characterized by a conceptual framework favoring absolute concepts and avoiding ambiguity. This belief system emerges in an autocratic environment requiring a person to adopt a set of beliefs about how the world functions, without critical consideration. The conceptualization of the world in rigid terms can be related to an Idealistic style of art in which the artist seeks refuge from a complex and changing world within the confines of absolute, static, and geometrically normalized forms. This mode of vision can therefore be associated with a highly linear style of art.

The second stage is characterized by ideas and behavior that challenge external established authority. This differentiation of the self from external sources of authority occurs in an environment where the social order is autocratic yet unstable, thereby providing the appropriate context for the appearance of "an antithetical, ambivalent, sense of life that expresses itself in apparently irreconcilable formal structures [Hauser, 1965, p. 152]." The inability of the artist to transcend the more rigid features of his heritage and to construct a new, directly expressive style leads to the distortion of the classical forms as the only vehicle for self-expression. The second stage is, therefore, reflected in works of art that are extreme on the multiplicity or tense end of the multiplicity-unity dimension.

The third stage involves a more empirical and accurate conception of the world in which social interaction is no longer conceptualized in absolute terms (Stage 1) or personal motives (Stage 2) but rather in terms of shared understanding and past experience. The greater mutuality and empathy is achieved in a democratic environment where cooperation and intimacy are stressed over obedience, and an integration of purpose and action is sought through an emphasis on independence. This heightened intimacy is associated with the somber-tonality end of the color dimension.

The fourth stage is reflected in the ability to shift perspective and to move freely from the conceptual to the empirical or the emotional. This flexibility is associated with a balance between social mutuality or cooperation and autonomy that is achieved in an environment favoring independence over emotional intimacy. This development lays the foundation for the emergence of novel conceptual schemata, which may be revealed in art approaching the abstract pole of the abstract-representational dimension.

The hypothesis that Visual art precedes Ideational or abstract art implies that the exploration of the empirical world will encourage a new level of understanding establishing the appropriate conditions for a major reorientation of artistic style. This perspective gives Ideational art (abstract art) a more creative role than the merely symbolic and socially cohesive function attributed to it by Sorokin. According to this interpretation, the new insight, associated with the abstract or Ideational style, becomes reified in Idealistic or Classical art, which rigidly adapts the already dated schema to new problems.

In sum, this model of stylistic development applies to West European art where the environmental factors such as authoritarianism and democracy are particularly salient. However, where other social factors and their attendant child-rearing patterns are more in evidence, the cognitive styles and, consequently, artistic styles should differ. This would be reflected in two possible ways. First, entirely new dimensions could underlie the works of art. Second, the works of art could cluster at different points of the four stylistic dimensions that have been discussed.

Stimulus Materials

The stimuli used in this investigation consisted of 16 color slide reproductions of paintings selected from the Department of Art History Library at the University of Wisconsin. Fifteen of the works were oil paintings executed in western Europe between the beginning of the seventeenth century and the early twentieth century. The remaining work was a Japanese screen painting by Taiga (1723–1776). Two expert judges selected four paintings to represent each of the four dimensions according to specified criteria. The paintings representing the linear-versus-painterly dimension (Group 1) ranged from a strong emphasis on outline to a predominance of merging color areas. The paintings on the abstract-versus-representational dimension (Group 4) varied from high selectivity of detail to high depiction of detail. The paintings on the multiplicity-versus-unity dimension (Group 2) ranged from complex or turbulent and tense to simple, harmonious, and calm. The paintings on the somber-tonality-versus-bright-color dimension (Group 3) ranged from an emphasis on orderly structure and tonality, through high tonality, to a more decorative use of light and color. A list of the titles, artists, and year of execution is presented in Table 1.

EXPERIMENT ONE: JUDGMENTS OF STYLISTIC SIMILARITY

The goal of the first experiment was to determine the dimensions underlying the perception of stylistic similarity among the set of 16 paintings. This was accomplished by requesting a group of judges to make pairwise dissimilarity ratings of all 120 possible pairs of the 16 paintings and then submitting these data to a nonmetric scaling analysis (INDSCAL). Since the criteria for making the judgments were not specified, it was possible to compare any spontaneously used dimensions with the four hypothesized dimensions.

Subjects

Thirty-eight Ss, including 22 females and 16 males, enrolled in the introductory psychology course at the University of Wisconsin, participated in this study in partial fulfillment of a class requirement.

Procedure

The 16 stimuli were divided into 120 pairs and each pair was randomly assigned a position in the presentation sequence. The Ss were randomly divided into two equal groups and each group saw the painting pairs in the same sequence but on two different days.

Ss were seated in a small lecture room and the instructions were read aloud to them. They were instructed to decide how stylistically similar or different each of the pairs of paintings were and to disregard specific content. A

TABLE 1

Paintings Used in Experiments 1 and 2

				Experiment 1 Coordinates on INDSCAL dimensions				Experiment 2 Mean factor scores			
Number	Artist	Date of execution	Title	1	2	3	4	I Classicism	II Subjectivism	III Complexity	IV Expressionism
Group 1											
1	David, J. L.	1784	Oath of the Horatii	-.30	-.11	.39	-.15	1.25	-1.00	.01	-.73
2	Cezanne, P.	1891	The Gulf of Marseille	.03	-.20	-.28	-.20	.40	.22	-.08	.59
3	Turner, J. M. W.	1840	The Slave Ship	.30	.03	.06	-.53	-.78	-.24	.85	-1.30
4	Monet, C.	ca. 1922	Japanese Footbridge and Water Lilies	.38	.04	-.11	-.23	-1.50	-.08	-.24	-.38
Group 2											
5	Heckel, E.	1913	Day of Glass	.08	.28	-.32	-.06	.23	.81	-.20	-.95
6	Van Gogh, V.	1889	Starry Night	.19	-.01	-.33	.06	-.49	.93	.19	-.64
7	Sisley, A.	1879	The Road in the Woods	.23	-.31	-.12	.09	-.61	-.66	.22	.83
8	Taiga	1763	Banquet at Lung Shan	.24	.14	.01	.32	.01	.24	-1.03	1.05
Group 3											
9	Vermeer, J.	1662	The Music Lesson	-.30	-.19	.24	-.17	.43	-.77	.69	.41
10	Steen, J.	ca. 1665	Feast of St. Nicholas' Eve	-.34	-.12	.40	-.24	.41	-1.09	.24	-.35
11	Fragonard, J.	ca. 1765	Bathers	.30	.01	.33	.13	-.60	-.40	-.16	.29
12	Klimt, G.	1917–18	Female Portrait, Unfinished	.11	.06	-.03	.54	-.37	.87	-.36	.70
Group 4											
13	Miro, J.	1953	Painting	-.19	.52	-.23	.20	.59	.90	-1.34	1.05
14	Picasso, P.	1921	Three Musicians	-.28	.49	-.23	.07	.92	.94	.61	-.04
15	Seurat, G.	1884	Sunday Afternoon on the Island of La Grand Jatte	-.25	-.31	-.08	.08	-.14	.49	1.48	-.07
16	Bouguereau, W. A.	1884	Crown of Flowers	-.19	-.31	.31	.23	.25	-1.16	-.88	.79

15-point scale ranging from 1 (extremely similar) to 15 (extremely different) was provided for the rating task. The scale was divided into five parts as follows:

Extremely similar			Somewhat similar			Neutral			Somewhat different			Extremely different		
1	2	3	4	5	6	7	8	9	10	11	12	13	14	15
(−1)	(0)	(+1)	(−1)	(0)	(+1)	(−1)	(0)	(+1)	(−1)	(0)	(+1)	(−1)	(0)	(+1)

Each part was further refined to reflect subtle nuances of judgment. Thus, within each of the five divisions (e.g., Extremely Similar), S could choose from three numbers to indicate the extremity of his evaluation. He entered a number in the answer space for each of the 120 pairs. Two practice trials using 4 paintings not in the original set of 16 were included to acquaint Ss with the rating task. They saw each of the 120 slide pairs for 8 seconds and had a 10-second interval to perform the similarity-rating task.

The experimental apparatus included two Kodak Carousel projectors (model 860), two Gerbrands shutters (model G1165), an Automated Data Systems Timer (model 1248A), and two 47-inch square Da-lite screens. Presentation of the stimuli was controlled by the timer, which advanced the slides during the interstimulus interval and triggered the shutters at the onset of the stimulus presentation period. E changed trays after each set of 40 pairs, and the entire session lasted 50 minutes.

Results

First, an analysis of variance was performed to determine intersubject consistency in the similarity-rating task. The F value for pairs of paintings was significant ($F = 24.06$; 119 and 4403 df; $p < .001$) and corresponded to a reliability coefficient of .96. Second, a nonmetric individual difference scaling analysis (INDSCAL) was conducted on the 16×16 matrix of mean similarity scores (Carroll & Chang, 1970).

An examination of the summed subject weightings associated with each of the dimensions in the four-dimensional solution reveals one dominant and three secondary dimensions. The dominant dimension distinguishes paintings which share an emphasis on outline (Steen, −.34; Vermeer, −.30; David, −.30; Picasso, −.28), and contrasts them with others that appear to emphasize surface qualities (Turner, +.30; Monet, +.38; Fragonard, +.30), and whose forms are blurred or indeterminate. In addition, the two works that were selected to represent the painterly style, the Monet (+.38) and the Turner

(+.30), are nearest one end of the dimension. The David (-.30), which was chosen as an example of the linear style, is located at the extreme opposite end of the dimension, but the Cezanne (+.03) is neutral on this dimension. It would therefore appear that this approximates the predicted linear-versus-painterly dimension.

The second dimension groups together paintings that emphasize tonal qualities, including Sisley, -.31; Seurat, -.31; and Bouguereau, -.31, and juxtaposes against them brighter and more colorful paintings (Miro, +.52; Picasso, +.49; Heckel, +.28). While the paintings chosen to represent the tonality-color dimension are correctly ordered, they are not strongly weighted on the dimension (Vermeer, -.19; Steen, -.12; Fragonard, +.01; Klimt, +.06). However, the properties of the two groups of paintings distinguished on the dimension indicate that the Ss have discriminated between tonal and colorful works.

The third dimension divided the paintings into those reflecting the deliberate selection of detail (Heckel, -.32; Van Gogh, -.33; Cezanne, -.28; Miro, -.23; and Picasso, -.23), and those characterized by a great deal of detail (Steen, +.40; Fragonard, +.33; David, +39; Bouguereau, +.31; and Vermeer, +.24). The two paintings chosen to represent the abstract style (Miro, -.23 and Picasso, -.23) oppose one of the paintings selected as an example of the representational style (Bouguereau, +.31), but the Seurat (-.08) was not strongly weighted. This dimension appears close to the hypothesized abstract-versus-representational dimension.

The fourth dimension distinguishes between paintings that are more turbulent or active (Turner, -.53; Steen, -.24; Monet, -.23; and Cezanne, -.20), and those that are simpler in composition and calm (Klimt, +.54; Taiga, +.32; and Bouguereau, +.23). An inspection of the two groups of paintings suggests that this is related to the hypothesized multiplicity-versus-unity dimension. However, the fact that only one of the selected paintings is of significant weight on this dimension (Taiga, +.32) renders this inference extremely tentative. In sum, while the findings suggest confirmations of the hypothesized dimensions, it was essential to obtain additional information about the paintings to aid in the identification process.

EXPERIMENT TWO: STYLISTIC SCALING

In this experiment, stylistic properties of the 16 paintings were judged on rating scales. A new group of judges with some degree of artistic sophistication was requested to rate the paintings on a series of 16 scales. The experiment was performed for two reasons. First, information was sought concerning the interrelations among the rating scales. Second, it was hoped that the data would help in identifying the dimensions derived from the first experiment.

Subjects

Eight *S*s, 3 males and 5 females, were chosen by the faculty members of the Fine Arts Department at the University of Toronto from among undergraduates enrolled in studio courses. These *S*s had already participated in Experiment 3 reported in Chapter 9 and were familiar with the rating procedure. Each *S* was paid $2.00 for participating in the study.

Scales

Two types of scales were included among the 16 used in this experiment. Ten bipolar seven-point scales (e.g., 1 = CLEAR, 7 = INDEFINITE) were

TABLE 2

Experiment 2: Stylistic Ratings
(Scales)

Importance of:

1. SHAPES
2. LINES
3. Composition or arrangement of elements (COMPOSITION)
4. Surface qualities or textures (SURFACE)
5. The artist's individual way of perceiving objects or the world as a whole (ARTIST'S PERCEPTION)
6. LIGHT
7. The artist's feelings or emotions (ARTIST'S FEELINGS)
8. Reproduction of the appearance of objects or people (REPRODUCTION)

(*Note:* Words in parentheses are abbreviations by which scales are designated in text.)

Bipolar scales:

9. CLEAR-INDEFINITE
10. CURVED-ANGULAR
11. ORDERLY-DISORDERLY
12. TENSE-TRANQUIL
13. TONAL HARMONY-COLOR HARMONY
14. WARM-COLD
15. OBJECTIVE IDEAS-INNER FEELINGS
16. SIMPLE-COMPLEX

used. Six unipolar scales measured the relative importance of a particular attribute on each scale (e.g., Importance of LINE). The 16 scales can also be divided into four groups, which pertain to different types of information related to the dimensions discussed in the Introduction. Seven stylistic scales were selected to describe the physical properties of the paintings (e.g., Importance of COMPOSITION). Three collative scales (e.g., CLEAR-INDEFINITE) were selected to reflect their informational properties. Four scales were included to determine whether objective or subjective information was conveyed through the paintings (e.g., OBJECTIVE IDEAS versus INNER FEELINGS). Finally, two affective scales were included (e.g., WARM-COLD) to determine the emotional connotations of the paintings. Table 2 lists the scales.

Procedure and Design

The judges performed the rating tasks separately. Each S saw the slides in a different order, corresponding to a randomly selected row of a 16×16 counterbalanced Latin square.

S was informed that the purpose of the experiment was to obtain information about the 16 paintings. E gave S an answer booklet, reviewed the scale labels, and explained the rating procedure. S rated all of the paintings on each question before continuing on to the next one. He also controlled the time for which each picture was exposed.

Results

An analysis of variance was conducted for each rating scale to determine whether the ratings of the paintings were consistent from S to S. A significant paintings effect at the .001 level was obtained for all but one of the scales (ORDERLY-DISORDERLY). The correlations of mean ratings over paintings on each of the scales are presented in Table 3.

A principal-components factor analysis, with Varimax rotation, was performed on the 15 scales that showed a significant paintings effect in the analysis of variance in the correlation matrix. A four-factor solution was extracted accounting for 84.03% of the variance. The factor loadings are presented in Table 4 and those with an absolute value greater than .5 are presented in bold face.

Factor I has high positive loadings on five scales: SHAPES, COMPOSITION, LINES, CURVED-ANGULAR, and WARM-COLD, and high negative loadings on four scales: ARTIST'S FEELINGS, SURFACE QUALITIES, CLEAR-INDEFINITE, and OBJECTIVE IDEAS-INNER

TABLE 3

Experiment 2: Descriptive Scales
(Correlations)

	1	2	3	4	5	6	7	8	9	10	11	12	13	14	15	16
1. SHAPES	—															
2. COMPOSITION	.78**	—														
3. LINES	.85**	.83**	—													
4. ARTIST'S PERCEPTION	.44	-.02	.20	—												
5. LIGHT	-.57*	-.07	-.37	-.40	—											
6. ARTIST'S FEELINGS	-.34	-.62*	-.43	.31	-.12	—										
7. SURFACE QUALITIES	-.69**	-.70**	-.59*	.08	.38	.37	—									
8. REPRODUCTION	-.23	.33	.14	-.78**	.61*	-.46	-.13	—								
9. CLEAR-INDEFINITE	-.36	-.76**	-.67**	.33	-.19	.59*	.49	-.64**	—							
10. CURVED-ANGULAR	.55*	.69**	.44	.06	.04	-.35	-.47	.07	-.36	—						
11. ORDERLY-DISORDERLY	-.30	-.55*	-.41	.08	-.08	.24	.30	-.44	.49	-.18	—					
12. TENSE-TRANQUIL	-.09	.11	-.04	-.36	.07	-.50*	-.03	.30	-.04	-.23	-.29	—				
13. TONAL HARMONY-COLOR HARMONY	.51*	.15	.47	.80**	-.46	.02	-.03	-.56*	-.04	.23	.09	-.46	—			
14. WARM-COLD	.69**	.55*	.71**	.27	-.59*	-.25	-.47	-.14	-.27	.44	-.25	.09	.49	—		
15. OBJECTIVE IDEAS-INNER FEELINGS	-.35	-.70**	-.44	.28	-.23	.92**	.37	-.50*	.60*	-.49	.43	-.45	.05	-.27	—	
16. SIMPLE-COMPLEX	.18	.29	.20	.07	.34	-.45	.27	.18	-.22	.21	.00	-.02	.11	-.17	-.40	—

*$p < .05$.
**$p < .01$.

TABLE 4

Experiment 2: Descriptive Scales

(Factor Analysis)

	I Class- icism	II Subject- ivism	III Complex- ity	IV Expres- sionism
1. SHAPES	.80	.52	−.06	.09
2. COMPOSITION	.94	−.04	.14	.17
3. LINES	.87	.27	.02	.10
4. ARTIST'S PERCEPTION	−.01	.89	.12	−.23
5. LIGHT	−.19	−.68	.58	−.14
6. ARTIST'S FEELINGS	−.54	.18	−.38	−.65
7. SURFACE QUALITIES	−.78	.06	.46	−.08
8. REPRODUCTION	.28	−.85	.19	.17
9. CLEAR-INDEFINITE	−.77	.39	−.18	−.05
10. CURVED-ANGULAR	.72	.03	.20	−.19
11. TENSE-TRANQUIL	−.10	−.22	−.07	.93
12. TONAL HARMONY-COLOR HARMONY	.29	.81	.17	−.23
13. WARM-COLD	.63	.45	−.30	.24
14. OBJECTIVE IDEAS-INNER FEELINGS	−.59	.24	−.40	−.56
15. SIMPLE-COMPLEX	.14	.06	.90	.10

FEELINGS. The findings imply that the paintings which display an emphasis on line are also clear and tend to be perceived as colder, while reflecting an emphasis on ideas rather than feelings. This description is consistent with the characterization of the linear style as "idealistic" and appropriate for expressing ideas or beliefs rather than subjective experiences. Factor I was therefore identified as a Classicism factor.

Factor II has high positive loadings on three scales: SHAPES, ARTIST'S PERCEPTION, and TONAL HARMONY-COLOR HARMONY, and high negative loadings on two scales: LIGHT and REPRODUCTION. These findings reveal that artist's perception is associated with a deemphasis on accurate reproduction and a heightened concern for color composition and shapes. The emphasis on artist's perception and its physical manifestation provides a basis for labeling this factor Subjectivism.

Factor III has high positive loadings on the COMPLEXITY and LIGHT scales and this factor is provisionally labeled Complexity.

Factor IV has a high positive loading on the TENSE-TRANQUIL scale and high negative loadings on the ARTIST'S FEELINGS and OBJECTIVE IDEAS-INNER FEELINGS scales. The emphasis on the artist's emotional experience and its reflection in a tense quality of the painting provides a basis for labeling the factor Expressionism.

It is noteworthy that factors I, II, and III resemble factors obtained by Berlyne & Ogilvie (Chap. 9, this volume) from their battery of stylistic scales, which had some items in common with the battery used in this experiment. Factor IV had high loadings on two scales that were not included in their stylistic battery.

COMPARISONS BETWEEN RESULTS OF EXPERIMENTS ONE AND TWO

All 16 paintings used in this study have scores on each of the four dimensions of the INDSCAL analysis of similarity judgments and also have mean scores on each of the 16 scales employed in Experiment 2, as well as a mean factor score on each of the four factors extracted from the factor analysis. Each stimulus therefore is represented by points in a 4-dimensional INDSCAL space, a 15-dimensional scale space and a 4-dimensional factor space.

Several questions can be asked about the relation between the structures of the similarity (INDSCAL) space and either the scale or the factor spaces. The most general question concerns the degree to which the location of a painting in either the scale space or the factor space is related to its location in the INDSCAL space. The maximum canonical correlation coefficient (R_c) represents this degree of relation (see Chap. 9, this volume). The canonical correlation between the 15-dimensional scale space (with ORDERLY-DISORDERLY omitted) and the 4-dimensional INDSCAL space is 1.00 $(x^2 = 169.65; 60 \ df)$, while R_c relating the 4-dimensional factor space to the INDSCAL space is .97 $(x^2 = 56.52; 16 \ df)$. Both correlation coefficients are significant well beyond the .001 level according to the appropriate x^2 test (Bartlett, 1941). The redundancy index (Stewart & Love, 1968) reflects the extent to which knowledge of a painting's location in the scale space (or factor space) reduces uncertainty about its location in the INDSCAL space. The redundancy is 1.00 for the 15-dimensional scale space and .71 for the factor space.

A more specific question concerns the degree of association between the mean scores for the paintings on each of the 15 scales or 4 factors and the 4-dimensional INDSCAL space as a whole. The appropriate index of this relationship is the multiple correlation coefficient (R). The results of this analysis, presented in Table 5, show that the multiple correlations are

TABLE 5

Experiments 1 and 2: Product-moment and Multiple Correlations

Variable (Experiment 2)	INDSCAL dimensions (Experiment 1)				
	1	2	3	4	R
1. SHAPES	−.58*	.58*	–	–	.88**
2. COMPOSITION	−.80**	–	–	–	.81*
3. LINES	−.77**	–	–	–	.89**
4. ARTIST'S PERCEPTION	–	.54*	−.72**	–	.77*
5. LIGHT	–	−.72**	–	−.64**	.94***
6. ARTIST'S FEELINGS	.63*	–	–	–	–
7. SURFACE QUALITIES	.57*	–	–	–	.77*
8. REPRODUCTION	–	−.72**	.83**	–	.95***
9. CLEAR-INDEFINITE	.84**	–	–	–	.89**
10. CURVED-ANGULAR	−.54*	–	–	–	.76*
11. ORDERLY-DISORDERLY	–	–	–	–	–
12. TENSE-TRANQUIL	–	–	–	–	–
13. TONAL HARMONY-COLOR HARMONY	–	–	−.70**	–	.84**
14. WARM-COLD	–	–	–	–	.76*
15. OBJECTIVE IDEAS-INNER FEELINGS	−.61*	–	–	–	–
16. SIMPLE-COMPLEX	–	–	–	–	–
1. Classicism	−.83**	–	–	–	.86**
2. Subjectivism	–	.66*	−.84**	–	.93***
3. Complexity	–	–	–	−.52*	–
4. Expressionism	–	–	–	.60*	–

*p < .05.
**p < .01.
***p < .001.

significant for 11 of the 15 scales and for the Classicism and Subjectivism factors.

Finally, it is possible to determine the degree of association between each of the scales or factors and each of the INDSCAL dimensions using the product-moment correlation coefficient. The results in Table 5 show that Factor I, (Classicism) is negatively correlated with Dimension 1 of the INDSCAL space. This provides support for the hypothesis that Dimension 1 contrasts linear styles of painting, which emphasize outline and composition, with painterly works, which are indefinite and warm and which reflect the artist's feelings. The second factor (Subjectivism) is negatively correlated with

INDSCAL Dimension 3. This supports the inference that Dimension 3 distinguishes between abstract works reflecting the artist's personal perception of (or selection of information from) the world, and works aimed at accurate reproduction. Factor II is also positively correlated with Dimension 2 of the INDSCAL space. This fits the earlier inference that Dimension 2 contrasts the artist's personal interpretation of events, as expressed through shape and color, with emphasis on tonal relations. Factor III (Complexity) is negatively correlated with Dimension 4, and Factor IV (Expressionism) is positively correlated with this dimension.

DISCUSSION

The findings indicate that at least four dimensions may underlie the perception of artistic style. The first dimension contrasts the pronounced use of outline with a more expressive adaptation of surface qualities that connote warm feelings and seems to correspond to Wölfflin's linear-versus-painterly dimension. A second, abstract-versus-representational, dimension reflects the artist's individual perceptions of events through the selection of the content or detail depicted in the painting. A third dimension contrasts paintings that include colorful shapes with those embodying more somber tones.

The fourth dimension may contrast complex with simple paintings and reflects the artist's feelings as expressed in the tension of the complex works and the tranquility of the simple works. While the process that mediates between complexity of the painting and the attribution of tension has not been investigated, it may be conjectured that a form of information overload is a significant factor. In other words, the attribution of tension to a painting results from the difficulty of interpreting or ordering a highly differentiated but unstructured set of events. This ordering problem could be associated with both the semantic (e.g., *Guernica* by Picasso) and syntactic (e.g., *Day of Glass* by Heckel) aspects of the work of art.

A final comment should be added concerning the utility of the four dimensions and four factors for objectively comparing paintings of different historical periods and cultures, and even of different artists. The two paintings that represent the extremes of each dimension might be used to represent poles of a scale for the evaluation of other paintings. Specifically, judges would be introduced to the scale represented by the two paintings and instructed to select a number to indicate where a new painting lies on this dimension. Alternatively, the verbal scales loaded highest on each factor could be used for rating new sets of paintings.

REFERENCES

Abell, W. *The collective dream in art: A psycho-historical theory of culture based on relations between the arts, psychology, and the social sciences.* Cambridge, Mass.: Harvard University Press, 1957.

Ariès, P. *Centuries of childhood.* New York: Knopf, 1962. (*L'Enfant et la vie familiale sous l'ancien régime.* Paris: Plon, 1960.)

Arnheim, R. *Art and visual perception.* Berkeley, Calif.: University of California Press, 1971.

Bartlett, M. S. The statistical significance of canonical correlations. *Biometrika*, 1941, 32, 29–38.

Berlyne, D. E. *Aesthetics and psychobiology.* New York: Appleton-Century-Crofts, 1971.

Berlyne, D. E., & Borsa, D. M. Uncertainty and the orientation reaction. *Perception and Psychophysics*, 1968, 3, 77–79.

Carroll, J. D., & Chang, J. J. Analysis of individual differences in multidimensional scaling via an N-way generalization of "Eckhart-Young" decomposition. *Psychometrika*, 1970, 35, 283–319.

Garner, W. R. *Uncertainty and structure as psychological concepts.* New York: Wiley, 1962.

Harvey, O. J., Hunt, D. E., & Schroeder, H. M. *Conceptual systems and personality organization.* New York: Wiley, 1961.

Hauser, A. *Mannerism: The crisis of the Renaissance and the origin of modern art.* Vol. 1. London: Routledge & Kegan Paul, 1965.

Kavolis, V. *Artistic expression: A sociological analysis.* Ithaca, N. Y.: Cornell University Press, 1968.

Moles, A. *Information theory and esthetic perception.* Urbana, Ill.: University of Illinois Press, 1966. (*Théorie de l'information et perception esthétique.* Paris: Flammarion, 1958.)

Posner, M. I., & Keele, S. W. On the genesis of abstract ideas. *Journal of Experimental Psychology*, 1968, 77, 353–363.

Riegl, A. *Stilfragen.* 1893.

Shapiro, M. Style. In M. Philipson (Ed.), *Aesthetics today.* New York: Meridian, 1961.

Sorokin, P. A. *Social and cultural dynamics.* Vol. 1. *Fluctuations of forms of art.* New York: Bedminster Press, 1962.

Stewart, D., & Love, W. A general canonical correlation index. *Psychological Bulletin*, 1968, 70, 160–163.

Wölfflin, H. *Principles of art history.* New York: Dover, 1950. (*Kunstgeschichtliche Grundbegriffe.* Munich: Bruckmann, 1915.)

Worringer, W. *Abstraction and empathy.* New York: International Universities Press, 1953. (*Abstraktion und Einfuhlung.* Munich: Piper, 1908.)

Zimmermann, R. *Geschichte der Aesthetik.* 1858.

12

A CROSS-CULTURAL STUDY OF EXPLORATORY AND VERBAL RESPONSES TO VISUAL PATTERNS VARYING IN COMPLEXITY [1]

D. E. Berlyne, M. C. Robbins, and R. Thompson

The vast majority of investigations belonging to the new experimental aesthetics, or for that matter the older experimental aesthetics, have been carried out with subjects from western Europe or North America. Furthermore, the subjects have generally been taken from the more highly educated social strata in those regions. They have more often than not been drawn, in fact, from readily available "subject pools," composed of undergraduates taking elementary courses in psychology.

In a field where norms differ so widely from culture to culture (and from subculture to subculture), and exercise such powerful sway over the tastes of individuals, the question of how far the findings reveal universal characteristics of the human species and how far they reveal peculiarities of human beings with a particular kind of upbringing and social background must remain a haunting one.

[1] The collection of Ugandan data by the second and third authors was partially supported by USPHS Research Grant MH 20210-01, for which they are grateful. They would also like to thank the Makerere Institute of Social Research, Makerere University, Kampala, Uganda for their hospitality, kind cooperation and assistance during their tenure there as Research Associates.

The collection of Canadian data and the analyses of data from both groups of subjects were supported by Research Grants A-73 from the National Research Council of Canada and S70-1570-X2 from the Canada Council. The data were collected by Mary Louise King, and the analyses were carried out by Patricia Hunter. The authors are indebted to them for their able collaboration.

The only way to answer this question is by extending research to other populations of subjects. Experiments by Francès (1970, 1974) illustrate how even an extension to nonstudent sections of western society can cast doubt on the generality of findings. He used verbal and nonverbal techniques, namely recording of Looking Time and judgments of interestingness and of preference, with both students (mostly not of psychology) and workers of a comparable age. The stimulus material consisted of visual line drawings of varying complexity taken from a collection used in many experiments over the last 15 years or so (beginning with Berlyne, 1958—see Berlyne, 1966, 1971; Chap. 14, this volume). It is the collection from which the stimulus material was drawn for the investigation to be reported in this chapter. The findings show significant differences between students and workers on some tasks and some pairs of patterns.

Other investigators, notably Child and Eysenck (see Child, 1969), have carried out cross-cultural research representing more traditional approaches in aesthetics to ascertain how the same works of art are evaluated by people of different cultures. On the whole, such work indicates some degree of intercultural consistency as well as some disagreement.

This chapter presents some experimental findings permitting comparisons between Ugandan and Canadian subjects. The opportunity was provided by a field trip to Uganda by the second and the third author. They presented Ugandan subjects of three different populations with visual patterns taken from the collection that has already been mentioned as having been used repeatedly in experiments on the motivational effects of visual complexity on western subjects. The procedures were based on some of those used most frequently in these experiments, but they were modified and simplified, as necessitated by the transfer from the laboratory to the field. Afterwards, exactly the same stimulus material, procedures, and experimental conditions were used with Canadian students, resembling the subjects of so many earlier investigations.

The results for the Ugandan and Canadian subjects will be presented separately, so that their salient resemblances and differences can be pointed out. Statistical analyses comparing the two will also be discussed, as well as some analyses relating both sets of data to results of some earlier experiments. Some results of an earlier experiment carried out in Uganda with the same stimulus material were mentioned in an earlier publication (Berlyne, 1972). They showed significant correlations over patterns between verbal judgments of Ugandans and verbal and nonverbal responses of North American subjects to the same patterns.

Stimulus Material

The 16 pairs of patterns used in the present experiment are reproduced in Figure 1, together with the letter-number combinations that are used to refer to them. In each pair, the LC (less complex, irregular or incongruous) pattern is on the left, and the MC (more complex, irregular or incongruous)

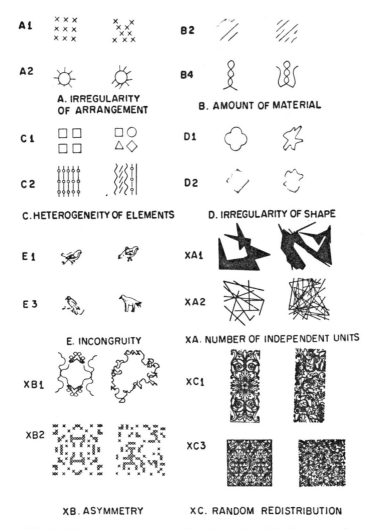

FIG. 1. Stimulus patterns used in the study. LC (Less complex, irregular or incongruous) member of each pair is on left and MC (More complex, irregular, or incongruous) on right.

on the right. The actual variable distinguishing LC patterns from their MC counterparts differs, however, from one category (denoted by the letter or letters preceding the number associated with a pair) to another. These variables are named in the figure.

DATA COLLECTION IN UGANDA

Subjects

Data were collected among the Baganda of Uganda. The Baganda are the predominant inhabitants of the rural and urban areas along the northwestern shores of Lake Victoria and, numbering well over a million persons, they comprise the largest and most socio-economically diverse population in Uganda. Buganda was formerly the largest and most centralized of the several surrounding Interlacustrine Bantu Kingdoms. The Baganda are among the most ethnographically well known populations in Africa, and several excellent accounts of their polity, economy, and society are available (e.g., Roscoe, 1911; Mair, 1934; Fallers, 1960; Southwold, 1965).

Most Baganda are rural peasant cultivators of a variety of subsistence and cash crops including plantains, cassava, sweet potatoes, cotton, coffee, and tea. The physical environment is benevolent and provides for a secure subsistence base. Because most subsistence and some cash farming is relegated to women, males are free to engage in trade, litigation, fishing, and today, pursue wage-earning occupations in towns and cities.

Beginning with Arab and European contact in the nineteenth century, the Baganda have displayed unusual receptivity to innovations and a keen desire to acquire the advantages of the outside world. This allowed them to achieve one of the most advantaged positions in East Africa. However, despite their modern and rapid development, they have retained a strong sense of their inherent cultural tradition and identity. Many of the political events and economic changes that have transpired in Uganda since independence have been interpreted by the Baganda as threats to their socio-cultural integrity.

Traditional forms of graphic and plastic art are underdeveloped in Buganda. Visual art consists mainly of simple symmetrical nonrepresentational geometric designs on baskets, mats, and other material items (cf. Fallers, 1960; Lugira, 1970). Forms of representational western and Asian art and photographs have diffused throughout Buganda. Individual exposure, however, varies directly with contact with mass media and urban experience (cf. Kilbride, 1970).

The research reported here was conducted in three areas of Buganda selected to represent "points" along a rural-intermediate-urban continuum.

Rural population. The rural community is located 40 miles southwest of Kampala, the major urban center. No electricity, telephone, or western medical services are available in this area. Battery-powered radios and twice-daily taxi service to and from Kampala are the major sources of information.

Farming and fishing are the major occupations, although the single primary school in the area employs local teachers. There is little apparent social or economic stratification, and significant interpersonal relationships tend to be based on kinship. Opportunities for recreation and entertainment are restricted to drinking parties, church attendance, visiting among friends and relatives, and traditional forms of music and games.

Intermediate area. The intermediate area consists of two communities which lie 7 and 20 miles southwest of Kampala along the road going on to and beyond the rural area. Modern medical facilities and electricity are available to residents. Both economically and culturally, the population is considerably more heterogeneous than the rural population. Three secondary schools and several primary schools are located in and around these communities, and public and private forms of transportation are always available. A variety of traditional and modern forms of music and entertainment are enjoyed in these communities.

Urban community. Kampala-Mengo (pop. 350,000) is the capital of Uganda and the commercial and geographical hub of Buganda. The city boasts numerous high-rise tourist hotels, banks, a major general hospital, large markets, the national theater, and a museum. The wide range of economic opportunities offered in the city attracts members of several ethnic groups from East Africa. Social relations in the city are both casual and uncertain. Status in Kampala is defined largely by material life-styles, education, and occupation. Entertainment in the form of numerous nightclubs, bars, cinemas, sports events, and celebrations is a major attraction of Kampala.

In addition to the qualitative differences noted above, results of our social surveys, administered in conjunction with the gathering of the data to be reported in this chapter, reveal that the three areas can also be distinguished by a variety of quantitative comparisons. Some of these data are presented in Table 1. These data rather clearly indicate that, beginning in the rural area and progressing through the intermediate to the urban area, one finds increasing amounts of formal education, literacy, a younger population, and greater exposure to mass media. In addition, data from these areas reported

TABLE 1

Ugandan Subjects

Intersubgroup Comparisons

	Rural	Intermediate	Urban	Total group
Age (years)	36.4	30.6	29.9	32.3
% Males	48	48	52	49
Education (years)	4.2	5.4	6.1	5.2
Household size*	4.7	4.2	4.2	4.4
% Own T.V.	–	03	10	04
% Own radio	53	63	65	60
% Read English	27	40	58	42
% Read Luganda	77	87	87	84
% Go to cinema	18	41	35	31
# Newspapers and magazines known	2.6	4.1	5.4	4.0

elsewhere reveal greater material wealth and higher incomes for the urban population (cf. Robbins and Thompson, 1972).

Procedure

The data reported in this chapter are derived from interview schedules administered in the Luganda language to random samples of 100 subjects in each of the rural, intermediate, and urban areas. The interview schedule, which took approximately 40 minutes to complete, was translated and back-translated to criterion several times by Baganda research assistants and administered with their aid after pretesting and modification.

The procedure comprised four successive phases:

1. Looking Time. Ss were allowed to sit in a comfortable position and were presented a single stimulus pattern mounted on 23 cm x 30 cm black paper inserted in a loose-leaf notebook. Viewing distance could not be rigorously controlled but fell within a range of 75 cm to 120 cm. The 18 stimulus patterns (see Table 2) were presented in a randomized order.

S was told in Luganda: "I have some pictures that I am going to show you. You can look at each for as long as you wish. When I show you a picture, you tell me when you are finished and I will change to the next one." *S* was then asked whether he understood the task and, if there was any doubt, the instructions were repeated and elaborated by *E*. The first pattern in the notebook was then displayed and a second *E* operated a stopwatch to record Looking Time to the nearest second.

2. Paired comparisons of attractiveness. Ss were presented 16 stimulus pairs mounted on 23 cm x 30 cm black paper in a loose-leaf notebook. The subject was told: "I have pictures in pairs (two by two). When I show them to you I want you to tell me which one you think is the more attractive (*okusikiriza*)." In presenting the stimulus pairs, the right-left presentation order for LC and MC stimuli was randomized.

3. Seven-point scales. Ss were shown six visual patterns (three pairs), each mounted separately on 9 in. x 11 in. black paper in a loose-leaf notebook. Three different sets of visual patterns were employed so that 100 Ss, distributed as evenly as possible among the rural, intermediate, and urban areas, responded to each set of six stimuli, comprising three pairs. Ss were then asked to evaluate the patterns against a set of seven bi-polar adjectival scales. In translating polar adjectives, antonyms were used when present (e.g., *kirungi-kibi*, good-bad). In cases where there were no sets of Luganda antonyms, a negative form of a positive was substituted (e.g., *kizimu-sikizimu*, complex-simple or difficult-easy). These scales include:

pleasant-unpleasant	*kisanyusa-sikisanyusa*
complex-simple	*kizimu-sikizimu*
familiar-unusual (new)	*kikadde-kipya*
strong-weak	*kimaanyi-kinnafu*
fast-slow	*kirimpola-kyangu*[2]
exciting-unexciting	*kikyamufu-sikikyamufu*
good-bad	*kirungi-kibi*

The polar adjectives were scaled to form a seven-point continuum. For instance, STRONG was scaled as "(1) very strong (2) strong (3) slightly strong (4) strong and weak (5) slightly weak (6) weak (7) very weak." However, when the data were analyzed, these numbers were subtracted from seven to produce scores varying directly with the attributes denoted by the left-hand adjectives.

4. Paired comparisons of pleasingness. The apparatus and procedures employed here were identical to those for the paired-comparison judgments of attractiveness, except that subjects were instructed to report which pattern "pleases you more" (*kisanyusa*).

[2] The word *kyangu* can mean "fast," "tight," "quick," or "easy," depending on the context. *Kirimpola* can mean "slow," "gently," or "quietly." Both the ratings on this scale of LC and MC patterns and the correlation with the Canadian subjects' ratings (reported below) indicate that the *Kyangu-kirimpola* scale reflected judgments of how fast or easily a pattern could be assimilated.

DATA COLLECTION WITH
CANADIAN SUBJECTS

Subjects

Thirty undergraduates taking elementary psychology courses participated.

Procedure

The same loose-leaf notebooks, containing reproductions of the patterns, as were used in Uganda were used in Canada. The procedure was kept as close as possible to what was done in Uganda, except that the interviews took place in a laboratory room and the English equivalents of Luganda words, as shown above, were employed. "Difficult-easy" was taken to be the best English substitute for *kirimpola-kyangu* (see Footnote 2). In the tables, the word EASY stands for this scale.

RESULTS

Looking Time

The mean time spent looking at each pattern was worked out for each of the three Ugandan subgroups of *S*s and for the Canadian group. The mean Looking Time over all patterns was 4.6 seconds for the

TABLE 2

Mean Looking Time (seconds) by Pairs of Patterns

Pair	Ugandan *S*s			Canadian *S*s		
	LC	MC	$F(1,297)$	LC	MC	$F(1,29)$
A1	4.2	4.1	0.24	3.1	4.4	11.34***
A3	4.0	4.2	2.50	2.4	3.8	29.87***
B4	4.2	‑4.6	6.28*	2.1	3.0	33.48***
C1	3.7	3.4	**6.78	1.8	2.5	24.84***
D1	3.9	4.2	4.26*	2.2	3.4	13.27***
E1	4.1	5.4	47.22***	2.8	4.6	35.39***
E3	5.6	4.9	***10.20	2.5	3.4	18.72***
XA1	4.3	4.7	11.80***	3.5	4.3	13.62***
XC3	7.0	5.3	***39.99	3.3	3.8	4.44*

Asterisks on left denote higher LC mean.
Asterisks on right denote higher MC mean.
  *$p < .05$.
 **$p < .01$.
***$p < .001$.

Ugandans and 3.2 seconds for the Canadians. This difference was significant: $t = 2.05, df = 328, p < .05$.

There are two ways to look for evidence of a tendency to devote more Looking Time to more complex patterns. One is to compare the means for MC and LC members of the same pair. The relevant means are shown in Table 2. As the table shows, the Canadian subjects showed a marked and statistically significant inclination to look longer at MC patterns, reproducing what has invariably occurred in experiments on Looking Time with western subjects (see Berlyne, 1971, Chap. 13). The Ugandans, on the other hand, looked significantly longer at the MC patterns of some pairs and the LC patterns of others. Over all pairs, their MC and LC means are close together and not significantly different. There is, however, a significant interaction between the MC/LC variable and subgroup membership among the Ugandans: $F(2,297) = 5.29, p < .05$. As can be seen from Table 3, the LC patterns attract longer Looking Time in the rural subgroup, the MC patterns attract longer Looking Time in the urban subgroup, and the means for MC and LC patterns are close together in the intermediate subgroup. In other words, increasing urbanization seems to mean devotion of an increasing proportion of Looking Time to MC patterns, thus bringing Ugandan Ss progressively nearer to the exploratory behavior characteristic of western subjects.

The second way to pursue the effects of stimulus complexity on Looking Time is to compare the means for both the MC and LC patterns of pairs A1, A3, B4, C1, and D1 with those of pairs XA1, and XC3. The patterns in the XA and XC categories were designed (see Berlyne, 1963) to represent material of a markedly higher order of complexity than the patterns of categories A to D. In fact, both the MC and LC patterns of the "X" categories

TABLE 3

Mean Looking Time (seconds) Over Categories of Patterns

Ss	All categories		LC + MC	
	LC	MC	A–D	XA–XC
Ugandan rural	4.4	4.1	3.8	5.0
Ugandan intermediate	4.6	4.6	4.0	5.3
Ugandan urban	4.7	4.9	4.4	5.6
All Ugandan	4.6	4.5	4.1	5.3
Canadian	2.6	3.7	2.8	4.2

would appear to exceed the patterns of the "non-X" categories in complexity more than the MC members of most pairs exceed their LC counterparts. Some corroboration of this conclusion, at least as far as subjective complexity is concerned, is to be found in some rank-ordering data collected by Day (1965, Table 10). When our Ss were asked to scale patterns for complexity in the second part of the experiment (whose results will be discussed more fully in due course), the mean ratings by the Ugandans came to 2.6 for patterns from categories A–D and 5.5 for patterns from categories XA and XC. The corresponding means for the Canadian subjects were 1.2 and 4.5, respectively. Unfortunately, the significance of these differences cannot be tested, since the comparisons were partly within-subjects and partly between-subjects.

As Table 3 shows, both Ugandan and Canadian groups tended to look longer at patterns from the "X" categories than at patterns from the "non-X" categories. The differences are significant: $t = 11.88$, $df = 297$, for the Ugandans, $t = 7.06$, $df = 27$, for the Canadians, $p < .001$ in both cases. As can be seen once again in Table 3, the ratio between the mean non-X looking time and the mean X looking time is remarkably constant between the two nationalities and among the Ugandan subgroups, varying between 40% and 44%. The correlation between mean Looking Times for the Ugandan and Canadian groups over patterns comes to +.33, which is not significant.

Paired comparisons

Table 4 shows the number of Ss in each group who selected the LC member of each pair as the more "attrative" and as the more "pleasing." Correlation coefficient over pairs of patterns between the number of Ss judging the LC member more attractive and the number judging the LC pattern more pleasing came to +.96 for both the Ugandan group and the Canadian group. So, even allowing for the possibility that prior judgments on one attribute may have influenced judgments on the other attribute recorded a few minutes later, we can conclude that the two judgments have to a large extent the same meaning.

We see that, in each group, there were significant tendencies for the LC members of some pairs, and the MC members of other pairs, to be judged more attractive. The significance levels derived from the sign test are indicated in Table 4. Ss of both groups, on the average, select more LC than MC patterns as more pleasing and more attractive. The F values, with 1 and 297 degrees of freedom, for the Ugandan group are 30.14 for pleasingness and 27.91 for attractiveness; $p < .001$ in both cases. There was no sign of an interaction with subgroups. The corresponding t values, with 29 degrees of freedom, for the Canadian group are 5.57 and 4.88; $p < .01$ for both. The mean numbers of choices of LC patterns for both pleasingness and

TABLE 4

Paired Comparisons:
Number of Subjects Choosing LC and MC Patterns and
Mean Numbers of LC and MC Choices

Pair	Pleasingness				Attractiveness			
	Ugandans		Canadians		Ugandans		Canadians	
	LC	MC	LC	MC	LC	MC	LC	MC
A1	**182	118	20	10	**175	125	*22	8
A3	**226	74	**29	1	**192	108	**28	2
B2	96	204**	7	23**	66	234**	5	25**
B4	77	223**	4	26**	72	228**	3	27**
C1	**177	123	19	11	150	150	15	15
C2	**205	95	**23	7	**177	123	*21	9
D1	**228	72	**25	5	**196	104	*21	9
D2	153	147	20	10	135	165	19	11
E1	152	148	19	11	**119	181	17	13
E3	160	140	**24	6	137	163	*22	8
XA1	*168	132	16	14	133	167*	15	15
XA2	**194	106	16	14	**189	111	18	12
XB1	**180	120	**25	5	139	161	**26	4
XB2	**208	92	**24	6	**214	86	**24	6
XC1	**260	40	**26	4	**247	53	**28	2
XC3	**211	89	**25	5	**192	108	**26	4
Mean no. of choices	9.6	6.4	10.7	5.3	8.4	7.6	10.3	5.7

Asterisks are placed next to significantly larger number.
*$p < .05$.
**$p < .01$.

attractiveness are significantly higher in the Canadian group than in the Ugandan group: with 328 degrees of freedom, $t = 1.97$, 3.71, respectively, $p < .05, < .001$.

Over pairs of patterns, the correlation between the number of Ugandan Ss and the number of Canadian Ss judging the LC pattern more pleasing is +.89, $p < .001$. The corresponding correlation coefficient for judgments of attractiveness is +.82, $p < .001$. In every single pair, the pattern judged more pleasing by more than half of the Ugandans is also judged more pleasing by more than half of the Canadians. The same holds for most pairs with regard to attractiveness, but there are five exceptions. So, apart from the overall tendency of Canadian Ss to favor LC patterns a little more than Ugandan Ss, there is a high degree of agreement between the two groups on which pattern of each pair is more pleasing or attractive.

Seven-point scales

Since three sets of patterns were judged, respectively, by 33, 33, and 34 Ss on the 7-point scales in each Ugandan subgroup, data from 3 randomly selected Ss were discarded. Consequently, data from 33 Ss were analyzed for each scale and each pattern. In the Canadian group, 10 Ss judged each set of 6 patterns. Each set of 6 patterns comprised LC and MC members of three pairs, so that LC/MC comparisons were always within-subjects.

Table 5 presents the mean scores on the scales for the LC and MC patterns of each pair. Whenever analysis of variance showed a pattern to have received a higher mean score on a particular scale than the other pattern of the same pair, this is indicated. When the data from Uganda were analyzed, some scales applied to some pairs of patterns produced significant differences among subgroups or significant subgroup × LC/MC interactions. Information on these instances is to be found in Table 6.

The data for the two groups were then subjected to separate correlational analyses. The mean score of each pattern on each scale was calculated, and the correlations over patterns among these scores appear in Table 7. It will be seen that corresponding correlation coefficients for the two groups are in general impressively close, apart from some involving the EXCITING and GOOD scales. Each set of correlations was subjected to principal-axes factor analysis, with Varimax rotation, using Veldman's (1957) FACTOR computer program. The factor loadings are presented in Table 8, with high loadings ($>.50$) in bold face. With each group of Ss, two factors emerge. They account together for 91.1% of the variance of the Ugandan data and 89.8% of the variance of the Canadian data. The two factor structures are remarkably similar. The same scales have high loadings on the same factors in the two sets of data, except that the STRONG scale is highly loaded on both factors in the Ugandan data and the EXCITING scale is highly loaded on both factors in the Canadian data. The two factors, which emerge in both groups and are evidently close to those appearing in other factor-analytic studies (see Chaps. 2, 5 and 14, this volume; Berlyne, 1972, 1973), are provisionally labeled Uncertainty and Hedonic Tone, respectively.

TABLE 5

Mean Ratings on 7-Point Scales

Pair		A1		A3		B4		C1		D1		E1		E3		XA1		XC3	
Scale		LC	MC	LC	MC	LC	MC	LC	MC	LC	MC	LC	MC	LC	MC	LC	MC	LC	MC
PLEASING	U	4.0	5.3	5.1***	3.7	3.0	3.5	5.0**	4.4	4.9***	2.9	5.0	4.7	4.4	4.5	4.4*	3.9	4.7	4.6
	C	3.1	2.6	4.0**	1.7	3.2	4.0*	2.6	3.2	4.7*	3.3	4.7*	1.9	3.3	2.9	3.7	4.5	5.5*	4.0
COMPLEX	U	2.6	2.6	2.2	2.9**	2.3	2.6	1.9	2.5**	2.5	3.7***	2.3	4.2***	2.7	4.0***	4.0	4.6**	4.3	4.9**
	C	0.9	2.5*	0.6	1.7	0.6	0.7	0.3	2.7**	0.8	1.8	0.8	5.3***	0.8	3.5**	3.1	4.8*	4.1	6.0*
FAMILIAR	U	3.3	3.4	3.3**	2.5	2.7*	2.0	4.0**	3.4	3.5**	2.1	4.3***	1.2	3.7**	1.4	1.8*	1.3	1.5	1.3
	C	6.0***	3.4	5.8**	3.2	4.4	3.6	5.7	4.3	5.6**	3.2	5.6***	1.2	5.2***	0.9	2.0	1.5	5.0**	2.3
STRONG	U	3.6	3.8	4.6	4.2	2.8	3.2*	3.9	4.0	3.9	3.9	4.2	4.8**	3.6	4.5***	4.3	4.5	4.9	4.8
	C	3.7*	2.3	3.5*	1.7	1.9	2.1	1.9	3.4	3.9	2.8	3.9	3.5	2.3	4.3	3.7	5.3*	4.8	3.7
EASY	U	3.9	3.7	4.0***	3.1	3.1	3.3	4.1*	3.5	3.7**	3.1	4.1***	2.8	3.6***	2.7	2.9	2.7	2.7	2.4
	C	5.9***	3.7	5.9*	4.3	5.7	4.6	5.8**	4.0	4.7	4.9	4.7*	1.6	4.4*	2.6	3.0	2.0	2.3*	0.4
EXCITING	U	4.0	4.2	5.0**	4.2	3.7	4.1	4.8***	3.8	4.9***	3.5	4.6	4.8	4.5	4.4	4.3*	3.8	3.9	4.1
	C	1.2	2.2	2.1	1.0	0.9	2.5*	0.9	2.8*	3.2	2.4	3.2	4.1	1.2	3.4*	3.2	4.4*	4.3	3.5
GOOD	U	4.3	4.4	5.1***	4.0	3.6	4.1**	5.1***	4.6	4.7***	3.6	5.0	4.7	4.6**	4.2	4.3	4.1	4.8*	4.4
	C	2.8	2.3	3.3	2.3	3.0	3.2	2.5	3.6	4.3*	2.7	4.3	3.3	3.3	3.2	3.7	4.5	5.2**	3.0

U: Ugandan subjects.
C: Canadian subjects.
  *Significantly higher mean at .05 level.
 **Significantly higher mean at .01 level.
***Significantly higher mean at .001 level.

271

TABLE 6

Mean Ratings on 7-Point Scales—Ugandan Subgroups

Scale	Pair	Subgroup	LC	MC	Subgroups main effect	Subgroups × LC/MC interaction
PLEASING	A3	R	4.1	4.3		
		I	3.7	3.9	*	
		U	4.2	4.4		
COMPLEX	A1	R	3.1	3.3		
		I	2.6	2.4	*	
		U	2.2	0.9		
COMPLEX	B4	R	1.9	2.8		
		I	2.4	2.8		*
		U	2.5	2.2		
COMPLEX	E1	R	3.3	3.8		
		I	1.8	4.3		**
		U	1.8	4.5		
COMPLEX	XAI	R	3.5	3.9		
		I	4.2	4.7	*	
		U	4.4	5.2		
FAMILIAR	A1	R	2.4	2.5		
		I	3.6	3.8	**	
		U	3.8	3.8		
FAMILIAR	D1	R	2.4	1.8		
		I	3.7	2.0	*	
		U	4.1	2.6		
FAMILIAR	E1	R	3.1	1.8		
		I	4.5	1.1		**
		U	5.1	0.7		
STRONG	D1	R	4.5	4.1		
		I	4.1	3.5		**
		U	3.2	4.0		
EASY	A1	R	3.3	3.4		
		I	3.8	3.4	*	
		U	4.5	4.3		
EASY	A3	R	3.7	3.4		
		I	3.7	3.1		*
		U	4.6	2.8		
EASY	E1	R	3.6	3.7		
		I	3.9	2.7		**
		U	4.9	2.1		
EXCITING	A1	R	4.7	4.8		
		I	3.6	3.7	**	
		U	3.7	4.1		

TABLE 6 *(Continued)*

Mean Ratings on 7-Point Scales—Ugandan Subgroups

Scale	Pair	Subgroup	LC	MC	Subgroups main effect	Subgroups x LC/MC interaction
EXCITING	C1	R	5.0	3.8		
		I	4.4	3.3	*	
		U	5.1	4.4		
EXCITING	XAI	R	3.9	3.1		
		I	4.1	3.8	*	
		U	4.8	4.5		
GOOD	A3	R	4.7	3.8		
		I	5.4	3.5	*	*
		U	5.3	4.6		
GOOD	D1	R	5.0	4.1		
		I	4.5	3.4	*	
		U	4.6	3.2		

R: Rural.
I: Intermediate.
U: Urban.
$*p < .05$.
$**p < .01$.

Interrelations

Looking Time and other measures. With respect to the nine pairs of patterns that figured in both the Looking-Time and the paired-comparison sections of the experiment, the following question was examined: Did Ss tend to look longer at whichever pattern of a pair they selected as the more (or less) pleasing or attractive? Each S was given a score, consisting of one point for each pair in which the pattern selected as more attractive was also the one looked at longer. When Looking Times were equal for the two patterns of a pair, .5 was added to the score. A similar score was worked out using pleasingness choices.

The resulting scores did not differ significantly from 4.5, the score expected by chance, for either pleasingness or attractiveness in the Ugandan group or for attractiveness in the Canadian group. The mean score for pleasingness was, however, 3.7 in the Canadian group ($t = 2.93$, 29 degrees of freedom, $p < .01$), indicating that the Canadian Ss tended to look longer at whichever member of a pair they judged less pleasing. This agrees with some previous findings. Western Ss invariably look at MC patterns for a

TABLE 7

Correlations between Mean Scores per Pattern

	PLEAS-ING	COM-PLEX	FAMILIAR	STRONG	EASY	EXCIT-ING	GOOD
			A. Ugandan subjects				
PLEASING							
COMPLEX	−.04						
FAMILIAR	.25	−.89**					
STRONG	.59*	.65**	−.46				
EASY	.30	−.90**	.94**	−.40			
EXCITING	.78**	−.32	.36	.27	.47*		
GOOD	.92**	−.28	.45	.41	.52*	.75**	
			B. Canadian subjects				
PLEASING							
COMPLEX	.05						
FAMILIAR	.29	−.75**					
STRONG	.61**	.56**	−.23				
EASY	−.12	−.96**	.74**	−.52*			
EXCITING	.51*	.75**	−.51*	.82**	−.77**		
GOOD	.83**	.26	.08	.77**	−.31	.71**	

Asterisks are placed next to significantly larger number.
*$p < .05$.
**$p < .01$.

TABLE 8

Factor Loadings

Subjects	Ugandan		Canadian	
Factor Scale	I (Uncertainty)	II (Hedonic Tone)	I (Uncertainty)	II (Hedonic Tone)
PLEASING	.00	.98	−.15	.93
COMPLEX	.98	−.05	.95	.20
FAMILIAR	−.93	.24	−.91	.20
STRONG	.71	.63	.43	.81
EASY	−.92	.32	−.93	−.24
EXCITING	.26	.84	.69	.68
GOOD	.24	.93	.09	.95

longer time (as shown in the present experiment and many others), but these patterns tend to be judged less pleasing (Berlyne, 1963). Harrison (1968), using different patterns, found likewise that his subjects tended to look longer at patterns that they said they liked less.

The correlations between the mean Looking Times for the 18 patterns with the mean scores for the same patterns on the 7-point scales, as well as with the mean estimated factor scores (computed with the help of the factor weights provided by the computer program), are displayed in Table 9. It is noteworthy that Looking Time is significantly correlated with the same scales and factors in both groups.

The right-hand column of Table 9 also shows correlations between mean scores of the Ugandan and Canadian Ss on the same measures. Here, it will be seen that the correlations are high and significant on four of the seven scales. There is also a high and significant correlatioñ between scores on Factor I (Uncertainty) but not between scores on Factor II (Hedonic Tone).

Finally, the opportunity was taken to compare the measures generated by our two groups of Ss and some earlier data obtained with the same patterns. These data were collected in Berkeley, California in 1957, although they were not reported until several years later (Berlyne, 1963). The Ss were

TABLE 9

Correlations

	Ugandan Looking Time and Ugandan ratings	Canadian Looking Time and Canadian ratings	Ugandan and Canadian ratings
PLEASING	.02	−.23	.28
COMPLEX	.61**	.69**	.91**
FAMILIAR	−.66**	−.66**	.73**
STRONG	.37	.30	.65**
EASY	−.61**	−.63**	.81**
EXCITING	−.17	.44	.04
GOOD	−.02	−.08	.30
Factor I (Uncertainty)	.56*	.74**	.80**
Factor II (Hedonic Tone)	−.04	.11	.44

*$p < .05$.
**$p < .01$.

undergraduates taken from psychology courses, and they were shown 54 patterns, including all of those that figured in the present experiments. Half of them had to rate each pattern on a 7-point scale for pleasingness and the other half had to rate them on a 7-point scale for interestingness. The correlations between the mean ratings made by these American subjects some 15 years earlier and various mean scores produced by our Ugandan and Canadian Ss are shown in Table 10. It is worth mentioning that, over the 18 patterns used in the present investigation, the correlation between the Berkeley pleasingness and interestingness ratings comes to $-.34$, which is not significant.

As can be seen in Table 10, there are several significant correlations between the Canadian and the American data and, despite a temporal distance of about 15 years, a spatial distance of about 10,000 miles and a great cultural distance, scarcely fewer significant correlations between the Ugandan and American data.

Only the Ugandan Looking Time scores and ratings on the PLEASING and EXCITING scales fail to show a significant correlation with either Berkeley score. The correlation between Ugandan STRONG ratings and Berkeley Interestingness ratings suggests, together with other considerations that the Luganda word for "strong" comes somewhat close in meaning to the English "interesting".

TABLE 10

Correlations with Mean Ratings Obtained in Berkeley in 1957

Berkeley ratings	Pleasingness		Interestingness	
Variable	Ugandans	Canadians	Ugandans	Canadians
Looking Time	.32	−.54*	−.26	.56*
PLEASING	.35	.54*	−.06	.22
COMPLEX	−.55*	−.59*	.78**	.72**
FAMILIAR	.67**	.79**	−.78**	−.52**
STRONG	−.20	.07	.48*	.62**
EASY	.70**	.57*	−.69**	−.76**
EXCITING	.30	−.16	−.22	.63**
GOOD	.52*	.38	−.11	.46*
Factor I (Uncertainty)	−.47	−.74**	.66**	.66**
Factor II (Hedonic Tone)	.43	.48*	.06	.37

*p < .05.
**p < .01.

CONCLUSIONS

All in all, this study has revealed more similarities than differences between the reactions of Ugandan and Canadian *S*s faced with the same stimulus material and the same tasks.

In western *S*s, Looking Time has been found regularly to increase with complexity, whether it is a matter of complexity according to objective criteria or of subjective complexity as revealed by *S*s' verbal judgments. The significant correlation between Looking Times and ratings on the COMPLEX scale and the comparison between Looking Time for the non-X and X categories of patterns provide evidence for the same tendency in Ugandans. However, Ugandans do not show the greater Looking Time for MC, as compared with LC, patterns that has regularly appeared when western *S*s have been studied. Since we find relatively more time spent looking at MC patterns as we progress from the rural Ugandans through the intermediate Ugandans and the urban Ugandans to the Canadians, we may suppose that the tendency to look longer at more complex stimuli, while present to some extent in human beings generally, becomes stronger with increasing westernization and urbanization.

There were also many resemblances between the verbal judgments of the Ugandan and Canadian *S*s, despite not only cultural differences but also the fact that the words denoting the attributes to be judged came from unrelated languages and, therefore, do not have exactly the same connotations. There were also striking similarities between the ways in which the various judgments were related to one another, as shown by the factor structure. The overall findings provide no support for those who believe that the search for generalizations in a field of research like experimental aesthetics is hopeless, on the grounds that variations in tastes from individual to individual and from society to society will alone be revealed when aesthetic reactions are probed. There clearly are differences among individuals and among ethnic groups, as some of our findings illustrate. But there are also impressive similarities in the ways in which people with markedly different cultural backgrounds respond to the same visual material. And when there are differences, it seems not too much to say that they are generally differences in degree. Apart from anything else, our findings confirm what a study of artifacts from a variety of periods and civilizations will demonstrate, namely that aesthetic reactions all over the world depend on common variables, notably the collative or informational variables that the patterns used in our experiments were designed to sample, even if the preferred values of these variables fluctuate.

Our findings highlight, however, the urgent need for more cross-cultural research in experimental aesthetics to supplement the comparative studies of aesthetic artifacts that are becoming increasingly frequent among anthropologists. Only with the help of all these methods can the human universals of artistic activity and appreciation, as well as their stylistic diversities, be illuminated.

REFERENCES

Berlyne, D. E. The influence of complexity and change in visual figures on orienting responses. *Journal of Experimental Psychology*, 1958, 55, 289-296.

Berlyne, D. E. Complexity and incongruity variables as determinants of exploratory choice and evaluative ratings. *Canadian Journal of Psychology*, 1963, 17, 274-290.

Berlyne, D. E. Curiosity and exploration. *Science*, 1966, 153, 25-33.

Berlyne, D. E. *Aesthetics and psychobiology*. New York: Appleton-Century-Crofts, 1971.

Berlyne, D. E. Ends and means of experimental aesthetics. *Canadian Journal of Psychology*, 1972, 26, 303-325.

Berlyne, D. E. Interrelations of verbal and nonverbal measures used in experimental aesthetics. *Scandinavian Journal of Psychology*, 1973, 14, 177-184.

Child, I. L. Esthetics. In G. Lindzey & E. Aronson (Eds.), *Handbook of Social Psychology*. (2nd ed.) Vol. 3. Reading, Mass.: Addison-Wesley, 1969.

Day, H. I. Exploratory behaviour as a function of individual differences and level of arousal. Unpublished Ph.D. thesis, University of Toronto, 1965.

Fallers, M. *The Eastern Lacustrine Bantu*. London: International African Institute, 1960.

Francès, R. Intérêt et préférence esthétique pour des stimuli de complexité variable. Étude comparative. *Journal de Psychologie*, 1970, 70, 207-224.

Francès R. Les choix et les jugements esthétiques. *La Recherche*, 1974, 46, 553-561.

Harrison, A. A. Response competition, frequency, exploratory behavior and liking. *Journal of Personality and Social Psychology*, 1968, 9, 363-368.

Kilbride, P. Baganda Modernization and Pictorial Perception. Unpublished Ph.D. dissertation, University of Missouri, 1970.

Lugira, A. M. *Ganda art*. Kampala: Osasa, 1970.

Mair, L. *An African people in the twentieth century*. London: Routledge and Kegan Paul, 1934.

Robbins, M., & Thompson, R. Socio-Cultural Bases of Gratification Patterns. Final Progress Report Grant # MH 20210-01, University of Missouri, 1972.

Roscoe, J. *The Baganda*. London: Kegan and Paul, 1911.

Southwold, M. The Ganda of Uganda. In J. Gibbs (Ed.), *Peoples of Africa*. New York: Holt, Rinehart & Winston, 1965.

Veldman, J. *FORTRAN programing for the behavioral sciences*. New York: Holt, Rinehart & Winston, 1957.

13

CORRELATES OF HUMOR: VERBAL AND NONVERBAL AESTHETIC REACTIONS AS FUNCTIONS OF SEMANTIC DISTANCE WITHIN ADJECTIVE-NOUN PAIRS[1]

M. Godkewitsch

If one were to distill the large number of philosophical theories of humor and the sporadic empirical attempts to explain the humor phenomenon, three sets of variables would emerge that alone, or in interaction, instigate humor responses and determine their strength:

1. Variables associated with the receiver. Tastes differ; individual differences in development, education, adjustment, and personality play an important role in which kind of humor people appreciate. For example, McGhee (1971) showed that liking for a given sample of cartoons was limited by children's level of cognitive development, and Levine & Redlich (1960) found that a joke whose content induced a moderate level of anxiety, would be greatly appreciated, but when that content became threatening the joke was liked less.

2. Variables associated with the social situation. Factors such as an expectation of being amused and some degree of inebriation probably help one to enjoy nightclub entertainers' humor, which at other times may not strike the receiver as convulsing wit. Malefijt (1968), describing "baiting and

[1]The author wishes to thank Ms. S. Byford of Toronto, and the Ontario Science Centre, Don Mills, Ontario, Canada, for their cooperation in collecting data for Experiment 1. The studies reported in this chapter were reported in a thesis submitted in accordance with the requirements of the Ph.D. degree of the University of Toronto.

279

biting," demonstrated how this Dutch form of playful communication between a husband and his wife's girlfriend represents a form of humor bound by social situation and culture.

3. Variables associated with the stimulus. The salience of the theme can contribute to the liking for a joke: Godkewitsch (1972) found, for instance, a positive relation between rated amount of sex in jokes and their rated funniness. In humor research, extremely little effort has been spent on unraveling the operation of stimulus variables in subsequent affect. In the 243 hitherto traced published and unpublished, more or less empirical, studies of humor, 135 dealt with receiver-associated variables, 43 dealt with situational variables, and, although stimulus variables were of some interest in 66 studies, they were the main target in only 16 studies, while the remaining 50 focused on interactions of stimulus—and receiver-associated variables.

What is Humor?

The term "humor" describes the subjective side of a set of responses, verbal and nonverbal, to complex verbal or pictorial stimuli. These responses have affective and exploratory components (e.g., eager anticipation), similar to other aesthetic responses. Berlyne (1972a) has made a case for dealing with humor within a framework of empirical aesthetics. Aesthetic behavior, as a highly sophisticated form of exploration, has been described as a consequence of the interaction of arousal-raising and arousal-reducing properties of the stimulus situation with the momentary arousal state of the receiving organism (Berlyne, 1960, 1971). Berlyne proposes that three classes of arousal-raising stimulus properties comprise a stimulus's arousal potential: psychophysical, ecological, and collative properties. While the first class, representing the distribution of energy in space and time, is important in visual art, it probably is of less importance in humor. For example, repeated presentations of a joke may affect its appreciation. Ecological properties, usually associated with the induction and reduction of primary drives, such as hunger, sex, and aggression, represent the thematic aspects of jokes and are of obvious importance in humor. Collative properties usually depend on the collation, or comparison, of information from different sources for their impact (Berlyne, 1963, p. 290).

Whatever "humor" is, the verbal and nonverbal measures used in these experiments are considered its correlates.

Collative Stimulus Properties in Humor

Such properties as the perceived likelihood or the oddity of the situation described in the body of a joke, or the surprisingness and fitness of the punchline, are examples of collative properties of jokes. They have been found to have reliable, but complex, relations to rated funniness. Kenny (1955) found that jokes are judged to be funnier the less unexpected the endings. Godkewitsch (1974) found that the funniness of sex jokes depended on a salient theme and a predictable, appropriate ending, while, in verbal "put-ons" and harmless wit, there had to be an unlikely, odd situation described in the joke body, followed by a punchline perceived to be appropriate to explain that situation.

In view of their seeming importance and the scarcity of empirical findings, explorations of the role of stimulus variables in the humor response seemed warranted.

Some formidable problems inherent in the use of jokes as stimuli in humor research immediately became apparent. First, the nature of the experiment cannot be hidden from the subject. His expectation of being amused by humor stimuli may confound the relation between stimulus properties and humor responses. Second, it is extremely difficult to define, measure, and subsequently manipulate those properties of genuine jokes that are relevant to their appreciation. Third, whenever any aspect of a joke is manipulated in order to test its contribution to some aspect of the humor response, both thematic and collative characteristics of the stimuli are probably altered, because both sets of properties are inextricably intertwined. For example, changing the punchline so that it becomes less unexpected may affect the salience of the main theme of the joke. Therefore, artificial stimuli were generated in order to attempt to synthesize some responses related to experienced humor.

Two Encouraging Precedents

Nerhardt (1970) recorded laughter in response to presentations of weights differing more or less from a pre-established range of weights in a quasi-psychophysical experiment. Since no jokes or cartoons were employed, the method assessed the contribution of a collative stimulus property to affect as distinct from the effect of themes. The study aimed to test the "incongruity" hypothesis. This view claims that humor results from the reduction through insight of the discrepancy between what was expected and actual stimulus conditions (cf. Maier, 1932). The hypothesis received support: frequency of laughter was found to be a positive function of the novelty and unexpectedness of the weights in relation to the ranges to which Ss were habituated.

Ertel's (1968) efforts came close to manipulating collative properties of verbal material with respect to humor. In one study, he investigated the influence of the approximation order of 12-word German sentences on the rated absurdity of the sentences. He found a linear relationship: the lower the approximation order (the larger the deviation from statistical sequential probabilities in normal discourse) the more absurd they were judged. In contrast, curvilinear relations between rated humor and approximation order were found: intermediate approximations were judged funnier and wittier than sentences that differed either very little or greatly from the structure of normal prose.

In another study, Ertel (1968) presented 50 nouns and 50 adjectives. The first group of Ss was asked to make up "humorous" pairings, while a second group created "witty" combinations. A third group of Ss made up "absurd" pairs, and a fourth formed "normal" pairs. The most frequently produced pairs of all categories were rated in a random order by a new sample of Ss for "connection" (*Zusammenhang*) of adjective and noun, and for "*Stimmigkeit*," best translated as "fitness." The average of connection and fitness ratings of the adjective-noun pairs (ANPs) decreased from the "normal" category via the "witty" and "humorous" categories to the "absurd" category. Although Ertel fails to present significance levels of the differences between categories of ANPs, his findings suggest a relation between perceived incongruity of juxtaposed verbal stimuli and their affective impact. However, because the classes of ANPs differed in content and composition besides varying in perceived incongruity, Ertel did not demonstrate an unequivocal relation between a collative stimulus property and a consequent motivational condition, uncontaminated by thematic stimulus properties.

Purpose of the Experiments Reported in This Chapter

The main purpose of the series of experiments reported in this chapter was to ascertain the relations between a structural, quantified, manipulable collative variable in verbal stimulus material and consequent verbal and nonverbal responses associated with the humor response.

THE MAIN INDEPENDENT VARIABLE

Berlyne (1972a) has noted that "while humor depends heavily, and at times exclusively, on the structure of the joke, the relations that constitute the structure are almost always ones obtaining between recognizable perceived objects or verbal meanings. A structure bereft of content may suffice for art and for mathematics, but rarely for humor."

A very simple set of relations between meanings is found in adjective-noun pairs (ANPs), whose composition can be quantitatively varied without altering the components. ANPs thus seemed appropriate stimulus material for experiments designed to explore effects of a collative stimulus variable, namely the degree of discrepancy in meaning between the two components of an ANP (their Semantic Distance, SD) on verbal and nonverbal correlates of experienced humor.

Each adjective and each noun can be represented by a point in a three-dimensional Euclidean space. The coordinates of the respective points represent projections of those points on the three orthogonal axes. These axes were Osgood's Activity, Evaluative, and Potency dimensions (cf. Osgood, Suci, & Tannenbaum, 1957), which have emerged time and again in factor analyses of semantic differential ratings of many different kinds of stimuli (Snider & Osgood, 1969). The independent variable of interest in this series of experiments was the distance between the points corresponding to a paired adjective and noun.

In three-dimensional semantic space, eight octants are defined by the intersections of three planes common to each pair of axes. Four kinds of pairings of adjectives and nouns are thus possible. First, both adjective and noun can be situated in a common octant, in which case their respective coordinates on all three of Osgood's dimensions have identical signs (positive or negative). Second, the two points can lie in two adjoining octants, and are then distant on one of Osgood's three dimensions, i.e., the coordinates of the adjective and the noun on that dimension have different signs. Third, the two octants containing the respective points have only one dimension in common, so that the two points are distant from each other on two dimensions: the coordinates of adjective and noun have different signs on two dimensions. Finally, the respective octants may only have the point of origin of the semantic space in common and therefore occupy opposite positions in that space. In that case, the coordinates of adjective and noun have different signs on all three dimensions and are distant on all three of them.

In summary, each adjective could be distant from the noun paired with it on zero, one, two, or three of Osgood's dimensions in semantic space. This distance was used as the independent variable in the experiments presented in this chapter.

THE MAIN DEPENDENT VARIABLES

Verbal Behavior

A traditional, convenient, and common method of recording responses indicative of direction and intensity of affect is the bipolar 7-point rating scale. In the present experiment, *Ss'* ratings for how HUMOROUS, WITTY, and FUNNY they judged the ANPs were collected. These verbal-jocularity ratings were related to a battery of other verbal rating scales. Some of these, such as IMPROBABLE-PROBABLE, NOT AT ALL PECULIAR-EXTREMELY PECULIAR, NOT AT ALL STRANGE-EXTREMELY STRANGE, and INAPPROPRIATE-APPROPRIATE were intended to explore how SD was perceived. Other scales tapped hedonic aspects of *Ss'* reactions: NO PLEASURE-EXTREME PLEASURE, DISPLEASING-PLEASING, and NO DISCOMFORT-EXTREME DISCOMFORT.

Three scales aimed to test the effect of SD on subjective feelings of arousal: RELAXED-TENSE, and DROWSY-ALERT, which, it has been suggested (see Berlyne, 1973), may be related to autonomic and cortical arousal respectively.[2] NOT AT ALL ACTIVE AND LIVELY-EXTREMELY ACTIVE AND LIVELY is a composite of adjectival self-reports that Thayer (1970) found to be related to general arousal, and that Godkewitsch (1974, 1975) found to be highly correlated with a composite of heart rate and GSR measures, as well as with rated funniness, in response to jokes.

The WEAK-POWERFUL, UNINTERESTING-INTERESTING, and SIMPLE-COMPLEX scales were used because they have been shown to be related to objective stimulus complexity (e.g., Berlyne, 1963; Crozier, 1973; Day, 1967). Their relation to hedonic ratings is less clear and seems to depend on the modality and range of objective complexity. Varied relations between interestingness and hedonic tone have been found (Berlyne, 1971, Chap. 13; 1972c).

Nonverbal Behavior

Obviously, verbal responses do not tell a complete story of the humor response. Of nonverbal components, physiological responses have been explored by Langevin & Day (1972) and by Godkewitsch (1974, 1975). Three other nonverbal humor correlates were investigated in the present series of experiments.

[2] This suggestion is discussed and qualified somewhat in Chapter 14.

Looking Time (LT), reflecting the duration of voluntary self-exposure to each stimulus, has been regarded as a measure of specific exploratory behavior (Berlyne, 1971). Because LT, like its auditory equivalent Listening Time, has been shown to vary positively with rated and objective measures of stimulus complexity (Day, 1966, 1968; Berlyne, 1957; Crozier, 1973; Chap. 2, this volume), it was also expected to vary positively with SD.

Facial Reactivity (FR) has been used as an index of the intensity and quality of subjective experiences (e.g., Ekman, Friesen, & Tomkins, 1971) and thus may well be related to other correlates of humor responses.

A measure of exploratory behavior indicative of the Reward Value (RV) of stimuli is the rate of performing an arbitrarily selected manual response causing them to appear (see Chap. 1, this volume). Some modifications and extensions of this method were used to explore the relation between SD and Reward Value. Since humor is believed to be pleasurable, one would expect more humorous stimuli to have greater Reward Value, as shown by effects on nonverbal behavior, as well as higher scores on verbal ratings indicative of hedonic tone.

EXPERIMENT 1

Stimuli

Forty-eight words, comprising three adjectives and three nouns located in each of the octants of semantic space, were selected from a list compiled by Heise (1965). This list gives the semantic profiles for the 1,000 most frequent English words and is based on semantic-differential ratings by a representative cross-section of 1,000 North Americans. Every word had an absolute standardized factor score of at least .40 on each of the three semantic dimensions and had a minimum polarization score of 2.00 standardized factor-score units from the point of origin, with a few minor exceptions.

Four categories of ANPs were constructed. In the first category every one of the 24 adjectives was randomly paired with a noun belonging to the same octant, which produced a mean SD of 1.52. Some examples are "happy child," "metal bridge," "impossible end," "quiet poet," and "poor sorrow."

To obtain the second SD category every adjective was paired with a different noun from an adjacent octant, i.e., a noun distant from it on only one dimension. Since each octant had three adjacent octants the pairings were random with the provision that every adjective in a given octant was paired with a noun in a different adjacent octant. The resulting mean SD was 3.68.

Some examples are: "heavy winter," "iron end," "dangerous progress," "bad building," and "hot door."

ANPs of the third category were constructed by randomly pairing every adjective in a given octant with a different noun, located in a different octant, distant on two semantic dimensions. A mean SD of 4.66 resulted. "Wise egg," "happy doubt," "wonderful tax," "broken victory," and "terrible stone" are some examples.

Finally, the mean SD of the fourth category, in which adjectives and nouns distant on all three dimensions of semantic space were paired, was 5.44. Some examples are: "successful sorrow," "wise failure," "silver war," "hot poet," and "nervous control."

As a check on the effectiveness of the pairing method in obtaining different SD categories, a posteriori multiple comparisons between the four mean SDs were made. Using Duncan's New Multiple Range Test, all differences between mean SDs greatly exceeded the minimum difference required for significance at the .01 level.

It should be noted that all four SD categories contained the complete set of 24 adjectives and 24 nouns. Every adjective and every noun occurred once in each of the four SD categories of ANPs, but they were paired differently.

Subjects

One hundred and twelve male, and the same number of female, adult visitors to the Ontario Science Centre, Don Mills (Metropolitan Toronto), Ontario, volunteered to take part in the experiment. Their ages ranged from 18 to 56 years of age with a mode of 28.

Each group of eight male and eight female Ss rated all 96 ANPs on one of the 14 rating scales only, in order to avoid contamination between scales. The rating scales are listed in Table 1. These Ss represented a less restricted sample than that employed in most other studies of empirical aesthetics, which should lend some generality to the findings, unlikely to be achieved when using exclusively undergraduate students as Ss.

Procedure and Design

The 96 ANPs were printed in one random order on eight pages of a test booklet, 12 ANPs to every page. The reverse order was similarly printed. Four of the eight Ss of each sex assigned to each scale received the stimuli in one order, and the other four in the reverse order. Within each order group, the four males and four females were randomly assigned to the rows of a

TABLE 1

Mean Verbal and Nonverbal Responses in Experiments 1, 2, and 3 per SD
Category, and ANOVA Main Effects and Linear and Quadratic
Trend Components across SD

Experiment 1					ANOVA effects of SD		
Categories of ANPs	1	2	3	4	Main effect	Linear component	Quadratic component
Mean semantic distance	1.52	3.68	4.66	5.44	$F(3,36)$	$F(1,12)$	$F(1,12)$
	Mean scores						
1 IMPROBABLE-PROBABLE	5.51	4.43	3.95	4.04	64.68***	124.54***	11.52*
2 NAA PECULIAR-EX PECULIAR[a]	2.55	3.72	3.97	3.68	75.63***	214.90***	42.17***
3 NAA STRANGE-EX STRANGE	2.57	3.48	3.89	3.61	55.94***	89.52***	23.51***
4 INAPPROPRIATE-APPROPRIATE	5.05	3.96	3.52	3.81	30.73***	60.41***	14.23**
5 NO PLEASURE-EX PLEASURE	3.84	3.61	3.29	3.42	12.48***	45.10***	
6 DISPLEASING-PLEASING	4.04	3.76	3.39	3.15	20.31***	46.29***	3.26
7 NO DISCOMFORT-EX DISCOMFORT	3.82	3.72	3.16	3.44	5.86**	5.18*	
8 DROWSY-ALERT	4.09	3.77	3.90	4.07	1.49		10.55**
9 RELAXED-TENSE	3.67	3.92	4.09	4.19	12.00***	36.31***	
10 NAA ACTIVE & LIVELY-EX A & L	4.19	3.97	3.91	3.76	4.42**	29.44***	
11 WEAK-POWERFUL	4.29	3.66	3.47	3.57	10.03***	19.48***	3.87
12 UNINTERESTING-INTERESTING	3.58	3.67	3.63	3.54			1.18
13 NAA HUMOROUS-EX HUMOROUS	2.98	3.34	3.33	3.37	2.85[b]	3.40	1.85
14 NAA WITTY-EX WITTY	3.43	3.62	3.91	3.83	2.95*	5.27*	
Experiment 2					$F(3,48)$	$F(1,16)$	$F(1,16)$
Looking Time (in seconds)	5.30	5.41	5.44	5.53	3.44*	7.84**	
Facial Reactivity	.26	.31	.29	.37	7.41***	16.53***	
NAA FUNNY-EX FUNNY	2.66	3.21	3.20	3.20	19.60***	32.23***	16.47***
Experiment 3							
SIMPLE-COMPLEX	2.62	3.86	4.02	3.72	63.44***	81.38***	62.11***

[a]NAA = Not at all; Ex = Extremely.
[b]$p = .051$.
*$p < .05$.
**$p < .01$.
***$p < .001$.

balanced 8 x 8 Latin square, whose columns represented the orders of the eight pages of the test booklet. The Ss were run in groups varying from one to seven people. They received oral as well as printed instructions explaining how they could express their reaction to each ANP by marking an appropriate section of the rating scale.

Results

Reliabilities of mean ratings. To warrant further analysis, the reliability of the mean ratings, averaged across the 16 Ss using a given rating scale, was estimated for every scale. Two-way analyses of variance showed that ratings of the 96 ANPs differed significantly at the .01 level for every rating scale, implying sufficient intersubject consistency.

Univariate analyses of variance. Every S's ratings for the 24 ANPs of each of the four SD categories were averaged. An analysis of variance with planned tests for linear and quadratic components of trend over the four SD categories, was performed for every rating scale. The mean ratings across SD are presented in Table 1, upper portion.

The main effect for SD was significant for most scales, and linear trend accounted for the bulk of the variance in the first four scales. Clearly, SD systematically affected Ss' perception of ANPs: they were rated less PROBABLE, more PECULIAR and STRANGE, and less APPROPRIATE, as SD increased. Results of the three hedonic scales indicated that hedonic value decreased linearly with increasing SD. Also, Ss reported feeling more TENSE, but significantly less ACTIVE AND LIVELY, with increasing SD, and they judged the ANPs having less semantic discrepancy as more POWERFUL.

While the WITTY scale appeared to be positively and linearly related to SD, as expected, the main effect of the HUMOROUS scale was marginally significant: $p = .051$.

Most of the significant quadratic components of trend across SD represented a flattening out of the linear relationship between SD and the pertinent rating scale rather than nonmonotonicity.

Multivariate analysis of the rating scales. The 14 rating scales were intercorrelated, taking the mean ratings across Ss for every ANP as observation pairs. These correlations, presented in Table 2, were thus calculated from data differing from those used for the univariate analyses of variance. Briefly, while the WITTY scale and the HUMOROUS scale were significantly correlated with each other, the former correlated strongly with those scales that were monotonically related to SD (PROBABLE, PECULIAR, STRANGE, and APPROPRIATE), and not to the hedonic scales,

TABLE 2

Product-moment Correlations between Rating Scales
(Numbering of Scales as in Table 1)

	1	2	3	4	5	6	7	8	9	10	11	12	13	14
2	-86**													
3	-87**	85**												
4	87**	-82**	-84**											
5	29**	-28**	-28**	34**										
6	34**	-37**	-31**	34**	90**									
7	20*	-15	-16	11	-42**	-38**								
8	13	-10	-13	28**	09	-07	00							
9	-16	12	18	-28**	-81**	-73**	49**	-25**						
10	38**	-40**	-38**	34**	47**	46**	-09	06	-11					
11	54**	-50**	-57**	59**	13	06	17	61**	-28**	12				
12	13	-15	-04	06	38**	35**	-07	19	-20*	49**	14			
13	-26**	18	32**	-26**	51**	43**	-38**	-10	-35**	21*	-23*	36**		
14	-39**	41**	40**	-38**	07	-06	-12	14	-08	-16	-19	11	31**	

*$p < .05$.
**$p < .01$.

while the latter correlated significantly with the hedonic scales (PLEASURE, PLEASINGNESS, and DISCOMFORT). The HUMOROUS scale also correlated substantially with RELAXED-TENSE, which fits the positive relation between physiological indices of arousal and rated funniness found by Langevin & Day (1972) and Godkewitsch (1975). Finally, the HUMOROUS scale was significantly correlated with the INTERESTING scale.

In order to reduce the data further, the intercorrelation matrix of the 14 rating scales was subjected to a principal-components factor analysis, whose initial solution was rotated to the Varimax criterion (Kaiser, 1958). The upper part of Table 3 presents the loadings of the rating scales on the first four factors. Only factors with eigenvalues of at least 1.0 were extracted.

Factor I accounted for 31% of the variance in the correlation matrix, and was characterized by high (over .50) loadings of the PROBABLE, PECULIAR, STRANGE, APPROPRIATE, and WEAK-POWERFUL scales. It was provisionally labeled "Perceived SD."

Factor II, accounting for 22% of the variance, was dominated by the three hedonic scales and the HUMOROUS and RELAXED-TENSE scales. It was therefore called "Hedonic Tone." While the first factor showed a close resemblance to Osgood's Activity factor, the second looked like Osgood's Evaluative factor. Factor III accounted for 13% of the variance, and showed high loadings for only the DROWSY-ALERT and WEAK-POWERFUL scales. It was much like Berlyne's (1972c, 1973) third factor, which he provisionally called "Cortical Arousal." Factor IV represented about 14% of the variance, and was mainly composed of the INTERESTING and ACTIVE AND LIVELY scales. It may be called "Attention," for lack of a better term.

Despite obvious differences in stimulus material, Ss, rating scales, and technique, these factors, especially the first three, show a strong resemblance to those described in Chapters 2, 5, 9, and 12.

Analysis of factor scores. To clarify the relation between the independent variable SD and each of the extracted factors, the factor scores were analyzed. For every ANP, a factor score was estimated for each factor by taking the sum of the normalized scores of the ANP on each rating scale, multiplied by that scale's factor weight for the factor in question.

For each factor, an analysis of variance of the mean factor scores and a planned trend analysis were performed. In Table 4, the mean factor scores and the significance levels of main SD effects and trend components are

TABLE 3

Varimax Rotated Factor Loadings of Rating Scales in Experiment 1, and
Product-moment Correlations of Mean Estimated Factor Scores with
the Dependent Variables of Experiments 2 and 3

Experiment 1	Loadings on varimax factors				
Rating scales	I	II	III	IV	Communality
1 IMPROBABLE- PROBABLE	.91	.04	.15	.14	87.7
2 NAA PECULIAR-EX PECULIAR	-.90	-.05	-.09	-.18	84.6
3 NAA STRANGE-EX STRANGE	-.92	-.06	-.16	-.05	87.7
4 INAPPROPRIATE- APPROPRIATE	.88	.14	.29	.03	87.4
5 NO PLEASURE-EX PLEASURE	.22	.86	.05	.35	91.4
6 DISPLEASING- PLEASING	.31	.81	-.12	.33	88.2
7 NO DISCOMFORT-EX DISCOMFORT	.23	-.71	.08	.08	57.2
8 DROWSY-ALERT	.01	.02	.92	.07	85.2
9 RELAXED-TENSE	-.10	-.90	-.29	.02	89.8
10 NAA ACTIVE & LIVELY-EX A & L	.37	.15	-.08	.75	72.8
11 WEAK-POWERFUL	.50	-.00	.76	.00	82.0
12 UNINTERESTING- INTERESTING	-.03	.13	.19	.85	78.3
13 NAA HUMOROUS-EX HUMOROUS	-.39	.54	-.14	.47	68.1
14 NAA WITTY-EX WITTY	-.62	.12	.28	.15	49.8
Percent of Variance accounted for	31.3	22.0	12.9	13.1	79.3%

	Correlations with mean estimated factor scores, all having 94 df.				
Experiment 2					
Looking Time	-.30**	.03	.01	.24*	
Facial Reactivity	-.42**	.06	.01	.19	
NAA FUNNY-EX FUNNY	-.54**	.35**	-.22*	.30*	
Experiment 3					
SIMPLE-COMPLEX	-.76**	-.13	-.35**	.08	

*$p < .05$.
**$p < .01$.

TABLE 4

Mean Estimated Factor Scores and Anova SD Effects across ANP Categories

Mean SD	Mean estimated factor scores				Main SD effect	Trend components of main SD effect	
	1.52	3.68	4.66	5.44		Linear	Quadratic
Factor I	.955	.102	-.326	-.730	$F(3,88) = 21.240***$	$F(1,88) = 63.515***$	
Factor II							
All	-.074	-.092	-.086	.252	$F(3,88) = 2.129$	$F(1,88) = 2.183$	$F(1,88) = 2.823$
Pos	1.038	.712	.809	.502	$F(3,44) = 3.271*$	$F(1,44) = 6.384*$	$F(1,44) = 1.689$
Neg	-1.186	-.896	-.981	.002	$F(3,44) = 3.960*$	$F(1,44) = 6.897*$	$F(1,44) = 2.377$
Factor III	-.086	-.326	-.196	.608	$F(3,88) = 4.610**$	$F(1,88) = 3.471$	$F(1,88) = 9.211**$
Factor IV	.154	.181	.075	-.410	$F(3,88) = 1.879$	$F(1,88) = 2.726$	$F(1,88) = 2.549$

$*p < .025.$
$**p < .005.$
$***p < .001.$

presented. Figures 1, 2, and 3 depict the relationships between SD and the mean estimated factor scores for Factors I, II, and III, respectively. Clearly, SD operated as an effective collative variable in that Perceived SD, Factor I, increased linearly with it, as evidenced by the highly significant linear trend component.

The main effect of SD on Factor II was not significant. To explore the lack of significance, analyses were performed separately on the factor scores of those ANPs whose adjective had a positive sign, and those of which the adjective had a negative sign on the Evaluative dimension of semantic space. This seemed a relevant distinction in view of the character of Factor II. The tetrachoric correlation between this division and the division between ANPs with positive and negative scores on the Hedonic Tone factor reached .97.

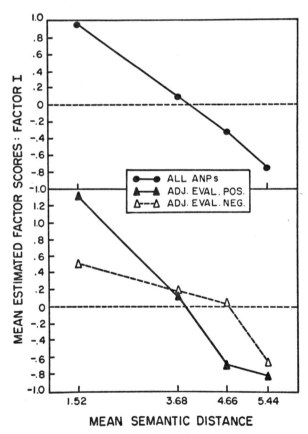

FIG. 1. Experiment 1: Mean estimated factor scores on Factor I (Perceived Semantic Distance).

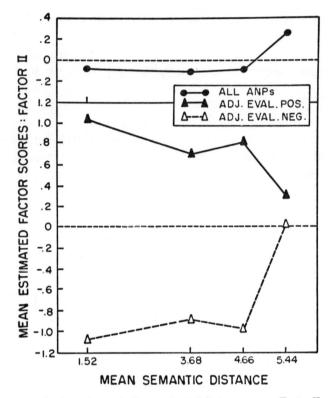

FIG. 2. Experiment 1: Mean estimated factor scores on Factor II (Hedonic Tone).

Thus, Hedonic Tone of ANPs in the present factor structure was entirely determined by qualities of the adjective and not by those of the noun.

Factor II then became more meaningful: initially attractive ANPs decreased in Hedonic Tone as the SD between their members increased (Table 4). That was probably due to the fact that the same positively evaluated adjectives were paired across SD categories with a systematically increasing number of negatively evaluated nouns. Similarly, initially unattractive ANPs, i.e., those having adjectives with a negative sign on the Evaluative dimension, gained in Hedonic Tone as SD increased, because the adjectives were paired across the SD categories with an increasing number of positively evaluated nouns. The lack of significance of the SD main effect could thus be ascribed to two opposing trends across SD categories, canceling each other out.

Factor III, Cortical Arousal, showed a significant quadratic trend, which seems to indicate that Ss felt most alerted by the smallest and the largest SDs. Factor IV, Attention, showed no significant SD effect.

Some implications of the factor structure will be discussed below.

EXPERIMENT 2

The second experiment had three purposes: first, to explore how Looking Time (LT) and Facial Reactivity (FR), nonverbal measures, respectively, of specific exploration and of a motor component of the humor response, would vary with SD.

Looking Time, as a measure of specific exploration, probably plays a more prominent role in problem-solving tasks such as puzzles and riddles than in jokes. However, the humor in nontendency jokes derives mostly from structural properties that such jokes have in common with conditions in which problem solving occurs (cf. Freud, 1905; Berlyne, 1972a).

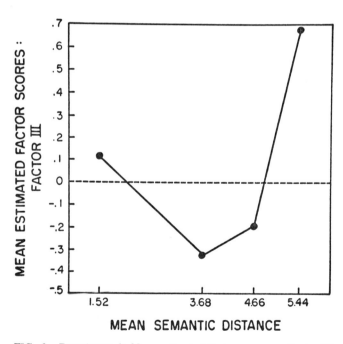

FIG. 3. Experiment 1: Mean estimated factor scores on Factor III (Cortical Arousal).

It was expected that both measures would increase as SD increased. Secondly, the prediction that verbal ratings on a NOT AT ALL FUNNY-EXTREMELY FUNNY scale would be related to other humor responses and to SD was to be tested. The third purpose was to test the "expectancy" effect: Ss' responses may be influenced by their expectation of being amused when they know that funny stimuli are about to be presented. When neutral stimuli are expected, on the other hand, the humor experience may be less intense (e.g., Bloom & Mayer, 1969; Schweizer, 1964). In this experiment, the impact on FR and LT of instructions inducing different expectations was assessed.

Stimuli, Subjects, and Procedure

Sixteen male and 16 female experimentally naive undergraduates taking an introductory psychology course voluntarily served as Ss. The 96 ANPs used in Experiment 1 were presented on white-on-blue slides in balanced order conditions. Ss were run individually. They were seated in a shielded room, and electrodes were attached to the ventral and dorsal sides of the nonpreferred hand, in order to make the situation resemble a physiological experiment.

First, Ss were instructed to look at every ANP on the screen as long as they wished and to press a button with the unwired hand to advance the slide tray and expose the next ANP. An event recorder automatically registered LT in units of 1/3 seconds. Then, after E had left the room, S opened an envelope containing one of the two expectation instructions. In the "funny" condition it read: "A number of these pairs were clipped from a humor magazine and some of the pairs you are going to see were judged to be quite funny by subjects in earlier experiments."

In the control condition, the instruction was: "All the words in the pairs were randomly picked from the dictionary, and a computer combined them randomly into pairs."

During this first run through the stimuli, E observed S through a hidden one-way screen and scored FRs on a 6-point scale adapted from Zigler, Levine, & Gould (1966). This scale ranged from a STRONG FROWN to OVERT LAUGHTER. In a pilot study the average interrater reliability over six judges was only .81, but, after the scale was reduced to four points, ranging from NO REACTIVITY to VERY MUCH REACTIVITY equating SLIGHT FROWN with SLIGHT SMILE, the average interrater reliability increased to a satisfactory .94.

Throughout the experimental session, E remained blind to S's expectation condition, and, although he could see when a slide was changed, he was unable to see which ANP was presented at any moment. During a second run, when E was present in the room, Ss were asked to rate every ANP for funniness on a 7-point scale ranging from NOT AT ALL FUNNY to EXTREMELY FUNNY.

The design for each dependent variable was identical: between-Ss variables were two order factors, Sex and Expectation Instruction, while within-S factors were SD and the sign of the adjectives on the Evaluative dimension of semantic space.

Results

In the middle part of Table 1, the mean LTs in seconds, mean FRs, and mean funniness ratings across the four SD categories are presented. In all three instances the linear component accounted for most of the significant SD main effect.

LT increased linearly with SD, as expected. So did the mean funniness ratings, although the curve flattened out at greater SD levels. FR score was also found to be a linear function of SD.

Warning that something funny was to be expected resulted in a greater amount of FR, .39 compared to .22 on the 4-point scale; $F = 6.629$, 1,16 df, $p < .025$. No effects on LT or Funniness ratings were observed.

In the middle section of Table 3, the correlations between mean estimated factor scores on each factor and the dependent variables of this experiment are presented. While FR seemed to depend on Perceived SD (Factor I) only, LT was also positively related to Attention (Factor IV). Rated Funniness was significantly correlated with all four factors and may thus be viewed as a complex response in which Perceived SD, Hedonic Tone, Cortical Arousal, and Attention all play a part.

The product moment correlations between the dependent variables showed an expected pattern. The FUNNY scale correlated significantly with FR ($r = .56$, 94 df, $p < .01$) and with the HUMOROUS and WITTY scales of Experiment 1 ($r = .74$, .32; $p < .01$ in both cases), but not with LT. LT, in turn, correlated significantly with rated Wittiness ($r = .34$, $p < .01$) but not with rated Humorousness. FR, finally, correlated significantly with the HUMOROUS and WITTY scales ($r = .48$, .36; $p < .01$) in both cases.

EXPERIMENT 3

While the two preceding studies showed that greater SD led to intensified exploratory behavior, the question remains of how rewarding stimulus events are. If humor responses are related to perceived structural stimulus properties and if they are also indicative of Ss' hedonic reactions, some positive relation may reasonably be expected between perceived structural stimulus properties and Reward Value (RV). Consequently, in the present experiment, RV was expected to increase with SD.

The measure of exploration representing RV of the stimulus is discussed by Berlyne (1972b; Chaps. 1, 5, and 10, this volume). Reward Value reflects the power of stimuli to reinforce learned stimulus-seeking behavior. Jokes and cartoons often attract similar behavior aimed at pleasure, e.g., the eager anticipation in the listener when "a good one" is announced, or the tendency of many newspaper readers to skip to the "funnies" before immersion in matters of greater import.

A secondary aim of this experiment was to establish the relation between rated Complexity and SD. Berlyne (1972b) found that RV of visual patterns varying in rated complexity was more closely related to objective measures of complexity than to Pleasingness. This led to the expectation that rated Complexity would linearly increase with the RV of the stimuli as well as with their SD.

Stimuli, Subjects, and Procedure

The same 96 slides, bearing one ANP each, that were prepared for Experiment 2 were used. Seven male and 17 female undergraduates taking an introductory psychology course volunteered to serve as Ss. The apparatus used is fully described by Berlyne (1972b; Chap. 5, this volume). S was seated in front of a horizontal board bearing two telegraph keys, while all programming, projecting, and recording equipment was placed in an adjoining room.

Every S went through two successive 8-minute phases. A different pair of SD categories was presented in each phase so that S was exposed to all four SD categories, two at a time. Eight Ss were assigned to each of three permutations of SD-category pairs. For half the Ss assigned to each condition, the higher SD category was associated with the right key in the first phase and the left key in the second phase, while the remaining Ss had the opposite arrangement. In general, complete balancing of all independent variables was achieved. Table 5 summarizes the design.

TABLE 5

Summary of the Design of Experiment 3

ORDR	POSN	Permutation	Subject	SD Categories		Phase 2	
				Phase 1		Phase 2	
Larger SD in Phase 2	Larger SD first Right, then left	1	1 2	0	1	3	2
		2	3 4	0	2	3	1
		3	5 6	0	3	2	1
	Larger SD first Left, then right	1	7 8	1	0	2	3
		2	9 10	2	0	1	3
		3	11 12	3	0	1	2
Larger SD in Phase 1	Larger SD first Right, then left	1	13 14	3	2	0	1
		2	15 16	3	1	0	2
		3	17 18	2	1	0	3
	Larger SD first Left, then right	1	19 20	2	3	1	0
		2	21 22	1	3	2	0
		3	23 24	1	2	3	0

Just as in Experiment 2, the purpose of the study was disguised by attaching electrodes to the palm and back of S's nonpreferred hand and telling S that physiological reactions were being recorded.

S was told to press the keys one at a time, whenever he wished, in any order he wished, and as often as he wished. Each key was independently scheduled to produce 5-second exposures of ANPs as reinforcers, according to a Variable-Interval schedule. Every reinforcement on a given key consisted of the appearance of a different ANP belonging to the SD category associated with that key. The orders of the slides were randomized independently for each S. The minimum interval between one reinforcement and the next reinforcement on the same key ranged from 5 to 35 seconds with a mean of 20 seconds. To discourage alternation, neither key could expose a slide for 5 seconds after a reinforcement, and a key could not produce reinforcement for 3 seconds after the other key had been pressed.

After this part of the experiment was completed, S was asked to rate the 96 ANPs in a random order on a 7-point SIMPLE-COMPLEX scale.

Innovations in the Technique

The present variant of Catania's (1963) technique for measuring relative RV differed considerably from Berlyne's (1972b). In the latter study, successive reinforcements on a given key consisted of repeated exposures of the *same* stimulus pattern. In each phase of the experiment, a single pair of reinforcing stimulus patterns was used. It is therefore not altogether clear how far peculiarities of individual patterns may have produced the observed effects, as distinct from degree of complexity as such.

In the present design, successive reinforcements on one key meant exposure of *different* stimuli from a particular category of ANPs. The only property that ANPs belonging to the same category had in common was the number of dimensions on which their elements were distant, i.e., SD. This was also the only variable distinguishing ANP categories. Thus, any systematic effect of SD on key pressing responses would imply that Ss were abstracting the relevant stimulus property, i.e., SD, and that their behavior was governed by it.

Results

Figure 4 presents cumulative curves of mean numbers of responses producing ANPs of lower and higher SD categories. The raw data were subjected to logarithmic transformation to reduce great inter-S variability. The mean numbers of key presses after eight minutes were, respectively, 147.9 and 187.8. An analysis of variance showed that these means differed significantly: $F = 35.23$, 1,12 df, $p < .001$, and in the predicted direction: greater SD meant more responses and therefore greater RV.

The design did not permit a parametric trend analysis across the four SD categories. However, a nonparametric trend analysis across SD categories (Ferguson, 1965) revealed a highly significant monotonic increasing trend: $z = 3.06$, $p < .005$. The mean numbers of responses for SD levels 0, 1, 2, and 3 were, respectively, 157.1, 167.5, 172.9, 174.0. Moreover, none of the interactions of SD with other variables was significant, so that the ratio

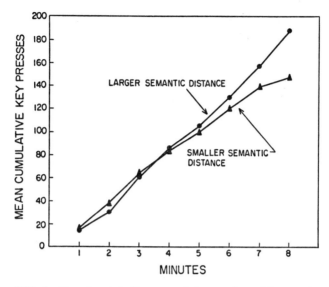

FIG. 4. Experiment 3: Mean cumulative numbers of key-pressing responses for ANPs with greater and smaller semantic distance.

of the number of responses for the higher SD category to the number for the lower SD category did not vary across pairs of categories. This indicates that the relation between SD and response rate is linear.

In conclusion, the stimulus categories that evoked verbal and nonverbal responses associated with humor and stronger exploratory responses (i.e., ratings on the WITTY, HUMOROUS, and FUNNY scales, FR and LT) had higher RV. In addition, all these variables increased with rated Complexity and with the independent variable, SD.

Complexity Ratings

The linear component of the main SD effect was highly significant (Table 1, lowest part). Its significant quadratic component indicated that complexity ratings reached a ceiling at an intermediate SD, since the downturn in the curve was not significant by Duncan's New Multiple Range Test. In Table 3, lowest part, the correlations between complexity ratings and factor scores on the four factors derived from Experiment 1, are reported. As expected, rated complexity varied directly with Perceived SD (Factor I) and with Cortical Arousal (Factor III).

CONCLUSIONS

Three verbal and three nonverbal correlates of experienced humor were all found to vary systematically with the semantic distance between elements of ANPs. While some humor indices (ratings on the FUNNY and HUMOROUS scales) appeared related to both Hedonic Tone and the independent variable, SD, the other humor correlates (ratings on the WITTY scale, Looking Time, Facial Reactivity, and Reward Value) were closely related to Perceived SD only. Apparently, people show stimulus-seeking behavior towards stimuli they profess not to like, even when they have a choice between stimuli with a positive and a negative Hedonic Tone. Such discrepancies between what people do (RV, LT) and what they say (Hedonic Tone) have recently been found by Berlyne (1971, 1972c) and Crozier (Chap. 2, this volume).

Following up on Berlyne's (1972a) position that "structure bereft of content . . ." does not suffice for humor, the present experiments have shown that, at least for adjective-noun pairs varying in semantic distance between their members, a structural attribute can indeed suffice to evoke some verbal and nonverbal correlates of the humor experience. This does not mean, of course, that other characteristics of real-life humor stimuli, such as their themes and format of presentation and various other ecological and psychophysical stimulus variables, as well as individual differences between recipients, do not contribute significantly to the evocation of affective responses. One may, however, conclude that these conditions other than stimulus structure are not necessary antecedents for the humor response, since it was demonstrated in the present series of experiments that correlates of humor can depend on quantifiable, manipulable, structural properties of simple verbal stimulus patterns alone.

REFERENCES

Berlyne, D. E. Conflict and information-theory variables as determinants of human perceptual curiosity. *Journal of Experimental Psychology*, 1957, 53, 399–404.

Berlyne, D. E. *Conflict, Arousal and Curiosity*. New York: McGraw-Hill, 1960.

Berlyne, D. E. *Structure and Direction in Thinking*. New York: Wiley, 1965.

Berlyne, D. E. *Aesthetics and Psychobiology*. New York: Appleton-Century-Crofts, 1971.

Berlyne, D. E. Humor and its kin. In J. H. Goldstein & P. E. McGhee (Eds.), *The Psychology of Humor*. New York: Academic Press, 1972. (a)

Berlyne, D. E. Reinforcement values of visual patterns compared through concurrent performances. *Journal of the Experimental Analysis of Behavior*, 1972, **18**, 281–285. (b)

Berlyne, D. E. Ends and means of experimental aesthetics. *Canadian Journal of Psychology*, 1972, **26**, 303–325. (c)

Berlyne, D. E. Interrelations of verbal and nonverbal measures used in experimental aesthetics. *Scandinavian Journal of Psychology*, 1973, **14**, 177–184.

Bloom, S., & Mayer, M. Enjoyment of humor stimuli under six conditions of socially induced sets. Paper read at the Western Psychological Association meeting, Vancouver, B. C., 1969.

Catania, A. C. Concurrent performances: A baseline for the study of reinforcement magnitude. *Journal of the Experimental Analysis of Behavior*, 1963, **6**, 299–300.

Crozier, J. B. Verbal and exploratory responses to sound sequences of varying complexity. Unpublished Ph.D. Thesis, University of Toronto, 1973.

Day, H. I. Evaluations of subjective complexity, pleasingness and interestingness for a series of random polygons varying in complexity. *Perception and Psychophysics*, 1967, **2**, 281–286.

Day, H. I. Some determinants of looking time under different instructional sets. *Perception and Psychophysics*, 1968, **4**, 279–281.

Ekman, P., Friesen, W. V., & Tomkins, S. S. Facial affect scoring techniques: A first validity study. *Semiotica*, 1971, **3**, 37–58.

Ertel, S. Eine psychologische Theorie des Komischen. Inaugural address, University of Muenster, 1968.

Ferguson, G. A. Non-parametric Trend Analysis. Montreal: McGill University Press, 1965.

Godkewitsch, M. The relationship between arousal potential and funniness of jokes. In J. H. Goldstein, & P. E. McGhee (Eds.), *The Psychology of Humor*. New York: Academic Press, 1972.

Godkewitsch, M. Verbal, exploratory and physiological responses to stimulus properties underlying humour. Unpublished Ph.D. Thesis, University of Toronto, 1974.

Godkewitsch, M. Physiological and verbal indices of arousal in rated humour. To be published in A. J. Chapman, & H. C. Foot (Eds.), *Research in humour and laughter*. Chichester, England: John Wiley & Sons, 1975.

Heise, D. R. Semantic differential profiles for 1000 most frequent English words. *Psychological Monographs*, 1965, **79**(8, Whole No. 601.)

Kaiser, H. F. The varimax criterion for analytic rotation in factor analysis. *Psychometrika*, 1958, **23**, 187–200.

Kenny, D. I. The contingency of humor appreciation on the stimulus-confirmation of joke-ending expectations. *Journal of Abnormal and Social Psychology*, 1955, **51**, 644–648.

Langevin, R., & Day, H. I. Physiological correlates of humor. In J. H. Goldstein, & P. E. McGhee (Eds.), *The Psychology of Humor*. New York: Academic Press, 1972.

Levine, J., & Redlich, F. C. Intellectual and emotional factors in the appreciation of humor. *Journal of General Psychology*, 1960, **62**, 25–35.

Maier, N. R. F. A Gestalt theory of humour. *British Journal of Psychology*, 1932, **23**, 69–74.

Malefijt, A. de Waal. Dutch joking patterns. *Transactions of the New York Academy of Sciences*, 1968, 30, 1181–1186.

McGhee, P. E. The development of the humor response: a review of the literature. *Psychological Bulletin*, 1971, 76, 328–348.

Nerhardt, G. Humor and inclination to laugh: Emotional reactions to stimuli of different divergence from a range of expectancy. *Scandinavian Journal of Psychology*, 1970, 11, 185–195.

Osgood, C. E., Suci, G. J., & Tannenbaum, P. H. *The Measurement of Meaning.* Urbana, Ill.: University of Illinois Press, 1957.

Schweizer, W. R. *Der Witz.* Berne and Munich: Francke, 1964.

Snider, J. C., & Osgood, C. E. *Semantic Differential Technique: A Sourcebook.* Chicago: Aldine, 1969.

Thayer, R. E. Activation states as assessed by verbal report and four psychophysiological variables. *Psychophysiology*, 1970, 7, 86–94.

Zigler, E., Levine, J., & Gould, L. Cognitive processes in the development of children's appreciation of humor. *Child Development*, 1966, 37, 507–518.

14
CONCLUDING OBSERVATIONS

D. E. Berlyne

It would hardly be feasible to present a comprehensive overview of the findings reported in the preceding chapters of this book. The experiments take up a variety of specific questions, which have already been discussed in conjunction with the relevant experimental data.

All that this final chapter can do is to consider some of the themes that run through this body of research and to touch on some of the basic problems that have cropped up during the first two decades of the new experimental aesthetics.

INFORMATION-THEORETIC CONCEPTS

First, our experiments, together with other work carried out in our own and other laboratories, can be said to have confirmed the importance of information-theoretic concepts for psychological aesthetics. Measures and manipulations derived from information theory have been shown consistently to have profound effects on aesthetic reactions. They are far from being the only variables that play a part in aesthetic behavior. But their role seems to be powerful and pervasive, so that continued attention to them, and their continued use by researchers in experimental aesthetics, are clearly advisable.

We have to say "measures *derived from* information theory," because of some distinctions that need to be made. What is now called "information theory" originated in an article by Shannon that was first published in 1948

(Shannon & Weaver, 1949). In this article, Shannon did not use the term "information theory," referring instead to the "mathematical theory of communication," and he did not use the terms "uncertainty," "redundancy," and "information content." But he introduced the measures that are nowadays labeled with these terms. He pointed out the applicability of these measures whenever there is a "discrete source" or "stochastic process," i.e., a "system which produces a sequence of symbols governed by a set of probabilities." Furthermore, he stated that the discrete sources he had in mind were "ergodic" sources. Ergodicity has a precise but cumbersome definition in probability theory and means roughly "statistical homogeneity." Subsequently, he extended the scope of these concepts to "continuous" sources, which produce continuously fluctuating signals. Such continuous sources are what telecommunications engineers usually have to deal with, but most applications of information theory to psychology and other behavioral sciences have been restricted to the discrete case.

Of all the kinds of stimulus material used in our experiments, only the random sound sequences mentioned in Chapters 2 and 3 and the visual sequences mentioned in Chapter 4 can be regarded as messages from discrete sources as Shannon conceived them. They alone consisted of sequences of stimulus events, each of which was randomly selected, independently of its predecessors and of its successors, from a specifiable set of alternatives with probabilities attached to them. The stimulus material of the other experiments, like the stimulus material used in most psychological experiments that have been inspired by information theory, was not produced by discrete sources of this kind. But the intention was to design them so that they might have been (cf. the matrix patterns and Smets patterns that were the subject of Chapter 5).

When we are dealing with spatial arrangements of elements, several of which are present simultaneously, it is difficult to determine whether each element should be regarded as a signal produced by a different discrete source or whether all the elements should be thought of as successive outputs from one source. In some cases, these two analyses will amount to the same. In some cases, they will not.

Broadbent's book *Perception and Communication* (1958) did much to encourage the use of information-processing language among psychologists. He pointed out, as one of the prime lessons of information theory, that a subject's response to a stimulus depends in large part on what other stimuli might have been there instead. In other words, the brain treats a particular stimulus as an item selected from a set of alternatives with corresponding frequencies of occurrence. But how can we be sure that the sample space—the set of alternatives—that the brain associates with a particular stimulus is the same as the one that the experimenter or the theorist had in mind?

Some of the early seminal information-theoretic analyses of perception, with a crucial bearing on aesthetics among other things, treated stimulus patterns as representatives of classes of patterns. In particular, they treated "better" or more structured patterns as representatives of smaller classes than other patterns (Hochberg & McAlister, 1953; Attneave, 1954; Garner, 1962). But a particular pattern can belong to numerous classes or sample spaces. The main assumptions made in these analyses have been open to the criticism that they are arbitrary and debatable (cf. Green & Courtis, 1966).

Such problems are especially acute when we leave stimulus patterns that are specially designed for the synthetic approach in aesthetics and turn to genuine works of art, as used in the analytic approach. Several writers have suggested plausibly that works of art in any medium can appropriately and instructively be analyzed in information-theoretic language. It seems reasonable enough to think of a work as an arrangement of elements, each of which has been selected from a particular sample space (alphabet, vocabulary). It seems clear enough that, wherever one kind of element appears, other kinds of elements might have appeared instead. But who can enumerate them with any confidence? In place of any single word in a poem, there are other words that the poet might have used and possibly has considered and rejected. But do these comprise all the words in the English language, or only words appropriate to the context, or words deemed appropriate for a particular style? In a piece of music, it might seem relatively easy to specify the notes or chords, each defined in terms of pitch, timbre, loudness, and duration, that could be heard at a particular moment. But is there not a much more restricted subset of these that would alone be conceivable at this location to both the composer and the listener? In the visual arts, the problem of identifying the repertoire of possible forms or depicted objects is obviously even more baffling for all except a few highly stereotyped genres.

Even before we face this troublesome problem, there is the even thornier one of deciding what should be regarded as an element of a work. In a poem, are the elements phonemes, words, statements, or images? Is a musical work composed of notes and chords or of motifs and melodies?

And in painting, are the elements spots of color, depicted objects, groups of objects, or larger formal arrangements?

These considerations and others bring us to yet another point. The measures that form the substance of what is usually called "information theory"—sometimes "objective information theory" or "statistical information theory"—are functions of objective probabilities, i.e., of how often events of particular kinds actually occur. They have nothing necessarily to do with the reactions of any human or animal observer of these events. But when these measures affect human behavior, as they have so often been shown to do, they must surely work through their subjective equivalents (Berlyne, 1960, 1974). This is surely of particular importance when we are considering their motivational effects, including their role in motivational aspects of aesthetics. Psychologically, the objective information content of an event, which is dependent solely on its frequency of occurrence, is surely less important than the degree to which the subject was expecting the event. The alternative events that the subject can anticipate or conceive of must matter more than the actual sample space from which the event is drawn. And the redundancies that can be computed from conditional probabilities can carry psychological weight only in so far as the subject recognizes similarities and interdependencies.

Various measuring operations have been introduced under the guise of subjective-uncertainty indices (e.g., Laffal, 1955; Driscoll & Sturgeon, 1969; Nicki, 1970; Lanzetta, 1971). But none of these indices has won general acceptance.

What is needed, especially for psychological aesthetics, is some simple device that reflects judgments made by subjects and produces scores that increase with objective uncertainty whenever this can be manipulated or estimated. Mean ratings on a 7-point SIMPLE-COMPLEX scale seem to fulfill these requirements to a remarkable degree. Take, for example, Figure 2 in Chapter 2. As already mentioned, the random sound sequences that Crozier used, following Vitz, can be regarded as successions of signals from an ergodic discrete source and thus of precisely the kind of events for which the information-theoretic measure of uncertainty was originally devised. The curve relating the mean complexity judgments of Crozier's subjects to objective uncertainty level in bits approximates a straight line. Even a specialist in information theory would be hard put to it to estimate in bits per tone the information content of the sound sequences as he heard them. Yet the brains of Crozier's subjects (or, more accurately, their averaged brain!), most of whom have presumably never heard of information theory, were doing something very much like that. Other experiments, using a wide variety of stimulus material (Chaps. 3, 4, 5, 6, 7, and 12, this volume; see also Berlyne, 1971, pp. 198–202; Berlyne, 1973), have also revealed close, monotonic relations between judged complexity and objective · uncertainty (or variations in stimulus material that imply differences in objective uncertainty).

Ratings on certain other scales, including CLEAR-INDEFINITE and DISORDERLY-ORDERLY, are invariably correlated with SIMPLE-COMPLEX ratings and thus likewise vary concomitantly with objective uncertainty. So, of necessity, do mean factor scores on factors in which these ratings figure prominently. Finally, measures of several other kinds, such as Looking Time or Listening Time, Rating Time, Interestingness ratings, and ratings presumably indicative of arousal (RELAXED-TENSE, DROWSY-ALERT), are commonly also correlated positively both with manipulations of uncertainty and with rated Complexity.

As pointed out in Chapter 1, there are four ways in which the uncertainty associated with a class of patterns (and consequently the information content associated with a pattern taken from that class) can be varied. All of these have been used in our experiments, viz., variations in the number of alternatives from which each elements is selected (Chaps. 2, 3, 4, 5, 6), in the number of elements per pattern (Chap. 5), in distributional redundancy (Chap. 6) and in correlational redundancy (Chap. 5). It is noteworthy that mean Complexity ratings, as well as other variables belonging to the same cluster, are affected significantly by all four kinds of manipulation. This constitutes evidence that these variables depend on a common underlying variable, viz., uncertainty.

One point of theoretical interest might profitably be taken up here. Birkhoff's (1933) pioneering mathematical theory invoked "complexity" and "order" as the two determinants of "aesthetic value," assuming that these two can, at least sometimes, vary independently of each other. This assumption was taken over by Gunzenhäuser (1968), when he offered an information-theoretic reinterpretation of Birkhoff's theory, identifying complexity with uncertainty and order with redundancy. Although, all things being equal, redundancy brings down uncertainty, uncertainty can vary when relative redundancy (expressed as a percentage) remains constant and vice versa.

Our own results with the DISORDERLY-ORDERLY scale do not confirm that whatever our subjects mean by "order" can be separated from judged Complexity. DISORDERLY-ORDERLY ratings show a marked tendency to vary inversely with SIMPLE-COMPLEX ratings, even when redundancy is absent from the stimulus material.

We can now see a possible way out of a difficulty that was considered earlier. There are reasons for supposing that information-theoretic measures, like uncertainty and redundancy, should be applicable to works of art, e.g., paintings, and that these measures should have a great deal to do with their motivational effects on appreciators. But it is virtually impossible to compute such measures with reference to works of art, because of the difficulties of identifying elements and of specifying sample spaces. Nevertheless, Complexity ratings, which show such a close affinity to uncertainty whenever uncertainty can be computed, can also be applied with considerable intersubject consistency to paintings (Chaps. 9 and 11). Furthermore, Looking Time and other verbal ratings that covary closely with rated Complexity and with uncertainty, whenever uncertainty is manipulable or assessable, do so when applied to paintings. We therefore have some basis for supposing that rating scales offer an indirect means of estimating information-theoretic attributes when they cannot be calculated directly.

Besides the verbal and nonverbal measures that vary monotonically with uncertainty and with judged complexity, there are others that follow nonmonotonic—unimodal (inverted U-shaped) or multimodal—curves. These include DISPLEASING-PLEASING ratings and other ratings, highly correlated with these, that are prominent contributors to what we have called the Hedonic Tone factor. In the case of paintings, these variables are generally uncorrelated with those that reflect complexity and uncertainty. Since the correlation coefficients that are used for factor analysis reflect only linear relations between variables, this lack of correlation is compatible with the possibility that indices of hedonic tone are curvilinearly related to indices of uncertainty and complexity. Since hedonic tone must depend on other properties of paintings besides information-theoretic and collative ones, our relatively small samples of paintings did not permit an adequate test of this hypothesis. Nevertheless, other experimenters (Rump, 1968; Wohlwill, 1968; Walker, 1970) have obtained inverted U-shaped curves relating ratings indicative of hedonic tone to rated complexity, using pictures that were selected to differ primarily in complexity.

FACTOR ANALYSES OF COLLATIVE AND EVALUATIVE RATINGS

A further objective common to several of our experiments, and one that deserves a high priority at the present stage of experimental aesthetics, is to study the interrelations among verbal ratings. In particular, it is necessary to find out how ratings on various collative and evaluative scales are related to one another, since these are indicative of motivational effects and of some of the main stimulus properties that are responsible for them. It is necessary to determine to what extent different scales are informing us about the same internal variables and, in other words, to identify major dimensions of verbal aesthetic reaction.

The appropriate technique for answering questions of this sort is factor analysis. In our experiments, we used a variant of what Cattell (1952) calls "P technique." Only those scales that showed significant intersubject consistency, e.g., a significant F value for the Stimulus main effect in an analysis of variance, were involved in the factor analyses. The mean rating on each of these scales for each stimulus pattern was calculated, and the correlations over stimulus patterns between pairs of scales were factor-analyzed.

Apart from the factor analyses of this kind reported in this book, there have been others applied to collative and evaluative ratings in our own and other laboratories. The results of 17 investigations of this kind are synopsized in Table 1.

This table omits factor analyses of stylistic scales (see Chaps. 9 and 11), since these concern different questions. Also omitted are factor analyses that yield essentially a single factor, as is apt to happen when stimulus material is confined to relatively low degrees of complexity. Furthermore, a few investigations using R technique are not included. In these latter investigations, subjects were required to rate one stimulus, usually an indoor or outdoor environment, on a number of scales, and correlations over subjects, rather than over stimuli, were analyzed. It is, however, worth mentioning that these R-technique analyses have generally produced similar factors to those using P technique (e.g., Küller, 1972). Finally, Osgood, Suci, and Tannenbaum (1957, Chap. 2) used words as stimuli with yet other factor-analytic procedures. These do not appear in Table 1. They produced factors corresponding to Osgood's well-known Evaluative, Activity, and Potency dimensions.

The following additional points must be made with regard to Table 1:

1. In some cases, there were more than five factors accounting for an appreciable portion of the variance, but, when this is so, only the five most important factors are shown.

2. The factors are not necessarily presented in the order in which they were extracted or in order of decreasing eigenvalue (percentage of variance

TABLE 1
Factor Analyses (P Technique)

	Evaluation	Activity	Potency	Balance	Clarity
1 Tucker, 1955 (Representational paintings)	**Evaluation** WET-DRY CHAOTIC-ORDERED BAD-GOOD CLEAR-HAZY VAGUE-PRECISE PLEASANT-UNPLEASANT	**Activity** PASSIVE-ACTIVE VIBRANT-STILL REPETITIVE-VARIED STATIC-DYNAMIC SIMPLE-COMPLEX RELAXED-TENSE	**Potency** SERIOUS-HUMOROUS SOFT-HARD STRONG-WEAK MASCULINE-FEMININE		
2 Ertel, 1973 (Miscellaneous visual patterns)	**Valency** ATTRACTIVE-REPULSIVE BEAUTIFUL-UGLY INTERESTING-UNINTERESTING	**Excitement** MOVING-STILL ENLIVENING-CALMING COMPLEX-SIMPLE INTERESTING-UNINTERESTING	**Potency** POWERFUL-TENDER MIGHTY-ORNAMENTAL	**Balance** BALANCED-UNBALANCED UNITARY-NONUNITARY	**Clarity** CLEAR-VAGUE DISTINCT-DIFFUSE
3 Evans & Day, 1971 (Random polygons)	**Evaluative** GOOD-BAD UGLY-BEAUTIFUL PLEASING-DISPLEASING	**Activity** GSR Looking Time Number of sides COMPLEX-SIMPLE INTERESTING-BORING CALMING-EXCITING DEFINITE-UNCERTAIN	**Potency** SMALL-LARGE WEAK-POWERFUL		
4 Libby & Selinger, 1971 (Black and white photographs)	**Pleasantness Evaluation** BEAUTIFUL-UGLY GOOD-BAD PLEASANT-UNPLEASANT Heart rate	**Curiosity (Attention)** CURIOSITY-PRODUCING/BLAH ATTENTION-GETTING/BLAND GSR Pupillary diameter	**Potency (Activity)** STRONG-WEAK ACTIVE-PASSIVE		

TABLE 1 (Continued)
Factor Analyses (P Technique)

Libby, Lacey, & Lacey, 1973	Pleasantness (Evaluation)	Attention (Interest)	Activity (Potency)	Complexity	
5 (Black and white photographs)	PLEASANT-BEAUTIFUL (Low cardiac deceleration)	INTERESTING ATTENTION GETTING FASCINATING (Cardiac deceleration) (Pupillary diameter)	FAST STRONG ACTIVE	FAIR. Many details COMPLEX	
Franke & Bortz, 1972	Valency	Variation	Structural order	Comfort	
6 (Residential areas)	GREY-COLORED BUILT/UP-ORGANIZED DREARY-ATTRACTIVE UGLY-BEAUTIFUL	VARIED-BORING IMPRESSIVE-NOTHING TO SAY MONOTONOUS-MULTIFARIOUS	ACCESSIBLE-CLOSED OFF CLEAR-BLURRED DISTINCT-CONFUSING	LUXURIOUS-POOR SOBER-OVERLOADED LOOKED AFTER-SHABBY	
Küller, 1972	Pleasantness (Evaluation)	Complexity (Activity)	Social status	Originality	Enclosedness
7 (Photographs of interiors)	STIMULATING PLEASANT GOOD BORING (–) REPULSIVE (–)	MOTLEY DISCREET	PRETENTIOUS EXPENSIVE SPLENDID	ORDINARY (–) CURIOUS TIMELESS (–)	AIRY OPEN CLOSED (–)
Küller, 1972	Pleasantness	Complexity	Potency	Unity	Enclosedness
8 (Photographs of interior & exterior environments)	PLEASANT UNINTERESTING (–) IMPERSONAL (–) UGLY (–) FRIENDLY	MOTLEY COMPOSITE COMPLEX	MASCULINE FEMININE (–)	FUNCTIONAL IMPRACTICAL (–) WHOLE	OPEN (–)

TABLE 1 (*Continued*)

Factor Analyses (P Technique)

	Evaluation	Activity	Potency
Evans 1973			
9 (Prose paragraphs)	GOOD-BAD	INTERESTING-BORING	COMPLEX-SIMPLE
	UGLY-BEAUTIFUL	SHARP-DULL	HARD-TENSE
	CALMING-EXCITING	WEAK-POWERFUL	HAZY-CLEAR
	PLEASING-DISPLEASING	PASSIVE-ACTIVE	RELAXED-TENSE
	EMG	LIKEABLE-DISLIKEABLE	SMALL-LARGE
	GSR		
Berlyne, 1973	Hedonic Value	Complexity-Uncertainty	Cortical arousal (Oblique to Hedonic-Tone factor)
10 (Visual patterns and paintings)	DISPLEASING-PLEASING	SIMPLE-COMPLEX	WEAK-POWERFUL
	UGLY-BEAUTIFUL	CLEAR-INDEFINITE	DROWSY-ALERT
	NO PLEASURE-EXTREME PLEASURE	UNINTERESTING-INTERESTING	UNINTERESTING-INTERESTING
		RELAXED-TENSE	RELAXED-TENSE
	(Looking Time)	(Looking Time)	(Looking Time)
Crozier, (Chap. 2, this volume)	Evaluation	Activity	Potency
11 (Random sound sequences)	AWFUL-NICE	SIMPLE-COMPLEX	WEAK-STRONG
	BAD-GOOD	REPETITIVE-VARIED	
	DISPLEASING-PLEASING	UNINTERESTING-INTERESTING	
	UGLY-BEAUTIFUL	PASSIVE-ACTIVE	
	UNMUSICAL-MUSICAL	DISSONANT-CONSONANT	
	UNINTERESTING-INTERESTING	(Listening Time)	

TABLE 1 (*Continued*)

Factor Analyses (P Technique)

	Hedonic Tone	Uncertainty/Arousal	
Berlyne, (Chap. 5, this volume)			
12 (Visual matrix patterns)	DISPLEASING-PLEASING	SIMPLE-COMPLEX	
	PLEASURE	CLEAR-INDEFINITE	
	DISLIKE-LIKE	DISORDERLY-ORDERLY	
	UGLY-BEAUTIFUL	RELAXED-TENSE	
	UNINTERESTING-INTERESTING	(Looking Time)	
	WEAK-POWERFUL		
	(Hanging on wall)		
	(Looking Time)		

	Hedonic Tone	Uncertainty/Arousal	
Berlyne, (Chap. 5, this volume)			
13 (Visual Smets patterns)	DISPLEASING-PLEASING	SIMPLE-COMPLEX	
	PLEASURE	CLEAR-INDEFINITE	
	DISLIKE-LIKE	DISORDERLY-ORDERLY	
	UNINTERESTING-INTERESTING	RELAXED-TENSE	
	WEAK-POWERFUL	UNINTERESTING-INTERESTING	
	DROWSY-ALERT	(Looking Time)	
	RELAXED-TENSE	(Hanging on wall)	
	(Hanging on wall)		

	Hedonic Tone	Uncertainty	Arousal
Berlyne & Ogilvie, (Chap. 9, this volume)			
14 (Western post-medieval paintings)	DISPLEASING-PLEASING	SIMPLE-COMPLEX	UNINTERESTING-INTERESTING
	UGLY-BEAUTIFUL	CLEAR-INDEFINITE	WEAK-POWERFUL
	DISCOMFORT	UNBALANCED-BALANCED	DROWSY-ALERT
	PLEASURE	DISORDERLY-ORDERLY	RELAXED-TENSE
	RELAXED-TENSE	RATING TIME	SIMPLE-COMPLEX
	(Looking Time)	(Looking Time)	(Looking Time)

TABLE 1 (*Continued*)

Factor Analyses (P Technique)

	Hedonic Tone	Uncertainty	Attention	Arousal	Perception of semantic distance
Berlyne, Robbins & Thompson, (Chap. 12, this volume) 15 [Line drawings (Ugandan & Canadian Ss)]	PLEASING-DISPLEASING STRONG-WEAK EXCITING-UNEXCITING GOOD-BAD	COMPLEX-SIMPLE FAMILIAR-UNFAMILIAR EASY-DIFFICULT			
Godkewitsch, (Chap. 13, this volume) 16 (Adjective-noun pairs)	PLEASURE DISPLEASING-PLEASING RELAXED-TENSE HUMOROUS (Funny)		ACTIVE AND LIVELY UNINTERESTING-INTERESTING (Looking Time) (Funny)	DROWSY-ALERT WEAK-POWERFUL (Funny) (SIMPLE-COMPLEX)	IMPROBABLE PECULIAR STRANGE INAPPROPRIATE WITTY (Looking Time) (Funny)
Berlyne, (unpublished) 17 pre-Renaissance and non-Western paintings	DISPLEASING-PLEASING UGLY-BEAUTIFUL PLEASURE DISCOMFORT RELAXED-TENSE UNINTERESTING-INTERESTING	DISORDERLY-ORDERLY UNBALANCED-BALANCED CLEAR-INDEFINITE		UNINTERESTING-INTERESTING WEAK-POWERFUL DROWSY-ALERT	

accounted for). The order is sometimes rearranged to draw attention to correspondences between factors emerging from different studies.

3. The variables with the highest loadings on each factor are listed, but these do not necessarily include all the variables whose loadings have absolute values exceeding .50.

4. The variables named in parentheses were not included in the factor analyses but turned out to have significant correlations with mean factor scores after being measured separately.

5. In some cases, the subjects were not English-speaking, so that the scale labels appearing in Table 1 are translations from other languages, and may in some cases be slightly debatable.

The 17 factor analyses used a great variety of stimulus material, both visual and auditory. They differed widely in the verbal scales that were included. They incorporated, however, enough common scales, or scales bearing closely synonymous labels, to enable their results to be collated with one another. It is hardly surprising that there are differences among the sets of factors yielded by these in many ways dissimilar studies. But the similarities are unmistakable and surely significant. As Herne (1973) has put it, "Belief in the results of multivariate analysis depends on a common picture consistently arising from very many separate data samples."

As we examine Table 1 then, the following points seem worthy of note (numbers in parentheses refer to entries in Table 1):

1. Hedonic Tone (Evaluative) factor. Ratings on DISPLEASING-PLEASING, UNPLEASANT-PLEASANT, NO PLEASURE-EXTREME PLEASURE, GOOD-BAD, and UGLY-BEAUTIFUL scales, and other scales with similar meaning, are invariably highly intercorrelated. In our own studies, we have generally applied the label "Hedonic Tone" to the factor defined by such scales. This is because we have adopted this term to denote those aspects of hedonic value that are revealed by verbal evaluative judgments. But the factor can safely be equated with the Evaluative factor that has emerged from the semantic-differential research of Osgood and his colleagues.

2. Uncertainty (Activity) factor. We regularly find high intercorrelations among the SIMPLE-COMPLEX, CLEAR-INDEFINITE, DISORDERLY-ORDERLY, and UNBALANCED-BALANCED scales. Of these, SIMPLE-COMPLEX is one that has more than once been found to have a high loading on Osgood's factor (cf. 1). Moreover, the factor defined by these scales, all of them reflecting properties associated with objective and subjective uncertainty, is shown by several studies to embrace two other scales that Osgood's group has linked with the Activity factor, namely ACTIVE-PASSIVE and RELAXED-TENSE.

Finally, this factor is shown to have a close relation with some nonverbal measures when they are either included in the factor analysis or recorded separately and compared with factor scores, namely Looking Time and Listening Time, psychophysiological changes indicating activation of the sympathetic nervous system, and objective complexity (3, 4, 5).

There are therefore indications that Osgood's Activity factor may represent the extent to which a stimulus pattern calls for information-processing effort. It incorporates (a) complexity, variety, and rate of change, which correspond to amount of information per element or per unit of time and thus to the uncertainty associated with the sample space (the class of patterns to which the pattern belongs), (b) properties like order and balance, which imply reduction of uncertainty through redundancy, and (c) properties like indefiniteness, which imply that some of the information needed for perceptual and intellectual processing is not readily available.

3. Arousal (Potency) factor. Whenever WEAK-POWERFUL and RELAXED-TENSE judgments were solicited, a high positive correlation between them appeared. They most often defined a factor distinct from the Hedonic Tone (Evaluative) and Uncertainty (Activity) factors, which can be identified safely enough with Osgood's Potency dimension.

In the two experiments by Libby (4, 5), there was a single factor that seemed to the authors to represent a combination of the Activity and Potency factors.[1] This is presumably because ACTIVE and STRONG judgments both had high loadings on it. In spite of this, it seems likely that this was the Potency factor and that another factor, labeled Curiosity-Attention and Attention-Interest by Libby and his colleagues, had more in common with the Activity factor. In three of our own studies (12, 13, 15), using visual material that might very well have been rather low in complexity and information content, the Potency factor merged with the Hedonic Tone factor.

4. Interestingness. The UNINTERESTING-INTERESTING scale has been used in a fair number of previous researches, as well as in several of the experiments reported in this book. Whereas judgments indicative of Hedonic

[1] Osgood and his colleagues (Osgood, et al., 1957, p. 74) have, in some of their studies, found the Activity and Potency factors to merge. They then refer to a "Dynamism" factor.

Tone usually reach a peak, or sometimes several peaks, at intermediate levels of complexity and uncertainty, judged interestingness tends to increase with complexity and uncertainty, at least until very high levels are reached when there is occasionally a hint of a leveling off or slight decline. Close monotonic relations have also repeatedly appeared between rated interestingness and Exploration Time.

It is therefore not surprising that in most cases the UNINTERESTING-INTERESTING scale has a high loading on the Uncertainty (Activity) factor. In three studies (10, 14, 17), whose stimulus material consisted wholly or partly of paintings, it was associated with the Potency factor, and, in four studies (8, 11, 12, 13), it was associated with the Hedonic Tone factor. Sometimes, in fact, it had high loadings on more than one factor. Previous research has suggested the possibility that judged Interestingness is high whenever there is a fair degree of subjective uncertainty or arousal potential and some prospect of relieving it promptly through perceptual and intellectual processing.

5. Arousal scales. Our own factor-analytic studies have incorporated two scales, RELAXED-TENSE and DROWSY-ALERT, that were intended as verbal measures of arousal. Self-ratings using these words, or others close to them in meaning, have turned out to possess quite high and significant correlations with psychophysiological indices of arousal (see Schönpflug, 1969; Thayer, 1967, 1970; Godkewitsch, 1974). It was thought (Berlyne, 1973, Chap. 1) that DROWSY-ALERT would reflect primarily cortical arousal and RELAXED-TENSE autonomic arousal. A number of lines of research (see Berlyne, 1967) indicate that cortical and autonomic indices of high arousal, while they often appear together, can sometimes occur independently of each other.

Now, however, an examination of our correlations and factor structures suggests that this interpretation might have been mistaken. The Uncertainty (Activity) factor is representative of properties that make demands on perceptual and intellectual processing and therefore, one would imagine, on the activity of the cerebral cortex. And, as in Table 1 shows, there is evidence for a closer connection between this factor and the RELAXED-TENSE scale than between this factor and the DROWSY-ALERT scale. The stimulus properties underlying the Uncertainty (Activity) factor include, in fact, some that are known to be conducive to vigorous orientation reactions (see Berlyne, 1960, 1963b, 1971a). The factor also encompasses electrocutaneous, pupillary, and circulatory changes that are recognized as indices of the orientation reaction (3, 4, 5). RELAXED-TENSE ratings may, therefore, signify something like the magnitude of the orientation reaction (Sokolov, 1958; Berlyne, 1960) occasioned by the initial impact of a pattern or, in other words, the arousal increment accompanying information-processing exertions. Since the RELAXED-TENSE scale sometimes (and more frequently than the DROWSY-ALERT scale) has a high negative loading on the Hedonic Tone factor, ratings approximating the TENSE pole may indicate arousal increments large enough to enter the unpleasant or aversive range (Berlyne, 1967, 1971).

On the other hand, the DROWSY-ALERT scale is closely connected with the Potency factor, which we have in our work often termed an "Arousal" factor. In the light of Osgood's research, stimuli scoring high on this factor are ones that are judged to be "strong," "big" "hard," etc. These sound like stimuli that are apt either to exert a violent impact on the subject or to resist his actions and thus give rise to frustration. One can therefore speculate that this factor characterizes threatening stimulus patterns that mobilize anticipatory arousal. The arousing properties of such patterns are presumably not ones that information-processing efforts are likely to resolve. To pursue a line of thought proposed by Dr. G. Cupchik at one of our laboratory meetings, what Osgood calls the "potency" of a stimulus may be its power to capture attention, to dominate the subject's perception, thought, and behavior, and to deflect him from other stimuli that might be present.

It is worth recalling once again, that in two studies (12 and 13) using relatively simple visual material, the Potency factor was combined with the Hedonic Tone factor. This is compatible with the view that maximum hedonic tone tends to coincide with intermediate demand on attention, so that the two curves will rise together over the lower reaches of the complexity or uncertainty continuum but will diverge as higher reaches, presumably not attained in these experiments, are entered.

FACTOR ANALYSES OF STYLISTIC RATINGS

The need for an objective taxonomy of pictorial style, derived from reactions of nonexperts is still a long way from accomplishment. But various techniques of multidimensional and multivariate analysis offer much promise in this connection, and some initial trials of their potentialities are reported in Chapters 9 and 11.

It is encouraging that three factors or dimensions, labeled Classicism, Subjectivism, and Expressionism, emerged from two factor analyses, reported in Chapters 9 and 11, respectively. This is especially noteworthy because of the differences between the two experiments in question. Both were devoted to post-Renaissance western painting, but one used a collection of paintings selected as a fairly representative sample, while the other used paintings intended to represent some dimensions suggested by art-historical writings and some theoretical notions. Furthermore, the batteries of scales were somewhat different. Further encouragement can be derived from the fact that these three dimensions correspond to those that Knapp had found serviceable when employing a quite dissimilar scaling procedure and the fact that they are evidently close to dimensions of variation that have loomed large in the discussions of art historians and critics.

On the other hand, the same stylistic battery as in Chapter 9 was recently applied to a collection of pre-Renaissance and nonwestern paintings. This is the collection that figures, with reference to collative and evaluative ratings, in row 17 of Table 1. With these paintings, the collative and evaluative factor structure was quite similar to the one obtained with post-Renaissance western paintings. But the rotated stylistic factor structure was different. Three factors appeared, which were labeled Stylization, Fantasy, and Decorativeness.

EXPLORATORY BEHAVIOR

Another major goal of our research program is to elucidate relations between verbal judgments and nonverbal forms of behavior. This goal can, of course, be pursued in two ways. One can examine correlations, over stimulus patterns, between verbal and nonverbal responses of the same subjects or of different subjects. Alternatively, or simultaneously, one can look for verbal and nonverbal responses that are affected by the same independent variables and in the same way.

Techniques

The principal nonverbal measures used in our experiments, as in the new experimental aesthetics generally, have been measures of exploratory behavior, i.e., measures of how strongly a subject is inclined to seek contact with particular kinds of stimulus patterns. The two main techniques for recording exploratory behavior that we have used, namely Exploration Time (Looking Time or Listening Time) and Exploratory Choice, have their counterparts in everyday aesthetic behavior. There are times when a visitor to an art gallery inspects the pictures on exhibition one by one, and the factors determining how long he spends on each may be of interest. Similarly, there are times when an individual selects one book to read, one recorded musical work to hear, or one painting to buy and hang on his wall, out of several that are available to him. A third technique, the so-called cafeteria technique, has sometimes been applied to problems with relevance to aesthetics (e.g., Jones, Wilkinson, & Braden, 1951). It permits a subject to change freely from one stimulus pattern to another, presenting them to himself in any order and for as long as he likes. We have avoided this technique, which also has its everyday counterparts, because it combines duration and choice and it seems advisable to look for the determinants of these two phenomena separately.

Exploration Time

Past work (see Berlyne, 1971a, Chap. 13) has virtually always found Exploration Time to increase with complexity, whether manipulated through information-theoretic variables or estimated by subjects, and to bear a close relation to judged interestingness. Our experiments corroborate these findings, with uncertainty varied in the different ways that have been pointed out. When factor analyses are carried out, Looking Time and Listening Time are always more highly correlated with the Uncertainty (Activity) factor than with any other. It is worth noting, however, that significant correlations with the Hedonic Tone factor also appear. This indicates that Exploration Time can be affected by hedonic tone when variations in complexity, uncertainty, and information content are held constant. This is a new finding, which previous experiments, using univariate procedures, could not reveal.

Exploratory Choice

The situation with regard to exploratory choice has always been more complicated and more puzzling (see Berlyne, 1971a, Chap. 13; 1972). The direction of exploratory choice is certainly dependent on complexity and uncertainty when other properties that might influence it are minimized. But there seem to be conditions in which the more complex of two patterns is more likely to be chosen and conditions in which the opposite holds.

If a subject can perform either of two responses that will lead to subsequent exposure of different patterns and if the properties of the patterns are to determine the choice, there must obviously be some way of informing the subject beforehand about the kinds of stimulation that will result from either response. There are four ways in which this has been done by experimenters: (1) exposing the subject, before he makes his choice, to the two patterns that can result from the two responses, (2) telling him beforehand what kinds of stimuli will result from different responses (e.g.,

McReynolds & Bryan, 1956), (3) presenting patterns that undergo gradual and progressive changes, so that the form they will take at a particular moment in the future can be anticipated (e.g., Kiekheben, 1966), and (4) causing distinct but similar patterns to result from the alternative responses on successive trials, so that the subject knows in advance to which class the pattern produced by a particular response will belong (e.g., Godkewitsch, Chap. 13). Of these, the first has been used most frequently.

Much more research will have to be done before we can understand why sometimes more complex stimulation and sometimes less complex stimulation is sought out. But the existing literature points to a number of factors that play some part:

1. Uncertainty and curiosity. The first is the quantity of information about the alternative patterns that the subject receives before making his choice and, in particular, the duration of their prechoice exposure. If two patterns are presented too briefly to enable the subject to grasp their principal characteristics, he will be left with appreciable subjective uncertainty and therefore perceptual curiosity (Berlyne, 1960) about them. Consequently, one would expect his choice to be governed largely by curiosity, which means that the more complex pattern, the one associated with more residual uncertainty and therefore, more curiosity, will tend to be chosen. On the other hand, if pre-exposure is long enough to eliminate curiosity, other factors, e.g., hedonic tone, may be decisive.

That exploratory choice may work in this way was suggested by what was apparently the first experiment to study it (Hoats, Miller, & Spitz, 1963). The subjects, consisting of normal and retarded children, first saw two patterns differing in complexity for the relatively long time of 3 seconds. They then chose one or the other for further viewing, and all groups chose to see the less complex pattern significantly more often. The suggestion was tested in an experiment (Berlyne, 1963a), which showed that undergraduate subjects tended to choose more complex patterns after brief (0.5 or 1 second) pre-exposures but less complex patterns after longer (3 second or 4 second) pre-exposures. The effects failed to appear in a later experiment (Berlyne & Lewis, 1963), in which each subject had 0.5 seconds pre-exposures on some trials and 3-second exposures on others. However, Ertel (1973), found that subjects having 0.5 seconds pre-exposures tended to choose pictures that other subjects had judged more "unbalanced, ununified," whereas subjects having 4-second pre-exposures chose pictures that had been judged more "beautiful, attractive."

Kiekheben's (1966) results, obtained with a rather unusual procedure, are congruent with what these findings indicate. His subjects saw continuously changing patterns, leaving no uncertainty about what would be seen at a particular moment. They could switch off the apparatus and stop the changes whenever they wished. They tended to do so, so that they could look at a static pattern for a few seconds, at times when maximum regularity and symmetry were reached.

It is conceivable that the preferred, i.e., most eagerly sought, level of complexity actually follows a (noninverted) U-shaped curve as a function of duration of exposure, so that relatively complex stimulation is particularly attractive after either very short or very long acquaintance. As contact with a particular pattern is prolonged to extreme durations, there is reason to believe (Dember & Earl, 1957; Walker, 1973) that the optimal level of complexity tends to increase.

2. Relation with Hedonic Tone. When curiosity becomes a minor factor, e.g., through relatively long pre-exposures, there are indications that moderately complex patterns are more likely to be chosen than patterns of greater or lesser complexity. Such nonmonotonic relations emerge from the experiment with sound sequences reported in Chapter 3 and the experiment with Smets patterns reported in Chapter 5. They resemble the relations that have emerged between hedonic tone and complexity.

These findings, together with those of Ertel just mentioned, point to an association between Exploratory Choice and hedonic tone in conditions where curiosity can be left out of account. This view is confirmed by other data in Chapter 5, i.e., answers to the question "How much would you like to have the pattern framed and hanging on your wall at home?" This is, of course, a somewhat dubious measure of actual behavior: subjects did not actually have to face, day after day, the patterns that they had rated high on this scale. Nevertheless, it provides some indication of how strongly inclined they were to accept the prospect of prolonged exposure to a pattern, presumably long after they would have become fully acquainted with it and curiosity would have died down. Moreover, the ratings were obtained after other experimental procedures that afforded an ample opportunity for examination of the patterns. Mean ratings in response to this question were significantly correlated with the Hedonic Tone factor alone when applied to matrix patterns, and more highly correlated with the Hedonic Tone than with the Uncertainty factor when applied to Smets patterns.

3. Prior information processing. A different interpretation of the effects of varying pre-exposure duration received some support from two experiments (Berlyne & Crozier, 1971; Berlyne, 1971b), in which pre-exposure stimulation differed from what could appear after the choice. It was found that stimulation demanding information-processing effort (a recorded story, colored slides of tourist attractions) made choice of more complex patterns less frequent, whereas other stimulation (white noise, light music) did not. The conclusion is that demanding, attention-capturing stimulation as such, as distinct from information about the patterns between which the subject must choose, may have some influence. However, in none of the conditions used in these experiments was the proportion of more-complex choices brought down below chance and, in any case, recognition of this additional factor does not exclude the hypothesized effect of presence or absence of curiosity. Finally, the subjects in these experiments had to choose between the same two patterns for 50 trials in succession. This is how they knew (after the first trial) what patterns the two alternative responses would expose. It constitutes another important difference as compared with other Exploratory-Choice experiments.

4. *Constancy or variability of side.* Yet another factor, and one by which the two experiments just mentioned were characterized, was investigated in an unpublished study, carried out in collaboration with Mary Louise King. This time, a different pair of patterns (30 pairs in all) was used in each trial as in most Exploratory-Choice experiments. For one group of 12 undergraduate subjects, however, the less complex pattern always appeared on the same side during pre-exposure and was thus always produced by pressing the same button. For another group of 12, the less complex pattern shifted randomly from side to side, as in most of the Exploratory-Choice experiments so far discussed. The pre-exposure duration was 5 seconds throughout. The group having the more complex patterns on the same side for every trial chose the more complex pattern more frequently. The group for which more and less complex patterns appeared equally often on either side made less complex choices more frequently. The difference was significant: $t = 5.99$, 22 *df*, $p < .01$.

5. *Individual differences.* Crozier's MDPREF analysis (Chap. 2, p. 83) shows that individuals differ in the degree to which their exploratory choices of sound sequences tend to follow complexity and uncertainty, on the one hand, or hedonic tone on the other hand. To the extent that they follow the first, more complex stimulus patterns will be chosen over less complex ones. To the extent that they follow the latter, patterns corresponding to intermediate uncertainty levels will be chosen in preference to others. Miller (1971), reanalyzing data from the already mentioned experiment of Hoats,

Miller, & Spitz (1963), showed likewise that some normal children are inclined to choose more complex patterns, while others have the opposite inclination.

It is obviously desirable to find out what other characteristics distinguish subjects who prefer exposure to relatively high and relatively low complexity, respectively. The developmental study described in Chapter 3 demonstrates that age can be one factor; the younger the subject, the lower the most frequently chosen uncertainty level.

Another likely possibility is that variations along the introversion-extraversion dimension have something to do with differences in exploratory choice. Eysenck (1963, 1973) has contended that introverts provide themselves with higher "levels of stimulation" (including novelty and complexity) than extroverts. He supports this contention with various pieces of evidence, most drawn from measures of everyday behavior and all drawn from situations differing from that of the usual Exploratory-Choice experiment. He has also argued that introverts have a higher prevailing level of arousal or are more arousable than extroverts. And several experimenters have found that heightened arousal makes both animals and human beings less inclined than usual to expose themselves to relatively novel or complex stimulation (Berlyne, 1967, 1971a, pp. 257ff).

Reward Value

Three of our experiments (Chaps. 5, 10, and 13) used the concurrent-variable-interval-schedule technique for comparing the reward value of visual patterns. When paintings and Smets patterns were used (Chaps. 5, 10), there was strong evidence for the close connection between hedonic tone and reward value that many theorists would expect. The other experiment (Chap. 13) warns us, however, that reward value can in some conditions follow other variables to the extent of running counter to verbal ratings associated with hedonic tone. So, this promising technique must be used to probe further the factors that govern reward value of visual and auditory patterns and especially relations between reward value and verbal characterizations.

INDIVIDUAL DIFFERENCES

Apart from the points made above with reference to Exploratory Choice, our experiments supplied a few findings on individual differences that affect aesthetic behavior. The experiments were, however, concerned only peripherally, if at all, with individual differences. This is because they concentrated on the development of research techniques and identification of crucial variables, which are necessary preliminaries to the fruitful investigation of interindividual variations.

Our cross-cultural study (Chap. 12) revealed quite astonishing similarities between verbal ratings on corresponding scales of patterns by Ugandan and Canadian subjects. The resemblances extended to correlations and factor structures. In both cultures, the repeatedly observed tendency for more complex patterns to attract more Looking Time appeared, but this tendency was less pronounced among the Ugandans than among the Canadians, and, among the Ugandans, its strength increased with degree of urbanization. On the other hand, Francès (1970, 1974) found some differences, using the same kind of stimulus material and somewhat similar tasks, between French students and French factory workers, as discussed in the introduction to Chapter 12.

Ways in which both the verbal evaluations and the exploratory responses of children differ from those of adults, at least with respect to randomized sound sequences, are presented in Chapter 3.

Crozier (Chap. 2) found, like several previous investigators, that relatively complex sound sequences are rated more favorably by subjects with specialized musical training than by others. Hare (Chap. 6) found the same to hold for subjects trained in the visual arts, thus providing what appears to be the first evidence for cross-modality transfer. But the effect did not appear when specialists in music were confronted with visual patterns.

FINAL COMMENTS

It is clear that the new experimental aesthetics has not yet gone very far beyond its first twitchings and gasps for breath. Some of the tasks that await it, as it grows into a sturdy adolescent, are self-evident. There seem to be good reasons for concentrating on collative and information-theoretic variables at this stage. But we must not forget either that the measurement and analysis of these variables still require a great deal of refinement or that these are far from being the only determinants of aesthetic reaction. Questions of content have received little attention in the reported experiments. This is not because they are not important. It is because the operative variables and measuring techniques are difficult to determine and because the motivational effects of structural factors seem a little more crucial and a little more puzzling.

As far as nonverbal responses are concerned, it may be felt that research confined to Exploration Time and other measures of the strength of stimulus-seeking behavior is woefully limited and even superficial. Nevertheless, how long an aesthetic pattern engages an appreciator's attention, and how effectively it competes with other stimulation to which he might direct himself, are important questions and seem suitable ones to take up initially. Later on, we must certainly edge our way towards the more elaborate forms of visible and audible behavior that center around art. These must include the diverse activities of the creative artist and the interpretative artist. They must also include the miscellaneous ways in which contact with art can affect an appreciator's reactions to many different situations, often after considerable delays. We must also analyze more minutely the activities through which the appreciator absorbs and processes what is in a work of art. Some of them, e.g., eye movements and reading out loud, can be observable directly. Others, being internal, must be traced through roundabout methods in conjunction with verbal and psychophysiological clues to what is going on inside the nervous system.

Still more work using multivariate techniques, such as factor analysis, is needed. The newer methods of multidimensional scaling offer themselves as adjuncts, with immense potentialities for psychological aesthetics. The verbal labels that we used in our experiments to define scales, and thus to elicit subjects' verbal characterizations of stimulus patterns, were only a few of those that could be used. They were chosen because of the part they had played in previous research and because of theoretical considerations. Some investigators using factor analysis (e.g., Osgood, Suci, & Tannenbaum, 1957; Küller, 1972) have made efforts to sample systematically from the whole stock of applicable adjectives that the language makes available. Their example must be followed up and extended.

It can hardly be reiterated too often that we need extensive study of ways in which nonverbal behavior can be predicted from the verbal judgments of the same or other subjects. Until such studies have been completed, totally unwarranted assumptions on this point are bound to be rife. Specialists in other areas besides psychological aesthetics, notably the social psychology of attitudes and marketing research, have assumed far too freely that what people will do is in line with what they say. Reviews of existing evidence pertaining to this assumption are sobering (e.g., Festinger, 1964; Bauer, 1966; O'Brien, 1971). They show that relevant empirical studies are very scarce and that the data produced by them provide little corroboration for the assumption.

And after the initial stages of looking for productive techniques and for crucial independent and dependent variables, a fresh and methodologically sounder attack on problems of individual differences is appropriate. The attack must be directed at the development of aesthetic appreciation in childhood, at relations between cultural differences and differences in style and preference, and at the personality correlates of variations in aesthetic taste. Cross-cultural studies using objective, rigorous data-collecting and statistical procedures are, as we have had occasion to note more than once, the only means to settling a troublesome question, namely, how far the observed reactions of readily accessible subjects are typical of the human species or peculiar to persons with our kind of cultural and educational background.

There is a sizeable suggestive, but far from unequivocal, literature on relations between personality and taste (see Berlyne, 1971, Chap. 15). But we need (1) reliable ways of classifying personality, (2) reliable ways of classifying artistic style, and (3) reliable ways of measuring "preference" or "taste" in the various senses that these terms have. Although many problems remain to be solved, specialists in personality theory have made a great deal of progress in providing the first of these. With the new techniques that are now at the disposal of psychological aestheticians, we are surely now on our way towards possession of the second and third of them.

Like another lusty infant called Gargantua (Rabelais, 1534), the new experimental aesthetics cries out immediately after birth for "Drink! Drink! Drink!" Its thirst is, however, not for wine but for solid research data. There are some who view its arrival with misgivings. They mistakenly fear it as a competitor who might threaten their own livelihoods. But it has no wish to harm anyone, least of all fellow-art-lovers. All it wants is its due place in the sun and an opportunity to insert its own unique patch into the multicolored fabric of human knowledge.

The principal conclusion coming out of our experiments is as follows. Powerful new research techniques are at our disposal, and we can confidently expect others to become available before long. The questions have been there for centuries. When they have been answered, both our understanding of art and our understanding of human psychology will have been advanced. We must get to work.

REFERENCES

Attneave, F. Some informational aspects of visual perception. *Psychological Review*, 1954, 61, 183–193.

Bauer, R. A. Attitudes, verbal behavior and other behavior. In L. Adler & I. Crespi (Eds.), *Attitude research at sea*. New York: American Marketing Association, 1966.

Berlyne, D. E. *Conflict, arousal and curiosity*. New York: McGraw-Hill, 1960.

Berlyne, D. E. Complexity and incongruity variables as determinants of exploratory choice and evaluative ratings. *Canadian Journal of Psychology*, 1963, 17, 274–290. (a)

Berlyne, D. E. Motivational problems raised by exploratory and epistemic behavior. In S. Koch (Ed.), *Psychology—A study of a science*. Vol. 5. New York: McGraw-Hill, 1963. (b)

Berlyne, D. E. Arousal and reinforcement. In D. Levine (Ed.), *Nebraska Symposium on Motivation*, 1967. Lincoln, Neb.: University of Nebraska Press, 1967.

Berlyne, D. E. *Aesthetics and psychobiology*. New York: Appleton-Century-Crofts, 1971. (a)

Berlyne, D. E. Effects of auditory prechoice stimulation on visual exploratory choice. *Psychonomic Science*, 1971, 25, 193–194. (b)

Berlyne, D. E. Ends and means of experimental aesthetics. *Canadian Journal of Psychology*, 1972, 26, 303–325.

Berlyne, D. E. Interrelations of verbal and nonverbal measures used in experimental aesthetics. *Scandinavian Journal of Psychology*, 1973, 14, 177–184.

Berlyne, D. E. Information and motivation. L. A. Silverstein (Ed.), *Human communication: Theoretical explorations*. Washington: Erlbaum, 1974.

Berlyne, D. E., & Crozier, J. B. Effects of complexity and pre-choice stimulation on exploratory choice. *Perception & Psychophysics*, 1971, 10, 242–246.

Berlyne, D. E., & Lewis, J. L. Effects of heightened arousal on human exploratory behavior. *Canadian Journal of Psychology*, 1963, 17, 398–411.

Broadbent, D. E. *Perception and communication*. London & New York: Pergamon, 1958.

Cattell, R. B. The three basic factor-analytic research designs: Their interrelations and derivatives. *Psychological Bulletin*, 1952, 49, 499–520.

Dember, W. N., & Earl, R. W. Analysis of exploratory, manipulatory, and curiosity behaviors. *Psychological Review*, 1957, 64, 91–96.

Ertel, S. Exploratory choice and verbal judgment. In D. E. Berlyne, & K. B. Madsen (Eds.), *Pleasure, reward, preference*. New York: Academic Press, 1973.

Evans, D. R. The factorial structure of responses to conceptual complexity. Paper presented at meeting of the Canadian Psychological Association, Victoria, June, 1973. 1973.

Evans, D. R., & Day, H. I. The factorial structure of responses to perceptual complexity. *Psychonomic Science*, 1971, 22, 357–359.

Eysenck, H. J. *Experiments with drugs*. New York: Macmillan, 1963.

Eysenck, H. J. Personality and the law of effect. In D. E. Berlyne, & K. B. Madsen (Eds.), *Pleasure, reward preference*. New York: Academic Press, 1973.

Festinger, L. Behavioral support for opinion change. *Public Opinion Quarterly*, 1964, 29, 404–427.

Francès, R. Intérêt et préférence esthétique pour des stimuli de complexité variable. Étude comparative. *Journal de Psychologie*, 1970, 70, 207–224.

Francès, R. Les choix et les jugements esthétiques, *La Recherche,* 1974, **46**, 553-561.

Franke, J., & Bortz, J. Beiträge zur Anwendung der Psychologie auf den Städtebau. *Zeitschrift für experimentelle und angewandte Psychologie,* 1972, **19**, 76-108.

Garner, W. R. *Uncertainty and structure as psychological concepts.* New York: Wiley, 1962.

Godkewitsch, M. Verbal, exploratory and physiological responses to stimulus properties underlying humour. Unpublished Ph.D. thesis, University of Toronto, 1974.

Green, R. T., & Courtis, M. C. Information theory and figure perception: The metaphor that failed. *Acta Psychologica,* 1966, **25**, 12-36.

Herne, H. Review of W. W. Cooley, & P. R. Lohnes, *Multivariate data analysis. Journal of the Royal Statistical Society,* 1973, **136**, 101-102.

Hoats, D. L., Miller, M. B., & Spitz, H. H. Experiments on perceptual curiosity in mental retardates and normals. *American Journal of Mental Deficiency,* 1963, **68**, 386-395.

Hochberg, J., & McAlister, E. A quantitative approach to figural "goodness." *Journal of Experimental Psychology,* 1953, **46**, 361-364.

Jones, A., Wilkinson, H. J., & Braden, I. Information deprivation as a motivational variable. *Journal of Experimental Psychology,* 1961, **62**, 126-137.

Kiekheben, F. Der Einfluss eines kaleidoskopischen Figurwandels auf das Erkundungsverhalten. *Psychologische Forschung,* 1966, **30**, 105-150.

Küller, R. *A semantic model for describing perceived environment.* Stockholm: State Institute for Building Research, 1972.

Libby, W. L., Lacey, B. C., & Lacey, J. I. Pupillary and cardiac activity during visual attention. *Psychophysiology,* 1973, **10**, 270-294.

Libby, W. L., & Selinger, S. The relative effects of attention-interest and pleasantness-evaluation. Paper presented at the 43rd Annual Meeting of the Midwestern Psychological Association, Detroit, May, 1971.

McReynolds, P., & Bryan, J. Tendency to obtain new percepts as a function of the level of unassimilated percepts. *Perceptual and Motor Skills,* 1956, **6**, 183-186.

Miller, M. B. Intrinsic motivation: Unlearned, learned and modifiable. In H. Day, D. E. Berlyne, & D. E. Hunt (Eds.), *Intrinsic motivation: A new direction in education.* Toronto: Holt, Rinehart & Winston of Canada, 1971.

O'Brien, T. Stages of consumer decision making. *Journal of Marketing Research,* 1971, **8**, 283-289.

Osgood, C. E., Suci, G. J., & Tannenbaum, P. H. *The measurement of meaning.* Urbana, Ill.: University of Illinois Press, 1957.

Rabelais, F. *Gargantua.* Lyon: Juste, 1534.

Schönpflug, W. Phänomenologische Indikatoren der Aktiviertheit. In W. Schönpflug (Ed.), *Methoden der Aktivierungsforschung.* Stuttgart: Huber, 1969.

Shannon, C. E., & Weaver, W. *Mathematical theory of communication.* Urbana, Ill.: University of Illinois Press, 1949.

Sokolov, E. N. *Vospriiate i uslovny refleks.* University of Moscow Press, 1958. *(Perception and the conditioned reflex.* New York: Macmillan, 1963.)

Thayer, R. E. Measurement of activation through self-report. *Psychological Reports*, 1967, 20, 663–678 (Monograph Supplement 1–V20).

Thayer, R. E. Activation states as assessed by verbal report and four psychophysiological variables. *Psychophysiology*, 1970, 7, 86–94.

Tucker, W. T. Experiments in aesthetic communication. Unpublished Ph.D. thesis, University of Illinois, 1955. (Summary in Osgood, Suci, & Tannenbaum, 1957.)

Walker, E. L. Complexity and preference in animals and men. *Annals of the New York Academy of Sciences*, 1970, 169, 619–652.

AUTHOR INDEX

Numbers in italics refer to the pages on which the complete references are listed.

Abel, T. M., 159, 160, *168*
Abell, W., 241, *257*
Albrecht, G., 86, *87*
Apel, W., 27, *87*
Ariès, P., 242, *257*
Arnheim, R., 86, *87*, 242, *257*
Arnoult, M. D., 165, *167*
Attneave, F., 28, 29, *87*, 165, *167*, 307, *329*
Avital, T., 21, *23*

Babbitt, M., 28, *87*
Barron, F., 160, *167*
Bartenwerfer, H., 17, *23*
Bartlett, M. S., 197, *225*, 254, *257*
Bauer, R. A., 328, *330*
Baumgarten, A. G., 1, *23*
Belar, H., 28, *89*
Bense, M., 6, 19, *23*
Berg, W. K., 53, *88*
Berlyne, D. E., 4, 5, 6, 8, 9, 12, 13, 14, 15, 16, 17, 19, 20, *23*, *24*, 31, 36, 44, 45, 54, 55, 57, 69, 77, 85, *87*, 97,

107, 124, 125, 126, 129, 138, 140, 153, 154, 156, *157*, 159, *167*, 172, *173*, 175, 176, 177, *179*, *180*, 182, 184, 192, 202, *225*, 227, 228, 232, *233*, 241, 243, *257*, 260, 267, 270, 275, *278*, 280, 282, 284, 285, 290, 295, 298, 300, *302*, *303*, 308, 309, 311, 312, 314, 315, 322, 323, 325, 326, 329, *330*
Bieri, J., 161, *167*
Birkhoff, G. D., 9, *24*, 124, *157*
Bloom, S., 296, *303*
Borsa, D. M., 13, 24, *25*
Bortz, J., 313, *331*
Braden, I., 160, *168*, 322, *331*
Brawley, J. G., 28, *88*
Broadbent, D. E., 306, *330*
Brooks, C., 3, *25*
Brooks, F. P., 28, *88*
Bryan, J., 323, *331*
Bush, R. P., 199, *226*

Campbell, D. N., 70, *88*

Cantor, G. N., 175, *180*
Carroll, J. D., 80, 81, *88*, 102, *107*, 189, 196, 218, *225*, *226*, 248, *257*
Catania, A. C., 15, *24*, 153, *157*, 300, *303*
Cattell, R. B., 16, *24*, 310, *330*
Chang, J. J., 80, *88*, 102, *107*, 189, 196, 218, *225*, *226*, 248, *257*
Child, M. S., 159, 160, *168*, 260, *278*
Cliff, N., 83, *88*
Coates, F. D., 9, *24*
Coffee, S., 160, *167*
Cooke, D., 70, *88*
Coons, E., 28, *89*
Copland, A., 70, *88*
Courtis, M. C., 45, *88*, 307, *331*
Crozier, J. B., 86, *88*, 93, 95, 97, 100, 103, 104, 105, *107*, 228, *233*, 284, 285, *303*, 308, 325, 327, *330*
Cunningham, K. M., 190, *226*

Dadson, R. S., 47, *89*
Day, H. I., 13, *24*, 132, *157*, 165, *167*, 268, *278*, 284, 285, 290, *303*, 312, *330*
Dell, P., 11, *25*
Dellas, M., 161, *167*
Dember, W. N., 160, *167*, 324, *330*
Diserens, C. M. 13, *24*
Doob, A. N., 86, *88*
Dorfman, D., 140, *158*
Driscoll, J. M., 169, *173*
Duke, A. W., 91, *107*

Earl, R. W., 160, *167*, 324, *330*
Edwards, A. L., 37, *88*
Egger, G. J., 160, *167*
Eisenman, R., 160, *167*
Ekman, P., 285, *303*
Ertel, S., 125, *158*, 282, *303*, 312, 323, *330*
Evans, D. R., 312, 314, *330*
Eysenck, H. J., 9, *25*, 326, *330*

Fallers, M., 262, *278*
Farnsworth, P. R., 91, *107*

Fechner, G. T., 2, 5, 18, *25*
Ferguson, G. A., 80, *88*, 102, *107*, 139, 152, *158*, 300, *303*
Festinger, L., 328, *330*
Finley, J. R., 228, *233*
Fletcher, H., 47, *88*
Francès, R., 260, *278*, 327, *330*, *331*
Frank, H., 6, 19, *25*, 76, *88*, 124, *158*
Franke, J., 313, *331*
Friesen, W. V., 285, *303*

Gaier, E. L., 161, *168*
Garner, W. R., 20, *25*, 29, 239, 240, *257*, 307, *331*
Garrett, H. E., 76, *88*
Gernet, S. K., 160, *168*
Godkewitsch, M., 17, 21, *25*, 228, 280, 281, 284, *303*, 311, 323, *331*
Goldstein, A. G., 46, *88*
Goude, G. A., 184, *226*
Gould, L., 296, *304*
Graham, F. K., 53, *88*
Green, R. T., 45, *88*, 307, *331*
Gullickson, G. R., 91, *107*
Gunzenhäuser, R., 9, 19, *25*

Hare, F. G., 161, *168*
Harman, H. H., 98, *107*
Harrison, A. A., 44, 46, *88*, 275, *278*
Harvey, O. J., 244, *257*
Hatton, H. M., 53, *88*
Hauser, A., 241, 242, 244, *257*
Heise, D. R., 285, *303*
Herne, H., 317, *331*
Hoats, D. L., 323, 325, *331*
Hochberg, J., 307, *331*
Hopkins, A. L., 28, *88*
Hunt, D. E., 244, *257*
Hutcheson, F., 9, *25*

Iminski, S. A., 160, *167*

Jellison, J. M., 175, *180*
Johnson, S. C., 190, *226*
Jones, A., 160, *168*, 322, *331*

Kaiser, H. F., 63, *88*, 290, *303*
Kaplan, R., 9, *25*
Karmel, B. Z., 140, *158*
Kavolis, V., 241, 242, *257*
Keele, S. W., 238, *257*
Kendall, M. G., 79, *88*
Kenny, D. I., 281, *303*
Kessen, M. L., 92, *108*
Kessen, W., 91, *108*, 109, *119*, 132, 160, 161, *168*, 228, *233*
Kiekheben, F., 323, 324, *331*
Killbride, P., 262, *278*
Knapp, R. H., 206, *226*
Konečni, V., 86, *88*
Kraehenbuehl, D., 28, *89*
Kruskal, J. B., 189, *226*
Küller, R., 311, 313, 328, *331*
Künnapas, T., 184, *226*

Lacey, B. C., 313, *331*
Lacey, J. I., 313, *331*
Lance, G. T., 190, *226*
Langevin, R., 284, 290, *303*
Levine, J., 279, 296, *303, 304*
Levy, E., 70, *89*
Lewis, J. L., 323, *330*
Libby, W. L., 312, 313, 318, *331*
Lomax, A., 27, *89*
Love, W., 197, *226*, 254, *257*
Lugira, A. M., 262, *278*
Lundin, R. W., 91, *108*

Maier, N. R. F., 281, *303*
Mair, L., 262, *278*
Malefijt, A. deW., 279, *304*
Marcus, S., 8, *25*
Matlin, M. W., 44, *89*
Mayer, M., 296, *303*
McAlister, E., 307, *331*
McDonnell, P., 14, *24*
McGhee, P. E., 279, *304*
McKenna, H., 140, *158*
McLaughlin, T. P., 46, 86, *89*
McReynolds, P., 323, *331*
Messick, S., 83, *90*
Meyer, L. B., 70, 86, *89*

Miller, M. B., 323, 325, 326, *331*
Mindus, L., 28, *89*
Moles, A., 6, 19, *25*, 29, *89*, 239, *257*
Morris, C., 8, *25*
Mosteller, F., 199, *226*
Munsinger, H., 92, *108*, 109, *119*, 132, *158*, 160, 161, *168*, 228, *233*
Munson, W. A., 47, *88*
Mursell, J. L., 91, *108*

Nerhardt, G., 281, *304*
Nerlove, S. B., 81, *89*, 182, 189, *226*
Neumann, P. G., 28, *88*
Newman, W. S., 53, *89*
Nicki, R. M., 14, *24*, 140, *158*
Norman, M., 184, *226*
Nowlis, V., 47, *89*
Nunnally, J. C., 63, 76, *89*

O'Brien, T., 328, *331*
Oeser, O. A., 202, *226*
Oglivie, J. C., 184, 190, *225*
Olds, J., 9, *25*
Olson, H. F., 28, *89*
Osgood, C. E., 8, 13, *25*, 37, 55, 59, 62, 66, *89*, 93, *108*, 125, *158*, 227, *233*, 283, *304*, 310, 328, *331*
Overmier, J. B., 28, 29, 34, 72, 75, *89*

Paradise, N., 160, *167*
Parham, L. C. C., 13, 14, *24*, 184, *225*
Peirce, C. S., 8, *25*
Petzeld, P. G., 91, *108*
Piaget, J., 92, *108*
Pierce, J. R., 28, *89*
Pinkerton, R. C., 28, *89*
Posner, M. I., 238, *257*

Quastler, H., 28, 29, *89*

Rabelais, F., 329, *331*
Raychaudhuri, M., 160, *168*
Redlich, F. C., 279, *303*
Riegl, A., 236, *257*
Robbins, M., 264, *278*
Robinson, D. W., 47, *89*

Romney, A. K., 81, *89*, 182, 189, *226*
Roscoe, J., 262, *278*
Rosen, J. C., 160, *168*
Ross, R. T., 78, *89*, 101, *108*
Roubertoux, P., 161, *168*

Saegert, S. C., 175, *180*
Schlosberg, H. A., 69, *89*
Schönpflug, W., 319, *331*
Schroeder, H. M., 244, *257*
Schweizer, W. R., 296, *304*
Selinger, S., 312, *331*
Shannon, C. E., 29, *89*, 305, 306, *331*
Shapiro, M., 236, 243, *257*
Shepard, A. K., 81, *89*, 182, 189, *226*
Simon, C. R., 27, 72, 75, 76, *89*
Skaife, A. M., 175, *180*
Smets, G., 140, 149, *158*
Snodgrass, J. G., 109, *119*
Sokolov, E. N., 320, *331*
Sorokin, P. A., 240, 243, 245, *257*
Southwold, M., 262, *278*
Sowa, J., 28, *90*
Spence, K. W., 15, *25*
Spitz, H. H., 323, 326, *331*
Staats, A. W., 228, *233*
Stevens, S. S., 45, *90*
Stewart, D., 197, *226*, 254, *257*
Stockhausen, K., 28, *90*
Sturgeon, L. B., 169, *173*
Suci, G. J., 37, 55, 62, *89*, 93, *108*, 125,
    158, 227, *233*, 283, *304*, 310, 328,
    331

Tannenbaum, P. H., 37, 55, 62, *89*, 93,
    108, 125, *158*, 227, *233*, 283, *304*,
    310, 328, *331*
Taylor, S., 91, *108*
Thayer, R. E., 17, *25*, 47, *90*, 284, *304*,
    311, *332*
Thomas, H., 92, *108*
Thompson, R., 264, *278*

Tischler, H., 70, *90*
Tomkins, S. S., 285, *303*
Tucker, W. T., 55, 59, 83, *90*, 97, *108*,
    312, *332*

Valentine, C. W., 5, *25*
Veldman, J., 63, *90*, 126, *158*, 270
Venturi, L., 3, *25*
Vitz, P. C., 28, 29, 30, 31, 34, 37, 47,
    56, 57, 72, *90*, 93, *108*, 109, 110,
    119, 122, *158*, 160, 161, *168*

Walker, E. L., 310, 324, *332*
Washburn, M. F., 159, 160, *168*
Weaver, W., 29, *89*, 306, *331*
Wedin, L., 184, *226*
Welsh, G. S., 160, *167*, *168*
Werbik, H., 27, *90*
Wilkinson, H. J., 160, *168*, 322, *331*
Williams, E. J., 37, *90*, 160, *168*
Williams, W. T., 190, *226*
Wimsatt, W. K., 3, *25*
Winer, B. J., 37, 48, *90*, 189, *226*
Winter, L., 160, *168*
Witryol, S., 228, *233*
Wohlwill, J. F., 27, 72, 75, 76, *89*
Wölfflin, H., 202, *226*, 235, 236, 243,
    257
Woods, J. M., 160, *168*
Woodworth, R. S., 35, *90*
Worringer, W., 236, *257*
Wright, W. V., 28, *88*
Wundt, W. M., 9, *25*

Youngblood, J. E., 28, *90*

Zajonc, R. B., 43, 44, 46, *88*, *90*, 175,
    180
Zigler, E., 296, *303*
Zimmermann, R., 236, *257*
Zink, S., 70, *90*

SUBJECT INDEX

Abstract-representational dimension, 240–241
Activity factor, 62–71, 93, 317–318
Adjective-noun pairs, responses to, 279–302
Aesthetic information, 6–7
Aesthetics, disciplines concerned with, 2–5
  empirical, 3–5
  experimental, 4–5
  philosophical, 3
  problem of defining, 1–2
  psychobiological, 4–5
  psychological, 4
  speculative, 2–3
Age and responses to sound sequences, 91–107
Analytic approach, 18, 20–21, 27–28, 181–184
Arousal, 8–12
  factor, 194–195, 227–233, 318
  potential, 9–12
Arousal-boost mechanism, 8–12, 232
Arousal-minimization position, 31–33
Arousal-reduction mechanism, 8–12, 232

Art:
  criticism, 3
  history, 3, 183
  problem of defining, 1–2
  theory, 3
Artistic training and responses to sound sequences, 161–164
Artist's year of birth, correlates of, 209

Baganda, description, 262–263
Beauty, 2
Behavioral measures, 14–15

Circular patterns, responses to, 169–173
Classicism factor, 203–207, 251–256, 320
Classicism/Order factor, 213, 215
Collative properties, 5, 8–9, 18–19
  and humor, 280–282
  and information theory, 19
Complexity/Curvilinearity factor, 213, 215
Complexity factor, 252–256
Concinnity, 9, 12
Correlational redundancy, 20, 140–157
Cortical-arousal factor, 290–295

Cross-cultural research, 23, 259-278, 327-329

Cultural information, 6, 202

Dependent variables, 13-15, 34-35
  relations among, 15-17
Descriptive ratings, 13, 310-320
  of adjective-noun pairs, 285-295, 301
  of circular patterns, 169-173
  of matrix patterns, 124-136
  of paintings, 192-198, 210-216
  of Smets patterns, 144-149
  of sound sequences, 36-71, 92-101,
    116-119
  of visual patterns, 265, 270-276
  of visual sequences, 109-119
Dimensions, of musical experience,
    70-71
  of paintings, 235-256
  of perception of paintings, 181-225
Distributional redundancy, 20, 169-173

Evaluation factor, 62-71, 93, 317
Evaluative ratings, 13, 310-320
  of adjective-noun pairs, 285-295
  of circular patterns, 169-173
  of matrix patterns, 124-136
  of paintings, 192-198
  of Smets patterns, 144-149
  of sound sequences, 36-71, 77-85,
    116-119
  of visual patterns, 265, 270-277
  of visual sequences, 109-115
Experimental aesthetics, new, 5-23,
    327-329
Exploration time, 14, 322
Exploratory behavior, 321-326
Exploratory choice, 14, 34-35, 322-326
  and matrix patterns, 138-140
  and Smets patterns, 150-153
  and sound sequences, 101-103
Expressionism factor, 213, 215, 253-254
Expressive information, 6, 202

Facial reactivity and adjective-noun
    pairs, 295-297
Factor analysis, 55-71, 97-99, 114-116,
    126-136, 144-149, 194-198,
    203-207, 251-254, 288-295,
Factor analysis, (*Cont'd.*)
    310-321
Factors:
  Activity, 62-71, 93, 317-319
  Arousal, 194-195, 227-233, 318
  Attention, 290-295
  Classicism, 203-207, 251-256, 320
  Classicism/Order, 213, 215
  Complexity, 252-256
  Complexity/Curvilinearity, 213, 215
  Cortical Arousal, 290-295
  Evaluation, 62-71, 93, 317
  Expressionism, 213, 215, 253-254
  Hedonic Tone, 126-136, 146-149,
    156, 194-195, 227-233, 288-295,
    317
  Impressionism, 203-207
  Potency, 62-71, 93, 318, 320
  Realism, 203-207, 320
  Realism vs. Subjectivism, 213, 215
  Subjectivism, 203-207, 252-256, 320
  Uncertainty, 194-195, 227-233
  Uncertainty/Arousal, 126-136,
    146-149, 156
Furthest-neighbor analysis, 190-191

Hedonic-tone factor, 126-136, 146-147
    156, 194-195, 227-233,
    288-295, 317
Hedonic value, 8-12
Humor, 279-282

Impressionism factor, 205-207
Incongruity, 35
Independent variables, 17-21
Individual differences, 22-23, 326-327
  and exploratory choice, 325-326
INDSCAL program, 189-192, 218-223,
    248-249

Information, 19-20
aesthetic, 6-8
cultural, 6, 202
expressive, 6, 202
semantic, 6, 202
syntactic, 6, 18, 202
Information-optimization position, 31-33
Information theory, 6-8, 29, 31, 305-310
Information theory,
and collative properties, 19
Internal-stage ratings, 13, 310-320
and adjective-noun pairs, 285-295
and circular patterns, 169-173
and matrix patterns, 125-136
and paintings, 192-198
and psychophysiological measures, 17
and Smets patterns, 144-149
and sound sequences, 46-55

Linear-painterly dimension, 236-240
Listening time, 14, 34-35, 322
and sound sequences, 71-77, 104, 107
Looking time, 14, 264, 266-268, 322
and adjective-noun pairs, 295-297
and matrix patterns, 136-138
and paintings, 198-200
and Smets patterns, 149-150

Matrix patterns, responses to, 122-146
MDPREF program, 80-84, 102-103,
218-223
Melody, 27-29, 86-87
Multidimensional scaling, of paintings,
181-192, 210-223, 246-249
of sound sequences, 80-84, 102-103
Multiplicity-unity dimension, 241-242
Musical training, 33-34, 36-87
and responses to visual patterns,
165-167

New experimental aesthetics, 5-23,
327-329
NMSCAL program, 189, 192
Novelty and interestingness, 175-179

Objectives of experiments, 12-23

Paintings, responses to, 175-179,
181-233, 227-233, 235-256
Paired comparisons of visual patterns,
265, 268-270
Polygons, responses to, 165-167
Potency factor, 62-71, 93, 318, 320
Psychophysiological measures, 13-14
Psychophysiological measures,
and internal-state ratings, 17

Rating time, 34-35, 67-68, 129
Realism factor, 203-207
Realism vs. Subjectivism factor, 213, 215
Redundancy, 306
correlational, 20, 140-157
distributional, 20, 169-173
Reward value, 14-15, 326
of adjective-noun pairs, 298-301
of paintings, 227-233
of Smets patterns, 153-155
R-R laws, 15-16

Semantic distance, 283-302
Semantic information, 6, 202
Similarity judgments of paintings,
188-192, 210-216, 246-249
Smets patterns, responses to, 140-157
Somber-Bright dimension, 242-243
Sound sequences, responses to, 27-87,
116-119, 161-164
S-R laws, 15-16, 20
Stylistic development and change,
243-245
Stylistic ratings, 13, 320-332
of paintings, 200-207, 249-256
of sound sequences, 46-55
Subjective uncertainty, 308
Subjectivism factor, 203-207, 252-256,
320
Symbols, 8
Syntactic information, 6, 18, 202
Synthetic approach, 17-20, 28

Tension, 9-12
Theoretical orientation, 5-12

Ugandan subjects, 262–265
Uncertainty, 19–20, 29–30, 306
Uncertainty/Arousal factor, 126–136,
　　146–149, 156
Uncertainty factor, 194–195, 227–233,
　　317–318
Uncertainty Level:
　of sound sequences, 27–87, 91–107,

Uncertainty level: (*Cont'd.*)
　　161–164
　of visual patterns, 121–157, 165–167
　of visual sequences, 109–119

Verbal ratings, 13
Visual sequences, responses to, 109–119,
　　121–157, 175–179, 259–278